MOTIVATIONAL THEORIES
AND PRACTICES

GRID SERIES IN MANAGEMENT

Consulting Editor
STEVEN KERR, The Ohio State University

Adams & Ponthieu, *Administrative Policy & Strategy, A Comparative Approach Casebook,* Second Edition
Anthony & Nicholson, *Management of Human Resources: A Systems Approach to Personnel Management*
Cassell & Baron, *Collective Bargaining in the Public Sector*
Chung, *Motivational Theories and Practices*
Deitzer & Shilliff, *Contemporary Management Incidents*
Knapper, *Cases in Personnel Management*
Lewis, *Organizational Communications: The Essence of Effective Management*
Murdick, Eckhouse, Moor & Zimmerer, *Business Policy: A Framework for Analysis,* Second Edition
Ritti & Funkhouser, *The Ropes to Skip and The Ropes to Know: Studies in Organizational Behavior*

OTHER BOOKS IN THE GRID SERIES IN MANAGEMENT

Adams, *Personnel Management: A Program of Self-Instruction*
Ahmed, *Quantitative Methods for Business*
Baker, *Environment 1984*
Bennett & Felton, *Managerial Decision Making: Case Problems in Formulation and Implementation*
Clover & Balsley, *Business Research Methods*
Rosen, *Supervision: A Behavioral View*
Seimer, *Elements of Supervision*
Steinhoff, Deitzer & Shilliff, *Small Business Management: Cases and Essays*
Swinth, *Organizational Systems for Management: Designing, Planning & Implementation*
Tersine & Altimus, *Problems & Models in Operations Management*
Walton, *Business in American History*
Wasmuth & deLodzia, *Dynamics of Supervision: Organizational Cases and Intrigues*

MOTIVATIONAL THEORIES AND PRACTICES

Kae H. Chung

Department of Administration
Wichita State University

Grid Inc., Columbus, Ohio

I.S.B.N. 0-88244-140-x
Library of Congress Catalog Card Number 76-44999

1 2 3 4 5 6 ⊠ 2 1 0 9 8 7

MOTIVATIONAL THEORIES AND PRACTICES *was edited by Jane C. Foss; stylized by Elaine Clatterbuck, production manager. Cover design was by Marcie Clark. The text was set in 10/11 Press Roman by Impressions, Columbus, Ohio.*

CONTENTS

v

ABOUT THE CASES

The textbook contains nine short cases pertinent to the theories and programs presented in the chapters. They are intended to stimulate class discussions and to bridge theory and application. Although most case situations sound relatively simplistic, they nevertheless defy simplistic answers. It is because the cases are taken from actual job situations where no easy solutions are available to the managers. What seems to be a good solution often produces undesirable side effects. Thus, it is suggested that students have an understanding of relevant theories and concepts before they attack the cases. These case materials can be used as a supplement to the text without a prior preparation by the students. However, the students will benefit more if they prepare case analysis and/or undertake research endeavors in advance and share their preparations with others in the class.

Although these cases can be discussed in any order, because there is no direct one-to-one relationship between cases and theories, they can be arranged in the following manner. Such an arrangement may enhance the relevancy of the case materials. The reader will find that the first two cases, "Recognition Won't Buy Bread" and "No Newspaper Story," will go well with Chapters 3 and 4. These cases deal with employee needs and the problems of satisfying them. The next two cases, "What Do You Do With Willie" and "Midwest Electronics," discussed the problems of employee satisfaction and the quality of organizational life. These two cases can be discussed in conjunction with Chapter 6.

"Great Pizza Fiasco" and "Continental Pipes" present the problems of designing financial incentive systems. Therefore, these two cases will go well with Chapter 7. Also, since the "Continental Pipes" utilizes the management-by-results as the performance appraisal tool, it can be discussed and compared with the management-by-objectives concept and its performance appraisal in Chapter 10. The case, "Every Employee Is An Associate" is an interesting managerial practice which helps to create an organizational climate conducive to a successful implementation of a job enrichment program. This case can be discussed in conjunction with Chapters 8 and 9. The cases, "Are You Satisfied With Your Job" and "Job Enrichment at AT & T," are closely related to job design. While one is concerned with the way of analysing the motivational potential of a job, the other suggests a strategy for enriching a job. The text materials from Chapter 9 can be utilized in discussing these cases. Finally, the text materials presented in Chapter 5—expectancy concepts—are relevant to all the cases.

PREFACE

Much progress has been made in recent years in the study of work motivation. Several important theories of motivation have been advanced and tested by numerous researchers. As a result, the level of understanding of work motivation has increased substantially, and an increasing number of employers are implementing various motivational programs in their organizations. However, a lingering problem with this development is that many theories are primarily concerned with a limited set of motivational determinants and fail to deal with complex motivational problems which involve a variety of determinants. This book is written in response to this problem. The book reviews major theories of motivation and integrates them into a comprehensive theoretical framework. Instead of listing theories atomistically, major theories will be related and integrated. In addition, an attempt has been made to blend these theories with actual applications in organizations.

The special features of this book are: first, the book reviews major theories of motivation (need, incentive and reinforcement, and expectancy theories) separately first and then integrated into a theoretical framework similar to Vroom's expectancy model. Unlike the Vroom's model which primarily deals with expectancy and valence, the proposed model recognizes and incorporates the differences in individuals' needs and organizational incentives for studying work motivation.

Second, theories are translated into specific motivational programs applicable to organizations. This integrative approach provides students and practitioners in management with sound theoretical foundations on which appropriate motivational programs can be developed for real-world applications. Theories outline underlying principles of motivational behavior, while motivational programs demonstrate various ways managers implement theories and concepts to achieve individual and organizational goals.

Finally, this book utilizes a systems or contingency approach to employee motivation. Instead of suggesting universal principles of motivation that can be applied to all organizational situations, the systems approach takes an attitude that the selection of a particular set of motivational programs depends on the nature of the task, individuals, and organizational realities. An effective motivational program balances the demands of various motivational components. When there is a "workable fit" between individual characteristics and organizational properties, both management and employees are able to maintain mutually reinforcing relationships.

The book is divided into two parts. Part I deals with major motivational theories while Part II presents motivational programs for developing a productive work force. Chapter 1 discusses the importance of studying motivation, strategies for developing motivation theories and programs, and related issues and problems. In Chapter 2 the classical interpretations of human behavior and motivational programs are briefly discussed to give readers an historical perspective of motivational theories and programs.

Contemporary motivation theories, which describe and explain the motivational process in organizations, are divided into three major categories: need theories, incentive theories, and expectancy theories. Need theories in Chapter 3 describe internal motivational causes, while incentive theories in Chapter 4 explain external causes of human behavior. The expectancy theories in Chapter 5 then explain individual differences in goal-oriented behavior. The relationships between motivation, job satisfaction, and performance are discussed in Chapter 6.

This book emphasizes that motivated behavior is influenced by many factors. Behavior is energized internally by needs, reinforced externally by incentives, and modified by the way the person perceives the "path-goal" relationship between his behavior and goal attainment. Thus, the theories presented in Chapters 3, 4 and 5 are complementary and inclusive in nature and can be integrated into a theoretical framework.

Motivational programs are presented in the remaining chapters. Chapter 7 deals with conventional ways of motivating employees and examines the relative effectiveness of various pay systems. Chapter 8 discusses the effects of organizational structure, leadership, and group process on employee interactions and relation-oriented need satisfaction. Affective interaction is important not only for achieving organizational goals but also for satisfying employees' relation-oriented needs. Chapter 9 presents basic principles and strategies for designing motivational work systems. Job enlargement, job enrichment, and flexible working hours are the major topics of the discussion. Chapter 10 emphasizes the goal-setting process and result-oriented managerial approach. Finally, Chapter 11 presents an overview of motivational theories and programs and suggests future directions in employee motivation.

Many individuals have contributed to the writing of this book. A very special note of gratitude goes to Steven Kerr, Ohio State University, for his insightful comments and diligent reviews of the manuscript. Leon C. Megginson, Louisiana State University, has provided the initial interest and encouragement for undertaking a writing project on work motivation. My colleagues at Wichita State University, especially Arthur Sweney, Gerald Graham, Guy McCormick, Leslie Fiechtner and George Beason, have served as sounding boards for formulating ideas and organizing materials. Also, I would like to recognize the assistance of Joe Sauer, Larry Brown, Monica Ross, Francis Kentling, and Barbara Ciboski. They were specially helpful in providing library research, reference checks, and editorial services. Kathy Jenkins, Cathy Martz, Nancy Mitchell, Ronni Oltersdorf, and Lois Wiles have contributed their typing skills to this project. Finally, I thank my wife, Young, and children for their love, encouragement, and patience.

Kae H. Chung

PART I

MOTIVATIONAL THEORIES

MOTIVATIONAL ISSUES AND PROBLEMS

Several recent studies on American workers and their work ethic generally agree that an increasing number of blue-collar as well as white-collar workers express unhappiness on their jobs (HEW, 1973; Sheppard and Herrick, 1974; Strauss, 1974; and Yankelovich, 1974). Young workers especially, reared in an affluent age, seem to find little virtue in holding jobs they consider menial or nonchallenging. Though young workers are as committed as their elders to work, they demand bigger payoffs in job satisfaction. They expect their jobs to be interesting and challenging, and desire more participation in shaping their work environment. The problem, however, is that these new expectations and demands, based on a humanistic and holistic view of the work world, are at odds with the work conditions and managerial practices of many organizations. For example, many factory jobs are dull, monotonous, and sometimes dangerous. Similarly, white-collar work involves many rudimentary and repetitive paper-shuffling activities.

Management's responses to job dissatisfaction are numerous. In an attempt to motivate workers, some managers offer better pay and job security only to find the effect short-lived and employee response discouraging. Workers demand higher wages and fringe benefits to compensate for the frustration and discontent with their jobs and/or to catch up with inflation. The net result may be that workers price themselves and their organizations out of the competitive marketplace. Other employers, in an effort to increase production efficiency, may further simplify and mechanize the work systems and exercise tighter control to counteract employee low motivation and poor productivity. Such an approach to job dissatisfaction further accentuates the job alienation, resentment, and low productivity. Consequently, managers often find themselves as frustrated as their workers.

There are, however, a few employers who have concluded that work, not the worker, must be changed and have introduced some changes in work content and managerial practices. Some have changed work methods or added more work components to the existing job (job enlargement), while others are delegating more managerial authority and responsibility to workers (job enrichment). Some allow their employees to participate in managerial decision-making (participative management), and others even permit their employees to participate in the goal-setting process (management by objectives). Although these motivational programs have different names and put emphasis on different managerial processes, they share the underlying theme that the survival of an organization depends on the attainment of both individual and organizational goals.

At the moment, however, work is not changing as fast as many industrial psychologists would like. Restructuring a work system is a time-consuming and costly endeavor and requires a high degree of sophistication to implement and manage it afterward. In addition, the introduction of a new work system can produce negative results; such failures have generated cautious attitudes toward implementation of the new motivational programs. Nevertheless, the new development in employee motivation has created considerable interest and enthusiasm among many employers who favor adopting these programs. As we gain more experience and knowledge in diagnosing motivational problems and in implementing and managing new work systems, the success rate should improve substantially.

IMPORTANCE OF MOTIVATION

The attainment of individual and organizational goals is mutually interdependent and linked by a common denominator—employee work motivation. Organizational members are motivated to satisfy their personal goals, and they contribute their efforts to the attainment of organizational objectives as a means of achieving these personal goals. In this respect, motivation is considered the key to individual well-being and organizational success. More specifically, there are several reasons why motivation is crucial for the survival of an individual, organization, or society.

FROM THE INDIVIDUAL'S STANDPOINT

Motivation is the key to an individual's productive life. Most workers spend a major portion of their waking hours in work organizations. Organizational life constitutes a central interest for many people in this society. The ways people manage their work lives differ. Some find their jobs interesting or make the jobs interesting; they become committed and involved. These individuals make creative use of their energies and organizational resources to accomplish more things for themselves and their organizations. In addition, they play productive roles in society by becoming good providers for their families, by contributing their fruitful skills and talents to produce goods and services, and by sharing their accomplishments with others in the society. There are, however, people who are bored and alienated from their jobs and search for every opportunity to decrease their work commitment. These individuals not only waste their energies but also consume organizational resources for nonproductive uses.

A person's job performance depends on factors other than motivation. For example, one's ability is as important as his motivation in determining the level of his performance. For this reason, many industrial psychologists suggest that job performance is a function of both ability and motivation (Vroom, 1964; Lawler, 1973). Ability determines what a person can do, while motivation determines what he will do. If job performance were the only function of ability, it would increase proportionally as the level of ability increased. However, because of the human element of volition, performance will not increase unless the person experiences the necessary motivation. It is inversely possible that no matter how well a person may be motivated to perform, good performance will not result if he lacks the necessary ability. Yet, motivation seems to play a more critical role in improving the level of performance because ability can be increased by learning which is facilitated by motivation within a hereditary limit.

FROM AN ORGANIZATIONAL STANDPOINT

Since labor costs usually comprise the largest expenditure in a firm, labor presents the greatest potential source of increased productivity and profitability. If productivity is increased, more goods and services can be produced at low costs which benefits consumers through lower prices. For the employer, higher productivity means greater profit; for the workers, it means greater economic rewards. But increased productivity does not necessarily reflect a greater expenditure of physical energy; it can be increased by more effective utilization of employee abilities and potentials. Just as the performance of an individual depends on factors other than motivation, the productive capacity of a firm depends on many factors other than employee motivation. Obviously, a firm's productivity is influenced by such production factors as technology, methods of production, materials and energy resources, capital equipments, management, and labor. However, these economic resources are inanimate unless they are transformed into productive uses by the human element. The development of economic resources, human as well as nonhuman, is the product of human effort, and the quality of human effort in large part depends on human motivation.

Over the years, there has been pressure for increased productivity and higher earnings for workers in industry. Employee earning can be increased by raising the selling price of the firm's products and services, reducing profits or costs of raw materials, or augmenting labor productivity. However, increasing employee earnings by means other than increased labor productivity jeopardizes the firm's competitive strength in the market. Higher prices usually mean fewer customers, reduced profit means less capital investment, and low-cost materials mean poor product quality. But, increasing labor productivity by enhancing skills and motivation creates an almost unlimited resource. It can be restricted only when employees are unwilling to exert their mental and physical energy. Fortunately, the nation's industrial productivity has increased over the years, and this increase has been reflected in employee earnings. According to the Bureau of Labor Statistics (1974), during the period of 1950–1973, the productivity measure (defined as output per manhour) has increased at the rate of 3 percent for all workers in the private sector of the economy, and their real earnings have increased commensurately.

Motivating employees with traditional authority and financial incentives has become increasingly difficult as employees become economically secure and their dependency on any one particular organization decreases. According to expectancy theorists (Lawler, 1973; Vroom 1964), the motivation to work increases when an employee feels his performance is an instrument for obtaining desired rewards. Nevertheless, in many organizations today employees are entitled to organizational rewards just by being employed. Unions, governmental regulations, and the nature of the job itself in some cases prevent management from relating rewards to performance. This is particularly true in administering financial rewards. People may be attracted to join and remain in organizations to receive organizational rewards, but being motivated to join an organization is not the same as being motivated to exert effort in an organization. The challenge to management is to find and administer alternative forms of incentives which will induce employees to improve work performance. Such alternative forms of reinforcement will require increased understanding of motivational theories and programs.

FROM A SOCIETAL STANDPOINT

The nation is facing many problems that demand effective utilization of human as well as nonhuman economic resources. First, shortages of energy, raw materials, and capital equipment are evident and have created a new urgency for utilizing human ingenuity. Rising labor costs, inflationary pressures, and the need to maintain a competitive position in the national and international markets have forced industrial organizations to use their resources more wisely. Our nation's rise in productivity has fallen behind other industrial nations, especially Japan and Germany, in recent years. The major hidden resource in this age of energy and material shortage is the untapped human potential of the work force in each organization in our society. The development and effective utilization of this resource may help counteract the shortage in natural resources.

Second, jobs in this advanced industrial society require more highly trained technical, scientific, managerial, and professional employees who have to pass through the necessary educational, training, and developmental processes. Such processes require motivation and long-term commitment on the part of individuals. Even in times of high unemployment, many jobs in this category remain unfilled due to a shortage of qualified personnel (*Wall Street Journal,* June 10, 1975). Many young people demand job challenge and satisfaction in their work environment, and yet seem impatient in preparing for careers in these demanding professional occupations. Motivational problems may arise when these people are employed in traditionally less challenging semi-professional occupations and yet demand job challenges that professional occupations can usually provide. The societal challenges are twofold. One is to motivate these young people to prepare careers in demanding occupations, and the other is to upgrade the jobs in semi-professional fields to provide job challenge and satisfaction to those young people who will be employed in these fields.

Finally, job alienation, especially among young workers, is a serious problem facing society. Job alienation is a national problem because it not only affects the nation's economic productivity but also significantly influences the quality of life in our society. Job alienation may have contributed to the heretofore mentioned slowdown in productivity. In addition, sociopsychological costs of job alienation can become exorbitant as a result of adverse effects on the mental and physical health of employees and eventually their families and communities. A recent study conducted by the University of Michigan's Institute of Social Research (1975) reported that assembly-line workers and others performing routinized tasks suffered more mental and physical health problems than doctors, scientists, and others in demanding professions (*Newsweek,* July 14, 1975, p. 64).

Sheppard and Herrick (1974) reported that one-third of the male union workers surveyed expressed feelings of job alienation and could not be motivated by financial incentives, shorter hours, or longer vacations. The HEW report, *Work in America,* confirmed Sheppard and Herrick's pessimistic findings. According to this report, more than half of American blue and white collar workers are dissatisfied with their jobs, and something has to be done to make work more attractive, interesting, and meaningful. This report assumes that people who are satisfied with their jobs would choose the same occupation again, while those who are not satisfied would not choose the same field. There are different degrees of job dissatisfaction; while some severe dissatisfaction may lead to dysfunctional behavior, a milder degree of dissatisfaction may not be avoidable or may even become a necessary condition for work motivation (see Chapter 6). Although the problem of job alienation may not be as catastrophic as the two reports pessimistically predict, it is a serious problem that has to be properly dealt with. Failure to do so will bear unpleasant consequencies in terms of lower productivity and poor mental health.

A study of motivation will help identify reasons why some people are well motivated and productive on their jobs while others are not. And it will help promote motivated behavior and at the same time minimize nonproductive behavior. Continued interest and research are needed to find organizational properties that ensure job satisfaction and a high degree of work commitment so that workers will be able to enjoy a high-quality organizational life while yielding high productivity. In short, the organizational and economic health of the nation's industries depends on the quality of the work environment.

MOTIVATIONAL PROCESS AND FACTORS

The term motivation refers to goal-directed behavior. Goal-directed behavior is characterized by the process of selecting and directing certain actions among voluntary activities to achieve goals. In general, human behavior can be classified into three major categories: *motivated behavior* which is characterized by persistent goal orientation, *frustrated behavior* which is aroused when goal-directed behavior is interrupted, and *physiological reflexes* which are automatic responses to external stimuli. Such a distinction is necessary for defining the scope of motivational study; this book is primarily concerned with goal-directed behavior.

The study of motivation is a complex task, for it deals with many factors that influence goal-oriented behavior. Motivated behavior is not only influenced by an individual's characteristics (needs, interests, attitudes, and goals) but also by organizational conditions (tasks, managerial practices, and organizational climate). To deal with this complexity, we need a conceptual scheme concerning the effects of these individual and organizational variables on work motivation. Such a theoretical framework serves as a vehicle not only for explaining motivational behavior but also for providing managers with a tool to promote productive behavior in organizations.

DEVELOPING MOTIVATIONAL THEORIES

Motivational theories are organized in such a manner to best describe and explain the motivational process in organizations, and are classified into three major categories: need theories of motivation, incentive theories of motivation, and cognitive theories of motivation. These theories are highly complementary. The need theories will explain the internal behavioral causes, while the incentive theories explicate the external determinants of behavior. The cognitive theories describe individual differences in responding to the internal and external behavioral determinants. Further, the relationships among motivational resultants (behavior, reward, satisfaction, and productivity) will be examined to guide managers to formulate motivational programs in their organizations.

The first step in studying motivational behavior is to understand how a person's needs are manifested into goal-directed behavior. Each individual has a set of needs, and satisfying these needs becomes his goal. The term *need* is defined here as an internal state of disequilibrium—physical as well as psychological—which causes the individual to pursue certain courses of action in an effort to regain equilibrium (Steers and Porter, 1975). The theories by Maslow (1954), McGregor (1960), and McClelland (1961) use the concept of need as a basic unit of motivational analysis. The study of needs helps explain and predict what, why, and when certain goals or outcomes become important to a person. The assessment of variations in human needs (existence, affiliation, and growth needs) and their relative strengths at a given moment becomes the initial step toward understanding what determines a person's effort and performance.

Individuals are attracted to work organizations because these organizations provide them with various means of satisfying their needs. For example, existence needs (biological, physical, and security) can be met with pay, physical working conditions, and job security, while affiliative needs (companionship, belonging, and affection) can be met with opportunities for socializing and participation; and growth needs (achievement, recognition, and advancement) can be met by performing enriched jobs. When these organizational properties are applied to encourage people to join and function in organizations, they are called organizational incentives. Whether these incentives induce organizational members to approach or to avoid organizational activities or tasks depends upon individual needs and how the incentives are administered.

The term *incentive* is defined as a stimulus existing in an organization, which can influence the behavior of its members. An incentive becomes a reward when given to workers. An organization has various incentives that can be used to induce employees to contribute their energies to organizational endeavors. These incentives are classified into three major categories: substantive (financial, job security, and working conditions), interactive (social, work group, leadership, supervision, and stractural factors), and effectance (job content, growth opportunity, and responsibility). These incentives can be intrinsically and extrinsically mediated to satisfy employees' needs.

Individuals respond differently to the same stimulus, depending on how they perceive the value of organizational incentives (valence), the belief that their task performance will be rewarded (instrumentality), and the belief that their effort will result in task accomplishment (expectancy). According to expectancy theorists (Atkinson, 1964; Lawler, 1973; and Vroom, 1964), an employee will be motivated to perform an organizational task when he feels the incentive rewards are attractive, his performance is a means of obtaining the rewards, and the chance of accomplishing the required task is favorable. One's perceptional pattern plays an important role in determining the valence of incentives, instrumentality, and expectancy. The study of perceptual mechanism and its influence on motivational variables will enhance our understanding of motivational behavior in organizations.

Motivation is the result of the interaction of needs, incentives, and perceptual patterns of an individual. Figure 1-1 visualizes the motivational process of an employee in an organizational setting. A person's needs push him to undertake a certain action for satisfaction, while organizational incentives pull the person toward a certain direction where behavior can be reinforced. The person's perceptual mechanism interprets the expectancy of his effort leading to task performance (E-P), the instrumental relationship between his performance and receiving incentive rewards (P-I), and the incentive value of these rewards for satisfying his needs (I-N). The person's level of ability influences his perceptions on these motivational components. A highly capable person will perceive the E-P expectancy more favorably than less capable persons. He may also experience more closer instrumental relationship between performance and reward. Ability also moderates the level of performance; which is considered a joint function of ability and motivation. Performance increases when both ability and motivation improve; it decreases when any one of the independent variables deteriorates.

MOTIVATIONAL INPUTS   **BEHAVIOR**   **MOTIVATIONAL OUTPUTS**

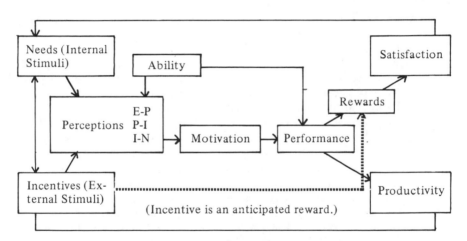

FIGURE 1-1. MOTIVATIONAL PROCESS IN ORGANIZATIONS

A selected behavior will take place as an outcome of perceptional interpretations. If one perceives the E-P expectancy, P-I instrumentality, and I-N valence favorably, he will be motivated to act. Expressed behavior then is either rewarded or not rewarded depending on his level of performance. Rewarded behavior leads to satisfaction and will be repeated, while nonrewarded behavior leads to dissatisfaction and will be discouraged. The amount of rewards and satisfaction achieved modifies the type and intensity of the person's needs. The modified need structure determines the nature of future behavior. Similarly, the level of productivity modifies the type and magnitude of incentives that can be utilized to induce employees to contribute their efforts to the attainment of organizational goals.

DEVELOPING MOTIVATIONAL PROGRAMS

Motivational theories cannot be put into practice until they are translated into workable programs. Understanding these theories helps explain and predict motivational phenomena, but it does not prescribe how managers should behave in dealing with motivational programs in their organizations. The fundamental difference between theory and a motivational program is that a theory of motivation describes a phenomenon, while a motivational program specifies a course of action; the former is based on a positivism while the latter takes a normative approach. The relationship between them is mutually inclusive in that an understanding of theories becomes a necessary initial step for developing sound action programs.

In developing workable motivational programs, the following points should be considered. First, work motivation depends on the personal commitment of an employee; a manager or an organization does not have direct control over an individual's motivation. However, an organization can influence the behavior of its employees through organizational incentives, intrinsic as well as extrinsic, which involve the following strategies:

1. An effort should be made to match organizational incentives to the needs of employees. This will not only enhance the incentive value but also result in greater employee satisfaction (I-N).
2. Organizational rewards should be related to task performance. Tying task performance to rewards, individually or collectively, will not only increase the value of performing the task, but also insure the mutual dependency of achieving individual as well as organizational goals (P-I).
3. The corollary to the second strategy is that the probability of obtaining rewards should be challenging but attainable. If it is either too pessimistic or optimistic to attain, it will lose its incentive value (E-P).

Second, there are a number of organizational properties that can be applied to generate organizational incentives. These organizational properties can be classified into three major categories: extrinsic or substantive (pay, working condition, and job security); social or interactive (group norms, trust and openness, risk-taking behavior, and supervision), and tasks or jobs (job enlargement, job enrichment, and flexible working hours). Although a set of organizational incentives can influence multiple needs, this particular set of incentives can have more direct and powerful instrumental relationships with the satisfaction of a certain set of needs than with others. For example, extrinsic incentives are closely related to the satisfaction of basic physiological needs, while organizational climate is more closely related to the satisfaction of relation-oriented needs such as companionship, belongness, and affection. The tasks that employees perform are better equipped to satisfy such high-order needs as self-fulfillment. More specifically, the motivational characteristics of these organizational properties are:

1. Extrinsic incentives will have a significant influence on employee motivation and productivity if they are applied to workers who are striving for lower-order need satisfaction (I-N); these incentive rewards are tied

to their performance, individually or collectively (P-I); and the expectancy of their efforts leading to task performance is challenging but attainable (E-P).

2. Organizational climate, defined as the psychological atmosphere of an organization or its subunits, has an impact on employee satisfaction and performance because it can satisfy relation-oriented needs (I-N), influences the perceptual relationships between task performance and incentive rewards (P-I) and influences the perceptual relationships between effort and performance (E-P). It has a stronger impact on emotional aspects of employee behavior than on rational decisions.

3. The task an employee performs leads to intrinsic motivation by directly generating motivational characteristics as a result of task accomplishment. Task performance produces feelings of success, achievement, and ego-involvement (P-I), and these intrinsic rewards satisfy such high-order needs as self-respect and self-actualization (I-N). In addition, the task elements such as variety, autonomy, and feedback directly control the expectancy or probability that effort leads to task accomplishment (E-P).

Finally, since motivated behavior is an outcome of the interaction of various individual and organizational motivational determinants, motivational programs should be viewed and developed in an interactive framework. An effective motivational program is one which balances the demands of various motivational determinants to enhance the value of incentives, the performance-reward tie, and the effort-performance relationship. The end result of the "fit" between these motivational determinants will be employee satisfaction and high productivity. Figure 1-2 depicts the relationships between motivational determinants and the outcomes of their interactions.

When there is a "fit" between individual characteristics and organizational properties, the organization and its members are able to maintain mutually reinforcing relationships. An oversimplified argument for such a fit runs as follows: workers who are primarily motivated to satisfy high-order needs will experience job satisfaction and high productivity when they perform enriched jobs in a flexible and supportive work environment. Workers who are primarily motivated to satisfy low-order needs may endure nonchallenging tasks under restrictive managerial systems as long as their activities lead to organizational rewards which will satisfy these needs. Their performance on these tasks and their compliance to formal organizational control systems can at least insure the minimum level of organizational goal attainment.

Motivational problems arise, however, when there is a lack of fit between individual needs or goals and the organizational characteristics. When maintenance seeking workers are assigned to demanding tasks which require a high degree of responsibility, initiative, and skills, they may be overwhelmed by organizational demands and expectations. It is predicted that they will be frustrated because they face a greater challenge than they can handle. Consequently, they withdraw from demanding tasks and perform inadequately. By the same token, those who seek higher-order need satisfaction will be frustrated when performing nonchallenging tasks with restrictive managerial controls; they may feel underutilized and overcontrolled. Such job dissatisfaction and frustration then lead to absenteeism, higher turnover, and inadequate job performance.

NEEDS	INCENTIVES	EXPECTANCIES	MOTIVATIONAL PROGRAMS
Growth-oriented Needs: Self-actualization Achievement Competence	Effectance Incentives: Growth Opportunity Challenge Job Content		Motivation Through Work Systems: Flexible Working Hours Job Enlargement Job Enrichment Management-by-Objectives
Relation-oriented Needs: Affiliative Companionship Competition Power and Status	Interactive Incentives: Social Reinforcers Work Group Leadership Supervision Structural Influence	E-P Expectancy P-I Instrumentality I-N Valence	Motivation Through Affective Interaction: Structural Design Leadership Process Group Process Organizational Climate
Existence Needs: Security Safety Physiological	Substantive Incentives: Job Security Pay Fringe Benefits Working Conditions		Motivation by Financial Incentives: Incentive Pay Salary Bonus Fringe Benefit Stock Option

FIGURE 1-2. MOTIVATIONAL COMPONENTS AND PROGRAMS

LINGERING PROBLEMS IN EMPLOYEE MOTIVATION

Finding a working fit among motivational components is a crucial managerial task. It is not an easy task because there are a number of external and internal factors which prevent this meshing. The roots of the difficulty lie not only in management's inability to change its work systems, but in sociocultural and economic forces that influence work motivation. The changing value of work, increasing economic well-being, climbing level of education, and other social forces have changed the needs and expectations of workers. People have become more expressive in demanding job satisfaction and more participative in the decision-making processes that affect their lives.

SOCIAL FORCES AND EMPLOYEE EXPECTATIONS

American work ethic has been changed through the three major historical stages: religious, economic, and psychological fulfillment. As Weber (1930) indicated, work was once considered a glorfication of God; hard-earned material success was a sign of God's blessing. In the early part of American history, new immigrants viewed the religious work ethic as primarily a means for survival while God showered his blessings on their pursuits. In contrast, the achievement of middle-class status by most people in the later part of the nineteenth century and the first part of the twentieth century developed a work value of a secular nature. The Great Depression once again reinforced the secular work ethic because people faced starvation unless they could find work. Reflecting a patriotic sentiment, during World War II, the nation's leaders were able to strengthen the work ethic because hard work was needed to produce war materials.

Today, many of the religious, economic, and social forces that sustained what was once considered the Puritan and then secular work ethic have been largely modified. The rising levels of economic security and education have contributed to the search for higher-order need satisfaction. The minimum wage is now approaching $2.50 an hour, which is ten-times higher than the initial minimum wage. People who are fully employed seem to enjoy good pay, job security, and the prospect of secure retirement. Furthermore, welfare and unemployment programs have reduced the absolute necessity of working. Even in times of high unemployment many low-paying and menial jobs remain unfilled.

The rising level of education produces more capable workers who are seeking high job satisfaction. The average worker in 1940 had an eighth-grade education, but now about 80 percent of the work force has gone beyond high school, and approximately 40 percent of high school graduates pursue some college education. Today's work force endorses conventional work values such as career development, hard work, and doing a good job. Yet, the reasons for its commitment to work seem quite different from its predecessors. Workers in the past viewed hard work and success in light of economic security, status, possessions, and enhancing the social mobility of their children. Young workers today, on the other hand, are actively pursuing careers to fulfill aesthetic and psychological needs, while the economic benefits are regarded more as an entitlement. Freed from economic hardship, they find it possible—as well as socially desirable—to seek self-fulfillment through meaningful work.

Finally, the changing life-style outside the job and increased social as well as geographical mobility of workers have influenced employee work behavior and commitment in organizations. The decreased emphasis on obedience to authority in churches, schools, and families has promoted a permissive attitude favoring individual freedom and self-expression on the job. Workers are more inclined to openly express their discontent in various forms, ranging from tardiness to active sabotage. Today's workers seem less patient in gratifying their needs and demand participation in controlling the means of satisfying them. It seems clear that new demands of employees in their jobs are not likely to revert to those of an earlier day; meanwhile, the traditional means of motivating employees by money, formal authority, and threats are becoming less effective. Hence, it is important to note that various work ethics prevail in our culture because work provides a means of satisfying human needs. However, as employees become better satisfied with, or at least have better opportunities for satisfying, lower-level needs, they begin searching for opportunities to satisfy higher-level needs such as self-respect and self-fulfillment.

ORGANIZATIONAL REALITIES

Modifications have been made in many social institutions such as family, marriage, church, and school to accommodate the changing demands of the populace. People become more participative in the decision-making process in these institutions. Yet, the world of work organizations has remained relatively unchanged. Despite considerable enthusiasm shown in the utilization of job enlargement and enrichment, many jobs in industry still remain fragmented and repetitive. Jobs are designed to increase engineering efficiency without considering such psychological costs as frustration and withdrawal. Work behavior is rigidly controlled by rules and regulations. Strict hierarchical structure often prevents natural flow of communication and interactions among organizational members and groups. Employee participation in managerial processes exists but is limited. Self-expression is often considered counterproductive and thus discouraged. Many conventional jobs and managerial practices are not able to meet the newly created demands and expectations of young workers in this changing time.

The dilemma in finding a workable fit between motivational components is that more workers search for the satisfaction of higher-order needs, but the availability of jobs where they can satisfy these needs are limited. In addition, many behavioral scientists seem to add more problems than solving them by sensitizing workers to believe that the utilization of new motivational concepts will provide them with job challenge and satisfaction. These motivational concepts are easy to talk about, but difficult to implement. As a result, more people may feel dissatisfied with their jobs and express their frustration by means of active or passive withdrawals. To combat this problem, it seems necessary to restructure many industrial jobs to make them more interesting and challenging, so that more workers are able to find job satisfaction.

A comforting view may be that not all workers demand job satisfaction. Some workers may be more tolerant than others in dull and repetitive job situations. Furthermore, many workers in a challengeless work environment seem to find ways of adjusting through socialization on the job, recreation, daydreaming, union activity, moonlighting, and various off-the-job activities. They are not overly dissatisfed but still are not satisfied. Although their performance will not be superb, they will do routine jobs in an acceptable manner. Such a neutral attitude is not likely to lead workers to aggressive behavior but does constitute an obstacle to higher productivity. The problem becomes serious when workers cannot satisfy their needs on or off their jobs, cannot sustain mental as well as physical health for long, and cannot continue to be productive members of society.

Unlike those employers who are contented with passively adjusted workers, a few industrial employers seem to conclude that productive workers are those who find their jobs challenging and, to this end, work must be changed. They have subsequently restructured organizational tasks and managerial practices so that workers can derive some job satisfaction. Restructuring work systems has taken three major approaches: job enlargement (technical expansion), job enrichment (power equalization, participation, and industrial democracy), and flexible work schedules. For instance, for job enlargement fragmented task components are incorporated into psychologically meaningful work units or modules, and workers then produce whole units or at least a major portion of the entire product. For example, Saab and Volvo auto manufacturing companies in Sweden broke up the assembly line into several work units, and workers perform their assigned work units as a group. Several companies in the United States (AT&T, General Foods, Proctor and Gamble, Texas Instruments, and TRW) have used job enrichment to allow employees to manage their own jobs.

Another development in recent years is redesigning working hours. For example, the four-day work week allows employees to fulfill their work commitment in fewer than the standard five-day work schedule. A survey by Wheeler, Gurman, Tarnowieski (1972) indicated that about 13 percent of the companies surveyed was using the four-day week, and another 22 percent is studying the possibility. About two-thirds of the companies which have adopted the program reported a significant increase in productivity, and more than two-thirds reported improvement in employee relations. The flexible work schedule is another example of restructured working hours. In West Germany, some 3,500 firms have adopted flexible work programs where workers can organize their work schedule to suit their personal needs and tastes without being forced to conform to rigid work schedules.

These new experiments in the work world have generated considerable interest among employers. However, the percentage of workers affected by them even among the experimenting companies is relatively low, and the introductory process of these programs into the work place is extremely slow. A study conducted by Luthans and Reif (1974) indicated that out of 125 major industrial firms surveyed, only five companies have made any formal and systematic attempt to enrich jobs. These five firms were large corporations in highly technologically oriented fields. Even in these companies, only a very small portion of their employees were included in the job enrichment programs. About 25 percent of the surveyed firms, however, reported an informal, limited use of these programs in which only a negligible percentage of their employees was affected by the new approach.

IMPLEMENTATION CONSTRAINTS

Why is it so difficult to implement these programs? There are several constraints that hinder widespread acceptance and utilization of the new programs. First of all, restructuring work systems is a costly proposition. Assembly lines need to be broken up and restructured into work modules, and managers and workers need to be retrained to adjust to new work systems. Outside consultants are usually invited to monitor the progress of implementation. Furthermore, the accompanying changes in managerial practices and organizational climate involve time-consuming efforts. Industrial experiences with these programs suggest that implementation may take years of struggle. Proponents of these programs, however, indicate, although redesigning work systems requires a substantial initial investment in terms of costs and time, it pays off in the long run in increased productivity and improved quality of worklife.

Second, the capitalistic economic system is to some extent at odds with power equalization in organizations. In a capitalistic economy, there is a distinction between labor, management, and ownership. Business owners take risk and invest their money for profits. The absolute power and responsibility of business endeavors resides in the hands of ownership. Workers are hired as helping hands and receive pay for their labor. Managers are representing the interests of business owners and are responsible for creating and maintaining profitable organizations. They are not particularly responsible for creating a happy work place for workers. They are not required to implement any motivational programs, but will be interested in them if these programs will boost organizational productivity. However, as a capitalistic society matures, more workers participate in the capitalistic system as business owners, through such motivational programs as stock options, pension plans, and employee stock ownership plans. Such a trend may facilitate the power equalization process in work organizations.

Power equalization programs can be more easily introduced in a socialistic economy where workers' participation in management is seen as a means of abolishing differences in economic classes. An outstanding example is the prevailing industrial democracy in Yugoslavian industries. Unlike the communists whose business property is state owned and managed, the property in Yugoslavia is socially owned and managed by the workers within the socialistic framework of self-government (Blumberg, 1968). Most production means and natural resources are socially owned with the exception of small agricultural holdings, handicraft, and similar establishments. The management of business enterprises rests with the workers of those businesses. The concept and practice of self-government seems to be a part of socioeconopolitical movements in Yugoslavia. It has spread from business organizations to all forms of institutional endeavors including local communes, labor organizations, and other work organizations.

Third, as a means of protecting workers' interests, unions and government have created various employee benefit programs, but they have also introduced various work rules which hinder experimentation with new motivational programs. Efforts made to implement these programs are often impeded by labor unions, especially if these efforts are suspected to be exploitative or a threat to the union's existence. For example, giving more responsibility to workers for the same pay in the name of job enrichment can easily be construed as exploitative. Furthermore, a successful job enrichment program may alienate workers from unions or at least reduce their dependency on union protection. In these situations, any unilateral attempt to implement such a program by management will meet with resistance from the unions. Thus, it is essential for management to consult with unions when implementing any new program.

Finally, assuming that both management and union are interested in changing work systems, the ultimate question to be asked is whether the proposed changes are effective in generating high productivity and job satisfaction. It has been more than two decades since industries have experimented with motivational programs such as job enlargement, job enrichment, and management by objectives. The result of these experimentations, though generally favorable, are somewhat mixed. Several companies in Europe and the United States (Phillips, Saab, Volvo, AT&T, General Foods, Proctor & Gamble, Texas Instruments, and TRW) have reported some improvements in employee job satisfaction, output quality, and in some cases output quantity, However, several companies (though not well publicized) have reported negative results and subsequent abolishment of their experiments. People abandon their institutions, customs, or habits only when it becomes evident that a more desirable substitute is available. Likewise, an organization will abandon existing motivational programs and introduce new ones only when the new programs can better serve its purposes.

SUMMARY AND CONCLUSION

Motivation is the key to individual success and organizational effectiveness. Yet, motivating employees with traditional authority and financial incentives becomes increasingly difficult as the employees become economically secure and their dependency on any one particular organization decreases. The challenge of management in the future is to find and administer alternative forms of motivational programs which will induce employees to improve work performance. The administration of such alternative forms of motivating employees will require better understanding of motivational theories and programs because it has to deal with a more complex set of motivational determinants than the traditional simplistic approach. Motivated behavior is not only influenced by personal characteristics of an individual but also the various conditions that exist in the organization. A theoretical framework is presented in this book so we can organize our thoughts concerning the relationships between the motivational determinants and their effects on work behavior. This theoretical framework contains need theories, incentive theories, and cognitive theories of motivation which are highly complementary in describing and explaining the motivational process in organizations.

Motivational theories cannot be put into practice unless they are translated into workable programs. Since motivated behavior is an outcome of the interaction of various individual and organizational motivational determinants, motivational programs should be viewed and developed in an interactive framework. An effective motivational program is the one which balances the demands of various motivational determinants by designing organizational tasks in such a way that moderate effort leads to task accomplishment, relating organizational rewards to task performance, and matching incentives to employee needs. The end result of the fit between these motivational determinants will be employee satisfaction and high productivity.

Many well-intended motivational programs fail because they are unable to find a workable fit between these motivational determinants. Most motivational tools suggested by industrial psychologists and practitioners have partial remedies for dealing with a limited number of motivational determinants. Partial remedies often do not deal with the entire process of employee motivation. Correct diagnosis of employee characteristics, the nature of their jobs, the kinds of rewards they receive, and the organizational climate are crucial steps for developing effective motivational programs in organizations. The purpose of this book is to help readers understand the complex phenomenon of human motivation in work organizations and develop motivational programs suitable to their organizations. No book can offer universal solutions to different organizational problems, but the conceptual framework suggested here can be an aid in finding a workable fit between various motivational components of a particular work group or organization.

2

CLASSICAL MOTIVATIONAL THEORIES AND PROGRAMS

What motivates human organisms and why they behave in certain ways have been asked since mankind began creating its own history. Knowing how these questions have been answered would enable us to better understand the changing explanations of human motivation and the origins of contemporary theories and programs of motivation. A review of the major classical doctrines, theories, and programs will give us some insight into the historical perspectives of human motivation. This chapter will discuss several classical doctrines and philosophical interpretations of human motivation, classical theories of motivation, and employee motivation from an historical perspective.

CLASSICAL DOCTRINES OF HUMAN MOTIVATION

Classical doctrines and philosophical interpretations of human motivation grew out of primitive religious beliefs, superstitions, and philosophical dogmas. Prior to the 1900s, the questions of what motivates people and why they behave certain ways were usually answered by such classical doctrines as Christian theologies, hedonism, physiological mechanism, capitalism, and altruism. Since these doctrines originated from religious and philosophical dogmas, they do not have scientific or empirical bases on which they can be tested. However, beginning in the early twentieth century, the development of motivational theories began to encompass the scientific approaches to explaining human motives.

CHRISTIAN DOCTRINE

Christian doctrine seems to combine primitive animism and the Greek philosophers' concept of virtue as a tool of explaining human motives. Primitive animism treated a spirit or mental cause of behavior as a carrier of motive. Spirits were classified as either good or bad; hence, in the religious teachings which grew out of the primitive animism we can easily find a clear-cut dualism of good and evil. Most primitive religious teachings were geared to direct human motives toward the form which would enhance the interests of society. Incentives toward the good and away from the evil were reinforced by the belief that good behavior would insure eternal life in heaven, while evil behavior would lead to punishment in hell after death. Christianity accepted much of the spiritual theory of animism and emphasized brotherly love over selfishness.

A group of Greek philosophers, including Socrates, Plato, and Aristotle, considered virtue the ultimate goal of human behavior and the source of all pleasures. They viewed man as an active and rational being consciously searching for the achievement of virtuous goals. While they recognized irrational parts of man's mind, they argued that such desires could be controlled by rational thinking. This doctrine of virtue not only dominated western philosophical thought via Christianity but also permeated eastern culture through Confucian teachings and other forms of religion. Further, the position of viewing man as a rational being who is aware of his goals and who acts to achieve them had a significant influence on the development of contemporary goal-path and learning theories.

Universal principles of right or wrong are derived from the exemplary behavior of God's figure; mandates come down to earth from heaven. Therefore, they are absolutes for human conduct with the only question being whether man can live up to them. Since Christianity places the highest value on brotherly love, the fulfillment of one's life will be achieved through service to others. This social responsibility of placing community interests ahead of personal interests seems to contradict the industrial ethic which justifies individual egoism. As soon as Christian businessmen begin to compete with other businessmen or try to make profits, they find themselves confronted with an ethical dilemma.

However, some elements in Protestantism, preeminently Calvinism, have successfully resolved the conflict between social and individual ethics in modern industrial societies. In Protestant ethics, work is seen as an asceticism absolutely necessary for life and salvation, and profit is regarded as a sign of God's blessing on the faithful exercise of one's calling. To quote Dunstan (1961):

> The capitalist is always a steward of the gifts of God, whose duty is to increase his capital and utilize it for the good of society as a whole, retaining for himself only that amount which is necessary to provide for his own needs. All surplus wealth should be used for works of public utility, and especially for purposes of ecclesiastical philanthropy (pp. 159-160).

Although the pure form of the Christian brotherly love has vanished from our daily lives, the Christian ethic has been permanently captured in our legal and judiciary systems and is today one of the theoretical bases for advocating the concept of social responsibility of managers in our economic system. Other evidence of the Christian influence appears in the law which provides churches with a special tax provision in hopes that churches will utilize the tax allowances to fulfill Christian missions of spreading brotherly love here and abroad.

DOCTRINE OF HEDONISM

Another group of Greek philosophers including Cyrenaics, Democritus, Epicurus, Lucretius, and Horace, was concerned with human motives. For them, the feelings of pleasure and pain were regarded as the only motives to action. It was assumed that the pursuit of pleasure and the avoidance of pain were the primary natural ends toward which all conscious living beings aimed. Unlike the virtuists who viewed that pleasures derived from the exercise of animalistic passions were ethically and morally inferior to those obtained from the exercise of virtuous conducts, the hedonists argued that all pleasures were equally good and that the maximum attainment of pleasure was considered ethical (Gomperz, 1904).

Similarly, earlier British philosophers like Hobbes and Spinoza, viewed the attainment of pleasure as a natural condition for self-preservation. According to them, all actions are motivated by the desire for pleasure or the desire to avoid pain. Hobbes argued that the pursuit of pleasure and the avoidance of pain are the only mechanisms that can move human organisms to act. Therefore, the question of whether the hedonistic tendency of mankind is ethical is irrelevant; men are irrefutably hedonistic by nature (Rand, 1912, pp. 147-207).

Bentham (1875) also formulated a hedonistic doctrine of motivation. He contended that man was placed under the governance of two masters: pain and pleasure. An individual is motivated to derive pleasure from his activities. But, the hedonism by Bentham was different from the classical hedonism in that Betham was more concerned with spreading pleasure on a social scale. The virtue of pleasure increases as more people in a society can enjoy it. In this sense, his hedonism can be called a social hedonism. Like Bentham, Mill (1865) stressed the concept of utilitarianism. According to him each man was an integral part of the society in which he existed. Such social hedonism seemed to represent prevailing social thought that influenced public policies during the nineteenth and twentieth centuries.

Spencer (1899) proposed another form of hedonism. However, unlike other hedonists who regarded the feeling of pleasure and pain as direct motives of behavior, Spencer considered them as reinforcers of the past. When a living creature is unaware of the consequences of actions, according to Spencer, he will go through a series of random movements. Some movements will be pleasurable and beneficial, while others will be painful and detrimental to the organism. Therefore, the body, after repeated movements, learns to make a movement that will lead to pleasure. This line of thought led to the development of the theory of learning and reinforcement.

DOCTRINE OF CAPITALISM

At the time of the Industrial Revolution in England, the concept of laissez-faire was given a broad and liberal interpretation synonymous with complete economic freedom. Smith (1776) in his book *The Wealth of Nations,* maintained that the wealth of a nation would be increased if government kept its hand out of private enterprise, and the energy and initiative of individuals were mobilized in the pursuit of self-interest. According to Smith, self-interest was the best guide to personal and social policy because each individual would try to create and produce as much as he could. Consequently, the wealth of a nation, which was the sum of the economic contributions made by all individuals, would be increased. The share of economic gains received by each individual would be based on his contributions to the wealth and on his capacity to compete in the free market.

This capitalistic morality was quite compatible with classical hedonism, the Darwinian notion of "survival of the fittest," and even the Christian doctrine. First, the concept of self-interest allowed the pursuit of pleasure as a prime motive of human behavior. Each individual would try to increase his share of economic gains which would be the means of ensuring pleasure. Second, the laissez-faire individualism was compatible with social Darwinism in that the stronger rose to lead while the weaker were submerged. Those who are strong in market competition will gain wealth and power; those who are weak will have less. Since competition is the basic law of a capitalistic society, those who cannot compete in the market do not survive. Third, as Weber (1930) indicated in his book, *The Protestant Ethic and the Spirit of Capitalism,* religious approval of the acquisitive motive in the Protestant ethic paved the way for acceptance of the spirit of capitalism. Especially the Calvinists and Puritan leaders emphasized the duty of individuals to God's will. Any action performed in business calling, as long as it involved honest and useful work, can be looked upon as one of the most righteous things a man could do; and its fruits, honestly acquired, were considered a direct sign of God's blessing.

Under this capitalistic movement, the mass of people has shared more materialistic benefits than any other system in man's experience. Yet, the very success of laissez-faire capitalism seemed to lead to its own downfall. During the later part of the nineteenth century and the early part of the twentieth, the rapid consolidation of industry and capital into monolithic industrial complexes boosted production rates and capacities but tended to weaken the bargaining power of the majority of workers and small entrepreneurs. The old moral order of a minority of wealthy individuals getting richer while the majority got poorer was challenged by many social scientists and policymakers, and a new capitalistic moral order spurred on by Roosevelt's New Dealism emerged as a result of this challenge. This new moral order required governmental intervention to protect the economic welfare of individual citizens and to ensure economic freedom for all socioeconomic groups so that the economic system could better serve the public interests. The government was considered by many as a necessary instrument to maintain full employment, to plan economic activities in the best interests of the public, and to maintain a balance of power among various economic groups.

CONFUCIANISM AND ALTRUISM

Unlike the individualistic and capitalistic philosophies in the Western cultures, the teachings of Confucian orthodoxy, which dominated Oriental philosophies for centuries, stressed the concepts of virtue and altruism as motivating forces of good men. The pursuit of pleasure was viewed as leading to moral decay, and a man pursuing this end was considered the enemy of the public. Denying the basic principle of hedonism, man's life was seen as a voyage through the "sea of pain."

A good society was based on the natural sympathy of men toward men for the sake of peaceful relationships. The art of establishing good relations involved the development of altruism in terms of "filial piety" on the part of children to their parents, on the part of a wife to her husband, and on the part of civilians to the emperor. In this ethical context, the Chinese society placed unquestioned value on piety, long life, good name, and saving face as motivators. The dominance of Confucian orthodoxy in the Oriental society, although it advocated faithful relations in the family and society, contributed in large part to the delay of industrialization in that part of the world, for the society as a whole did not place high value on material well being.

Since the introduction of Western culture into Oriental society, Confucian orthodoxy has been modified and dethroned in the search for scientific and capitalistic revolution. To modify the moralism of the old culture, the Orientals set higher levels of aspiration in achieving economic goals, individually and collectively. The new cultural system in the Oriental society now adopts the methods of Western civilization but retains the religious and moral bases of Confucianism.

PHYSIOLOGICAL MECHANISM

As a departure from philosophical and religious interpretations of human behavior, some scholars attempted to explain human behavior by finding biological and physiological bases or causes of action. For example, Descartes (1956-1650) developed a mechanical interpretation of animal behavior and modified his theory to analyze the behavior of man (Rand, 1912, pp. 168-190). He held that all physical phenomena could be adequately explained mechanically, for behavior was caused by internal and/or external forces acting upon the living organism. Unlike those scholars who relied on spiritual and mental elements in explaining human behavior, Descartes argued that internal forces were caused by agitations within the physical organism. He recognized the dichotomy of mind and body in explaining human behavior, but he held that man's actions were caused by the interactions of mind and body wherein the mind was subject to certain passions arising from activity of the pineal gland. The primary passions were wonder, love, hate, desire, job, and sadness. For Descartes, these passions were very important because in combination they could give rise to a large number of feelings which were considered introspective.

Another theory of physiological mechanism was found in Darwin's biological determinism and animal psychology developed during the nineteenth century. Darwin (1906) viewed man as only one stage in the development of an entire evolving world of living organisms. Man had advanced one degree further than other living beings. Darwin's doctrine of natural selection via innate instincts assumed that the most critical instinctive response could be evolved through the struggle for existence and the survival of the fittest. The doctrine of evolution did not need teleology or divine intervention to explain the process of creation and evolution of living organisms.

A group of physiologists and animal psychologists such as Carus and Romanes at the end of the nineteenth century attempted to find the mental faculties of man by studying animal activity. They expected to find the same kind of mental faculties in man and animals. Although their approach was challenged by psychologists who charged that the physiologists downgraded man to the level of animals by seeking to explain all behavior mechanically, their works gave great impetus to the development of concepts of physical refelex, instincts, and drive.

Although the pure form of physiological mechanism theory failed to survive, it was an important step for the development of empiricism and behaviorism in the study of human behavior. Some behaviorists, especially physiological behaviorists and reductionists, believe that knowledge of human behavior can be derived from empirical observations of responses which correlate to certain stimuli. Successful developments in biology and biochemical science seem to convince them that the mechanical explanation is possible not only for the physio-biological phenomena but even for the introspective and mental phenomena of human behavior. At this moment, however, they are not yet capable of describing and analyzing certain intervening variables such as perception and judgment which distort the simplified relationships between stimuli and responses.

Although these classical doctrines and interpretations of human motivation have not been empirically tested, their ideas about human behavior have contributed to the development of modern and contemporary psychological theories of motivation. For example, the view that man is a rational being who searches to achieve his goals is seen in the expectancy theories of motivation of Tolman and Lewin. Physiological interpretations of human motivation had helped to develop the conceptuation of instinct and drive. Hedonistic principle is applied to the reinforcement theory of modern behaviorism. Modern psychologists, employing scientific and systematic methods, have expanded their search for cause-and-effect relationships between mental and physical aspects of human beings and their actions.

CLASSICAL THEORIES OF MOTIVATION

Traditionally, the primary concerns of motivation theories have centered around three major questions: What are the forces energizing and arousing behavior? How can one influence or manipulate human behavior toward certain desirable objectives? Why are individuals different in their responses to the same stimuli and how they can be influenced?

The first question has led to the study of internal stimuli (or needs) which institute the motives of behavior. Answers that have been addressed to this question are grouped under the topic of *instinct, drive,* or *need theories of motivation.*

The second question has been involved in the study of external stimuli (or incentives) which influence or direct the behavior of individuals toward certain objectives. Answers to this question are placed under the heading of *learning* or *incentive theories of motivation.*

Finally, the third question has led to the study of such personal variables as cognitive style and personality which make each individual unique in his response to the stimuli. Studies concerning personal variables relative to motivation are discussed under *expectancy* or *cognitive theories of motivation.*

Several classical theories of motivation will be discussed in the following sections while contemporary theories of needs, incentives, and expectancies will be discussed in the following chapters. The subjects presented in the following sections—instinct and drive theories, classical learning theories, and classical expectancy theories—correspond to the contemporary theories of needs, incentives, and expectancies in coming chapters respectively.

INSTINCT THEORIES

Unlike the rationalists and hedonists who viewed man as a rational and goal-pursuing being, the instinct theorists (McDougall, 1908, and Freud, 1915) viewed man as governed by powerful instincts which demand gratification. For example, Freud (1915) conceived three instinctive forces in all human minds, namely, the id, the ego, and the superego. The id is the source of instincts and the home of the life energy seeking pleasure and avoiding pain. For all practical purposes, he regarded the sex instinct as the basis of all physical energy and called it *libido*. The id rests in the unconscious level and is governed by the extreme pleasure principle which itself is based upon hedonism. But man's conscience, the superego, when it confronts reality at the conscious level, repressed the instinct forces, for the erotic tendency is subject to severe repression in the ordinary social environment. Freud called this repressing agent the *censor* which stands on the threshold between the conscious and the unconscious levels of the mind.

Freudian theory, at this level, operates on the reality principle which, in turn, requires a safeguard mechanism for the self. The severe repression and objection to the instinct forces cause grave conflicts in the minds of people which may damage the self. Therefore, the ego arranges the process of the mind in a temporal order consistent with reality and brings the demands of the id in line with the restrictions imposed by the superego. Nevertheless, the Freudian system as it stands is essentially hedonistic in its main stream, and it is deeply rooted in the unconscious level of the mind. To quote Peters (1958):

> Freud claimed that the reality principle safeguarded but did not dethrone the pure-pleasure principle. The latter can do nothing but wish and work towards the gaining of pleasure and the avoiding of pain; but the former strives for what is useful and guards the Ego against damage (p. 73).

McDougall (1908) viewed the instincts as the prime motivators of human activity. He distinguished between instincts and emotions, regarding instincts as semi-physiological entities and emotions as psychological effects. He also correlated lists of instincts and emotions and found that emotions were aroused from the specific instinctive processes. To him, however, the instinctive forces were the essential springs or motives of all thought and attitudes from which character of individuals was gradually developed under the guidance of intellectual facilities.

Veblin (1914) also regarded instincts as the prime movers of human behavior. His concepts of instincts were closely related to work motivation and classified into four major categories: the acquisitive, the parental, the workmanship, and the idle curiosity. The acquisitive instinct leads a person to acquire property and to consider his own self-interest above the welfare of others. The parental instinct causes an individual to think of others first such as the family, the community, the nation, and mankind in general. The workmanship instinct encourages a person to work on materials so he can create useful products and services. The idle curiosity instinct leads man to inquire into the nature of his world. Unlike McDougall and Freud who viewed instincts as innate forces, Veblin viewed them as learned forces internally energizing behavior. According to Veblin, these instincts do not directly lead to action but are modified by habit and group action. The repeated urgings of an individual's instincts begin to take on a form of habitual responses, and these habitual responses are modified by the immediate environmental influences.

The notion of unconscious motivation is closely associated with that of instinct. According to Freud (1915), individuals were not always aware of their desires and needs and behaving in their best interests. Rather, their actions were governed by unconscious instincts which might be manifested in their dreams and fantasies. McDougall (1908) was, however, different from other instinct theorists in viewing instincts as purposive, inherited, and goal-seeking forces.

Undoubtedly, the instinct doctrines contributed to the development of drive and need theories of motivation, but their approach to human motivation lacked universal applicability for the following reasons. First, the concept of instinct was based on the homeostatic principle. According to this principle, an organism is active only when aroused needs or tensions exist to reduce them, but once these stimuli are reduced, the organism ceases to be active. This passive hedonistic principle overlooks the fact that some behavior may actively search for pleasure without having tensions within the organism—an active hedonistic principle. Second, the concept of instinct was limited to the study of such innate needs as sex, self-preservation, and other organic needs, and thus neglected the learned or acquired needs which are more dominant determinants of human behavior. Finally, the concept of instinct offered a pseudoscientific explanation of behavior, but it was not an explanatory concept because it could not explain a complex combination of motivational processes. Thus, the concept of instinct was dropped from among the generally accepted beliefs of psychology.

DRIVE THEORIES

The concept of drive was similar to that of instinct in that both were considered to motivate behavior and were assumed to have physiological bases. The drive concept, however, was preferred by those who searched for empirical bases for motivational behavior over the descriptive doctrine of instinct. The term *drive* refers to a physiological determinant of behavior which is aroused by a deprivation condition or need of an organism. The theory of drive generally assumes that a physiological need in an organism causes an urge or drive for a certain action which promises to gratify the need and hence reduce the level of drive. The need serves as an antecedent condition of drive, and the drive then determines the level of motivated behavior.

The relationship of need-drive-action constituted the major theme of the psychological theories around 1930, and this homeostatic principle was the subject of many experimental studies during that period. Major findings of the studies by Dashiell (1925), Richter (1927), and many others generally supported the generalization that when an organism, human or animal, is deprived of something necessary for its well-being, the organism is led to engage in an activity more rigorously than any organism which is satiated. For example, an organism deprived of food will try to find water, and so on. In general, the physiological needs of both animals and human beings cause some drives for action which will tend to satisfy these needs, and the force of a drive tends to be stronger when the organism is deprived.

The most comprehensive theory of drive was developed by Hull. In his book, *Principles of Behavior* (1943), Hull tried to accommodate the concept of habit within the framework of classical learning theory. To this end, he formulated the following equation:

$$sEr - (sHr) \times D$$

where *sEr* is an effort or reaction potential, *sHr* is habit, and *D* is drive. The concept of drive is defined as an energizing force which determines the intensity of behavior and which theoretically increases with the level of deprivation. Habit is defined as the strength of relationship between stimulus and response that was experienced in the past. Hull hypothesized that the habit strength depends not only upon the closeness of the S-R event in the process of drive reduction or reinforcement, but also upon the magnitude and numbers of such reinforcements. Hull's concept of drive, as seen in this hypothesis, has its root in the classical learning theory to be discussed later. The drive theory by Hull up to this point was based primarily upon the classical homeostatic principle of motivation. Hull (1952), however, in his later book, *A Behavior System,* developed an incentive theory of motivation which recognized the function of incentive; the primary function of incentive is to pull the organism toward the attainment of its goal.

The theory of drive is, however, not so simple as the homeostatic generalization suggests. It involves more complex relationships between the antecedent conditions (or needs), the drive, and the energizing force of drive (or motivation). For example, a strong need or deprivation does not necessarily instigate a strong drive for a higher level of motivation. Hull (1952) and Dufort and Wright (1962) indicated that the level of motivation sharply increased to a certain point as deprivation continued, but beyond that point the driving force leveled off as seen in the hunger drive. However, the patterns of responses vary for different drives. For example, the studies by Warner (1927), Jenkins (1928), and Beach and Jordan (1956) showed that the level of sexual motivation sharply increased to a certain point after ejaculation; but beyond that point the sexual drive, though it showed a slight decline, did not vary much with the duration of sexual deprivation.

A complicating factor is that not all physiological needs elicit drives for action. A person deprived of vitamin C or B_{12} is not necessarily motivated to satisfy the vitamin deficiency. Unless the person feels the need for vitamins, he will not be motivated to correct the deficiency. In addition, the concept of drive is limited to the organic states which lead to the development of goal-directed behavior. In the drive concept, the psychological bases of internal stimuli are neglected. The homeostatic principle can be applied to explain the process of reducing the force of drive, but it is not able to explain some psychological bases of behavior aroused in the absence of physiological tension.

EARLY INCENTIVE THEORIES

The concept of incentive was used by Hull and Spence to reflect the quantitative value of a reward. As will be discussed in Chapter 4, the level of performance is generally higher the greater the amount of a reward, the better the quality of reward, and the shorter the time of delay of reinforcement. An incentive theory assumes that an organism is capable of anticipating a reinforcement, and such an anticipation serves to facilitate an instrumental behavior. Hull (1943) previously treated an incentive as an antecedent which determined the habit strength. Then, he revised the concept of the antecedent condition of habit strength and introduced the incentive variable (K) as a separate motivational determinant (Hull, 1952). He defined the reaction potential (sEr) as a multiplicative function of drive (D), incentive (K), and habit strength (sHr):

$$sEr = D \times K \times sHr$$

A similar motivational equation was advanced by Spence (1956). Spence proposed that the excitatory potential (E) is a function of the sum of drive (D) and incentive (K) multiplied by the habit strength (H):

$$E = (D + K) \times H$$

Several studies (Reynold and Pavlik, 1960; Weiss, 1960; and Karczower, Freygold, and Blum, 1962) supported Spence's view that the two variables, D and K, are additive rather than multiplicative. However, in other studies (Seward and Proctor, 1960; Seward, Shea, and Davenport, 1960; and Marx, 1967), the multiplicative relationship between D and K were reported. When the subject had no drive, the mere presence of incentive could not instigate any action or elicit a weak action.

CLASSICAL LEARNING THEORIES

Classical learning theories attempted to formulate behavioral principles that might explain the influence of external stimuli or incentives on animal and human behavior. For example, Thorndike (1911) formulated two basic principles of learning that explained the relationship between stimulus and responses: the law of effect and the law of exercise. The law of effect states that satisfaction strengthens an associative bond between stimulus and response, and that discomfort weakens the bond. To quote Thorndike (1911):

> Of several responses made to the same situation, those which are accompanied or closely followed by satisfaction to the animal will, other things being equal, be more firmly connected with the situation, so that, when it recurs, they will be more likely to recur; those which are accompanied or closely followed by discomfort to the animal will, other things being equal, have their connections with that situation weakened, so that when it recurs, they will be less likely to occur. The greater the satisfaction or discomfort, the greater the strengthening or weaking of the bond (p. 244).

Thorndike's formulation of the law of effect is reflected in the tenets of classical hedonism. But, the difference between these two concepts is that the hedonistic behavior is undertaken to experience a feeling of pleasure (or to avoid discomfort) in the future, while Thorndike's law of effect is applicable only to the extent that it is based on the past experience of satisfaction or discomfort. Because of this, it is called "hedonism in the past."

Thorndike's law of exercise makes no reference to the affective aspect of response but refers only to the number of connections between stimulus and response. To quote Thorndike (1911):

> Any response to a situation will, other things being equal, be more strongly connected with the situation in proportion to the number of times it has been connected with that situation and to the average vigor and duration of the connections (p. 244).

The law of exercise paved the way for developing the concept of conditioned learning. A neutral stimulus becomes a conditioned stimulus by pairing with a primary or secondary reinforcer. The work of Pavlov (1927) was best known to many psychologists who were interested in the association between stimulus and response.

Pavlov (1927) carried out experiments on the salivary reflexes of dogs. In these experiments, the dogs secreted saliva when food was introduced into the mouth. The secretion was purely a reflex. When some other stimulus, such as the sound of a bell, was introduced simultaneously with the feeling, the secondary stimulus was able to arouse salivation even in the absence of food. The arousal of salivation by the secondary stimulus was called a "conditioned reflex." The conditions under which the secondary stimulus was effective were when the experimenter applied the conditioned stimulus before the injection of the primary stimulus, or when the conditioned stimuli was concurrent with the primary one. These experiments empirically supported the idea of association of stimulus and response, and demonstrated the fact that the association principle was physiologically as well as psychologically applicable.

However, Pavlov's further observations showed that in some cases the establishment of a conditioned reflex became difficult, if not impossible, especially when the dogs were drowsy. In fact, in some instances all conditioned reflexes suddenly disappeared in favor of other stimuli such as the attraction of the opposite sex (Pavlov, 1927, pp. 28-47).

The classical learning theories provided a starting point for the development of dominant incentive theories. Thorndike's law of effect and Pavlov's conditioned reflex paved the way for more refined principles of behavior such as the principles of primary and secondary reinforcement, the theory of approach-avoidance conflict, and the principles of reward and punishment.

However, there are some built-in limitations in these theories. First, Thorndike's law of effect and Pavlov's conditioned reflex can be applied only to situations where the meanings of the stimulus are already learned or experienced by the subject. When the subject is not consciously aware of the pleasantness or unpleasantness associated with the stimulus, he cannot respond to the stimulus as predicted in the simple S-R (stimulus-response) theory. During the unlearned period and/or when the subject is not aware of the meaning of the stimulus, the subject develops cognitive expectations of the consequences of attaining the goal. This latent-learning phenomenon which determines performance is treated as an intervening variable in the cognitive theories of motivation discussed in a later section. Second, the theories are applicable only when a subject has an aroused need which can be reduced by the application of the incentive. For example, when the subject is well fed, the food incentive does not elicit any reaction from the subject. The theories of learning frequently ignore the importance of needs or internal stimuli in the motivational process.

CLASSICAL EXPECTANCY THEORIES

Unlike the learning theories that viewed motivated behavior as a function of past satisfaction or reinforcement, the expectancy theory of motivation analyzed the function of expectation or anticipation concerning the person's future action. Whereas the simple S-R theory viewed behavior as a passive homeostatic response, the expectancy theory viewed it as a purposeful and goal-directed action based on conscious intention. Thus, unless a response is seen as an instrument of reducing a perceived need or drive, action will not take place.

Prior to the development of expectancy theories by Tolman and Lewin, considered pioneers in this field, Woodworth (1918) speculated that an organism's internal organic state might interfere with the simple S-R relationship in the classical learning theory. According to him, this internal organic state would cause multiple responses to the same stimulus, mutual exclusion of incompatible responses, selection of one alternative over others, and shifting of reaction from one stimulus to another.

Later, Tolman developed a more comprehensive theory of intervening variables that interfere with the simple S-R relationship. According to Tolman (1936), behavior was viewed as a function of demand for goal and expectancy of goal attainment. These two variables (demand for goal and expectancy) were considered intervening variables between stimuli and responses at any behavioral decision point. Figure 2-1 depicts the role of intervening variables in differentiating various responses to the antecedent stimuli.

Lewin (1938), whose interest was more in human behavior than animal behavior, introduced the concepts of valence and psychological distance to equate them with the concepts of demand for goal and expectancy in Tolman's model of motivation. According to Lewin, the strength of motivation is proportionate to the valence but is inversely proportionate to the psychological distance. In other words, motivation increases as the magnitude of valence (or attractiveness of goal-attainment) increases, and becomes stronger as the psychological distance decreases or the expectancy of goal attainment increases.

The cognitive theories of motivation by both Tolman and Lewin were ahistorical, yet they did not reject the importance of past experience in shaping a behavior. Past experiences of a person could have an impact on his present behavior to the extent that these experiences modified the valence and expectancy of an event. But, the primary strength of these cognitive theories lies in the thesis that behavior is not only affected by past experience or habit, as suggested by the learning theorists, but also by anticipation of future events. Especially when the subject does not have any experience with a task, he utilizes his perceptual mechanism to assign the utility of, and the probability or expectation of, accomplishing the task.

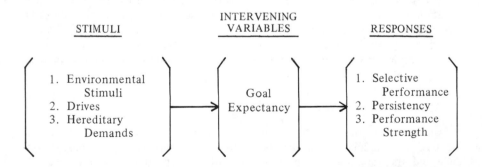

FIGURE 2-1. TOLMAN'S COGNITIVE THEORY OF MOTIVATION

(Modified from Atkinson, J.W., *An Introduction to Motivation.* Princeton, N.J.: Van Nostrand, 1964, p. 145).

These theories of intervening variables have become known as expectancy, valence, instrumentality, or path-goal theory by contemporary cognitive theorists (Atkinson, 1964; Galbraith and Cummings, 1967; and Vroom, 1964). For these contemporary theorists, motivation is seen as a multiplicative function of valences and expectancies. Valence refers to the strength of an individual's desire for a particular outcome and increases when the person perceives a close relationship between his performance and the outcome. Expectancy refers to the person's subjective likelihood that a particular effort will result in the accomplishment of a performance perceived to be an instrument of obtaining the outcome. These contemporary cognitive theories of motivation will be discussed further in a later chapter.

EMPLOYEE MOTIVATION FROM HISTORICAL PERSPECTIVE

Just as there has been an evolutionary process in the development of motivational theories, so has there been an evolutionary development in the ways managers in organizations approach the problem of employee motivation. Managerial strategies to high productivity and employee job satisfaction have been evolved through various historical stages: traditional approaches (scientific management and bureaucracy); human relations movements; and contemporary approaches (behavioral science, synthesis, and contingency). Although it is difficult to relate the classical theories of motivation to classical managerial programs of motivation on a one-to-one basis, several doctrines and theories of motivation are reflected in some motivational programs in organizations. For example, the Greek philosophers' rationalism can be seen in the traditional approaches to employee motivation, and the hedonistic philosophy was implied in the human realtions movement.

SCIENTIFIC MANAGEMENT APPROACH

The underlying thinking of scientific management in the earlier part of the 1900s was that employees were considered economic factors of production (Taylor, 1895 and 1911). Like other factors of production such as land and capital, human resources were used to produce goods and services for consumption and were subjected to the same economic analysis as the other factors. The worker was viewed as an interchangeable part that could easily be replaced by others and programmed to perform a specific task designed on the basis of motion and time studies. Scientific management specifically adopted the assumption of classical economic theory that the worker was an "economic man" basically motivated by his desire for economic ends. He was assumed to be a passive element in the production process and was characterized by a predictable degree of performance variation.

To motivate and coordinate the efforts of atomized human parts in a plant, elaborate performance standards and corresponding incentive systems were instituted, and highly detailed coordinating and controlling systems were called into play as exemplified in most mass production systems. The motivational principles of scientific management were to discover the best way of performing the tasks, determine the optimum daily production standards, train the workers to perform the tasks in the prescribed manner and at the prescribed pace, and then reward their performance by using an incentive system (piece-rate or differential wage incentive).

Interchangeable parts and the subdivision of human labor instigated the era of mass production which revolutionalized the industrial world and proliferated consumer goods for consumption. Better pay and a higher standard of living were realized as a result of the industrial revolution, but the very success of this mass production era ushered in a new set of problems that demanded changes in production methods and managerial practices. These production methods are now criticized as being incongruent with human needs as these jobs are usually dull and destructive to workers' self-esteem.

The scientific management approach to industrial problems still prevails as an integral part of modern management techniques. The need for high efficiency and reliable work measurements, and the persistence of incentive pay necessitate the use of industrial engineering techniques such as motion and time study, work method analysis, work sampling, and ergonomics. However, it is interesting to note there is a new generation of industrial engineers hard at work considering work psychology as well as physiology in designing work systems. To make industrial jobs more efficient, some industrial engineers go beyond the realm of ergonomics or work physiology and accommodate the knowledge of work psychology in task design and work measurement. Industrial engineering techniques can be valuable tools for designing jobs with optimal levels of motivational elements.

BUREAUCRATIC APPROACH

The bureaucratic approach, while distrusting individual egotistic behavior in organizations, turned to rationalism for finding a means of insuring organizational goal attainments. If employees were left alone, they would personalize organizational activities to satisfy their selfish goals even at the expense of organizational welfare. To avoid the personalization of organizational behavior, a formal and rational organization has to define the patterns of organizational relationships in which every series of actions is functionally related to the achievement of the organizational goals. Organizational activities are divided into offices or bureaus based on the principles of specialization and hierarchy. These offices are run by bureaucrats whose duties and responsibilities are closely defined by a set of limited and specific rules. Authority to carry these duties and responsibilities is granted to the office in charge rather than to the particular person who performs the official role.

Official actions are usually taken within the framework of prescribed rules and regulations. Impersonal rules and regulations serve to minimize personalization of organizational behavior and conflicts between bureaus and hierarchical levels, and consequently facilitate interactions between them, despite the differences in the occupants' attitudes and feelings. Bureaucrats who occupy the offices are professionally trained, and salary-paid experts are usually granted vocational tenure to insure the devoted performance of their official duties without subjecting themselves to extraneous pressures.

Weber (1947) conceived bureaucracy as an administrative apparatus that could maximize organizational efficiency. The chief merit of bureaucracy is its technical efficiency with emphasis on rationality, continuity, order, speed, and precision. However, bureaucratic practices can be at odds with human nature which searches for freedom and new learning experiences. Especially, the principles of specialization and impersonality minimize opportunities for organizational members to search for freedom, new experiences, and personalized relationships in organizations. Rigid hierarchical structure, departmentalization, and impersonal rules and regulations serve to decrease individual motivation to exercise initiative and risk-taking behavior in organizations.

Individual adjustments to bureaucratic practices are frequently dysfunctional from an organizational standpoint. Organizational members do not always behave in ways that maximize the accomplishment of organizational objectives. They can passively comply with organizational demands or proactively misuse bureaucratic properties for their personal benefits even at the expense of organizational goals. Passive adjustments take the form of ritualization of organizational practices, avoiding responsibility, buck-passing, and internalization of rules and regulations rather than organizational goals. Proactive bureaucratic sabotages then take the form of deliberate information withholding, empire building, and bureaucratic red tape and stalemate.

HUMAN RELATIONS MOVEMENT

As a reaction to the dehumanizing aspects of scientific management and bureaucratic organizational practices, the human relations movement in the 1940s and early 1950s advanced motivation theories which emphasized human elements in organizations. The worker was considered a person with emotions and feeling, motivated not only by economic factors but also by social factors. Mayo (1933, 1945) and Roethlisberger and Dickson (1939) pointed out that the increased routinization of organizational tasks carried out by the industrial revolution reduces the opportunities for workers to find socialization need satisfaction. As they receive higher wages due to increased productivity and incentive pay, they begin to search for satisfaction from interaction with co-workers. Further, managerial practices based on distrust, which are often dishonest, consolidate workers to side against management. As factories become more efficient, fewer workers are needed to perform the jobs, and production standards are often revised so that wages cannot increase proportionally.

Mayo revealed, based on the Hawthorne Experiments, that an organization is a social system as well as an economic entity. Social cliques, grapevines, norms, and informal status systems develop as a result of human interactions in organizations. These social demands in the group have significant influence on individual behavior, including production activities. Unlike the traditionalists who believed that productivity is a function of incentive pays and physical working conditions, the human relationists argued that productivity is more a function of social demands of the group. Thus, they believed that effective management involves leading workers rather than manipulating them. As workers bring to their organizations their attitudes, values, and goals, these human elements need to be satisfied before workers will contribute their efforts to the achievement of organizational goals.

The motivational strategies that management employed during this period were designed to satisfy employee needs. A number of fringe benefits such as paid vacations, sick leave, unemployment benefits, severance pay, health insurance, and pensions became common practices; and office parties, company picnics, the buddy system, and better supervision were advocated and widely practiced by an increasing number of companies. Management assumed the responsibility to establish a happy workplace where workers felt useful and important and to satisfy social needs. Thus, the management attention was shifted from the study of motion and time in the man-machine system to a better understanding of interpersonal and group relations at work.

Probably the major contribution of the human relations movement is that it generated a great deal of interest in human problems in organizations. The human relations movement provided the impetus for the contemporary behavioral science approach in management and motivational theories. However, the basic assumption and strategy underlying the movement have been criticized by many behavioral scientists. First, the human relationists assumed that employee morale leads to higher productivity. Contrary to the belief that satisfaction causes performance, most empirical studies did not find a significant relationship between satisfaction and performance (Brayfield and Crockett, 1955; Cherrington, Reitz, and Scott, 1971; Likert, 1961; Katz, Maccoby, Gurin, and Floor, 1959; and Vroom, 1964). High performance may be caused by intrinsic job satisfaction, but intrinsic job satisfaction is usually realized as a result of good performance. Thus, it can be said that performance causes satisfaction rather than the reverse. In some cases, high satisfaction may reduce motivational behavior due to the reduction in the importance of expected rewards which may follow as a result of that behavior.

Second, the human relations approach was accused of being as manipulative as the traditional approach. It gave the worker the illusion of control and power without substance. Human relations training was given to the supervisor so he might be able to relax his authoritarian supervisory style and widen his manipulative grip by understanding employees better and by controlling or exploiting informal group solidarities. The basic goal of management under this strategy was the same as under the traditional approach which aimed at the employee compliance with managerial manipulation (Miles, 1965).

CONTEMPORARY APPROACHES

The contemporary approaches to employee motivation take three overlapping forms: behavioral science or neo-human relations approach, synthesis of scientific management and human relations orientations, and contingency or systems approach. Like the human relationists, the behavioral scientists assume that satisfying employee needs is the key to high productivity (Argyris, 1957; Maslow, 1954; Herzberg, 1959; and McGregor, 1960). The difference between them, however, is that the behavioral scientists give more emphasis to satisfying high-order needs such as self-respect and self-actualization, whereas the human relationists were more concerned with need satisfaction of socialization and job security. To satisfy high-order needs, interesting and challenging jobs should be developed using job enlargement, job enrichment, participative management, and other forms of power equalization.

The synthetic approach recognizes the contributions of scientific management and human relations orientations. According to this approach, the scientific management and human relations orientations are not necessarily opposed. For example, Blake and Mouton (1961) have shown that the most effective managers are neither human relations oriented nor production oriented (scientific management). Rather, the most effective managers are those who show high concern for production as well as for people.

Unlike both the behavioral and synthetic approaches which suggest the best ways of managing and motivating employees, the contingency approach suggests that the selection of specific managerial and motivational programs should be based on thorough analyses of the nature of task, traits of organizational members, and other organizational realities (Dalton and Lawrence, 1971). The underlying theme of this approach is that there is no one best way to motivate and manage employees. People have different reasons for working and often seek different goals in their jobs. Consequently, they will not be motivated by the same incentive or motivational program. Some strive for extrinsic motivation while others are interested in intrinsic job satisfaction. Tasks that employees perform are also different; some jobs can be enriched while others cannot. Social climates of work groups are also different; some groups are responsive to a certain motivation program while others are not. Thus, a motivational program suitable for one situation may be unsuitable for another organizational situation. What is needed then is to find a motivational program suitable to the task requirements, employee expectations, and other organizational realities such as organizational climate, availability of resources, and expertise.

SUMMARY AND CONCLUSION

Most theories of motivation, both early and modern, find their origins in the classical doctrines and philosophical interpretations of human behavior. For example, the theory of learning and reinforcement has its root in the doctrine of hedonism, and the expectancy theory of motivation finds its origin in the Greek philosophers' view of man who is rational and goal-directed.

The classical theories of motivation (instincts, drives, learning, and perceptual theories) pave the way for the development of contemporary theories of motivation. The instinctive and drive theories of motivation attempted to explain internal forces of man's energizing and arousing behavior. The studies of internal stimuli led to the development of currently held theories of motivation. The classical theories of learning were primarily concerned with the manipulation of external stimuli that instigate needs or motives within the organism. The studies of external stimuli evolved into current theories of incentives and reinforcement. Finally, the classical perceptual theories of motivation concerned intervening variables between stimuli and responses. The studies of these intervening variables led to the development of currently held cognitive theories of motivation.

Several classical doctrines and interpretations of human motivation were reflected in the management of human resources in organizations in the latter part of the nineteenth and the early part of the twentieth centuries. For example, the mechanical view of man by physiological psychologists, the Greek rationalism and the hedonistic view of man as a goal-oriented being, and the doctrine of capitalism all influenced the development of scientific management principles by Taylor (1895 and 1911) and that of bureaucratic organizational practices by Weber (1947). The hedonistic philosophy and Christian doctrine of brotherly love seems to be manifested in the human relations movement.

The relationships between theories and practices become much clearer in modern and contemporary periods. Need and incentive theories of motivation are closely related to the human relations and behavioral science approaches to employee motivation, while the cognitive theories of motivation seem to be closely related to the contingency or systems approach to motivation. Need and incentive theories of motivation are primarily concerned with need satisfaction of employees, which is the major concern of the human relationists and behavioral scientists. Cognitive theories of motivation (expectancy and path-goal), on the other hand, suggest that the performance of organizational activities is the instrument of receiving organizational rewards or incentives. In addition, the types of jobs and incentives should match the needs and expectations of employees in order to enhance the effectiveness of organizational reward systems. The contingency or systems approach to employee motivation can be strengthened by utilizing the major themes of the cognitive theories in an organization. These contemporary theories of motivation and motivational programs in work organizations will be further discussed in the following chapters.

3

NEED THEORIES OF MOTIVATION

In an effort to answer the question of what energizes and arouses human behavior, many psychologists have studied the internal stimuli (instincts, drives, needs, and motives) as the prime causes of human action. Classical instinct and drive theorists, discussed in Chapter 2, assumed that these internal stimuli have physiological bases in the human organism. They used the concept of homeostatic principle to explain the process of stimulus arousal and its reduction. However, these instinct and drive theorists failed to explain psychological bases of behavior which are aroused in the absence of physiological tensions. Some internal stimuli do not lessen at their gratification as the homeostatic principle would predict. Contemporary psychologists prefer the terms "need" and "motive" to explain the internal causes of behavior which have physiological as well as psychological bases.

The concepts of need and motive have been deeply imbedded in motivational psychology, but they have been the sources of confusion. To some, the term "need" means a condition of physiological disequilibrium, while to others it connotes psychological wants. Needs can be classified into dynamic and nondynamic. Dynamic needs become the determinants of behavior, while nondynamic needs do not. A need is defined as the internal stimulus which causes a person to act and has physiological and/or psychological bases. Motive refers to a particular class of reasons for action directed to a goal or a set of goals. The relationship between needs and motives is that needs become the antecedent conditions for instigating the motives to function. The concepts of need and motive, however, are used here interchangeably unless they are specified otherwise.

This chapter will discuss the importance of studying needs as a unit of motivation, the major motivation theories of needs, the classification of motivational needs, and dominant needs and behavior manifestation in organizations. The relationships between need satisfaction and job performance and the effects of nonsatisfaction on employee behavior will be presented in Chapter 6.

IMPORTANCE OF NEED THEORIES

The study of needs as a unit of human motivation is important for understanding work motivation for several reasons. First, understanding the need structure of employees is essential for the manager to understand and predict their behavior in an organization. If the manager wants to influence the behavior of employees, he must understand the nature of the dominant needs that motivate them. People are motivated by a variety of needs, and in time their needs change due to maturation and satisfaction of certain needs. Since employees have different needs, they will respond to the same organization incentive (financial, social, or task) in a variety of ways. Some will positively respond to a piece-rate incentive system, while others may despise it. Thus, it is necessary for the manager to diagnose the nature of employees' needs to prescribe the right kinds of incentives if he wants to influence the behavior of employees in a desired direction.

Second, the valence of outcomes (the motivational value of incentives) is determined by their abilities to satisfy employees' needs. The mere existance of incentives will not influence the behavior of employees unless they can satisfy existing needs. The study of needs is important for effectively managing organizational incentives and for understanding the concept of valence in expectancy theory of motivation. The concept of valence is defined as the strength of an individual's desire for a particular outcome in expentancy theory (Vroom, 1964), but the expentancy theory does not spell out why the individual desires or values a certain outcome or incentive. A need theory will indicate that the individual values a particular outcome because it satisfies his needs.

Third, the contingency model suggests that tasks must be differentitated in their motivational characteristics and matched with individuals with different need strength. Some jobs can provide intrinsic motivation if they are assigned to workers with achievement-oriented needs. On the other hand, workers with lower-achievement needs can be motivated to perform less demanding jobs that provide financial incentives. An organization has a variety of jobs with different sets of motivational characteristics and is composed of people with different sets of needs. The manager should match employees to jobs where their needs can be satisfied. The need theory of motivation helps managers to differentiate between people's needs and assign them where they can be motivated.

Fourth, the organization does not have any direct control over the need structure of its employees. An individual's need structure very much depends on his hereditary factors and history of need satisfaction. However, it can indirectly influence the need structure by manipulating the means (incentives) of satisfying needs. By providing the means of satisfying the currently dominating needs of an employee, management can then help the employee search for the satisfaction of other needs. Also, as McClelland (1961, 1967) pointed out, a strong motivational need (achievement-oriented need) can be developed by manipulating one's family, educational, or work environment where achievement-oriented behavior is encouraged and rewarded. Understanding of the need theory may help managers select and develop people with certain types of needs.

Finally, people sometimes are motivated to do something just for the sake of doing it, without any apparent extrinsic rewards. There is no consummatory act which satisfies any particular need. Motivation is to arouse and maintain a certain level of activation rather than to search for a homeostatic equilibrium state. White (1959) called such a behavioral state *effectance motivation.* Its energy lies in the internal stimulus generated from the living cells that make up the nervous system. Its behavior tends to be exploratory and experimental. If one studies motivation only in the framework of reinforcement or incentive theory, he will fail to recognize the existence of effectance motivation. Although incentive theories view environmental factors as the causes of behavior, these theories recognize the existence of internal stimuli in the theoretical context that reinforcement reduces the potency of drives or needs upon their gratification.

In summary, need theory of motivation is a content theory which focuses on the internal stimuli that energize, direct, and sustain behavior. Behavior is motivated to satisfy these needs. Needs are satisfied by receiving incentive rewards; the motivational value of incentives is determined by needs. Thus studying need theories is important not only for understanding why people behave a certain way but also for increasing the effectiveness of an incentive system. The effectiveness of an incentive system will increase when it relates to the need structure of employees.

MOTIVATIONAL THEORIES OF NEEDS

A number of early scholars have contributed to the development of need theory of motivation. For example, Allport (1924) saw needs as the cause of behavior, stating that some needs exist in the human organism, and the organism acts to satisfy these needs. Need satisfaction refers to a biological readjustment. Although he recognized the social aspect of behavior, he related the social aspect to nonsocial behavior. To him, a person's social behavior is directed toward the fulfillment of biological needs. Lewin (1963) distinguished between genuine needs and quasi-needs. Genuine needs arose from biological conditions such as hunger, thrist, and other biological deficiencies; quasi-needs arose from psychic conditions such as intension and will power. Quasi-needs usually are manifested in the form of tension; a state of tension is created as a direct result of inability to satisfy a need. Lewin introduced the concepts of force and valence. Force refers to the strength of internal stimuli which demand satisfaction; valence refers to the desirability of a means of satisfying the stimuli. The concept of valence was used to relate the internal stimuli (needs) to the external stimuli (incentives) in Lewin's theoretical framework of motivation.

Murray (1938) advanced the theory of needs by listing a number of social or psychogenic needs. He classified needs into two categories: viscerogenic (primary) and psychogenic (secondary). The former includes the need for air, water, food, sex, lactation, urination, and defecation—all of which have known physiological bases. Psychogenic needs are derived from primary needs and are characterized by a lack of focal connection with a specific organic process or physiological satisfaction. Some of Murray's social needs include abasement, achievement, affiliation, aggression, autonomy, counteraction, defendance, dominance, and so forth. Murray had a significant influence on the development of motivational psychology by exploring the basic configuration of psychogenic needs derived from his studies of normal people.

The problems with these early need theories are that the explanation of behavior is based on the homeostatic principle that behavior is activated only to reduce the needs aroused in the organism, and the secondary needs are derived from the process of satisfying physiological needs. While some secondary needs are assumed to be derived from the process of satisfying the primary needs, most secondary psychogenic needs become major determinants of behavior far removed from any particular physiological base. Also, the homeostatic need-reduction theory does not recognize the existence of human behavior which is aroused in the absence of stimulation.

HIERARCHICAL THEORIES OF NEEDS

Maslow's Need Hierarchy. Maslow (1954) viewed an individual's motivation in terms of need hierarchy. Man's needs are arranged in the hierarchy of pre-potency in the order of 1) physiological, 2) safety, 3) social, 4) self-esteem, and 5) self-actualization needs. (Figure 3-1). Physiological needs are those associated with hunger, thirst, rest, sex, and other biological needs; safety needs are needs for protection from danger, threat, and deprivation; social needs are needs for expression of love, friendship, and a gregarious nature; self-esteem needs are those composed of autonomy, dignity, and respect from others; and self-actualization needs are the needs for realizing one's own potentialities in forms of creativity and capacity, for continuous self-development.

According to his analysis, as modified by McGregor (1960), man is a wanting creature and rarely reaches a state of complete satisfaction. Therefore, the organism will search continuously for need satisfaction. The process of animating the organism is the emergence of less potent needs from the gratification of

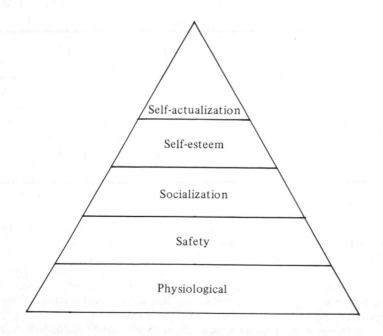

FIGURE 3-1. MASLOW'S HIERARCHY OF NEEDS

more potent needs such as physiological and safety. The emerging needs become major motivators of behavior. As soon as the needs on a lower level are reasonably satisfied, those on the next higher level will emerge as the dominant need demanding satisfaction. As an individual moves up to higher levels of the hierarchy, satisfaction of these needs increases their importance rather than reducing it (Maslow, 1970; and Wahba and Bridwell, 1976).

Another important proposition about human motivation is that a satisfied need is no longer a motivator of behavior. When people are deprived of something, they will crave it. Deprivation can be the motive of behavior. This concept is significant, for it limits the frequent use of certain incentives that cannot be motivators beyond a certain level of satisfaction. Only those needs that have not been satisfied exert any appreciable force on behavior. For healthy and mature individuals the nature of secondary needs including social, self-respect, and self-actualization, are such that they can never be fully satisfied. Therefore, no matter how much management wants to satisfy employees' needs there will remain some continued needs for satisfaction for which people strive.

Although Maslow is best known for his concept of need hierarchy, this is only a small, though important, portion of his total theory. To fully appreciate Maslow's theory of needs, one should consider the basic characteristics of the need system (Chung, 1969). First, Maslow (1954) proposed that the system of needs must be studied as a whole rather than as individual needs. Needs are rarely found in isolation but are found in a variety of combinations. A certain behavior can be caused not by one but many needs; conversely, one action can satisfy not one but a set of needs. To emphasize the multiplicity of the need system, Maslow introduced the concept of holism. This concept refers to the interrelated wholeness of an organism as one of the basic concepts of motivational theory.

Second, the clusters of needs in the holistic need system are "being contained within" rather than "being separated from." Maslow rejected the atomistic classification that listed various needs in a series of separated and independent parts. Various clusters of needs are interwoven within the holistic system, having varying effects on behavior and on each other. Maslow borrowed the concept of *syndrome* from medicine to describe the joint effects of interrelated needs on behavior. Syndrome refers to a pattern of behavior influenced by a number of causes simultaneously. As the levels of the hierarchy are not rigidly boxed but overlapping, it is possible that a higher-order need can emerge before lower-level needs are satisfied.

Finally, the order of needs in the hierarchy varies from one individual to another, especially when one moves from one culture to another. Some people never develop above the first or second level of the hierarchy, while others are absorbed by higher-order needs even when they are not satisfied with lower-order needs. The satisfaction of needs from one level to another is only a tendency, not a certainty. Thus, when an individual is satisfied with a given need, he may move to satisfy higher-order needs (not necessarily the next higher level need alone), and/or move back down the scale to better satisfy lower-order needs by upgrading the means of satisfying them. The flexibility in the hierarchy underlies the concept of interchangeability among needs. Thus, when direct achievement of a particular need is blocked, the person may develop a substitute goal or seek to gratify other alternative needs.

Two-level Theory of Needs. Despite the considerable amount of attention given to the need hierarchy theory, only a few attempts have been made to test the hierarchical arrangement of needs. The multiplicity, interrelatedness, and flexibility of the need system seem to make it difficult to experimentally test the prediction that the satisfaction of one need causes the strength of its next higher-order need. Testing the hierarchical concept can be done through a longitudinal data collection. However, as Maslow (1970, p. 20) pointed out, the hierarchy may take an entire life span to unfold. These difficulties seem to account for the lack of research data concerning the hierarchical concept.

Nevertheless, a number of studies are directly and indirectly related to the hierarchical concept. There is some evidence that lower-order needs must be satisfied before higher-order needs emerge as motivators. Keys, Brozek, Mickelsen, and Taylor (1950), Wolf (1958), Hampton, Summer, and Webber (1973, pp. 1-24) reported that when people are hungry or thirsty, they are preoccupied with the satisfaction of these needs and can think of little else other than food or water. Cofer and Appley (1964) presented data on animals and humans showing that as lower-order needs become reasonably satisfied, they become less important. Alderfer (1969), Goodman (1968), Porter (1964), and Porter and Lawler (1965) have shown that workers at lower-levels of organizational echelons tend to be more concerned with lower-order needs (especially job security), while managers at higher-levels are more concerned with higher-order needs. Alderfer (1966) also found that employees' satisfaction with fringe benefits is associated with increasing desire for satisfactory peer relations. These studies directly or indirectly support the importance of satisfying lower-order needs (biological and safety) before higher-order needs function as motivators of behavior.

However, it is not clear whether socialization needs have to be satisfied before higher-order needs (self-esteem and self-actualization) become important. Lawler and Suttle (1972) found that the satisfaction of lower-order needs were inversely related with their importance. However, no such relationship was found for socialization and higher-order needs. In a longitudinal study, Hall and Nougaim (1968) found that as managers advance in organizations, their need for safety decreases with an increase in their needs for social interaction, achievement, and self-actualization. These studies indicate that it is not necessary for socialization needs to be satisfied before higher-order needs become important. Socialization, self-esteem, and self-actualization can become simultaneously important upon the satisfaction of lower-order needs. This two-level theory of needs seems to receive support from other researchers. Waters and Roach (1973) factor-analyzed Maslow need categories and identified two factors: higher-order needs including esteem, autonomy, prestige, and self-actualization, and lower-order needs such as security, pressure, and friendship. Herzberg's two-factor theory (1959) of organizational incentives coincides with the two-level theory of needs. The dichotomization of intrinsic and extrinsic motivation generally support the position of the two-level theory. Herzberg's two-factor theory and intrinsic-extrinsic motivation will be further discussed in Chapter 4.

Three-Level Theory of Needs. Alderfer (1969, 1972) condensed the Maslow need hierarchy into existence, relatedness, and growth needs which he called the ERG theory. Existence needs include Maslow's physiological and safety needs; relatedness needs encompass socialization and self-esteem; and growth-oriented needs include the individual's desire to be self-confident, creative, and productive—Maslow's self-esteem and self-actualization. The self-esteem needs are divided into external (relatedness) and internal (growth) components. Alderfer, like Maslow, arranges needs in a hierarchy in the order of their importance. The satisfaction of a need not only influences its own importance but also affects the importance of higher-order needs. He agrees with Maslow that the satisfaction of higher-order needs (growth) make them more important rather than less important. However, Alderfer differs from the Maslow's theory that the lack of higher-order need satisfaction makes lower-order needs more important. He assumes that all needs can be simulataneously active; it is not necessary that lower-order needs have to be satisfied before higher-order needs emerge.

Alderfer (1972) provided some longitudinal data for supporting his view that the satisfaction of relatedness needs influences the importance of growth needs. He indicated that the basic ingredient of relatedness needs is sharing or mutuality. They are distinguished from existence needs in that the process of satisfying existence needs prohibits sharing. The historical perspective of motivational programs, discussed in Chapter 2, also provides an indirect support for the three-level theory of needs. The economic-rational concept of man in Adam Smith, *The Wealth of Nations* (1776), Taylor's scientific management in the 1920s, and Weber's bureaucracy in the 1920s emphasized the importance of lower-order needs and the economic efficiency in organizational operations. According to them, man works primarily for money. The importance of economic gains usually encourages competition rather than sharing.

The human relations movements in the 1930s and 1940s emphasized the importance of socialization needs (Mayo, 1945, Roethlisberger and Dickson, 1939). For most workers, the desire for acceptance, communication, friendship, and support on the job during the work hours became more important than earning extra money by being rate busters. Only recently has a significant portion of the populace been concerned with such higher-order needs as autonomy, growth, and self-actualization. The concept of man as a self-actualizing organism has essentially developed in the 1960s and 1970s. As the standard of living is rising and the level of education is increasing, people are more concerned with the satisfaction of higher-order needs.

Although higher-order needs become important for many workers, there is no evidence that lower-order needs are not important. Job security and needs for affection and acceptance are very much a part of the need structure for most people. However, there are some differences in the order of importance of various needs between managers and workers. For example, Porter (1964) pointed out that managers are mostly satisfied with lower-order needs and higher-order needs are important to them. Porter and Lawler (1965) reported that pay and other lower-order needs are more important to workers than managers. Reif and Luthans (1972) found that unskilled workers prefer the jobs that provide them with opportunities to socialize.

Researchers on need hierarchy have failed to support the view that needs are arranged in the five-hierarchical levels as suggested by Maslow (Wahba and Bridwell, 1976) Rather, these researchers suggest that needs are arranged in two or three levels. Alderfer (1972) and Yinon, Bizman, and Goldberg (1976) are more specific in saying that there are three levels of needs—existence, relatedness, and growth. These three levels of needs become the bases for developing the theories and programs of extrinsic, interactive, and intrinsic motivation.

McCLELLAND'S SOCIALLY ACQUIRED NEEDS

McClelland (1955, 1965) indicated that many needs are not physiological and universal as Maslow suggested. Rather, these are socially acquired and vary from culture to culture. Based on his research, he identified three types of acquired needs: the need for achievement (n Ach), the need for affiliation (n Aff), and the need for power (n Pow). The need for achievement reflects the desire for setting moderate task goals, taking responsibility, and receiving performance feedback. The need for affiliation reflects the desire for interaction with other people, a concern for the quality of interpersonal relationships, and a desire to be accepted by others. The need for power reflects the desire for interaction with other people, a concern for the quality of interpersonal relationships, and a desire to be accepted by others. The need for power reflects the desire of influencing others, exercising contol over others, and maintaining a superior-subordinate relationship. Most people have some aspects of all of these needs, but seldom in the same strength. All can be found in a person with varying degrees of strength. Depending on how these needs are structured, motivation will take different forms.

Since these needs are learned through coping with one's environmental realities, behavior which is rewarded tends to be repeated. Thus, people can acquire the need for achievement under conditions which encourage achievement-oriented and risk-taking behavior. The need for affiliation can result from a history of being reinforced for amiable and sociable behavior. Similarly, the need for power can be developed by rewarding dominant or inspirational behavior. Organizations can influence the configurations of employees' needs by manipulating work environment. By identifying and influencing the incentive associated with a specific motive or need, it is possible to strengthen the aroused behavioral tendency.

The strength of these motives or needs can be assessed by using the Thematic Apperception Tests (TAT). The TAT was originally developed by Murray (1938) as a tool for assessing personality. McClelland and his associates have modified the original form of TAT to make it suitable to the study of the socially acquired motives. Researchers ask their subjects to write a story about a set of pictures which usually show people in relatively ambiguous social and work situations. The subjects look at a picture for about ten to fifteen seconds and have about five minutes to write an imaginary story about the picture. The following questions can serve as guides for writing the story: 1) What is happening and who are the people? 2) What has led up to the situation? That is, what has happened in the past? 3) What are they talking or thinking about? 4) What will happen or will be done in the future?

The stories can be analyzed for the subjects' concerns for n Ach, n Aff, and n Pow (Kolb, Rubin, and McIntrye, 1971, pp. 51-83). If a story concerns a standard of excellence, task accomplishment or any achievement, and personal or task goals and plans, it will be scored higher on n Ach. If a story concerns emotional relationships, personal likes or dislikes, and socializing activities, it will be scored higher on n Aff. If a story concerns controlling or influencing people, controlling the means of influencing others, and superior-subordinate relationships, it will be scored higher on n Pow. It is possible that a story can be higher or lower on all of these three needs or motives.

The implications of McClelland's theory are significant for motivating managers. Different motives express themselves in different behavioral patterns. Tasks in an organization require different behavioral patterns. The organization can improve its selection and placement processes by matching the motivational characteristics of individuals with the requirements of the task. For example, an employee with high n Ach can be placed in a position where he can compete against high standards of performance. Such a position can be found in sales and entrepreneurial jobs. A manager with high n Pow should be placed in a mangerial position where he can inspire or control other people. Political offices provide such an opportunity. Similarly, a manager with high n Aff can be placed in a leadership position that requires a high degree of interaction among members and between hierarchical levels and democratic leadership style. A manager with highs on all these needs can be a versatile manager who can effectively function in all managerial situations. Such an organizational fit between individual predispositions and task requirements will result in high employee satisfaction and job performance.

EMPLOYEE NEEDS AND WORK MOTIVATION

Individuals in an organization have a variety of needs that they want to satisfy through organizational endeavors. Following the three-level theory, employees' needs are classified into existence, relatedness or relation-oriented, and growth needs. All these needs will influence work motivation. However, not all needs are equally instrumental for arousing work motivation. Growth needs are said to be the most powerful in arousing intrinsic motivation, while existence needs are the sources of extrinsic motivation. Affiliation needs then influence the effective reactions of employees to their jobs, co-workers, and management. It is generally hypothesized that workers motivated by growth needs tend to yield higher performance than those motivated by either existence or affiliation needs. The validity of this hypothesis will be questioned in the following discussion.

EXISTENCE NEEDS AND EXTRINSIC MOTIVATION

Physiological needs. The existence needs include physiological and economic maintenance needs. Common physiological needs are hunger, thirst, sex, sleepiness, and physical safety. These needs are:

1. Universal to most people
2. Vital for maintaining biological health
3. Operating on a homeostatic principle
4. Satisfied before other needs emerge as motivators
5. Continuously recurring
6. Satisfied through extrinsic means

Physiological needs are so universal and vital that everyone must first satisfy these needs. Failure to satisfy them usually means poor health and threat to survival. These needs are continuously recurring and temporarily satisfied by such external substances as food and water. However, since most people in industrial societies have the means of satisfying these needs, they are not usually considered important motivators. Most people do not have to work full-time to satisfy these needs; only a fraction of their working hours can serve their satisfaction.

Security needs. Security needs concern economic and psychological health maintenance. Economic downturns frequently create high rates of unemployment at all occupational levels. The problem of unemployment is not limited to uneducated and unskilled people. Frequently, the shift in technological orientation and the temporary oversupply in certain professional fields lead to unemployment of professionally trained people. Losing a job not only means a loss of income to support the family and their standard of living, but also a threat to maintaining mental health. People satisfy a variety of needs through work; unemployment cuts off the sources of satisfying these needs. Even employed people are adversely affected by the emotional climate in which their co-workers and neighbors worry about job security.

Job security is frequently rated by employees as one of the most important aspects of their jobs. For example, Herzberg, Mausner, Peterson, and Capwell (1957) found that the average worker ranks job security first in importance among sixteen job factors. Pay is ranked sixth in their study. Pay is closely related to job security and economic needs and is usually ranked high in its importance. Lawler (1971) surveyed forty-one studies on the relative importance of job factors and found that pay ranked third in importance.

Like physiological needs, security needs are maintenance needs; they must be satisfied so that other needs can function as motivators. However, these needs are more difficult to satisfy than physiological needs because they involve more than physiological satisfaction: they involve the mental and psychological sense of security. Maintaining a healthy psychological environment in an organization is important for releasing physical and psychic energies for productive purposes. Yet, it is difficult to create a psychologically healthy work environment because the work environment is affected by a number of factors other than pay. Pay may satisfy physiological needs. But, a sense of job security is influenced by the person's psychological makeups, employment condition, interpersonal relationship, and general economic condition.

Satisfying existence needs can be motivational factors for some people if they are not reasonably satisfied with these needs. But, once these needs are satisfied, they lose motivational power. Reward systems are directly related to the satisfaction of existence needs. Motivational principles and programs affecting the effectiveness of extrinsic reward systems will be discussed in Chapters 4 and 7. The satisfaction of these lower-order needs is usually a prerequisite for increasing intrinsic motivation. When workers are reasonably satisfied with these needs, they will positively respond to any motivational programs designed to increase intrinsic work motivation.

RELATION-ORIENTED NEEDS AND AFFECTION MOTIVATION

Relation-oriented needs include affiliative motive, power motive, and competitive motive. These needs concern man's desire to relate oneself to other people for socializing, competing, and influencing. The basic ingredients of these needs are that the process of satisfying them involves people as the major source of need satisfaction and people exchange feelings and emotions as the major units of interaction. Satisfying biological needs primarily involves materials and things rather than feelings and emotions. Satisfying growth needs then involves the performance of interesting and challenging tasks. The satisfaction of existence and growth needs usually appeals to man's desire for rational behavior. However, the expression of relation-oriented needs involves the rational and emotional aspects of a human being. These needs can be instrumental in achieving rational goals. But, at the same time, they influence the affective reactions of employees for their jobs, co-workers, and management. These affective reactions influence employees' work motivation.

Affiliative Motive   *Social*

Affiliative motive concerns companionship, belonging, love and affection, and emotional support from others. The following studies show that the affiliative motive has an influence on behavior. First, the Hawthorne Studies at Western Electric (Roethlisberger and Dickson, 1939) found that the attitudes and sentiments in a social situation at work influence workers' performance. Physiological factors are less important than sociopsychological factors on the job. Group pressures have a greater impact on productivity than economic incentives.

Second, Schachter (1959) has shown that people seek companionship of others when they are in anxious and confused situations. People have a tendency to seek out others to relieve the stress of uncertainties. In his experiment, the subjects were told that they would experience some pain as a part of the experiment and then they were given the opportunity to be with others while they were waiting. Most subjects preferred to be with others. Epley (1974), however, pointed out that the presence of others may reduce fear or anxiety, but not the instrumental response to the aversive stimulus itself.

Third, workers prefer a supportive leadership style when they are performing highly structured and nonchallenging jobs. Several path-goal leadership theorists (House and Dessler, 1974; House and Mitchell, 1974; and Stinson and Johnson, 1975) indicated that supportive leadership is positively correlated with employee satisfaction under conditions of high task structure, but not under low task structure. When tasks are highly structured, an effective leader provides his subordinates with consideration and support to relieve frustration resulting from performing routinized and uninteresting tasks. The leader becomes the major source of employee satisfaction.

Fourth, Hackman and Lawler (1971) reported that workers on jobs with few opportunities for social interaction experience less social need satisfaction than workers with ample opportunities. Vroom (1964) pointed out that workers who have greater opportunities for socialization tend to show lower absenteeism and turnover rates than those who do not. Persons with high n Aff will be more sensitive to the opportunity for social interaction and even take steps to promote such opportunities.

Finally, some studies suggest that affiliation needs may be innate, and are different from physiological needs. Harlow (1958) provided infant monkeys with surrogate mothers in lieu of their natural mothers. One surrogate mother was made out of wire and the other was terry cloth. The study found that the infant monkeys fed on the wire mother, but spent most of their time with the cloth mother. Monkeys developed their attachment to mothers based on comfort rather than on biological need satisfaction. A similar study by Harlow and Suomi (1970) reported that the infant monkeys spent more time clinging to the cloth surrogate than to rayon, vinyl, and sandpaper surrogates.

The affiliative motive does not directly influence work motivation. However, a person's desire to comply with the norms of his reference group can influence his performance if the norms concern performance levels. If group norms are higher than management's expectations, the tendency to conform to group norms may lead to high productivity. Conformity per se is neither good nor bad; the quality and intensity of group norms to which people conform determine the outcomes of group activities. It also has been hypothesized that the supervisor's expectation of excellence from his subordinates, and the subordinates' desire to meet that expectation, motivate employees to strive for high levels of performance (Oxley and Oxley, 1963). Since employees depend on their superiors for motivational opportunities, they will be willing to comply with supervisors' wishes. Thus, work motivation becomes the responsibility of supervisors.

Power Motive

Power motive involves man's desire to control or influence other people. The concept of power carries a negative connotation in American society; it is associated with fascist, Machiavellian, dictatorship, Watergate coverup, corruption, and dishonesty. People are suspicious of a person who seeks power, even if he does so to help other people. However, power is an important element in running organizations. Organizations cannot function without people who want to exercise power and have influence over others. If management is getting things done through other people, there should be someone who can influence other people to work together. McClelland (1970) articulated the need for power in organizations as follows:

> Since managers are primarily concerned with influencing others, it seems obvious that they should be characterized by a high need for Power, and that by studying power motive we can learn something about the way effective managerial leaders work. — Thus, leadership and power appear as two closely related concepts, and if we want to understand better effective leadership, we may begin studying the power motive in thought and action (p. 30).

McClelland identified two faces of power motive: the negative personalized power and positive socialized power. The negative personalized power is characterized by the dominance-submission relationship. The personalized power motive is associated with aggressive impulses, heavy drinking, and collecting prestige symbols. It does not lead to an effective leadership because a person with such a power drive tends to treat other people as pawns rather than as equals.

The positive socialized power is characterized by a concern for group goals, helping group members to find and achieve meaningful group goals, and giving them the necessary support, strength, and competence. People with such a power motive tend to be interested in informal sports, politics, and holding offices. The leader must learn that his role is not to dominate and treat people like pawns, but to give them the necessary strength and treat them as equals. The concept of power equalization is an example of promoting the positive socialized power in organizations.

The socialized power motive may cause a person to assume the leadership role, by which he influences other organizational members to strive for high productivity. A leader does not necessarily have to be a high achiever himself. The quality of a good leader lies in his ability to develop, encourage, and motivate other poeple to achieve. Studies found that persons with low n Ach still could lead highly productive work groups by exhibiting positive n Pow (McClelland, 1970).

Competitive Motive

The competitive urge has been deeply imbedded in people's lives and has been a leading motive in striving for high performance. Competition becomes a strong motive of behavior for several reasons. First, most of the means of satisfying human needs are scarce. Economic resources are limited, and people compete for these limited resources. As they are limited, winners get more of these resources at the expenses of losers. The fact that organizational structure is pyramidal indicates the scarcity in power positions in organizations. Thus, persons with high n Pow are driven to compete for the limited power positions.

Second, the ability to keep up with or get ahead of others determines one's ego. People compare their economic or power possessions with others as a basis for determining self-esteem and social status. People tend to compete with others whom they consider as equal or a little bit better. Many people do not concern themselves with people they cannot relate to. But, if their neighbors buy new campers or their colleagues received higher wages, they may be concerned with their deficiency and be motivated to correct it. Adam's equity theory (1965) indicates that people compare their ratios of outputs with others' ratios to determine the feeling of equity in resource distribution systems. Any discrepancy will motive them to minimize the feeling of inequity.

There are two kinds of competition in organizations: competition against people and competition against standards of performance. The first type of competition in a part of relation-oriented needs and is related to the power motive, while the second type is seen as an expression of growth-oriented needs and is closely related to the competence motive and achievement motive. The first type of competition concerns man's desire to win and control other people.

Organizational members compete with other members for limited economic resources or power. Work groups may compete with each other for the same reasons that individual members compete. Although competition may cause individuals and groups to perform their jobs well, it may in some cases lead to unnecessary destruction of cooperation and coordination among group members. Creating a sense of mastery over other organizational members or groups in an organization is dysfunctional for creating a supportive organizational climate. Especially, when the jobs require high degrees of interaction among work group members and between functional groups, competition is a destructive managerial tool. However, if individual jobs are relatively independent of others, a sense of competition among members can positively affect the level of performance.

The relatedness needs affect the quality of interactions among work group members and between functional work groups. If their interactions lead to the satisfaction of relatedness needs, they may lead to productive organizational outcomes—job satisfaction and performance. Relatedness needs become the sources of affective motivation. Affective motivation creates an organizational climate in which people develop affective reactions to their jobs, co-workers, supervision, and management. People draw psychological contracts regarding job involvement based on these affective reactions. Various organizational factors influencing affective motivation will be discussed in Chapter 8.

GROWTH NEEDS AND INTRINSIC MOTIVATION

Growth needs deal with man's desire to be competent, productive, and self-actualizing. The major characteristics of these needs are that satisfaction does not reduce their importance, and successful task performance becomes the major source of satisfying these needs. Unlike physiological needs which operate on a homeostatic principle, the strength of these higher-order needs can increase as a result of satisfying experiences. They become a continuous source of motivational energy, and their satisfaction ties to performance. An extrinsic reinforcement can be given to workers in addition to intrinsic reinforcement. However, the primary source of higher-order need satisfaction is derived from performing a task successfully rather than from receiving extrinsic rewards. A number of higher-order needs can be explored to stimulate intrinsic motivation and high performance.

Competence Motive

Competence refers to the ability to cope with one's environment and get what he wants from it (White, 1959). Its energy source lies in the central nerve system which instigates the organism to search for an optimal level of stimuli and to conquer the stimuli. Thus, a behavior motivated by this need tends to be exploratory and experimental. However, it is different from an existential nihilism that is not particularly goal directed. While the competence motive concerns with the desire for being competent and conquering, an existential behavior is lacking such a goal orientation.

Behavior aroused to satisfy the competence motive is called effectance motivation. As indicated earlier, its reinforcement is derived from an arousal of activity rather than in returning to the equilibrium state. Effectance is innately satisfying and is not necessarily learned through experiencing external reinforcements. Hunt (1965) suggested that people need an optimal amount of incongruity or productive tension and that this need is the psychological basis of intrinsic motivation. When this incongruency is minimized as a result of effectance behavior, the organism will search for a new level of incongruency. Thus, searching for and conquering the productive stimuli is an ongoing process.

Through this active and continuous process of seeking and conquering the challenges, people learn to effectively deal with their environment and gain a greater degree of automony. The sense of competence is strong or weak depending on the balance of successes and failures one has experienced in his encounters with his environment. In this sense, competition is closely related to the feeling of competence because people gain what they want from their environment through successful competition with other people or certain standards of task performance. Especially, competition against high standards of performance will greatly enhance one's sense of mastery over his work environment.

Effectance motivation involves learning, which is a continuous and never-ending process. A learning environment that has the characteristics of exploration and experimentation seems to arouse effectance motivation. People encounter continuous challenges and conquer them in a learning environment. Effectance motivation has a practical implication for designing jobs in organizations. Job enlargement and job enrichment programs that introduce a variety of task skill requirements are to arouse effectance motivation. These programs will require a variety of responses from workers and thus sustain their attention and interest. And, the introduction of skill variety in work environment creates a learning environment. When tasks provide such a continous learning opportunity, workers will be motivated to perform effectively without increased extrinsic rewards.

Achievement Motive

A desire to achieve what one wants to accomplish is one of the strongest motivators that stimulate high performance. McClelland (1961, 1962) indicated that people with high n Ach tend to be gravitated toward business where the need can be satisfied. He found that successful executives from such countries as the United States, Italy, and India generally scored higher on the n Ach than did people in other professions with compatible education and background. Stories written by middle-management executives contained more references to the n Ach than did other executives at lower and higher management levels. The n Ach propels a man into upper level management, but once the person reaches the top-management level, this need seems to be satisfied.

McClelland (1961) indicated that high n Ach is associated with entrepreneurial behavior, innovative risk-taking, and business success. A person with high n Ach tends to seek high degrees of personal responsibility, set realistic goals, take moderate risks, seek and use performance feedback, and search for achieving opportunities. Since he is highly task-oriented, he would rather choose a stranger known to be an expert than a friend as a working partner, whereas those with high n Aff chose a friend over an expert. He is more interested in getting the job done than being sensitive to other people's feelings.

His sense of personal responsibility may keep him from sharing authority and power with others. However, if he sees that being sensitive to and sharing power with others are the means of achieving his goals, he will develop the necessary qualifications. Contingency theory of leadership implies that an effective leader will change his behavioral patterns to be instrumental for achieving his and his subordinates' goals. If the goal-attainment requires him to be supportive or directive, he will modify his leadership style to suit the situation.

As indicated earlier, work environment influences the development of achievement motivation. By creating a work environment in which people can pursue the satisfaction of n Ach, the organization can increase the level of achievement motivation of its members. Stringer (1966) pointed out that the level of achievement motivation can be increased in an organization where 1) goal-setting behavior is encouraged, 2) personal responsibility for task accomplishment is demanded, 3) performance feedback is given to workers, 4) workers are allowed to take moderate risks, and 5) rewards are given according to their performance.

McClelland and his associates at Harvard have developed a set of techniques developing achievement motivation (McClelland, 1966). These techniques involve four main goals. First, they are designed to teach the participants to think, talk, and act like a person with high n Ach. For example, they learn to fantasize being successful persons and score high on n Ach. Second, they learn to set higher but realistic task and life goals for themselves. They check their actual performance or accomplishment with the goals. Third, the techniques teach them to learn more about themselves by TAT or ring-toss games. Group discussions often reveal a person's life goals and methods of achieving these goals. Finally, group techniques are used to create the esprit de corps from learning each other's hopes and fears, successes and failures, and limits and strengths. The participants not only learn about themselves and others but also build up emotional strength from their group therapeutic experiences.

The n Ach training was given to executives in a United States firm, businessmen in India, managers in Mexican firms, and underachieving high school boys. In every instance except one Mexican case, it was demonstrated that persons who had the training had done better than others with similar backgrounds in terms of earning more money, getting promotions, and expanding their business (McClelland, 1966). Several other studies support McClelland's findings. Durand (1975) reported a similar result from a training program designed to increase entrepreneurial activities among blacks. This study indicated that the participants receiving achievement motivation training increased their TAT scores and perceived the locus of behavioral causality (control) to be more internal. The participants who received both achievement motivation and regular management training became more active in their business endeavors than those who received only management development training. Aronoff and Litwin (1971) also reported that the executives in the achievement motivation training program had performed significantly better than those who attended a regular executive development program as measured by changes in job level and salary. Steers (1975) also reported the positive effect of n Ach on job performance. In his study, a sample of first-line supervisors with high n Ach demonstrated higher levels of job satisfaction, job involvement, and performance than did those supervisors with low n Ach.

Self-actualization Need

The highest-order need that stimulates people to excel is probably the desire to actualize one's own ambitious self-image and the desire to become what one is capable of becoming. Maslow (1954) articulated and popularized the concept of self-actualization by perceiving the need to be the most powerful motivator of performance-oriented behavior. As this need is situated at the pinacle of the need hierarchy, it becomes important for an individual when he is reasonably satisfied with his lower-order needs. Persons who are motivated by this need are in general economically, psychologically, and professionally independent so they are able to pursue self-actualization as their life goals.

Self-actualizing behavior is solely motivated by sheer enjoyment of doing and accomplishing what a person enjoys. He enjoys using and developing his capacities and talents for what he does. Such a behavior is intrinsically motivated and is independent of extrinsic rewards. However, extrinsic rewards may follow as a result of self-actualizing behavior but not as the conditions for such a behavior. Maslow (1970) also indicated that unlike lower-order needs operating on a homeostatic principle, higher-order needs become more important as people experience growth and self-fulfillment. Thus, these needs can serve as the continuing source of work motivation in an organization.

Not all people are motivated by this self-actualization need. It is because not many people are economically, psychologically, and professionally capable of pursuing the satisfaction of this need. Self-actualizing behavior is commonly found among managerial and professional people who have achieved social and economic status in and out of their professions. Porter (1962) found that managers at all levels, except the top management, felt some degree of deprivation of higher-order needs. However, as they are mostly satisfied with lower-order needs, such higher-order needs as autonomy and self-actualization become important for these managers.

Professional people seem to have more opportunities to satisfy this higher-order need. The HEW report *Work in America* (1973) found that more than 80 percent of professional personnel, including urban university professors, mathematicians, physicists, biologists, chemists, lawyers, and journalists, are satisfied with their jobs. It reported that these professional people would choose the same or similar work again if they were to repeat their careers. They are in general reasonably well satisfied with existence and relatedness needs, and their jobs seem to provide them with opportunities to satisfy high-order needs.

Presently, organizational tasks and managerial practices tend to limit the opportunity for blue and white-collar workers to realize their full potentials and talents. Many of them seem to find their jobs unrewarding and want to pursue other occupations if they have such opportunities (HEW, 1973). Especially, these employees are often deprived of lower-order need satisfaction and will divert their energies to satisfy them. However, as more people are better satisfied with existence and relatedness needs, they will demand need satisfaction of a higher-order. More jobs must be designed to provide them with opportunities to satisfy higher-order needs (Maslow, 1970; and Argyris, 1973). Motivational programs designed to provide such opportunities will be discussed in Chapters 9 and 10.

DOMINANT   NEEDS AND EMPLOYEE BEHAVIOR

People join and work in organizations to satisfy their needs. They will behave in a manner that will satisfy their dominant needs. At a given moment, an individual has a variety of needs; some can be satisfied in a particular organization while others cannot. An organization cannot satisfy the multiple needs of an individual simultaneously because different activities are necessary to satisfy each of the needs. At the same time, the organization is limited in terms of providing its members with the means necessary to satisfy all of these needs. What makes it more difficult is the fact that each individual has a unique set of needs that search for gratification. However, if the person's dominant needs can be satisfied as a result of his work, he will remain a member and contribute to the organizational success. Thus, a task of a manager is to identify a set of dominant needs of employees and create a work environment in which these can be satisfied.

EXTENT OF NEED FULFILLMENT

To what extent are people satisfied in organizations? What dominant needs do they strive to satisfy? Evidence thus far suggests that people in this society are relatively well satisfied with physiological needs, but the need for economic security is not yet fulfilled for many people. Thus, existence needs still can instigate work motivation if the extrinsic rewards satisfying these needs are contingent upon their work behavior.

Relatedness needs are satisfied through interaction with other people. As more people are better satisfied with existence needs, they become more sensitive to affiliation needs. And yet, as the society becomes more complex and mechanized, the opportunities for satisfying these needs seem to be diminishing. In addition, as more people are economically and psychologically independent, it becomes more difficult to lead and govern them. On the other hand, as more organizations are keenly aware of the importance of relation-oriented needs, more managerial personnel receive training in interpersonal skills, leadership, and behavioral sciences in general. Consequently, these trained managers counterbalance the difficulty of dealing with complex human problems in organizations.

Growth-oriented needs seem to offer excellent opportunities for management to stimulate employees' work motivation. More people are searching for fulfillment of these needs, and yet it is one of the least exploited areas of human motivation. Once activated, these needs will produce self-generating motivational power without apparent external stimuli.

Figure 3-2 describes the extent to which people are satisfied with their needs in organizations. Maslow (1954) indicated that an average working adult has satisfied 85 percent of his physiological needs, 70 percent of security and safety needs, 50 percent of socialization needs, 40 percent of self-esteem needs, and 10 percent of self-actualization needs. Although there is no evidence to support this proposition, many studies (Alderfer, 1969; Porter, 1964; Porter and Lawler, 1965; and Lawler and Suttle, 1972) generally agree that people are more satisfied with lower-order needs than higher-order needs.

The high degree of deprivation of need satisfaction at the higher-order levels implies that these unfulfilled needs present greater opportunities for management to motivate employees by appealing to higher-order needs than lower-order needs. Although not all people can be motivated by these higher-order needs, more people seem to consider the satisfaction of them important. The unfulfilled needs, if they are considered important, will become a major source of motivational energy. On the other hand, if these needs are unfulfilled over a prolonged period of time, people will be frustrated and may display stress signals such as ulcers, emotional disturbances, nervous breakdowns, and develop unhealthy attitudes toward their jobs, co-workers, and management. The possible consequences of need satisfaction and deprivation and their relationships to job performance will be investigated in Chapter 6.

PATH TO NEED SATISFACTION

People satisfy their needs through various paths. Existence needs (physiological and security) are satisfied primarily by such substantive reinforcers as pay and job security. Substantive reinforcers are externally mediated by others and can be applied to workers independent of work behavior. Thus, if these

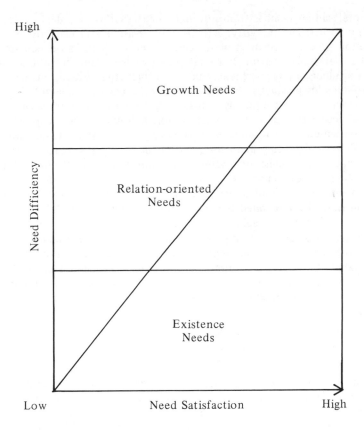

FIGURE 3-2. NEED DIFFICIENCY AND NEED SATISFACTION

reinforcers   are to be used as motivational incentives to increase work performance, they should be contingent upon work performance. When people work for substantive rewards, the locus of behavioral causality is said to be external. This means that they are motivated by incentives mediated by external agents. Extrinsically motivated behavior will cease when the rewards are absent. The power of substantive incentives to evoke behavior also decreases as workers become satisfied with existence needs.

Relation-oriented needs can be satisfied on the job through interaction with other people. Not content with satisfying merely existence needs, some employees may strive to satisfy such relation-oriented needs as affiliation, power, and competition by joining groups, interacting, accepting, competing, persuading, and influencing others. Work group, informal social group, managerial position, contest, and promotion all present opportunities for satisfying the relation-oriented needs. The locus of behavioral causality can be either internal or external. Affective motivation can be aroused by either sheer enjoyment of being with others (internal locus) or as a means of obtaining other outcomes such as praise, increased pay, or promotion (external locus). When the perceived locus of behavioral causality shifts from internal to external, it may destroy feelings of affection, trust, and integrity. Affective motivation also can influence the manifestation of existence or growth needs. It either reduces or increases the threshold for evoking behavior. For example, a worker wants to produce more units of a product to increase his pay under an incentive system, but he voluntarily withholds his productive behavior because he fears the rejection by other group members. People frequently refuse to get involved in intrinsically motivating jobs because they do not particularily like fellow workers or supervisors.

Growth-oriented needs (competence, achievement, and self-actualization) can be satisfied by undertaking interesting and challenging tasks. Behavior is motivated to experience a sense of mastery, accomplishment, and self-fulfillment. The primary locus of behavioral causality is internal; intrinsically motivated behavior is initiated without apparent extrinsic rewards. Deci (1975) pointed out that intrinsically motivated behavior falls into two general classes: 1) behavior that seeks out challenging situations or stimuli (effectance motivation), and 2) behavior that aims to conquer the challenges (achievement motivation). Intrinsic motivation involves the ongoing seeking and conquering of challenges. Once activated the behavior requires a continuous interaction between human organisms and their environment, providing the challenges and stimuli. The roles of substantive, interactive, and effectance incentives on specific behavior will be further discussed in Chapter 4.

DOMINANT NEEDS AND BEHAVIOR MANIFESTATION

Need theories of motivation are basically content theories and do not usually explain the processes by which dominant needs and their aroused states (motivation) are manifested into specific behavior. They seem to assume that if a certain need becomes dominant and aroused, an instrumental behavior will be naturally initiated to satisfy the aroused need. The aroused need may cause a response, but the selection of a specific behavior depends on the person's past history of reinforcing experience (instrumental relationships between needs and need satisfying agents), cognitive evaluation of behavioral outcomes (valence), and perceived probabilities of experiencing satisfactory behavior (expectancy).

Depending on their differences in reinforcement history and cognitive evaluation, people respond to the same set of needs in different manners (see Costello and Zalkind, 1963; pp. 64-66; and Graham, 1975; pp. 90-93). The differences in behavior manifestation are as follows. First, the same need can lead to different behavioral responses. Individuals with the same need with equal potency may behave differently to achieve the same goal. For example, their goal is to obtain promotion. One person may demonstrate high performance to impress his boss, while the other may ingratiate to please the boss. Second, the same need can be satisfied by different reinforcers. Hunger need can be met by different foods. The need for self-esteem can be satisfied by a promotion in rank, by exercising informal power over the people, or by joining a prestigeous social club. Third, the same behavior is caused by different needs. One person may play a musical instrument for fun, while another plays for money. Finally, behavior can satisfy a number of needs of a person. A musician can satisfy his existence, affiliation, and growth needs with music.

The above illustrations lead to the conclusion that the study of needs alone is not enough to understand the dynamic and complex processes through which dominant needs are manifested into specific behaviors. Since a specific behavior is manifested as a result of interaction between needs, incentives, and cognitive processes, it is necessary to study the functions and interactions of these motivational variables. Unlike those scholars who attempt to explain motivated behavior by studying only need theories (Maslow, 1954; McClelland, 1961), incentive or reinforcement principles (Skinner, 1953, 1975; Kazdin, 1975), or perceptional processes (Patterson, 1964; Vroom, 1964), the argument here suggests that these partial theories of motivation (needs, incentives, and perceptions) be integrated into a comprehensive theoretical framework. However, the partial theories need to be studied separately before they are thrown into a comprehensive theoretical model. Partial theories explain the motivational determinants and their functions in each particular motivational domain.

SUMMARY AND CONCLUSION

Needs are defined as internal stimuli that energize or cause people to interact with their environment to satisfy their dominant needs. These needs are classified into three major categories: existence, relation-oriented, and growth-oriented. The existence needs include physiological and security needs. These needs are primarily satisfied by such extrinsic rewards as pay and job security. When people are deprived of these needs, they are motivated by them. But, once these needs are reasonably satisfied, they become less important as motivators.

The relation-oriented needs include affiliative motive, power motive, and competitive motive. These needs are satisfied through interaction with other people. Unlike existence and growth needs that appeal primarily to man's rationality and goal-orientation, the relation-oriented needs involve feelings and emotions as basic units of interaction. The outcomes of their interactions influence affective motivation of workers which in turn affect their commitment to jobs, co-workers, and supervisors.

The growth-oriented needs include the desire for being competent, achieving, and self-actualizing. These needs can be satisfied by undertaking interesting and challenging tasks. The satisfaction of these needs does not reduce their importance; the strength of these needs can increase as a result of satisfying experiences. People who are motivated by these needs undertake their tasks for the sheer enjoyment of feeling competent, accomplishing, and developing their capacities. Behavior is manifested without apparent extrinsic rewards. The thrust of behavior is coming from man's desire to search for challenging situations and to conquer the challenge.

Need theories of motivation occupy a central position in motivational studies. However, the study of needs alone cannot explain the complex motivational processes through which dominant needs are expressed in specific behavior. Specific behavior manifestation, in addition to being influenced by man's dominant needs, is governed by external stimuli or incentives, and is influenced by his cognitive evaluation of behavioral outcomes and their expectancies. In essence, there are many behavioral determinants other than needs. Other motivational determinants will be discussed separately and integrated into a theoretical framework in the following two chapters.

4

INCENTIVE THEORIES OF MOTIVATION

To discover how to control and influence human behavior toward a certain desired direction, many scholars have studied the effects of environmental factors on behavior. Unlike need theorists who search for behavioral causes in the internal states of needs, incentive theorists turn their attention to the external factors that influence behavior. Incentive theorists are interested in finding contingency relationships between behavior and its consequences, rather than trying to explain why behavior is energized and how it is directed once it is energized. Behavior is said to be a function of its consequences (reward or punishment). People behave to receive rewards and avoid punishment. Thus, by manipulating the potential consequences or incentives, one can control the behavior of other people.

The term *incentive* is defined in this chapter as external stimuli that influence the behavior of employees, or the conditions in jobs that are capable of influencing or altering their behavior. Organizations have a variety of incentives that induce and influence their employees' behavior. Employees are induced to organizations for pay, job security, and/or professional growth. Students are influenced by grades, instructions, and/or course materials. Punishment also affects their behavior by discouraging them from certain undesirable activities. Knowledge about the relationships between behavior and its consequences provides managers with a set of principles and guidelines that can be applied for shaping, altering, and directing the behavior of employees toward the attainment of organizational goals.

This chapter deals with 1) theories of learning and reinforcement, 2) principles or mechanics of managing reinforcement systems, 3) types of incentives or reinforcers, and 4) application of reinforcement in organizations. Since organizations are primarily interested in managing their incentive-reward systems for the purpose of increasing employee productivity, more detailed discussions on various incentive-reward systems (extrinsic, affective, and intrinsic) will be presented in Chapters 7, 8, 9, and 10.

LEARNING AND REINFORCEMENT

The classical learning theories (Thorndike's law of effect and Pavlov's conditioned reflex), discussed in Chapter 2, paved the way for developing more refined theories of learning and reinforcement involving the application of incentives in organizations. The classical learning theories indicated that behavior is learned through affective and repeated associations between stimulus and response. Rewarded behavior tends to strengthen the association between stimulus and responses (law of effect). In the absence of such an affective S-R bond, repetitive pairings of stimulus and response can strengthen the S-R association (law of exercise or conditioned reflex). Skinner (1953) looked beyond the S-R association as a way of learning behavior. He made the distinction between S-R respondent behavior and operant behavior. Operant behavior is not emitted as a response to stimulus but is controlled by its consequences.

RESPONDENT CONDITIONING

Respondent conditioning concerns behavioral responses elicited by prior stimulation. There are two types of respondent behavior: unconditioned response and conditioned response. Certain stimuli existing in one's environment such as foods, noises, and shocks elicit reflex responses. These responses are generally thought of as being involuntary and unconditioned reflexes. Reflexive behavior comes naturally and does not have to be learned. For example, foods placed on the tongue cause salivation. A tap on the knee produces jerking. Such unconditioned responses are not a great concern of motivational study; the study of motivation primarily is concerned with voluntary behavior.

Conditioned responses learned as a result of classical conditioning present a behavioral technique for producing specific responses to otherwise neutral stimuli. Through a classical conditioning technique, stimuli which previously did not influence behavior can become a source of behavioral control. To produce a conditioned response, a neutral stimulus is repeatedly paired with an unconditioned stimulus which produces an unconditioned response. The neutral stimulus becomes a conditioned stimulus when it elicits a conditioned response by itself. For example, the classical conditioning by Pavlov (1927) illustrates the learning process. When the sound of a bell is repeatedly paired with feelings, the conditioned stimulus can elicit salivation.

The classical conditioning process has some practical implications for managing people in organizations. First, many emotional feelings such as likes or dislikes, anxieties, and fears which are associated with a number of external stimuli in organizations are learned through the classical learning process. For example, people like money because it is repeatedly paired with materials such as foods that produce unconditioned responses. People dislike or even fear the stern faces of their supervisors because such expressions are frequently associated with negative actions and produce unpleasant emotional responses. Such emotional feelings and responses are considered involuntary reactions. Second, the S-R association facilitates the operant learning process. External stimuli often present cues that behavior will be followed by certain consequences. When the consequences which follow behavior occur in the presence of a particular set of stimuli, the stimuli alone can increase the likelihood that the behavior is emitted.

OPERANT CONDITIONING

Operant behavior is controlled by its consequences. It is different from respondent behavior in that the former is voluntary behavior controlled by its consequences, while the latter is involuntary reflexes emitted by stimuli. Operant behavior acts on the environment to produce consequences, while respondent behavior is a passive response to an environmental stimulus (Skinner, 1953). Behavior controlled by altering consequences is called an operant. Operant is defined as behavior that produces effects. The concept of operant conditioning can be traced back to Thorndike's law of effect which emphasizes the effect of behavioral consequences. If the behavioral consequence is rewarding, the behavior which produces this particular consequence will be repeated. If it is not rewarding, the behavior will be discontinued. However, the difference is that while the law of effect still operates in the passive S-R framework, the operant conditioning actively acts on the environment to produce consequences.

Most behaviors in organizations are operant behaviors that are learned, controlled, and altered by the consequences that follow them. Thus, understanding of operant conditioning will help managers either increase or decrease the rate of a response by manipulating behavioral consequences (reward or punishment). Generally, the behavioral consequences that are rewarding increase the rate of a response, while the aversive consequences decrease the rate of a response. To make the management of behavioral consequences (reward systems) effective, it is necessary to make the consequences contingent upon responses. If the consequences are not contingent upon the rates of a response or performance (behavior), an unplanned behavior or response can be reinforced. For example, if the same rate of pay increase is applied to all employees regardless of their performance, the pay system may reinforce tardy employees while discouraging high performing employees.

Luthans and Kreitner (1975) advocated the application of operant conditioning principles for modifying behavior in organizations. These principles have been successfully used in clinical, hospital, school, family, and industrial settings in recent years (see Bandura, 1969; Kazdin, 1975; Luthans and Kreitner, 1975; and Sherman, 1973). Strategies for modifying organizational behavior can be implemented by positive reinforcement, negative reinforcement, punishment, and extinction. Various principles and rules governing the management of these behavioral consequences will be discussed in a later section. These reinforcement principles will specify the contingency relationships between operant behavior and its consequences.

INCENTIVE, PERFORMANCE, AND REWARD

Learning a behavior involves both classical and operant conditoning processes. Behavior can be emitted by a stimulus and then followed by a consequence. If the consequence is rewarding, the behavior is reinforced and will be continued. If it is not rewarding, it will be discouraged. People in organizations learn a set of behavioral responses in the same fashion. They respond to various organizational incentives. These incentives stimulate people's behavior, and then the expressed behavior either is or is not rewarded. A rewarding consequence increases the motivational power of an incentive which in turn increases the rate of a response. An aversive consequence increases the repellent power of a negative incentive which in turn decreases the rate of a response. Through this stimulus-behavior-consequence association, people learn a set of appropriate responses that will result in increased rewards and reduce aversive consequences. Figure 4-1 illustrates the contingency relationship between stimulus, behavior, and consequence.

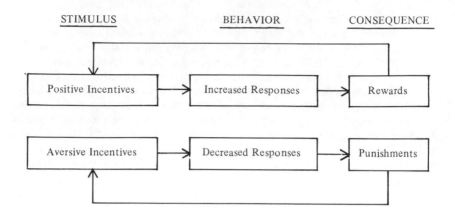

STIMULUS   BEHAVIOR   CONSEQUENCE

FIGURE 4-1. RELATIONSHIPS BETWEEN INCENTIVE, BEHAVIOR, AND CONSEQUENCE

Although the terms incentive and reward are used interchangeably, the differences between them are as follows. First, an incentive is an anticipation of reward and becomes a reward when it is awarded. Incentive is different from reward in that an incentive pay system can be applied to all employees, but not all of them receive the same amount of pay. Second, an incentive stimulates people to act, while a reward satisfies a need; the former induces, while the latter reinforces. When the power of a reinforcer increases, the motivational power of the incentive increases. A reward can be a reinforcer when it increases the rate of a response. Not all rewards are capable of reinforcing the response rate. Finally, incentives serve as cues that certain behaviors will be followed by a particular set of consequences. For example, a result-oriented performance appraisal system signals employees that high performers will be rewarded by increased pay and promotion.

In an organizational setting, there are a number of incentives capable of in-fluencing employee behavior. Positive incentives can be classified into three major categories: substantive incentives (pay, working condition, job security, and fringe benefits), interactive incentives (attention, praise, work group, super-vision, status, power, and influence), and effectance incentives (job content, challenge, responsibility, and accomplishment). Aversive incentives are the opposite of positive incentives: negative substantive incentives (pay docking, demotion, and termination), negative interactive incentives (social sanction, ostracism, reprimand, and domineering), and negative effectance incentives (fragmented job, stagnation, lack of challenge, and no freedom).

The effectiveness of an incentive primarily depends on its ability to satisfy a need or needs and the degree to which it is contingent upon performance. For example, fringe benefits have a limited reinforcement power to increase the performance rate because they usually are not contingent upon performance. The effectiveness of incentive systems to a large extent depends on an effective management of the contingency relationships between incentives, responses, and rewards (stimulus-behavior-consequence). Understanding of operant princi-ples will help to specify these contingency relationships.

PRINCIPLES OF OPERANT BEHAVIOR

The concept of contingency is important for managing a system of behavioral consequences (rewards or punishments) because operant behavior is controlled by the management of contingencies. People behave or work in organizations to receive a reward. Work is instrumental for obtaining the reward. To insure that people work and contribute their efforts to the attainment of organizational goals, the reward and punishment systems have to be contingent upon their work performance and contribution. The principles of operant conditioning describe the contingency relationships between stimuli (incentives), behavior (job performance), and consequences (rewards or punishments). The operant principles discussed in the following deal with different types of contingency relationships between behavior and environmental events (incentives and rewards).

REINFORCEMENT STRATEGIES

There are four major strategies of reinforcement: positive reinforcement, removal of punishment (often called negative reinforcement), punishment, and nonresponse or extinction. Also, these strategies can be combined to increase the effectiveness of a reinforcement system. The first two strategies can be used to increase the rate of performance and are considered reinforcers. In positive reinforcement, a reward is given after a response is performed. In negative reinforcement, an aversive event or punishment is removed after a response is performed. The last two strategies can be used to depress the frequency of undesirable behavior. Undesirable behavior can be reduced by an active application of an aversive event (punishment) or by a removal of a positive reinforcer (reward). Extinction refers to the cessation of reinforcement of a behavior. It can be accomplished when a response is followed by neutral stimuli.

Positive Reinforcement

Positive reinforcement strengthens the association between an incentive and behavior (performance) and increases the frequency of performance. Positive reinforcement occurs when a response is immediately followed by a reward. However, not all rewards are capable of being positive reinforcers. For a reward to become a positive reinforcer of a behavior, at least two conditions have to prevail. First, the reward should be contingent upon the rate of performance; the higher the performance, the greater the size of the reward. If the reward is not contingent upon performance, it cannot strengthen the motivational power of undistributed reward (incentive). Second, the reward should also be matched with the need or desire of the performer. If the reward is not matched with the need, it cannot satisfy the employee's need and thus cannot reinforce his behavior. Organizational members have a variety of needs (existence, relation-oriented, and growth) that they want to satisfy in organizations, and these needs can be matched by appropriate organizational incentives (substantive, interactive, and effectance).

There are two categories of positive reinforcers: primary or unconditioned and secondary or conditioned. A primary reinforcer innately satisfies a person's need and directly reinforces the behavior that generates the reinforcer. For example, food is a primary reinforcer that satisfies hunger need and reinforces the food-producing behavior. Cuddling can be a primary reinforcer satisfying a child's affiliation need. Work and play can be primary reinforcers that satisfy the compentence need. The major characteristics of primary reinforcers are that they are unconditioned, natural, and unlearned stimulus.

A secondary reinforcer results from previous association with a reinforcing event. Whereas primary reinforcers are innately satisfying, secondary reinforcers must be learned. Many organizational incentives are secondary reinforcers. Money is a secondary reinforcer by its association with daily necessities of satisfying existence needs. A mother who cuddles her child is a secondary reinforcer for the baby. Numerous social stimuli serve as secondary reinforcers in organizations. Praise, a smile, attention, and a pat on the back are secondary reinforcers.

The conditioned learning process has several implications for managing organizational incentives. First, an incentive can be paired with more than one primary or secondary reinforcer and become a generalized conditioned reinforcer. Generalized conditioned reinforcers are effective in modifying behaviors because they can be used to reinforce a variety of responses (Kazdin, 1975, p. 28). Money, trading stamps, attention, and praise are a few examples of generalized conditioned reinforcers. For example, money is associated with the means of satisfying existence, socialization, and self-esteem needs. Thus, it can be used to reinforce behaviors that will be followed by such things as food, shelter, job security, parties, and prestigious materials.

Second, a favored behavior with high frequency can be applied to promote a less favored behavior with low frequency. If the former is contingent upon the completion of the latter behavior, the frequency of the latter behavior will be increased (Premack, 1965). For example, children like to play outside with their friends rather than preparing homework. If playing outside is contingent upon the completion of homework, their studying behavior can be improved. This phenomenon is called the Premack Principle and has some practical implication for improving lower frequency behavior in organizations. For example, paid vacations, expense-paid trips, coffee breaks, and chatting with friends can be contingent upon the completion of various drudgery activities.

Removal Of Punishment

This strategy is often called a negative reinforcement and increases the frequency of a response by removing an aversive stimulus or punishment. A requirement is that removal of a punishment must be contingent upon the behavior to be reinforced. The termination of an aversive stimulus, rather than a presentation of a reward, is the reinforcer. Negative reinforcement also requires an existence of an aversive event (punishing or threat of punishment) that can be removed after a specific behavior is performed. For example, demotion can be reversed when the demoted person has performed a satisfactory job and thus reinforces his behavior. By reducing criticism upon satisfactory behavior of his subordinates, a supervisor can promote a desirable employee behavior.

Although both positive and negative reinforcement increase the frequency of a response, there is a clear distinction between these two strategies. In positive reinforcement, an employee actively approaches the reinforcer to gain pleasure. In negative reinforcement, the employee does something to avoid the aversive event. People learn a negatively reinforced behavior through an avoidance learning process. Both classical and operant conditionings are operative in avoidance learning. People learn avoidance behavior through past aversive experience with a punishment (conditioned and unconditioned) or through a conditioned stimulus signaling that if one does not escape from it, an aversive consequence will follow.

Punishment

Punishment involves the presentation of an aversive consequence after a response is performed. It is used as a method of reducing the frequency of undesirable behavior. The presence of an aversive stimulus itself can discourage a target behavior that will be followed by the aversive consequence if the behavior is expressed. The threat or actual application of punishment is widely used in organizations to discourage undesirable behavior. However, punishment is not an efffective method of controlling behavior for several reasons (Nord, 1969). First, the frequency of an undesirable response may be reduced only when the threat of punishment is perceived to exist. Once the punishing agent is away, the undesirable behavior may reoccur at its initial rate. Second, punishment only reduces the frequency of a target behavior. It does not necessarily promote a desired behavior. However, a negative reinforcement can occur if the punishing agent or threat is removed contingent upon a desirable performance.

Third, a punishment may interfere with a desirable behavior associated with an undesirable behavior. The punishment is targeted to reduce the frequency of the undesired behavior, but it also may discourage the desired behavior because they are not easily separable. Fourth, punishment may only frustrate the punished person, especially when the person cannot find the solution to the problem. Fifth, punishment may lead to avoidance and dislike of the punishing agent. This effect can be detrimental to managers who are striving to build supportive relationships with their subordinates. Sixth, punishment sometimes reinforces a behavior rather than reduces it (Reynolds, 1968). If a teacher pays attention to a student in forms of punishment only when the student is disruptive, his attention may reinforce the disruptive behavior, assuming that the student desires the teacher's attention. Finally, punishment requires a closed system from which people cannot escape. As people increase their mobility in an open society, they will leave an organization which heavily relies on punishment for controlling behavior.

Extinction

The frequency of a response can be decreased as a result of nonreinforcement. It can occur when responses are followed by neutral consequences, or when removal of a reinforcer continues. Since a behavior is not reinforced, the frequency of this behavior decreases and eventually disappears. In everyday life, one exercises extinction by ignoring others' behavior. A supervisor can reduce the frequency of an employee's complaints by ignoring the person. A teacher ignores a noisy student and the student drops his attention-getting behavior. Extinction is generally considered to be an effective method of controlling undesirable behavior and is less painful than punishment. While extinction involves neither positive nor aversive consequences, punishment usually involves the application of aversive consequences.

Extinction can be dysfunctional in some cases. Many desirable behaviors can be extinguished as a result of extinction. For example, a subordinate may attempt to bring his supervisor's attention to some potential problems. If the supervisor repeatedly ignores the subordinate's attempts, the latter's behavior will cease as a result of nonreinforcement. However, if the problem is serious, extinction may serve as a stimulus to pursue a further action. Extinction may create a suspicious feeling that stimulates a person to act. It also can be interpreted as a punishment that causes negative reactions.

Combined Strategies

The aforementioned operant strategies basically involve the manipulation (presentation or removal) of reward and punishment. Reward increases the attracting power of the rewarding event, while punishment increases the repellent power of the punishing event. When these two strategies are used simultaneously in combination, as shown in Figure 4-2, the resultant power to reinforce a behavior will be substantially augmented. The tendency to move toward the rewarding event will be doubled. This combined strategy is commonly called the "carrot and stick" approach and is the most widely used method of influencing people in our society. It is a simple and easy concept for many people to understand, and is a plausible means of influencing people.

In reality, many jobs in work organizations contain some unpleasant elements in varying degrees. The unpleasantness in task performance may reduce the tendency toward the rewarding event. The removal of any unpleasantness from task performance will strengthen the tendency to perform the task that will be followed by a positive reinforcer. Also, to augment the tendency toward the rewarding event, an aversive incentive or punishment can be introduced at the opposite end of the rewarding event. The aversive incentive will push the person toward the reinforcing event. This strategy combines the positive reinforcement with the negative reinforcement.

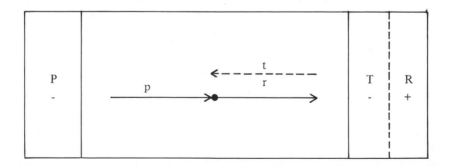

R = rewarding event; T - potential unpleasantness in task performance;
P = punishment or aversive incentive

FIGURE 4-2. COMBINED REINFORCEMENT STRATEGY

PRINCIPLES OF REINFORCEMENT

The aforementioned reinforcement strategies deal with the manipulation of rewards and punishments to either increase or decrease the frequency of various responses. These strategies specify what kinds of consequencies should be followed after certain responses are performed but do not specify how they should be administered. The following reinforcement principles are more definite in specifying the contingency relationships between behavior and consequences. The amount, quality, and timing of reinforcement will be contingent upon performance or behavior. These principles are to increase the effectiveness of specific reinforcement strategies.

Amount Of Reinforcement

The level of performance is said to be a function of the amount of reinforcement. The larger the amount of reinforcer given to a response, the higher the frequency of the response will be. An early study on the effect of quantitative variation of reinforcement on performance showed that when holding the hunger need constant, rats which were given a larger food incentive ran faster than rats which were given a smaller food stimulus during the training period (Crespi, 1944). After a number of trials, the amount of reward was shifted. The rats that received a reduced food incentive decreased their speed while the group that received more food increased their running speed. Similar studies by Donahoe, Schulte, and Moulton (1968), Platt and Gay (1968), and Wolf, Giles, and Hall (1968) have supported the principle of amount of reinforcement.

However, there is a limit to the effect of reinforcement amount on performance rate. The rate of performance increment decreases as the amount of reinforcement increases. There are two reasons for the leveling off effect. First, as the organism gets increasing amounts of reward, his marginal satisfaction or utility from the consumption of each additional reward will be decreased. Therefore, he will be less motivated to receive additional rewards. This is called a satiation effect. Second, the technical capacity of the subject tends to reduce the rate of performance increment. A person's hereditary elements and level of ability tend to limit the rate of performance as the person reaches a high level of performance.

Quality Of Reinforcement

The level of performance is said to be a function of reinforcement quality. In an experiment with rats, Guttman (1955) found that the level of performance increased when the rats received the same amount of food but with increased concentration of sucrose. The increase in sucrose, not the nutrition value, seemed to serve as a stimulant and resulted in the shifts of performance level. The increase of sucrose concentration led to a higher performance, and the reduction led to a depression effect. Similar findings have been reported by other investigators such as Rosen and Ison (1965), and Collier and Bolles (1968).

Quality of a reinforcer is often determined by the preference of the subject. Highly preferred reinforcers lead to greater performance (Kazdin, 1975, pp. 108-109). In an experiment by Hulse and Firestone (1964), the use of saccharin with the absence of nutritious values produced the equivalent amounts of reinforcement values that had been obtained with sucrose. It was concluded in the study that the sensory stimulation was created by the sweetness of the food stuff rather than by its nutritious value.

Although empirical evidence is lacking in human domain, it is conceivable that people are attracted to a reinforcer not only by its size but by its quality or preference. A better quality reinforcer provides a sensory stimulation that causes a positive effective arousal. This positive affective arrousal instigates a person to act to obtain the reward.

Delay of Reinforcement

The level of performance is a declining function of the time of reinforcement. A reinforcer should be given immediately after a response is performed. If it is delayed, it loses the reinforcement effect (Logan, 1960; Skinner, 1953; and Kazdin, 1975). When the reinforcement is delayed, a variety of alternative responses can interfere with the instrumental behavior. Such interferences confuse the contingency relationship between the instrumental behavior and its consequences. When the reinforcer is eventually delivered, it may reinforce an alternative response rather than the instrumental behavior. For example, a supervisor wanted to reward his subordinates for completing a market research project. However, due to the red tape in the administrative process, the performance bonus could not be paid for a few months. Meanwhile, the subordinates performed a number of other activities, some of which were successful and others mediocre. Eventually, when the bonus payment was paid, the subordinates might have had difficulty relating it to the project completion. The bonus payment could reinforce the alternative behaviors including the mediocre ones rather than the instrumental behavior.

The immediacy of reinforcement is more important for conditioning a new behavior than for reinforcing a learned behavior. If the reinforcement is delayed, it can be perceived as a period of extinction during which learning does not occur. After a response is learned, the amount of time between the response and reinforcement can be increased with performance decrement. However, it is important to note that the delay of reinforcement should not blur the contingency relationship between the reinforcer and its instrumental behavior.

SCHEDULES OF REINFORCEMENT

The scheduling and timing of reinforcement operationalizes the principles of reinforcement discussed in the preceding section. When, how, and how often reinforcers are applied can greatly influence the effectiveness of an incentive and reward system. There are three major types of reinforcement schedules—continuous, intermittent, and partial (Kazdin, 1975; Luthans and Kreitner, 1975; and Skinner, 1967). If every response is reinforced on a continuous basis, the schedule is called a continuous reinforcement. Each time a person touches a hot stove, his finger burns. Burning does not wait. If all responses are reinforced but the actual delivery of reinforcements occurs only after a number of responses are performed, the schedule is called an intermittent reinforcement. A check comes periodically, but the reinforcement applies to all the responses made during the pay period. If only a portion of responses are reinforced irregularly, the schedule is called a partial reinforcement. A supervisor may pat a subordinate on the back occasionally for a few randomly selected responses. Gambling activities are partially reinforced.

Continuous Reinforcement

A continuous reinforcement schedule (CR) is effective for developing and maintaining a higher rate of performance during the reinforcement phase. However, when the reinforcement accidentally or intentionally ceases, the behavior acquired or reinforced by a continuous schedule quickly diminishes. For example, each time a person puts a quarter in the vending machine, he is reinforced by candy bars. However, if the machine misses a reinforcement, the person quickly ceases to put quarters into it. CR follows the principle of delay of reinforcement; the immediacy of reinforcement strengthens the instrumental relationship between a response and its consequence. However, the high frequency of reinforcement can easily lead to a satiation point where the rinforcer cannot serve its function. Thus, it can be said that CR is an effective tool for shaping and developing a new behavior. Once a behavior is shaped or developed, it can be maintained by other reinforcement schedules.

Intermittent Schedules

Intermittent reinforcements are the most common forms of administering reward systems in organizations. Organizational rewards such as pay, promotion, recognition, award, and task completion are some prime examples of intermittent reinforcements. Since it is almost impossible to reinforce all desirable responses each time they are performed, the intermittent reinforcement schedules seem to be most appropriate for managing reinforcement systems in organizations. There are four major ways of scheduling intermittent reinforcements: fixed-ratio (FR), variable-ratio (VR), fixed-interval (FI), and variable-interval (VI). Figure 4-3 shows different types of reinforcement schedules and their effects on performance.

1. *Fixed-ratio Schedule (FR).* FR requires that a fixed number of responses must be performed before a reinforcement is delivered. A common example of this schedule is the piece-rate incentive system. A worker is paid on a basis of how many units he has produced. FR increases the instrumental relationship between performance and its consequences, and tends to produce a steady and high rate of performance. Studies show that performance is higher under FR than under a fixed-interval schedule (FI) (Chapter 7). CR is a special case of FR when the required number of responses for reinforcement is one (FR1).
2. *Variable-ratio Schedule (VR).* Under a VR, a reinforcement occurs after a number of responses, but the number varies between reinforcements. A sales commission is an example of VR. The number of responses generally varies from occasion to occasion, but the size of reinforcement is contingent upon performance. Studies indicate that the performance under VR is higher than that under CR or FR (see Logan, 1960; Reynolds, 1968; and Yukl, Wexley, and Seymore, 1972), and the resistance to extinction is higher under VR than under CR or FR (see Underwood, 1966; and Williams, 1973).

Schedule	Decription	Effects on Responding
Continuous (CRF)	Reinforcer follows every response.	1. Steady high rate of performance as long as reinforcement continues to follow every response. 2. High frequency of reinforcement may lead to early satiation. 3. Behavior weakens rapidly (undergoes extinction) when reinforcers are withheld. 4. Appropriate for newly emitted, unstable, or low-frequency responses.
Intermittent	Reinforcer does not follow every response.	1. Capable of producing high frequencies of responding. 2. Low frequency of reinforcement precludes early satiation. 3. Appropriate for stable or high-frequency responses.
Fixed ratio (FR)	A fixed number of responses must be emitted before reinforcement occurs.	1. A fixed ratio of 1:1 (reinforcement occurs after every response) is the same as a continuous schedule. 2. Tends to produce a high rate of response which is vigorous and steady.
Variable ratio (VR)	A varying or random number of responses must be emitted before reinforcement occurs	1. Capable of producing a high rate of response which is vigorous, steady, and resistant to extinction.
Fixed interval (FI)	The first response after a specific period of time has elapsed is reinforced.	1. Produces an uneven response pattern varying from a very slow, unenergetic response immediately following reinforcement to a very fast, vigorous response immediately preceding reinforcement.
Variable interval (VI)	The first response after varying or random periods of time have elapsed is reinforced.	1. Tends to produce a high rate of response which is vigorous, steady, and resistant to extinction.
Partial	Only a fraction of responses are randomly reinforced	1. Slow to produce a learned behavior. But, once learned, the behavior tends to be vigorous and resistant to extinction. 2. An effective reinforcement schedule when the total amount of reward to be applied is relatively small.

FIGURE 4-3. SCHEDULES OF REINFORCEMENT
Adopted from Luthans, F. and Kreitner, R., *Organizational Behavior Modification.* (Glenview, Ill.: Scott, Foresman and Company, 1975, p. 51.) Partially reprinted with permission.

3. *Fixed-interval Schedule (FI)*. Interval schedules are based on the amount of time that passes before a response is reinforced regardless of the level of performance. FI requires that a fixed amount of time has to elapse before a reinforcement is administered. It is the most common way of administering pay systems in organizations. Most workers are paid hourly, weekly, or monthly based on a certain number of hours or days. FI is commonly used in a situation where performance cannot be easily measured in identifiable units or being on the job is considered to be important.

4. *Variable-interval Schedule (VI)*. Under a VI, reinforcement is administered after a certain amount of time is elapsed, but the time interval is not fixed. Unscheduled sales contests, pop quizzes, and promotions are a few examples of VI. As in the case of VR, behavior learned under a VR tends to show a high degree of resistance to extinction. However, it is more difficult to shape or develop a new behavior under VI than under CR, FR, or VI.

Partial Reinforcement

Partial reinforcement (PR) can be considered a special case of VR or VI where reinforcement varies extremely from occasion to occasion. PR is constrained by neither the number of responses nor the amount of time interval; it varies in amount and/or time of delay of reinforcement. Unlike CR which reinforces all operant responses or intermittent schedules which reinforce all responses on a fixed rate or time schedule (FR and FI), PR reinforces a limited number of operant responses on an irregular rate or time schedule. Payoff schedules adopted by gambling establishments are a prime example of PR being used as a means of motivating players to bet. Sweepstakes are another example of PR that are used as a promotional means to boost merchandise sales. Although the use of PR in work situations is a relatively new phenomenon, Nord (1969, 1970) argued that a system of PR can be a powerful tool to those managers who are in charge of controlling and motivating employees in industrial settings.

Performance characteristics of PR are basically twofold: 1) PR schedules are more effective in producing and maintaining a high rate of performance than are CR schedules for a given magnitude of reward (Logan, 1960; Reynolds, 1968). For example, Yukl, Wexley, and Seymore (1972) investigated the effectiveness of pay methods under variable ratio and fixed ratio schedules in a repetitive task situation. The subjects (college students) worked under one CR and two PR or VR conditions. The results indicated that the subjects under the PR schedules performed better than those under the CR schedule. 2) Behavior acquired under PR continues for a longer period of time when the positive reinforcement is discontinued than does behavior acquired under CR. In other words, PR schedules produce greater resistance to extinction than CR schedules (Underwood, 1966; Williams, 1973). A study by Lambreth, Gouaux, and Davis (1972), which investigated the effects of PR in an instrumental conditioning task with college students, reported that the PR group proved to be more resistant to extinction than the CR group. Warm, Hagner, and Meyer (1971) also found that the response time performance in the PR group was better than that of the CR group in a vigilance task situation.

REWARD SIZE, FREQUENCY, AND PR

Several observations can be made regarding the amount, frequency, and scheduling of reinforcement. First, the effectiveness of PR seems to be a function of the average size of reward and the probability or frequency of obtaining the reward. The size of reward is inversely related to the probability of obtaining that reward. When subjects are rewarded frequently, the total reward is divided into smaller pieces, thereby reducing its value. Thus, to make the partial reinforcement more attractive, for a given amount of total reward, the frequency of reinforcement must be reduced so that the size of each reward is large enough to be attractive to the recipient. However, an extremely low frequency of reinforcement will reduce the effectiveness of partial reinforcement because people pessimistically perceive the chance of reinforcement and consequently do not respond to it.

Second, the trade-off point between the attractiveness of reward and the frequency of reinforcement can be influenced by the total size of reward to be distributed and the amount of investment or effort required. Although the effects of varying the amount of reward and investment are somewhat complex, the following speculations may be made regarding the trade-off point: 1) When the sum of the reward to be distributed is relatively small in comparison with a large number of participants and the required effort or investment by the participant is relatively insignificant (lottery systems or sweepstakes), a low frequency of reinforcement with a high variation in amount of reward is preferred over a high frequency of reinforcement with small sized rewards. In this case, a low frequency of reinforcement is needed to make the size of a given reward attractive to the receiver. 2) When the total reward amount is relatively large and the required investment is relatively substantial (investment in bonds or utility stocks), a high frequency of reinforcement with a low degree of variation in amount of reward is preferred over a low frequency of reinforcement. For example, Yukl and Latham (1975) found that when relatively large sized rewards ($4 and $8) were involved in an industrial setting that required substantial physical effort, productivity was higher under CR than PR conditions. In a previous study by Yukl, Wexley, and Seymore (1972), relatively small sized rewards ($.25 and $.50) were involved in a laboratory setting requiring a minimal effort. Under this circumstance, a low frequency reinforcement (VR) was preferred to a high frequency reinforcement (CR). When the total reward is large, a high frequency of reinforcement can still make the average size of rewards distributed attractive. 3) When the total reward size is intermediate and the required investment or effort is moderate, intermediate degrees of reinforcement frequency and reward size variation are preferred over very high or low degrees of reinforcement frequency and variation of rewarded amount.

Third, the resistance to extinction following training with PR has an inverted-U relationship with the percentage of reinforcement; 100 percent and 0 percent reinforcement show little resistance to extinction, while the peak of the inverted-U appears around 50 percent reinforcement (Lewis, 1960; Koteskey, 1972). When the percentage of reinforcement ranges between 100 percent and 50 percent in partial reinforcement schedules, there are opportunities for the subject to learn the conditioning elements so that more of these elements can be retained. However, as percentage of reinforcement decreases from 50 percent to 0 percent reinforcement, there will be too little reinforcement for sufficient conditioning to take place. Thus, further decrease in the percentage of reinforcement will result in less conditioning as well as less resistance to extinction. A theory of discriminative cognition indicates that when the subject clearly recognizes the difference between reinforcement and extinction conditions, he ceases to respond (Williams, 1973, pp. 53-54). At the extreme point near the 100 percent or 0 percent level of reinforcement, the distrinction between reinforcement and extinction will be most clear. However, subjects trained with a PR schedule with 50 percent reinforcement may perceive acquisition and extinction as similar and thus expect reinforcement in extinction.

Finally, the effectiveness of partial reinforcement also depends on the personality makeups of participants. An achievement-oriented person may prefer a choice with an intermediate degree of reinforcement frequency or risk (Atkinson, 1964). Whereas an assurance-conscious individual wants a choice with a high frequency of reinforcement, a gambler may prefer a low frequency of reinforcement. While the former is obsessed with a certainty in payoff, the latter is motivated by substantial payoffs even when they are not certain.

TYPES OF ORGANIZATIONAL INCENTIVES

Organizations can influence the behavior of their members by properly managing the means of satisfying their needs. The major tasks of managing a reinforcement system are twofold: 1) the selection of powerful reinforcers or incentives and 2) the proper use of these reinforcers. The first task can be accomplished by matching incentives with appropriate needs. The reinforcement power of an incentive increases when it appeals to and satisfies a particular need or a set of needs. To facilitate the matching process, organizational incentives or reinforcers are arranged into a hierarchical system which is compatible to the hierarchical system of needs. As the needs of employees are classified into three major categories, so are the incentives in organizations (substantive, interactive, and effectance). The second task can be accomplished by properly designing the work and organizational environment so that the reinforcement system can induce and reinforce desirable behavior. The principles and schedules of reinforcement can be utilized as a guide for designing an effective incentive system.

Since the management of a reinforcement system constitutes the major portion of organizational work motivation, the process of matching incentives with needs and the task of designing motivational reinforcement systems will be fully discussed in Chapter 7 (extrinsic motivation), Chapter 8 (affective motivation), and Chapters 9 and 10 (intrinsic motivation). The present discussion outlines different types of organizational incentives and their functional relationships as a prelude to the discussions in later chapters. Mostly, studies in the 1950s and 1960s are reported here; more recent studies will be reported in later chapters. The early studies set the general tone of the motivational characteristics of organizational incentives, while the recent studies are concerned with new developments in managing these incentives.

SUBSTANTIVE INCENTIVES

Substantive incentives refer to most tangible reinforcers capable of satisfying existence needs (physiological and security) and some of relation-oriented needs (power, competition, and esteem). Money, physical working condition, and job security are the prime examples of the substantive incentives. Although these incentives are capable of satisfying a variety of employees' needs, they do not reinforce work-oriented behavior unless the application of these reinforcers is contingent upon task performance. When people work to gain these incentives, they are said to be extrinsically motivated.

Financial Incentives

The use of money as a primary motivational tool has been emphasized by many scholars and practitioners. Taylor (1910) concluded that workers will put forth extra effort on the job to maximize their economic gains if wages are differentiated by differential outputs. Taylor devised what he called the *differential piece rate,* based on the assumption that different increments of income will produce direct and proportional increments of effort.

Viteles (1953) reported that surveys of companies experienced with wage incentive plans showed substantial increases in productivity following the installation of the incentive wage system. A comprehensive study about the effects of incentive plans on productivity showed that productivity increased an average of 63 percent during the years of incentive wage installation (Dale, 1959).

Opsahl and Dunnette (1966) summarized the theories of the role of money in affecting the job behavior of employees. Their summaries, combined with some other interpretations, are as follows: First, money acts as a generalized conditioned reinforcer because of its repeated pairings with other reinforcers. Such a reinforcer can be effective because some deprivation will usually exist for which the conditioned reinforcer is appropriate.

Second, repeated pairings of money with other incentives establishes a new learned drive for money. Presumably, money could become a generalized conditioned incentive by many pairings with different types of incentives. Third, money is an anxiety reducer. People learn to become anxious in the presence of a variety of cues signifying the absence of money. Thus, having money serves to reduce anxiety related to the absence of money.

Fourth, money is a hygiene factor serving as a potential dissatisfier if it is not appropriately administered, but not as a potential satisfier when employees are well paid. The acceptance of Herzberg's satisfiers-dissatisfiers theory of motivation (1959) appears to destroy the concept of pay as a motivator. However, Herzberg and his associates also recognized the fact that "money earned as a direct reward for outstanding performance is a reinforcement of motivators of recognition and achievement." Fifth, money acquires valence as a result of its perceived instrumentality for obtaining other desired outcomes. Money itself has no intrinsic value but acquires significant motivating power when it comes to symbolize tangible goals.

The findings of the above research, except Herzberg's hygiene factor concept, are inclined to emphasize the motivational value of financial incentives. However, some other views attach less importance to the motivational value of financial incentives. First, human relationists view man as a "socio-psychological" being who stresses the importance of the satisfaction of social and ego needs. Second, money is not the only reward, nor lack of money the only punishment. Job satisfaction is an outcome of the total work environment where employees satisfy a number of their needs. Money plays a small but important part in satisfying these needs. Finally, man has risen above the mundane demands of a physiological existence. Above the level of economic subsistence, monetary incentive tends to lose its importance as a motivator, and other incentives tend to become more important.

Physical Working Conditions

The study of the effects of physical working conditions on productivity was the original hypothesis of the Hawthorne Experiments. The result, however, turned out to be quite contrary to the original hypothesis. The experiments concluded that neither deterioration nor improvement of physical working conditions had significant effects on productivity. Many studies thereafter minimized the importance of the effects of physical working conditions on productivity and ranked them as least contributors to productivity.

Interpreting this trend in terms of Herzberg's factory theory, it may be concluded that physical working conditions are hygienic factors which have no motivational value when they are adequate, but become detriments to productivity when they are not adequate.

In some cases, however, improvement of physical environment beyond an adequate level contributes to high productivity. One study showed that an installation of a music facility had favorable effects on productivity, although the effect of music varied from one industrial situation to another (Uhrbrock, 1961).

INTERACTIVE INCENTIVES

Interactive incentives refer to social reinforcers capable of satisfying such relation-oriented needs as affiliation, companionship, emotional support, influence, and power. Attention, praise, physical contact, smile, social control, work group, and leadership process are the prime examples of the interactive incentives. Interactive reinforcers exert considerable influence on employee behavior. People develop effective reactions to their jobs, co-workers, supervision, and management based on their interactions with other people in organizations. Psychological contracts regarding job, work group and institutional commitments are influenced by these affective feelings. Interaction-oriented behavior can be intrinsically and/or extrinsically motivated. People may engage in social interactions for the sake of experiencing affective feelings and/or as a means of obtaining social acceptance, power, and mastery over other people.

Social Reinforcers

Social reinforcers such as attention, praise, and pat on the back are mostly conditioned reinforcers acquired by associating with other learned reinforcers. For example, if a praise or a pat on the back is frequently followed by a pay increase or promotion, such a social reinforcer increases the incentive value of the instrumental behavior. Social reinforcement has been used to develop and improve desirable behavior while discouraging undesirable behavior. Madsen, Becker, and Thomas (1968) reported that praise has improved attentive study behavior of students while disruptive behavior was gradually decreased by ignoring it plus praising appropriate behavior. Kazdin and Klock (1973) also reported an improvement of classroom behavior when nonverbal attention and/or verbal praise are contingent upon appropriate behavior.

Kazdin (1975, pp. 119-120) pointed out several advantages of using social reinforcers. First, they can be easily administered by anyone who supervises people. Anyone can deliver social reinforcement without special preparation. Second, social reinforcement does not disrupt the behavior being reinforced. For example, praise can be delivered while the instrumental behavior is being performed. Third, social reinforcement is a generalized reinforcer which can be associated with many reinforcing events. It can be paired with exhibiting inter-active behavior or task accomplishment. It also is less subject to satiation because it can be paired with a variety of reinforcing events. Fourth, social reinforcers are naturally occurring phenomenon in everyday life. Behavior developed with social reinforcement can be readily maintained outside the laboratory setting. However, Meyer, Kay, and French (1965) indicated that praise has little effect on behavior unless the praised person internalizes the instrumental behavior.

Work Group Influence

Early in the 1930s, the Hawthorne Experiments revealed that the perfor-mance of individual workers was affected by their relationship with other co-workers. In the relay assembly room experiments, the continued increases in productivity was due to the group cohesiveness that developed in the group. On the other hand, in the bank wiring room studies, the informal work group was the cause for restricting productivity (Reothlisberger and Dickson, 1939).

There are some research findings about the group influence on individual performance that have been reported since the Hawthorne Experiments. First, if the work group is believed by an individual to be instrumental to the attain-ment of positively valent outcomes, it will acquire positive valence for him (Vroom, 1964, p. 120). The attractiveness of the group for a given person de-pends upon the strength of his needs and upon the perceived suitability of the group for satisfying these needs.

Second, the cohesiveness of a group enforces its group norms on the behavior of the group members. Thus, a higher productivity was obtained in highly co-hesive groups with positive standards regarding productivity, while a lower productivity was found in highly cohesive groups with negative standards regard-ing productivity (Seashore, 1954).

Third, a group norm or standard serves as a guide for the behavior of the group members. Thus, individual productivity varies according to the rewards received from the group and management. If an individual is rewarded both by the group and management, he will produce close to the standard set by the group. If the worker is rewarded by management but not by the group, he will produce close to the standard set by the management. When the workers are rewarded by the group, but not by management, he will produce close to the group norm but lower than when he will be rewarded both by management and the group. When he is not rewarded by either the group or management, he becomes a lower producer (Zaleznick, Christensen, and Roethlisberger, 1958).

Finally, one of the fascinating aspects of group dynamics is that the group process of decision making and supervision can lead to the most effective organi-zation. According to Likert (1961, 1967), when the supervisor allows his work group to participate in the decision making and supervising process of the group activities, he can create a cohesive work group in which the involvement of individual members in the organizational activities leads to the most effective work group.

Leadership and Supervision

According to Myers (1964), the role of supervision in motivating employees is important for two reasons: it provides conditions for releasing such motivational needs as recognition, achievement, and responsibility; it provides the means of satisfying such maintenance needs as pay, working conditions, and socialization of employees.

Many studies of supervisory behavior have been concerned with the effect of supervision styles on productivity. These studies usually contrasted production-centered supervision with employee-centered supervision. The production-centered supervisor is interested almost exclusively in getting jobs done; the employee-centered supervisor is more interested in satisfying the needs of his subordinates. Some studies showed that production-centered supervision led to low productivity, while employee-centered supervision led to high productivity (Likert, 1961; and Katz and Kahn, 1960). However, in other studies employee-centered supervision was more of a liability than an asset, especially in the combat situations studied by Halpin and Winer (1957) and in the production divisions studies by Fleishman, Harris, and Burtt (1955).

It appears there are some inconsistencies in research findings from one study to another. These differences in findings may reflect the fact that the supervision styles which will result in effective group performance depend upon such variables as the traits of the supervisor, the traits of the group, and the job situation (Tannenbaum and Schmidt, 1958).

As a solution to the supervision style problem, Blake and Mouton (1961) suggested that the best managers are those who combine people-centered and production-centered supervision. They developed the concept of *managerial grid* which tests the manager's approaches to the two independent dimensions of supervision style. The management grid shows that the manager's score on supervision can be obtained by combining his people-centered and production-centered supervision scores. Misumi and Shirakash (1966) also reported that productivity proved highest under first-line supervisors of the people-centered and production-centered type, second highest under the production-centered type, and lowest under the people-centered type.

Structural Influence

Organizational structure influences the way people interact and satisfy their needs in organizations. It also can facilitate or hinder the necessary interactions among organizational members required for carrying out interrelated activities. A number of structural considerations influence the affective responses of employees toward their work environment. First, the size of the work group influences employee satisfaction. In a larger size group, there are fewer opportunities to satisfy the affiliation need (Porter and Lawler, 1965). Second, the bureaucratic organizational structure produces such undesirable consequences as a reduction in the amount of personalized relationships, a tendency to internalize rules and regulations rather than goals, and a reduction in the amount of behavioral alternatives to solve organizational problems (March and Simon, 1958). Third, the departmentalization leads to increased conflict and competition between organizational subunits. As these subgroups develop their own subgroup norms, their members tend to internalize their subgroup norms and goals rather than the organizational goals. Fourth, the increased level of education and standard of living of the work force changes the value they place on work. People will be more intellectually committed to their jobs and will require more involvement, participation, and autonomy in their work. A change in organizational structure from the bureaucratic to a more flexible organic structure seems to be inevitable to enhance the congruence between employees' needs and structural requirements (Bennis, 1966, pp. 10-14). Finally, as more people are better satisfied with existence needs, they become more sensitive to the satisfaction of relation-oriented needs. However, as the industrialized society becomes more complex and mobile, the opportunity for people to satisfy their relation-oriented needs seems to diminish. Structural changes are needed to accommodate the demands for expressing such needs.

EFFECTANCE INCENTIVES

Effectance incentives refer to those reinforcers capable of satisfying growth-oriented needs (competence, achievement, and self-actualization). The job itself and growth opportunity in organizations constitute the effectance incentives. These reinforcers are called effectance incentives because they are capable of producing motivational effects from their own influences without particular external reinforcers. When the job is challenging and interesting, people are motivated to perform more than required to justify their extrinsic gains. They exert extra effort to experience a sense of accomplishing something worthwhile and fulfilling their potential.

Job Content

The motivational consequences of job content have been highlighted by Herzberg and his associates (1959). They have studied job factors that lead to satisfaction and dissatisfaction. Their study concluded that job factors causing satisfaction are different from factors causing job dissatisfaction. Job satisfaction results primarily from the jobs that provide such factors as achievement, recognition, challenge, responsibility, advancement, and growth. Hackman and Oldham (1975) indicated that the job factors contributing to motivating potential include such task elements as skill variety, task identity, task significance, autonomy, feedback from the job itself and other persons, and opportunity to interact with other people. The presence of such job factors influences the psychological states of the worker and determines the affective reactions of the worker toward the job. The affective reactions to the job eventually influence internal work motivation and job performance of the worker. The effects of these job factors on employee motivation and performance will be further discussed in Chapter 9.

In addition to the above job factors, there are several job elements frequently studied in connection with job satisfaction. First, there is a positive relationship between job level and job satisfaction. Gurin, Veroff, and Feld (1960) reported that job satisfaction declined with the descending order of job level — professionals, managers, clericals, sales, skilled workers, semiskilled workers, unskilled worker, and farmers. The interpretation of this finding is that the positive relationship between job level and job satisfaction is due to the fact that positions at high levels provide employees with more opportunities for satisfying motivational needs that are associated with personal growth.

Second, increased specialization during this century took intrinsic work value from the jobs. Fragmentation of jobs has destroyed the meaning of work for employees, especially at the level of factory workers.

Third, an individual derives satisfaction from jobs which permit him to use skills and abilities. Vroom (1962) reported a positive relationship between the extent to which jobs permit employees to use their abilities and gain job satisfaction.

Finally, overall job satisfaction and the meaningfulness of the job, as Argyris (1962), Alderfer (1969), Lawler (1969), and Myers (1970) pointed out, are usually higher in enlarged and enriched jobs than nonenlarged jobs. Enriched jobs contain some job elements that serve as a motive arousal function, and successful performance on these jobs will result in outcomes that involve feelings of achievement, growth, and self-actualization.

Growth Opportunity

The worker needs to perceive the opportunity to grow and advance in his chosen profession. Professional growth and advancement provide the person with opportunities to engage in challenging and interesting jobs on a continuous basis. A job that is challenging and interesting at the time may not be the same in the future. Learning new skills and knowledge can be productively utilized in professionally advancing positions. Intrinsically motivated workers are interested in promotion and professional advancement, not for the sake of obtaining more financial gains or power, but because these extrinsic rewards are associated with intrinsically motivating jobs. Gellerman (1963) indicated that promotion offers an employee the opportunity for further personal and professional growth. It enlarges his sense of competence and realizes his desire for autonomy. In addition, it brings such extrinsic rewards as prestige, power and increased income. In essence, professional growth provides workers with an expectation that there will be a continuous supply of intrinsically motivating jobs. The employees whose growth-oriented work behaviors are continuously reinforced will remain in the organization as productive workers more often than those who are not continuously challenged in their work situations.

An attempt has been made to classify organizational incentives in a hierarchical system compatible to the need system. It has been pointed out that when incentives match with appropriate needs, the motivational value of the incentives increase. However, one should not be misled to believe that there is a direct one-to-one relationship between an incentive and a need. As indicated in Chapter 3, a need can be satisfied by different reinforcers. For example, the power need can be met by increasing financial gains (substantive incentive), by becoming an influential leader or a powerful dictator (interactive incentive), or by gaining the mastery over one's profession. When a path to a goal attainment is blocked, a substitute goal requiring a new set of outcomes or incentives can emerge as a motivational force. Many organizational reinforcers are generalized and can be associated with other reinforcing agents to produce new sets of conditioned reinforcers. For example, money is a generalized reinforcer capable of satisfying physiological, security, self-esteem, and power needs. The implication of the multiplicity of a reinforcer is that an organization can be flexible in utilizing its reinforcers for influencing employee behavior. If a set of reinforcers are lacking, the organization should be able to develop and utilize alternative sets of reinforcers.

INTRINSIC, EXTRINSIC, AND AFFECTIVE MOTIVATION

Organizational incentives or reinforcers influence employee behavior intrinsically or extrinsically. The characteristics of intrinsic motivation are that it is derived directly from performing the job (Saleh and Grygier, 1969; Herzerg et al., 1959), internally. mediated by the worker, or the locus of behavioral causality is internal (Deci, 1972); and usually associated with the satisfaction of higher-order needs (Solcum, 1971). The characteristics of extrinsic motivation are the opposite. It is derived from the environment peripheral to the job, externally mediated by someone other than the worker himself, and usually associated with the satisfaction of lower-order needs (Dyer and Parker, 1975).

Although most substantive incentives are extrinsically reinforced, some can be intrinsically reinforced. Some people seem to enjoy earning money for the sake of earning and accumulating it. They seem to gain sheer enjoyment from earning and accumulating money rather than from consuming it. By the same token, not all effectance incentives are internally or intrinsically reinforced. No matter how enjoyable a job may be, if one's task accomplishments are not extrinsically reinforced, his job performance will eventually suffer. When the job is intrinsically motivating, the worker will exert extra efforts beyond the performance requirement expected by management. However, if the intrinsically reinforced behavior is not accompanied by extrinsic reinforcement, the frequency and intensity of the behavior will be reduced.

EFFECTS OF AFFECTIVE MOTIVATION

Interactive incentives can be intrinsically and/or extrinsically reinforcing. People are gregarious; they seek opportunities for socializing for the sake of being with other people. Affiliative needs are even considered innate; being affilated with and accepted by other people is intrinsically reinforcing. On the other hand, some people are friendly to others as a means of obtaining what they want. Politicians are friendly to the voters during the election year. Subordinates ingratiate themselves to their supervisors around the performance appraisal time. Some supervisors become permissive hoping that their subordinates accept them. While a behavior seeking friendship and group affiliation is intrinsically motivated, organizational structure and group process externally impose constraints on interpersonal and group interactions. Figure 4-4 illustrates the extent to which various incentives intrinsically and/or extrinsically reinforce behavior.

The upper triangle in Figure 4-4 represents the motivational region where incentives intrinsically reinforce behavior. The lower triangle represents the area

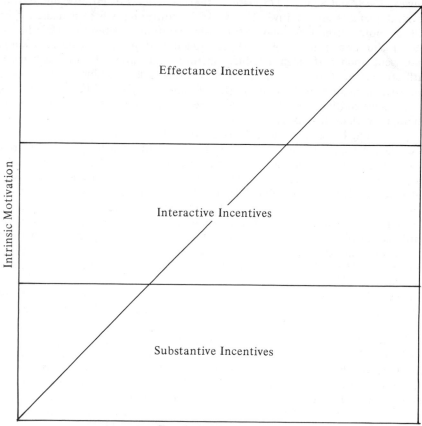

FIGURE 4-4. INTRINSIC AND EXTRINSIC INCENTIVE MEDIATION

where various incentives extrinsically reinforce behavior. The rectangular area in the middle of the figure represents the area where interactive incentives exert affective influence on job-oriented behavior. Within this area people are sensitive to their own as well as others' feelings and emotions and their behaviors are influenced by these affective responses. Below the lower threshold line, only those individuals not sensitive to these affective responses will undertake even an unpleasant task mainly for substantive rewards. For example, a mobster hitman engages in killing for money. Above the upper threshold line, some people will undertake what they consider to be intrinsically motivating jobs regardless of whether they are socially or financially reinforced.

EFFECT OF EXTRINSIC MOTIVATION ON INTRINSIC MOTIVATION

There has been a controversy over whether the introduction of a performance contingent reinforcer decreases the strength of intrinsic motivation. Most reinforcement and expectancy theorists (Hamner and Foster, 1975; Porter and

Lawler, 1968; and Scott, 1975) assume that the effects of intrinsic and extrinsic reinforcement are additive. The worker's motivation will be increased if he will be both intrinsically and extrinsically reinforced. However, De Charms (1968) and Deci (1971, 1972, 1975) argued that making extrinsic rewards contingent upon performance reduces intrinsic motivation. In his experiments with students performing intrinsically motivating tasks (matching puzzle pieces and writing newspaper headlines), Deci found that paying the subjects on a performance-contingency basis tended to reduce the amount of time they were willing to work on the tasks.

Interpreting his research findings, Deci proposed a cognitive evaluation theory to explain the shift in the locus of behavioral causality. When a person performs an intrinsically motivating task, the locus of causality is within the person himself. However, when a performance-contingent reinforcer is externally imposed, the perceived locus of causality shifts to his environment. He perceives himself working for money rather than for sheer enjoyment. Deci's findings are quite plausible in laboratory or real world situations where small sized extrinsic rewards are involved. If the task is interesting and challenging and is something the person really cares about, he would rather do it for free than get paid nominally for it. The insignificant amount of pay only makes him feel cheap and obligated.

However, if the size of the extrinsic reward is psychologically significant to the individual, the performance-contingent reinforcement will increase the rate of performance, intrinsically or extrinsically instigated, rather than repressing it. Several studies (Dermer, 1975; Hamner and Foster, 1975; and Hofstede, 1968; and Salancik, 1975) failed to support the Deci theory. Instead, these studies found that intrinsic motivation was increased in the presence of performance-contingent extrinsic reinforcement. These studies, combined with other research on reinforcement and expectancy theories (Cherrington, Reits, and Scott, 1971; Lawler and Porter, 1967; and Porter and Lawler, 1968), suggest that the effects of intrinsic and extrinsic reinforcers are additive in nature rather than offsetting. Deci's theory is also under criticism from methodological standpoints (Hamner and Foster, 1975; and Scott, 1975). For example, Scott argues that the reduction of performance can occur under a performance-contingent reward system, not because the reward system reduces intrinsic motivation, but because it is poorly designed and not attractive. A poorly designed incentive system can impair extrinsic motivation.

ORGANIZATIONAL APPLICATION OF REINFORCEMENT

The carrot and stick approach (reward and punishment) is widely used in organizations as a way of influencing and motivating their employees toward the attainment of organizational goals. Piece-rate incentive, performance appraisal, sales contest, pat on the back, promotion, demotion, pay docking, and disciplinary action are all familiar examples of applying the carrot and stick approach. Rewards are offered for acceptable behavior, while punishment or extinction are used to discourage undesirable behavior.

There are several problems with this simplistic approach. First, it is frequently used without systematic efforts to specify contingency relationships between behaviors and consequences. Management often rewards one behavior, while hoping for another behavior to occur (Kerr, 1975). For example, American voters punish candidates concerned with the sources of financing while rewarding those who speak of programs requiring a large sum of fundings. Yet, people hope that their elected officials will be financially restrained. Second, as pointed out previously, punishment produces a number of undesirable consequences. Yet, there is a general tendency for managers to pay more attention to their subordinates when they are doing something wrong than when they are doing something right. Positive reinforcement can be more effective in promoting productive behavior than punishment. Third, an incentive must be perceived to be valuable, and the reward should be perceived to be contingent upon performance in order to make the reinforcement system more effective. Expectancy theory can be operative in increasing the effectiveness of reinforcement systems (Pritchard, DeLeo, and Von Bergen, 1976). Finally, unlike rats in a cage, people in organizations are being offered a number of reinforcers from various nonmanagerial sources such as social groups, family, and hobbies. These nonmanagerial reinforcers compete with the operation of managerial reinforcers, reducing their effectiveness (Jablonsky and DeVries, 1972).

In light of the stated problems, it is necessary to understand and apply reinforcement theories and principles in specifying the contingency relationships between required behaviors and organizational rewards. The application of positive reinforcement at Emery Air Freight clearly demonstrates the need and benefits of using a systematic approach to reinforcement (Feeney, 1972). First, a performance audit was conducted to identify a few major performance areas that had greater influences on the company's profits. For example, as a freight company, Emery uses a large volume of containers. An effective utilization of containers was identified as the target behavior to reinforce. Second, management established a realistic performance goal for each worker and gave performance feedback to the worker. Employee involvement in goal-setting and getting feedback was encouraged. Third, increases in performance were positively reinforced. The positive reinforcement was directly related to the performance. Finally, reinforcement schedules were manipulated to facilitate the learning process and to maintain the learned behavior. Frequent reinforcements were given at the outset, then a variable-ratio schedule was followed. The positive reinforcement program saved the company $2 million in three years.

As demonstrated in Emery Air Freight, the application of reinforcement is different from the simplistic carrot and stick approach. Rather, it is a deliberate and systematic application of positive reinforcement usually requiring the following steps. These steps essentially involve the behavioral analysis of the contingency relationship between stimulus, behavior, and consequence (or incentive, performance, and reward).

Step 1. *Identify and Study the Target Behavior.* The target behavior refers to specific employee behavior that management wants to influence. Usually, this is the behavior that has a greater impact on job performance. The behavior must be observable, measurable, and performance related. Attendance, customer service, and actual production are a few examples of target behavior. The rate of response or performance should be studied to see if it is at an acceptable level. The study of the contingency relationship between behavior and its consequences may reveal the possible cause of the performance problem.

Step 2. *Match Incentives with Needs.* The motivational value of incentives increases when they are matched with appropriate needs. If management primarily relies on monetary incentive for those employees who want a job challenge, the incentive will quickly lose its effectiveness. Employees have a variety of needs which they want to satisfy by their contributions to the organization. On the other hand, the organization has various types of incentives which can be used to motivate its employees. Congruence between these two sets of variables (needs and incentives) is one of the critical conditions that lead to an effective incentive system.

Step 3. *Match Rewards with Performance.* Unless reinforcement is contingent upon performance, the reward system quickly loses its motivational effect. A system of rewards is one way of recognizing valuable contributions and thus serves as a stimulant to strive for excellent performance. Since most people regard rewards as a scale upon which to measure the excellence of their performance, the rewards should be commensurate with the productivity of employees if the system is to have the greatest motivational value. It is therefore important to design a reward system in such a way that organization members perceive a direct relationship between their productivity and the rewards they receive. Appropriate reinforcement schedules can be adopted to insure the performance-reward tie.

SUMMARY AND CONCLUSION

Incentive theories of motivation depart from internal theories which search for behavioral causes within the organism. Rather, emphasis is placed on studying the effects of external stimuli or incentives on behavior. Although the study of need and expectancy theories (internal) may help managers better understand why and how behaviors are energized and selected, these theories do not provide them with a set of working principles and techniques with which they can formulate productive incentive systems. Managers cannot directly influence the behavior of employees by changing their internal states (needs and perceptions). However, they can indirectly influence employee behavior by effectively managing organizational incentives. The need for studying incentive theories is succinctly expressed by Luthans and Kreitner (1975, p. 61) as follows:

> The internal approach to organizational behavior would suggest that managers be trained in psychiatry or perhaps even parapsychology. Obviously, this would not be realistic or desirable from either a societal or an organizational viewpoint. The external approach is much more realistic for practicing managers, regardless of educational background, experience, or current position. By understanding and applying what is embodied in O.B. Mod. (Organizational behavior modification), the practicing manager, in a sense, can become a behavioral scientist.

However, the problem with the external approach is that it generally assumes that reinforcers can be uniformly applied to all people under all circumstances.

It does not recognize the fact that an incentive may appeal to one person but not to another. Also, an incentive may appeal to one person under some circumstances but not under other circumstances. The differences in need structure of individuals and the change in need structure of a person may alter the motivational value of incentives. The external approach also does not recognize the differences in perceptional patterns among individuals. Two persons may have the same need with similar intensity and be offered the same incentive, but their responses may differ from one another. Depending on how they perceive the chance of obtaining the outcome or incentive, one may act while the other may not. The differences in individual perceptions that affect work motivation in organizations will be discussed in Chapter 5.

5

EXPECTANCY THEORIES OF MOTIVATION

To explain individual differences in motivational responses, scholars have developed expectancy theories of motivation. Rather than attempting to find a set of principles governing the instrumental relationships between stimuli and responses, expectancy theorists direct their attention to individual differences in motivational responses. They attempt to explain the cognitive process in which people select, organize, and interpret sensory stimulation into a meaningful picture of their own work environment, and choose a set of behavioral alternatives instrumental to the attainment of their own goals. Even if two persons with similar educational and socioeconomic background are subjected to the same job with similar incentive values, they will differ in motivational responses if they perceive the job's motivational values differently.

Expectancy theorists are interested in studying perceptional responses to the following motivational elements: 1) the expectancy that effort leads to task accomplishment or performance (E-P), 2) the instrumentality that task performance results in incentive rewards (P-I), and 3) the valence of incentives that will satisfy employees' needs (I-N). Work motivation is generally considered to be a multiplicative function of these perceived motivational elements. This chapter 1) reviews existing expectancy theories, 2) proposes an integrative expectancy theory, 3) discusses the determinants of valence and expectancy, 4) looks at the individual differences in motivational responses, and 5) discusses various ways of influencing perceptual determinants. Since the perceptual determinants are affected by internal as well as external stimuli (needs and incentives), the theories of needs and incentives can be integrated into the theoretical framework of expectancy theory.

DEVELOPMENT OF EXPECTANCY THEORY

The cognitive theories of motivation advanced by Tolman (1936) and Lewin (1938) emphasized the importance of perceptual variables moderating the relationship between stimulus and response. Unlike the need and incentive theories which view motivation as a response to aroused needs or stimulant incentives, the cognitive theories view motivation as a goal-directed behavior involving an active process of evaluating the valence of outcomes and the expectancy of goal attainment. Valence refers to the attractiveness of an outcome or incentive. Expectancy refers to the likelihood that an action leads to an outcome. From this early work of Tolman and Lewin, several cognitive theories have been developed: subjective expected utility, achievement motivation, and expectancy-instrumentality.

SUBJECTIVE EXPECTED UTILITY THEORY

Classical economists proposed a theory of decision making based on the assumptions that man is a rational being who wants to maximize the payoff of his effort, and he has all the information necessary for making a rational choice (Von Neumann and Morgenstein, 1957; Miller and Starr, 1967). The rational man chooses among risky courses of action in such a way to maximize the expected value. The expected value (EV) is the sum of possible outcomes (V) multiplied by their probabilities (P): $EV = \sum_{i=1}^{n} Vi \times Pi$, where i runs from 1 to a finite number of outcomes. The assumptions of rationality and perfect information imply that the decision maker has known the objective values and probabilities of behavioral outcomes.

However, psychologists discovered that people rarely make decisions based on objective values and probabilities; rather, they make decisions based on their subjective utilities of possible outcomes and the probabilities as they perceive them. The utility of an outcome can vary from individual to individual. Also, in reality, people usually do not have perfect information regarding the objective value of an outcome and the objective probability of its occurance. In the absence of such an information, individual decision makers rely on their subjective judgment for estimating the value and probability. This subjective judgment may be based on their past experiences with the outcome or sheer hunches. Then, based on this subjective judgment, they will select a course of action that will maximize their subjective expected utility (SEU). The subjective expected utility is found by multiplying the subjective utility of an outcome (SU) and the subjective probability of its occurance (SP): $SEU = f(SU \times SP)$.

The SEU theory generally assumes that the subjective utility is inversely related to the subjective probability: $SU = 1 - SP$. An outcome that is useful and has a lower probability has a higher utility than the same outcome if it had a higher probability of occurance. While the scarcity of an outcome or incentive increases its subjective utility, its plentifulness reduces the subjective utility. The subjective expected utility will be the highest when the subjective probability is intermediate, and it will be the lowest if the probability is either extremely high or low. When the probability is either high or low, its utility will be inversely low or high. The subjective expected utility, which is a multiplicative product, turns out to be low. This theory was originally proposed by Lewin et al. (1944) and thus could be called the Lewin SEU theory. Empirical studies testing the validity of this theory will be reported in the next section where the theory of achievement motivation is discussed.

THEORY OF ACHIEVEMENT MOTIVATION

Atkinson (1957, 1964), adopting the concepts of expectancy and valence of Lewin, advanced the achievement theory of motivation. Atkinson and Reitman (1956) originally stated that the goal-directed action tendency is a joint function of the strength of the motive and the expectancy of the goal attainment. Later, Atkinson recognized the influence of incentives on behavior and added the incentive variable to his achievement motivation model. Thus, achievement motivation is considered a function of motive, incentive, and expectancy. According to Atkinson, the tendency to act or perform is an outcome of the desire to achieve success and the desire to avoid failure. The tendency to achieve success (Ts) is considered a multiplicative function of the motive to achieve success (Ms), x the subjective probability (expectancy) of the goal attainment (Ps), and the incentive value of success (Is): $Ts = f (Ms \times Ps \times Is)$. The tendency to avoid failure (Tf) is considered to be a multiplicative function of the motive to avoid failure (Mf), the subjective probability of failure (Pf), and the incentive cost of failure (If): $Tf = Mf \times Pf \times If$. The resultant tendency to undertake a task is then the difference between Ts and Tf: $Tr = Ts - Tf$. If Ts is stronger than Tf, the person will undertake the task. If otherwise, the person will avoid the task performance.

The achievement theory assumes that people develop both the tendency to achieve success and the tendency to avoid failure at the time of performance. The resultant tendency to undertake a task is positive and strongest when the expectancy of success is intermediate. As in the case of Lewin's SEU theory, the incentive value of success is inversely related to the expectancy of success: $Is = 1 - Ps$. If the expectancy is high, the value of success will be low because the task does not provide the performer with any challenge. In addition, the motive and the tendency to avoid failure tend to be greater when the task appears to be easy to perform than when it appears to be difficult. Any failure to perform what appears to be an easy task creates a feeling of shame and embarrassment.

When the task appears to be difficult, the expectancy of success will be low. Normally, little or no stigma is attached to any failure to perform a difficult task. However, a person will not be motivated to undertake a task if it has a low probability of success. He may feel that no matter how hard he tries, he cannot achieve success. The tendency to undertake a task will be the highest when the expectancy of success is about 50 percent or intermediate. At this risk preference level, the performer may feel that his effort can result in task accomplishment.

Several studies empirically support the achievement theory of motivation. Atkinson (1958) found that the level of performance of female college students was significantly higher when the probability of winning a small monetary prize by getting a high score was half (1/2) than when the expectancy of winning was either very high (3/4) or very low (1/20). McClelland (1958) also found that children in kindergarten and second grade who were judged to be more highly motivated to achieve on a graphic expression measure of need achievement (n Ach) preferred an intermediate degree of risk than children presumed to be low in n Ach. The latter group more often than the former group preferred to do the tasks that were either very easy or very speculative. The major findings of Mahone (1960) and Atkinson (1964) confirmed these studies. Atkinson and Feather (1966) and Morris (1967) also reported that persons low in achievement motivation chose as if they were avoiding an intermediate degree of risk.

However, other studies do not support the inverse relationship between incentive value and expectancy of success. For example, Irwin (1953), Edwards (1953), and Feather (1963) argued that the incentive value of success (Is) is an independent function of the expectancy of success (Ps). They implied that the incentive value could be determined both subjectively and objectively independent of the probability of receiving the incentive. Another variation is that people have a tendency to overestimate the likelihood of desirable events and underestimate the likelihood of undesirable events. Thus, they perceive the probability of obtaining rewards more favorably when these rewards are valued by them than when they are not valued (Irwin, 1953; Crandall et al., 1955; and Edwards, 1953).

A possible explanation for these discrepancies may be that the inverse relationship between valence and expectancy can exist in performing achievement-oriented tasks where people experience anxiety, shame, and humiliation if they fail to achieve them. On the other hand, the independent relationship and the positively correlating relationship may occur in less distressing task situations where the success or failure does not produce considerable anxiety (Feather, 1963). The controversy over the relationship between valence and expectancy will be further discussed later.

Indik (1966) and Chung (1968) adopted the achievement motivation model to measure the work motivation for job seekers and students respectively. Indik reported that the motivation measures (motives, incentives, and expectancies) were significantly correlated with job seeking behavior. Chung also reported that the motivation measures were predictive of students' scholastic performance. Investigating the relationships between the motivational measures, Chung found that the motive measure was positively correlated with the incentive and expectancy measures. This result can be interpreted as: 1) the stronger the motive or need to perform a task, the higher the incentive value of the task performance outcome to the person; and 2) the stronger the motive or need to perform a task, the higher the expectation that the task is likely to be achieved. The correlation between the incentive measure and the expectancy measure was not significant. However, when subjects were divided into high, middle, and low performer groups, the incentive measure had a significant inverse relationship with the expectancy measure in low and middle performer groups. The incentive value was high, but the expectancy was low. For high performers, all three measures were high. This finding supports the view that the incentive value can be determined both subjectively and objectively independent of the expectancy of task performance. Also, the differences in performers moderate the relationship between incentive value and expectancy.

Atkinson's theory of motivation integrated the three major determinants of motivational behavior. It recognizes the motivational strength of achievement motives, the instigating power of incentives, and the effort-outcome expectancy. However, it is primarily a content theory of motivation which lists motivational components. It is not all clear how each component influences the strength of motivation. As it fails to explain the instrumental relationships between motivational components, it falls short of a process theory. A process theory explains how a motivational component is related to other components and to motivational effort and outcome.

VROOM'S EXPECTANCY THEORY

The basic concepts of expectancy and valence have been used in general psychology for some time, but Georgopoulos, Mahoney, and Jones (1957) were the first group of scholars who applied the expectancy concept in work organizations. Their major theme was that workers' motivation to produce could be predicted from the way they perceive their performance as a path to the attainment of their goals. If their path-goal perception is positive, their productivity will be high; if negative, productivity will be low. Their studies supported the goal-path hypothesis. First, high productivity was associated with the perception that high performance leads to each of the three goals (making money, getting along with others, and promotion). Second, performance was higher for workers who ranked goal-attainment as being important to them personally. Third, performance was higher for workers who perceived them to be autonomous. In general, productivity was positively related to perceived instrumentality for goal-attainment, and the degree of attraction to the goals and autonomy mediated the relationship between productivity and the perceived instrumentality.

The more complete treatment of expectancy theory was presented by Vroom (1964). Vroom articulated and popularized the cognitive theory of motivation commonly known as expectancy theory. His theory is based on four basic premises (Lawler, 1973, p. 49):

1. People have preferences (or valences) for various outcomes or incentives that are potentially available to them.
2. People have expectancies about the likelihood that an action or effort on their part will lead to the intended performance.
3. People understand the instrumentalities that certain behaviors will be followed by desirable outcomes or incentive rewards.
4. The action a person chooses to take (motivation) is determined by the expectancies and the valences that the person has at the time.

Vroom's theory of motivation includes three related models: the valence of outcome, work motivation, and job performance. The valence model states that the valence of an outcome is an increasing function of the algebraic sum of the valences of all outcomes and the person's perceptions about the instrumentalities between his performance and the outcomes. Instrumentality is defined as the degree to which the person sees the task performance as leading to the attainment of the outcomes or incentives.

The work motivation model states that the force to perform a task (M) is an increasing function of the algebraic sum of the products of the valences of all outcomes (V) and the expectancies that effort and performance will be followed by the attainment of these outcomes (E): $M = f(V \times E)$. Since the valence concept contains the instrumentality concept, Vroom's motivation model basically involves three core concepts—valence, instrumentality, and expectancy.

The motivation to perform a task starts from a person's desire to obtain preferred outcomes or incentive rewards in an organization. Since the organization dispenses the incentive rewards in return for an employee's task performance, the task performance becomes a means of obtaining the incentive rewards. Thus, if the employee perceives an instrumental relationship that good performance leads to increased incentive rewards (P-I), he will exert extra effort to accomplish the task in order to obtain more incentive rewards. However, the employee will not be motivated to perform the task unless he perceives that his effort leads to task performance (E-P). If the task performance does not depend on one's effort, the employee will not find the reason for extra effort.

The performance model (P) is considered to be an interactive or multiplicative function of ability (A) and motivation (M): $P = f (A \times M)$. Ability determines what the person can do; motivation determines what he wants to or will do. It follows from this performance model that, if either ability or motivation is low, performance will suffer. If both ability and motivation increase, performance will be higher. This performance model will be further discussed in Chapter 6.

GALBRAITH AND CUMMINGS' MODIFICATION

The original Vroom's model has been modified by several researchers. Modifications were made to improve the predictability of expectancy theory. Modifications by Galbraith and Cummings (1967), Campbell, Dunnette, Lawler, and Weick (1970), and Michell (1974) will be discussed in the following sections. Galbraith and Cummings made distinction between first and second level outcomes. First-level outcomes refer to workers' performance levels or performance characteristics which are the major concern of an organization. Second-level outcomes are the incentive rewards obtained by workers as a result of task performance. These second-level outcomes include money, fringe benefits, promotion, supportive supervision, and group acceptance which are extrinsically mediated. The attainment of the first-level outcomes is viewed as a means of obtaining the second-level outcomes. A person's perception of the relationship between the first-level and the second-level is called instrumentality. Their expectancy model is shown in Figure 5-1.

These researchers also distinguished intrinsic and extrinsic valences of performance outcomes. Intrinsic outcome valences are derived from work behavior itself and task accomplishment. These outcomes are mediated internally within the person performing the task independent of any extrinsic rewards. On the other hand, extrinsic rewards do not bear inherent relationship to work behavior and task performance. They are externally introduced to influence work behavior and task performance. They can influence work behavior by making rewards contingent upon performance.

Incorporating into the Vroom's expectancy model, Galbraith and Cummings defined motivation as a function of the expectancy that effort results in task performance (E), the valence of the second-level outcomes (V), and the instrumentality relationships between first-level and second-level outcomes (I). Their study generally supported the performance prediction of Vroom's expectancy model. Their analysis showed that at least two second-level outcomes, including supervision and monetary incentives, had positive instrumental relationships with first-level outcomes.

CAMPBELL'S HYBRID EXPECTANCY MODEL

Campbell, Dunnette, Lawler, and Weick (1970) further elaborated the Vroom's expectancy model. First, the effort-reward expectancy has been divided into Expectancy 1 and Expectancy 2. Expectancy 1 refers to the perceived belief that effort leads to task performance (E-P), while Expectancy 2 refers to the belief that task performance is instrumental for receiving valued outcomes

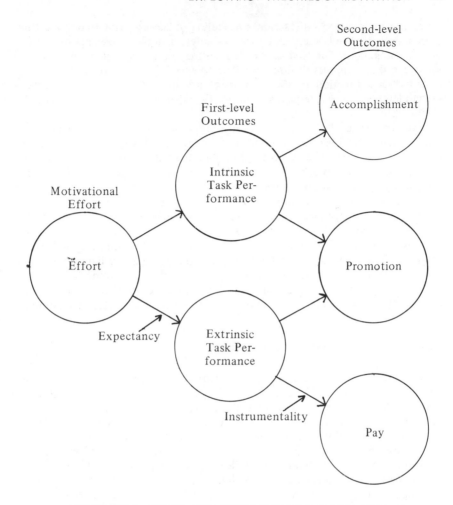

FIGURE 5-1. FIRST AND SECOND-LEVEL OUTCOMES

or incentives (P-I). The differentiation of the effort-reward expectancy into Expectancy 1 and Expectancy 2 is important for studying the impact of the E-P expectancy and that of the P-I instrumentality on employee motivation separately.

Second, they divided the characteristics of task performance or task goals into intrinsic and extrinsic components. Extrinsic task goals are imposed by the organization or the work group, while intrinsic goals are set by the individual himself. The examples of task goals include production quotas, project targets, quality standards, institutional loyalty, attitudes, and training goals. They also made a distinction between first and second level outcomes. The first-level outcomes are contingent upon achieving a set of task goals. They are those incentive rewards desired by the worker. Like task goals, the first-level outcomes or incentive rewards can be internal or external. Some external incentives granted by the organization include pay, job security, promotion, recognition, and granting autonomy. The worker also can set up his own internal incentive outcomes such as ego satisfaction and feeling of success. The second-level outcomes are basic needs such as for food, shelter, material things, status and freedom from anxiety. The first-level outcomes may or may not be instrumental for satisfying the second-level outcomes. The valence of a first-level outcome or an incentive is a function of the instrumentality of that outcome for satisfying second-level outcomes or needs. Campbell's expectancy model is presented in Figure 5-2.

Campbell et al. defined work motivation as a function of a person's belief that he can accomplish the task (E-P), his belief that his task performance will be followed by incentive rewards (P-I), and the valence of the first-level outcomes or incentive rewards (I-N). Although the hybrid expectancy theory does not clearly specify various contingency relationships between task goals, incentive rewards, and needs, it nevertheless makes unique contributions to the development of expectancy theory. First, it recognizes the differences in task performance goals. Task goals produce not only different incentive valences but also require different levels of effort exertion. Second, the addition of needs to the expectancy model enhances its motivational predictability. Atkinson's achievement motivation model has shown that the strength of motives is a reliable predictor of motivation and performance. In addition, the valence of incentives can be increased when these incentives are matched with appropriate needs.

EXPECTANCY AND MOTIVATIONAL EFFORT

Vroom's expectancy theory (1964) predicts that the higher the E-P expectancy, the higher the effort level will be. Kopelman the Thompson (1976) found that the expectancy predicition of performance was higher under the condition of high ability and low task difficulty (high E-P expectancy) than under the condition of low ability and high task difficulty (low E-P expectancy). Graen (1969) also found that the E-P expectancy is a reliable predictor of performance. However, a number of studies have failed to increase performance predictability by adding the E-P expectancy as a predictor or have found the P-I instrumentality to be a more reliable predictor than the E-P expectancy (Lawler and Porter, 1967; Porter and Lawler, 1968a; Mitchell and Albright, 1972).

Mitchell (1974) suggests that the levels of effort and expectancy may have to be differentiated to increase the predictability of expectancy theory. The level of effort may increase with an increase of E-P expectancy to a certain point as long as the valence of an outcome or incentive holds a certain value. However, beyond this point, the valence of the outcome approaches zero with an increase of the E-P expectancy. For example, air and water are vital for our survival, but our effort to get them is relatively low when they are plentiful. The valence or subjective utility of air and water for most of us is low because they are easy to get.

As pointed out earlier, Atkinson's achievement motivation and Lewin's SEU theories predict that the level of motivational effort has an inverted-V relationship with the E-P expectancy. Generally, the motivational effort will be the highest when the task requires a moderate level of difficulty or risk of success and failure. It will be the lowest when the task is either extremely difficult or easy to perform. There are several reasons why such an inverted relationship can occur between motivational effort and E-P expectancy. First, when the perceived

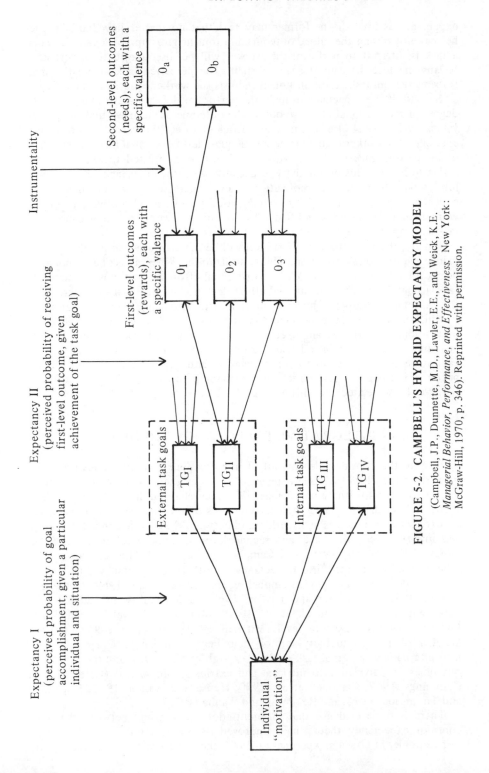

FIGURE 5-2. CAMPBELL'S HYBRID EXPECTANCY MODEL

(Campbell, J.P., Dunnette, M.D., Lawler, E.E., and Weick, K.E. *Managerial Behavior, Performance, and Effectiveness.* New York: McGraw-Hill, 1970, p. 346). Reprinted with permission.

expectancy is low, the performer may feel that no matter how hard he tries he may not obtain the valued outcome and thus he gives up. For example, when a task is difficult to perform, the worker will be discouraged to undertake it because he feels he cannot accomplish it. The perceived lack of positive reinforcement from task accomplishment reduces the worker's motivational effort.

Second, if the expectancy is high, the performer does not have to exert a high degree of motivational effort to obtain the outcome or incentive that the person values. A low level of effort may be sufficient to get the valued outcome. For example, if a worker is guaranteed an adequate level of annual income regardless of his performance level, the worker will not be motivated to exert an extra effort to increase his productivity, especially when the job is lacking of intrinsic job satisfaction. If the motivational level increases with an increase of expectancy, most simplified jobs paying good wages should motivate people to work harder. However, simplified jobs do not motivate workers because their task accomplishment does not require extra effort exertion.

Finally, the motivational effort level will be the highest when the task performance requires one's effort and ability utilization. When a task has a moderate degree of difficulty or risk, one's motivational effort is most closely related to task accomplishment. Motivational effort does not increase with an increase of the expectancy. Rather, it increases up to a certain point, but beyond that point, it will decrease as the expectancy approaches a level of certainty. When the motivational effort has an inverted-V relationship with expectancy, the expectancy theory, assuming a linear relationship between expectancy and valence, cannot be a reliable predictor of motivation and performance. If the E-P expectancy is going to serve as a reliable predictor, effort levels have to be differentiated to be correlated with different levels of expectancy.

INTEGRATIVE EXPECTANCY THEORY

Despite the considerable amount of modifications and extensions presented by various theorists, the basic cores of expectancy theory (expectancy, valence, and instrumentality) have not changed. What has changed, however, is that these theorists have differentiated the characteristics of the basic cores of expectancy theory. Differentiation is seen within and between these basic cores. Distinction was made between first level and second level outcomes (Galbraith and Cummings, 1967; Graen, 1969; and Campbell et al., 1970); the effort-outcome relationship was divided into Expectancy 1 (E-P) and Expectancy 2 (P-I) (Galbraith and Cummings, 1967; Campbell et al., 1970; Graen, 1969; House and Wahba, 1972; and Porter and Lawler, 1968); and needs were added to the expectancy model (Campbell et al., 1970). Motivational level is divided into high and low effort exertion levels (Mitchell, 1974); performance characteristics are divided into productivity and job-incumbent components (Graen, 1969) or into internal and external task goals (Campbell et al., 1970); and the valence of outcomes are divided into intrinsic and extrinsic components (Galbraith and Cummings, 1967; Campbell et al., 1970; House and Wahba, 1972; Kopelman and Thompson, 1976; and Reinharth and Wahba, 1975).

There is some evidence that differentiations within and between the basic cores of expectancy theory have improved its predictability of performance. For example, in Graen's experiment (1969), the achievement group was rewarded for prior performance, and the incentive group was paid for subsequent performance. The study found that the achievement-treated group rated the P-I instrumentality for achievement and recognition higher than did the incentive-treated group. The incentive-treated group rated the P-I instrumental relationship between job-incumbent work role and money higher than did the achievement-treated group. The differentiation in incentive reward systems has improved the predictability of expectancy model. A study by Reinharth and Wahba (1975) showed no support for the Vroom expectancy model. However, when the sample groups were differentiated by their demographic and environmental characteristics, the expectancy model showed some predictive power.

Kopelman and Thompson (1976) also studied the effects of various reward levels on the theory prediction. They found that job performance was more closely related to extrinsic outcome valences than to intrinsic outcome valences among design and development engineers. However, intrinsic valences are reliable predictors of performance among high-pay respondents, while extrinsic valences were better predictors of performance among low-pay subjects. Although intrinsic valences were reliable predictors, they were not better performance predictors than extrinsic valences. These researchers support the contingency approach to incentive application indicating that the effectiveness of intrinsic valences depends on the level of extrinsic need satisfaction.

The differentiations within and between the basic cores of expectancy theory have improved its performance predictability. But, the correlation coefficients between the predicted effort levels and the actual performance are still low, ranging between .20 and .70 (see Mitchell, 1974; Reinharth and Wahba, 1975; and Kopelman and Thompson, 1976). A lot of variances are still left unexplained. Indeed, the subject of motivation and performance is so complex and nebulous that we may never be able to capture them into a nice, neat theoretical model. However, it is hoped that an integration of these differentiations may further improve the predictability of expectancy theory and enhance the understanding of complex work motivation.

PROPOSED EXPECTANCY MODEL

An integrative expectancy model is proposed to enhance the predictability of expectancy theory and an understanding of motivational behavior in organizations. A number of suggestions and concerns expressed by various expectancy theorists are integrated into this model. Furthermore, the proposed expectancy model incorporates need and incentive theories discussed in Chapters 3 and 4. The primary features of the proposed expectancy theory are listed in the following. Figure 5-3 depicts the major themes of the proposed theory.

1. The levels of motivational effort are divided into high, medium, and low. It will vary according to the perceived level of effort requirement needed to carry out the task (E-P). It is hypothesized that (a) motivational level will be the highest when the E-P expectancy is .50, and (b) motivational level will be low when the expectancy approaches either 1.00 or zero. (c) If the expectancy is independent of the valence, the motivational level will increase as the expectancy increases.
2. The characteristics of task performance are divided into intrinsically, affectively, and nonmotivating dull jobs. Intrinsically motivating tasks

98

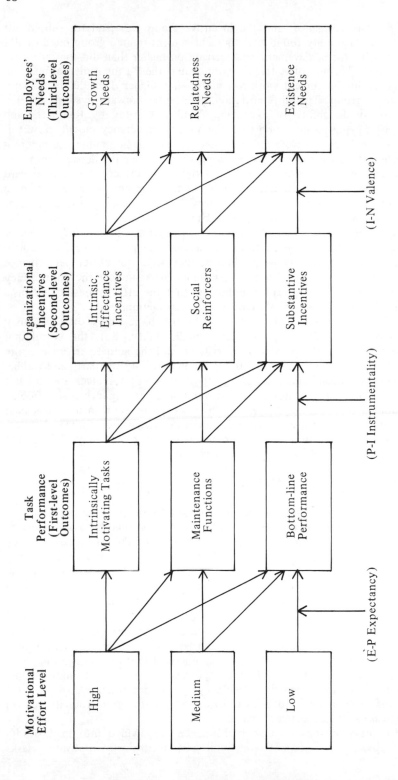

FIGURE 5-3. INTEGRATIVE EXPECTANCY MODEL

tend to produce ego-involvement, effort exertion, and ability and skill utilization. Affectively motivating tasks tend to serve the maintenance function of an organization—socialization, power and influence, and release of psychic energy. Nonmotivating jobs do not possess intrinsic motivational value. Their source of reinforcement primarily depends on extrinsic rewards.

3. Incentive rewards are divided into effectance, interactive, and substantive reinforcers. The motivational value of tasks depends on the perceived instrumentality that the characteristics of task performance are matched with the types of incentive rewards (P-I). The performance of intrinsically motivating tasks directly leads to effectance incentive rewards, while the instrumental relationships between nonmotivating jobs and substantive incentive rewards are externally manipulated.

4. Needs are divided into growth-oriented, relation-oriented, and existence. Existence needs are primarily satisfied by substantive incentives, relation-oriented needs are met by interactive incentives, and growth-oriented needs are satisfied by effectance incentives. The valence of incentives increases when these incentives are matched with appropriate needs (I-N).

5. The motivational force to perform a task (M) is then a function of the E-P expectancy, P-I instrumentality, and I-N valence, the strength of needs (N), the magnitude of incentives (I), and the nature of task performance (P). The mathematical relationships between them can be either additive or multiplicative. If the value of any of these motivational components is zero, the motivational force will be reduced to zero. Zero values substantiate the multiplicative relationship. If these values are nonzeros, additive relationships tend to be more realistic from theoretical and operational standpoints (Heneman and Schwab, 1972; Schmidt, 1973). The integrated expectancy model can be expressed as: $M = f(N, I, P, E-P, P-I, I-N)$.

The proposed expectancy model has a number of advantages over other expectancy models. Some of the characteristics of the proposed model are:

1. It integrates major theories of motivation (needs, incentives, and expectancies) into a more comprehensive theoretical framework. Actual motivational behavior involves all these motivational elements, so they need to be incorporated into a theoretical framework rather than polarized between theories. These theories are basically complementary to each other rather than competitive.

2. It should be able to increase the predictability of motivation and performance. It accommodates more salient motivational components or elements which have proven to be predictive of performance. The addition of the strength of needs, the motivational charcteristics of task performance (P), and the instrumental relationship between incentive rewards and needs (I-N) will enhance the predictability of motivation. Ability factor then will be added to this motivational model to predict the level of performance: Performance = f (ability and motivation).

3. The motivational components are divided into two major categories: content-oriented valence factors (needs, incentives, and performance characteristics) and process-oriented expectancy factors (E-P, P-I, and

I-N). Content factors imply that the worker should possess proper need strength, the amount of incentive rewards should be attractive, and the task performance should have some motivational characteristics. Process factors suggest that task performance should be a function of effort utilization, task performance leads to receiving appropriate incentive rewards, and these rewards should be matched with appropriate needs.

EXPECTANCY THEORY AND OPERANT CONDITIONING

There are some similarities and differences between expectancy theory and operant theory in explaining individual behavior in organizations. What appear to be diametrically opposing theories make similar performance predicitions. According to expectancy theory, people make work performance decisions based on the perceived importance of rewards (valence), the perceived relationship between performance and reward (instrumentality), and the belief that effort leads to performance (expectancy). Operant theory, on the other hand, predicts that performance is a function of the amount of reward and the learned connection between reward and performance (instrumental behavior). Both theories are similar in the theme that performance is seen as a function of the importance of reward and the reward-performance contingency.

The differences between them are found in the way these theories explain how the importance of reward and the instrumental relationship are acquired by the individual. They differ in two counts. First, expectancy theory views man as an autonomous being who actively selects and interprets the valence, instrumentality, and expectancy of behavioral outcomes. On the contrary, operant theory views man as an organism passively responding to contingencies of his environment. Second, expectancy theory stresses the importance of forward-looking belief about what will occur, while operant theory emphasizes the importance of learned stimulus-response connections in making behavioral decisions (Lawler, 1973). Expectancy theory indicates that in the absence of learned S-R connections, people have to rely on their cognitive judgment regarding the valence, instrumentality, and expectancy.

Which theory is correct in describing human behavior? A few studies (Mawkinney and Behling, 1973; and Berger, Cummings, and Heneman, 1975) have attempted to compare the relative merit of expectancy and operant theories. Mawkinney and Behling pointed out the difficulty of comparing the relative merit of these two theories, but Berger et al. indicated that their study did not show any superiority favoring any particular theory. Berger et al. reported that when additional pay was contingent upon performance, performance increased substantially. The performance-contingency reward is a major theme of both expectancy and operant theories. They indicated that both environmental and perceptual variables have to be studied for better understanding of work behavior.

It can be pointed out that both theories are correct in describing a portion of work behavior. Expectancy theory is primarily concerned with ahistorical and conscious choice behavior, while operant theory primarily deals with historically learned behavior. Work behavior can be influenced by both historical and ahistorical events, and can be internally as well as externally controlled. Thus, it is necessary to accommodate both theories for better understanding and explaining the complexity of human motivation.

A few attempts are made to integrate these two theories into a theoretical framework. First, Boles (1972) argued that learning is not based on learned S-R connections, but rather on two kinds of expectancies. One is environmental stimulus-outcome contingencies, and the other is a set of response-outcome contingencies. The stimulus-outcome expectancy has an incentive value which arouses an anticipation of desired outcomes, while the organism determines the direction of behavior that leads to desired outcomes. Operant procedure merely permits both kinds of contingencies to be learned. The second attempt was made by Lawler (1973). Lawler recognized the importance of past learning experience and habitual response as influencing factors of the E-P expectancy and the P-I instrumentality, and he included these historically learned variables in his expectancy theory. His expectancy theory is more historically-oriented than Vroom's original expectancy theory.

While it is feasible that the major ingredients of operant theory can be integrated into the theoretical framework of expectancy theory, a few researchers are quick to point out that expectancy theory prediction does not agree with one of the major findings of operant theory (Mawkinnery and Behling, 1973; and Berger et al., 1975). Operant theory predicts that performance will be higher under variable or partial reinforcement than under continuous reinforcement conditions. Expectancy theory, on the other hand, predicts that performance will be higher under continuous reinforcement than variable or partial reinforcement conditions. If one assumes an independent relationship between expectancy and valence, the expectancy will be higher under continuous than partial reinforcement conditions, assuming the valence of reward remains unchanged. Under a continuous reinforcement condition, the expectancy of receiving a reward is a certainty. Since the valence of total expected rewards will be constant, motivational effort will increase with an increase of expectancy.

However, as indicated previously, the independency postulate has been under criticism. Several researchers (Mitchell, 1974; and Starke and Behling, 1975) suggest that the relationship between valence and expectancy tends to be more dependent than independent. Under the dependency postulate, the valence of a reward decreases with an increase of its expectancy. Especially, when a relatively small sized reward has to be divided into smaller pieces in order to pay employees under a continuous reinforcement schedule, the valence of divided rewards will become almost meaningless. Under this circumstance, while the expectancy of receiving rewards increases, their valence decreases. Consequently, motivational effort will be lower under continuous reinforcement than the original expectancy theory predicts.

On the other hand, partial reinforcement can increase the average size of rewards making them more attractive to the receivers. Under partial reinforcement, although the expectancy of obtaining an incentive may decrease, its valence increases due to the increase in size of the incentive. Furthermore, as indicated earlier, the subjective probability of obtaining a reward can be higher than its objective probability. People have a tendency to favorably perceive the likelihood of desirable events and perceive unfavorably the likelihood of undesirable events. Therefore, it can be expected that performance will be higher under variable or partial reinforcement than under continuous reinforcement conditions. The dependency postulate of the modified expectancy theory is in agreement with operant theory performance prediction.

FACTORS INFLUENCING EXPECTANCY AND VALENCE

There are a number of influences on the content-oriented factors (needs, incentives, and task properties) and the process-oriented factors (E-P expectancy, P-I instrumentality, and I-N valence) in the proposed expectancy model. Specific influences on these motivational components are discussed in appropriate chapters. The following discussion focuses on several general factors not stressed elsewhere.

INTERNAL INFLUENCING FACTORS

The subject's needs influence the valence of incentive outcomes. For example, hungry persons tend to perceive foods and cooking utensils from a blank screen (McClelland and Atkinson, 1948). Words having a sexual connotation tend to be more quickly perceived when they are used in sexual context than when they are used in nonsexual context (Wiener, 1955). The sizes of valuable coins tend to be overestimated, while less valuable coins are underestimated in children's drawings (Bruner and Goodman, 1947). Subjects frustrated in their goal attainment tend to perceive pictures of money more often and overestimate the size of money more than subjects who are not frustrated (Knott, 1971). An implication of these findings is that when people desire an outcome they tend to overestimate its valence and expectancy.

The subject's ability influences the E-P expectancy. A person with high ability may perceive the E-P expectancy more favorably than a person with low ability. Kopelman and Thompson (1976) reported a positive correlation between ability and expectancy. High ability and low task difficulty were associated with high expectancy. A person with high ability will experience more successful task accomplishments than a person with low ability. Successful performances reinforce the person's E-P expectancy. Since the E-P expectancy of performing a task influences the level of motivational effort, tasks need to be differentiated for individuals with different ability levels. The need for task differentiation will be further discussed in Chapter 9.

The person's self-concept influences his perception. Self-concept refers to the way a person perceives the self. It determines the level of self-competency and serves as an ego-defense mechanism. If the person perceives himself to be capable, he tends to set and strive to achieve high performance goals; otherwise he may set and achieve lower performance goals. People seldom achieve more than what they expect to achieve because they usually do not try to achieve more than what they think they can. The degree of self-competence determines the level of aspiration that a person actually tries to achieve. People tend to set realistic goals so they can experience a feeling of success and accomplishment. A failure to achieve goals creates a feeling of incompetence and inferiority. To avoid such an averse feeling, they tend to set goals they think they can achieve.

Role perception influences a person's threshold for evoking behavior. Role perception refers to the way a person defines his job and the role he plays in organizations. If a person's role perception is compatible to that expected by the organization, his expectancy on the P-I relationship will be favorable. Consequently, his motivational effort can be easily evoked by the presence of organizational incentives. If the person's role perception is in conflict with that of the organization, he may sooner or later find that his effort will not be reinforced by the organization and thus his P-I expectancy deteriorates (Porter and Lawler, 1968). Role perception can be internally or externally oriented. Those individuals who are self-directed will define their own roles regarding what they should be doing to perform their jobs effectively. On the other hand, those individuals whose role perceptions are externally directed will be more sensitive to external pressures in defining their roles in an organization. Graen (1969) indicated performance level can be predicted from these two types of role perceptions—internally felt and externally pressured.

Personality influences a person's perception on the valence of organizational incentives and the E-P expectancy. Costello and Zalkind (1963) summarized the effects of personality on perception in social context: 1) Secure people tend to perceive other people as warm rather than cold. 2) Thoughtful people are less likely to view things in black and white and express extreme judgments about others. 3) Persons who accept themselves are more likely to perceive others more favorably than those who reject themselves. 4) People tend to perceive others more accurately when their characteristics are similar than when they are not. In motivational context, Sweney (1975) points out that personality influences a person's threshold for evoking behavior. For example, a passive individual is highly restrictive and unfavorable in perceiving his behavioral outcomes and thus requires a high level of stimulation to act. On the other hand, an impulsive individual is unconstrained and favorable in perceiving his behavioral outcomes and thus readily responds to a low level of stimulation. While an adventurous individual likes to undertake tasks with high degrees of risk, an assurance-oriented person will prefer tasks with payoff certainty.

Past experience of success or failure affects a person's perception on the E-P instrumental contingency. People formulate the E-P expectancy based on their past experiences with task performance or by observing others' experiences. If they experience successful task performance, their E-P expectancy will be strengthened. If they or others experience failure, the E-P expectancy will be weakened. The strengthened E-P expectancy tends to raise the level of aspiration or the goal of the subsequent task performances. The weakened expectancy tends to lower the level of aspiration or the goal for subsequent trails. As people experience success, the E-P is getting higher. What used to be challenging tasks are becoming less challenging as the E-P expectancy is getting higher. Thus, people search for higher goals where they can find their jobs to be challenging again.

EXTERNAL INFLUENCING FACTORS

The size, intensity, novelty, movement, repetition, and familiarity of the external stimuli or incentives influence the E-P expectance and the valence of these stimuli. The larger the incentive, the more likely it will be valued (Crespi, 1944; Donahoe et al., 1968; and Platt and Gay, 1968). The more intense the external stimulus, the more likely it will be perceived. A repeated stimulus is more likely to attract the perceiver's attention. People pay more attention to moving objects than to stationary objects. Either familiar or novel stimuli attract more attention than nonfamiliar or common stimuli. The proximity of a stimulus determines its perceived characteristics. Stimuli close together in space and time are perceived to belong together. The law of exercise discussed in Chapter 4 explains the association principle of proximity. The materials presented in Chapters 4, 7, 8, and 9 deal with the effects that organizational incentives have on employees' perceptions on the valences and expectancies.

Finally, the social situation in which a stimulus is perceived affects the valence and expectancy of the stimulus. The social situation refers to an organizational climate or psychological atmosphere in an organization. Employees will perceive the E-P expectancy more favorably in a trusting and supportive climate than in a distrusting and nonsupportive climate. A supportive leader may help his subordinates to clarify the path-goal relationships of both E-P and P-I expectancies. They also will perceive the P-I instrumentality favorably when a sense of equity prevails. The norms existing in reference groups influence a person's threshold for evoking behavior. For example, even if an employee wants to maximize his economic gains by producing more, he may not do so because he fears potential rejection by his co-workers. The motivational influences of organizational climate are further discussed in Chapter 8.

INDIVIDUAL DIFFERENCES IN MOTIVATIONAL RESPONSES

People differ in their motivational responses because they are motivated to satisfy different needs and are reinforced by different organizational incentives. Even if they have the same needs to satisfy and are offered the same organizational incentives, they will differ in their motivational responses because they differ in perceiving the valence and expectancy of their behavioral outcomes. Perceiving is not a passive process of imprinting sensory stimulation. Rather, it is an active process of selecting, organizing, and interpreting the meaning of sensory stimulation to serve the purpose of the perceiver. The perceived world is different from the real world; it is a personalized view of the real world. Consequently, no two persons will have the same perceptual responses, the same stimulus or incentive can evoke different responses from different individuals, and the threshold for evoking action will vary. The following discussion focuses on individual differences in their motivational responses within the theoretical framework of intrinsic and extrinsic motivation.

INTRINSIC AND EXTRINSIC BOUNDARY

People engage in a certain activity for its own end or as a means of obtaining other ends. If one performs a task for its own end (enjoyment, accomplishment, and development), it is called intrinsically motivating and its locus of behavioral causality is said to be internal to the performer. On the other hand, if one performs a task as a means of obtaining other ends such as money, job security, power, status, and promotion, it is extrinsically motivating and its locus of causality is said to be external. The same task can be either intrinsically or extrinsically motivating depending on how the performer perceives the locus of causality.

The distrinction between intrinsic and extrinsic sources of motivation is important because their impacts on behavior are producing different motivational results. First, when a task is intrinsically motivating, people enjoy performing it without apparent extrinsic rewards. They even sometimes pay to experience enjoyment or challenge resulting from such a task performance. Second, if one wants to motivate someone to perform an intrinsically motivating task extrinsically, the amount of extrinsic reward must be substantial to evoke the necessary response from the performer. If the amount is psychologically insignificant, the person will do it for free rather than be nominally reinforced.

Third, if a task is not intrinsically motivating, it is necessary to use extrinsic reinforcements to evoke the desired behavior. The amount of extrinsic reward necessary for evoking behavior depends on the performer's need strength, the incentive value to him, and his perception on the effort-reward expectancy. Usually, when the performer is repeatedly reinforced with a reinforcer, its incentive value tends to decrease. Thus, it takes more of the same reinforcer to produce the same motivational response. Finally, since a task can either intrinsically or extrinsically reinforce a motivated behavior but with different efficacy, it can be very helpful for management to understand the types of individuals who tend to possess internal locus of causality and the organizational situations under which people tend to perceive intrinsic sources of motivation.

As indicated in Chapter 4, while effectance incentives are intrinsically motivating, substantive incentives influence behavior extrinsically. Intrinsically motivated behavior can be rewarded extrinsically, but extrinsic rewards are posterior rather than antecedent conditions for behavior. Social or interactive incentives are both intrinsically and/or extrinsically influencing behavior. Some people may exhibit affectional behavior for sheer enjoyment of liking others, while others do so as a means of obtaining other valued outcomes.

The boundary between intrinsic and extrinsic motivation is not distinctive because the same incentives can be extrinsically or intrinsically motivating depending on how these incentives are perceived and interpreted by different individuals. For example, money is generally considered to be an extrinsically motivating reinforcer. However, if the individual perceives money to be endogenous to a task performance, which is a direct consequence of his own action, money can be seen as a source of intrinsic motivation. In essence, the boundary is reflected by individual differences in perceiving the locus of behavioral causality rather than by the nature of incentives. If the individual perceives the locus of causality to be internal, his behavior is considered to be intrinsically motivated. If he perceives it to be external, his behavior is said to be extrinsically motivated. Individual differences play an important role in perceiving the valence and expectancy of outcomes and in manifesting motivation into actual behavior.

THRESHOLDS FOR BEHAVIOR AND CONSIDERATION

Normally people are motivated to perform tasks both intrinsically and extrinsically motivating. However, at some point some people are motivated to perform a task for the sheer enjoyment of performing it without expecting extrinsic rewards. Sweney (1975) defines this point as the *threshold for action or behavior*. Threshold refers to the way in which motivation is transformed into behavior. On the other extreme, people will not be motivated to perform a task regardless of how much it extrinsically pays. Sweney calls it the *threshold for consideration* below which behaviors are not considered as viable options. However, there are some people who will undertake a task below the threshold for extrinsic rewards. Figure 5-4 illustrates the threshold lines for behavior and consideration.

The area which lies above the threshold for behavior can be identified as a region of volition where behavior can be evoked without the aid of extrinsic rewards. Behavior is said to be self-motivated in this region, and the individual acts upon behavioral options without seeking approval or encouragement from others. The area which lies below the threshold for consideration is called the region of self-restriction where no amount of extrinsic reinforcers will induce the person to act. The area which lies between the thresholds of behavior and consideration is called the region of manipulative susceptibility where all types of organizational incentives (substantive, interactive, and effectance) can be manipulated to influence the behavior of organizational members. In this region, a person's action will be influenced by all types of organizational incentives.

The thresholds for behavior and consideration are different from individual to individual and situation to situation. The more passive the person, the higher the level of extrinsic reinforcement needed to evoke an action. An impulsive person may respond to relatively lower levels of intrinsic rewards. People who are sensitive to social acceptance will not undertake a task unless it is socially acceptable. Other people may perform a socially unacceptable job purely for money. Organizational climate can alter the thresholds for behavior and consideration. In an organization where its members are allowed to control and manage their own jobs, they may positively respond to technically less interesting tasks. In a status-oriented work group, its members will be afraid of performing a low-status job due to a fear of rejection.

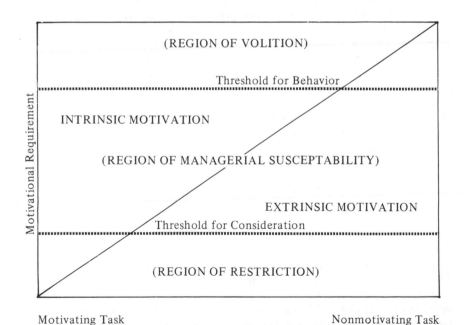

FIGURE 5-4. SWENEY'S THRESHOLDS FOR BEHAVIOR AND CONSIDERATION

INFLUENCING THRESHOLD FOR ACTION

A person's thresholds for action and consideration are largely a function of how the person perceives the performance outcome of his effort (E-P), the instrumental relationship between performance and rewards (P-I), and the valence of rewards for satisfying his needs (I-N). However, management can positively influence these instrumental contingencies by properly designing work systems, organizational relationships, and reward systems (see Chapters 7, 8, 9, and 10). Several specific suggestions can be made to either lower or raise the thresholds for action and consideration to suit the organizational situation. Since a desirable motivational style differs from situation to situation, modification of thresholds may be needed to find a workable fit between organizational demands and individual motivational styles.

Lowering Threshold For Behavior

By lowering the threshold for behavior, organizational members can exert initiative on their jobs and freely undertake organizational tasks that they prefer. The use of positive reinforcement rather than punishment makes it possible for an individual to act on a lower threshold for behavior. Fear of failure and punishment often discourages people from performing either demanding or easier tasks. A demanding task increases the chance of failure, while failure to accomplish an easy task leads to a feeling of humiliation and shame. A supportive organizational climate allows people to take risks without fearing punishment and repercussion. Recent developments in management such as organizational development and job enrichment efforts are aimed at lowering the threshold for behavior.

Raising Threshold For Behavior

By raising the threshold for behavior, management can reduce the region of volition for its employees and in turn increase its control over the employees. The threshold for behavior can be increased by demanding high performance from employees. External pressure tends to shift the locus of behavioral causality from internal to external. Overemphasis on extrinsic rewards produces the same effect; it tends to shift the locus of causality from internal to external. A nonsupportive punishing climate also discourages people from taking an initiative and risk in their task performance. People tend to perceive and fear the increased likelihood of failure and its accompanying punishment in a punishment-oriented climate. Zero-defect program has been a failure because of its tendency to create a punishing climate. Traditional management techniques (Scientific Management, Theory X, bureaucracy, and incentive systems) tend to raise the threshold for behavior.

Lowering Threshold For Consideration

By lowering the threshold for consideration, management can increase the region of manipulative susceptibility in which organizational incentives can be applied to influence and elicit broader behavioral options from workers. The threshold for consideration can be lowered by being flexible, open-minded, and less self-righteous in imposing formal controls systems. Individual differences in the value system and goals should be tolerated to accommodate various behavioral options. A paradox of the traditional management tools is that while management wishes to increase the region of manipulative susceptability (the area of managerial influence), these tools tend to narrow this region by imposing a number of prohibitions and inhibitions on employees' behavioral options.

Raising Threshold For Consideration

It is often necessary to raise the threshold for consideration to protect the image of a company or the reputation of a profession. An organization may prescribe a set of behavioral guides for its employees to limit their behavioral options. The number of behavioral options for consideration can be reduced by work group norms, rules and regulations, budgets, and time limitations. As these social and organizational controls impose a limit on behavioral options, they tend to raise the threshold for consideration. Organizational members restrict behavioral options which they fear will invite extrinsic punishments. The use of negative sanctions against members tends to raise the threshold for consideration.

The concept of threshold is closely related to expectancy theory. It explains how people transform their motivational pressures or tensions into action. The threshold for behavior and consideration depends on perceptions of the E-P, P-I, and I-N instrumental contingencies. While a person's needs and his external stimuli or incentives arouse motivational pressures, his perceptions of the instrumental contingencies help him to select a certain set of behavioral options. Positive reinforcement experiences and instrumental perceptions tend to lower the threshold for behavior and increase the likelihood of occurance of intrinsically motivated behavior. Similarly, the threshold for consideration is affected by past reinforcement history and the instrumental perceptions.

SUMMARY AND CONCLUSION

Motivation theory generally assumes that people are rational beings who want to maximize their gains. To have the rational choice of behavior, the person must have all the alternatives of choice, know all the consequences attached to each alternative behavior, and have the ability to order the priority for all possible sets of consequences. One can hardly expect that people possess such cognitive requirements for making rational choices of behavior. In the absence of the necessary information to make rational decisions, people respond to a limited set of stimuli which are subjectively processed by their perceptual mechanisms.

Perception is not a passive process of imprinting sensory stimulation. It is an active cognitive process by which sensory stimuli are selected, organized, and interpreted to give the meaning to the perceiver. Through this perceptual process, people estimate the degrees to which task performance is a function of effort exertion (E-P); task performance leads to incentive rewards (P-I); and incentive rewards satisfy employees' needs (I-N). These instrumental relationships constitute the major theme of expectancy theories and explain why a particular set of behaviors is selected as motivational responses. Perception serves as the threshold for evoking or withholding behavior. The decision to act or not to act toward a certain stimulus will be based on the perceptual outcomes.

The proposed expectancy model in this chapter integrates the needs and incentive theories into the theoretical framework of expectancy theory of motivation. The argument for this integration is that needs, incentives, and perceptions are all integral parts of motivation; they should not be treated as exclusive theories. While internal and external stimuli (needs and incentives) arouse motivational tension, the instrumental perceptions (E-P, P-I, and I-N) influence the thresholds for action and consideration. The concept of threshold explains the way in which motivational tension is manifested into action.

6

MOTIVATION, SATISFACTION, AND PERFORMANCE

Does motivation lead to high performance? Is a satisfied worker a productive worker? What happens if an employee is not satisfied with his job? These questions have been the major concerns of practicing managers and organizational researchers for the past several decades. Several theoretical propositions are advanced by scholars regarding the relationships among motivation, satisfaction, and performance:

1. Performance is a function of ability and motivation (Viteles, 1953; Vroom, 1964; and Lawler, 1966).
2. Unsatisfied needs cause motivation (Maslow, 1954 and 1970; McGregor, 1960).
3. Satisfaction causes performance (Roethlisberger and Dickson, 1939; Herzberg et al., 1957).
4. Performance causes satisfaction (Porter and Lawler, 1968; Vroom, 1964).
5. Reward causes satisfaction (Cherrington et al., 1971).
6. The satisfaction-performance relationship is moderated by other organizational variables (Schwab and Cummings, 1970; Sheridan and Slocum, 1975).
7. There is no relationship between satisfaction and performance (Brayfield and Crockett, 1955; Kahn, 1960; Locke, 1970).

In addition, there is a theoretical position that job dissatisfaction causes such dysfunctional behavior as absenteeism, turnover, accident, and strike (Herzberg et al., 1957; Vroom, 1964; and Flanagan et al., 1974).

Although some of these theoretical propositions are contradictory to each other and thus cause confusion, they nevertheless present some truth about the relationships among motivation, satisfaction, and performance. What these propositions have failed to show, however, is that they have not specified the contingencies under which their theoretical positions can be sustained. The primary purpose of this chapter is to review these theoretical positions and attempt to specify contingencies under which a particular theoretical position can be supported. This chapter discusses the relationship between motivation and performance, some theories of job satisfaction, the relationship between satisfaction and performance, and consequences of nonsatisfaction of various needs.

MOTIVATION AND PERFORMANCE

Traditionally, the study of job performance has been based on two somewhat independent assumptions: first, performance can be understood in terms of the individual's ability to perform the task; second, performance depends solely upon the level of motivation. Several scholars recognized the significance of the interaction between two variables in determining the level of performance. Viteles (1953) distinguished between the "capacity to work" and "the will to work" and proposed that both determine the level of performance. Maier (1955) and Vroom (1964) hypothesized that performances (P) is a function of ability (A) and motivation (M): $P=f(A \times M)$. According to this formula, if either ability or motivation is absent, performance has a value of zero and increases as either factor rises in value. When ability has a low value, increments in motivation will result in smaller increases in performance than when ability has a high value. When motivation has a lower value, increments in ability will result in smaller increases in performance than when motivation has a high value.

Investigating the relationship between ability and motivation jointly and independently, one can draw the following hypotheses. First, if the level of performance is only a function of ability, it would increase directly and proportionally with the increase of ability (see the straight line in Figure 6-1). Second, because of the element of motivation in job performance, performance is affected by the types of motivation. Positive motivation enhances the level of performance, while negative or weak motivation lowers it (Megginson, 1967). Third, the relationship between motivation and performance has an inverted-U function (Vroom, 1964). Performance is lower at low levels of motivation, reaches its maximum level with moderate degrees of motivation, and then drops off with higher levels of motivation (see the inverted-U curve in Figure 6-1).

There are several reasons for this inverted-U-shaped relationship. First, increased motivation tends to produce anxiety. A high level of anxiety produces such involuntary autonomic responses as perspiring, insomnia, and emotional disturbances. These responses interfere with performance; people tend to be less effective under conditions of high anxiety and stress (Atkinson, 1964). Second, a highly motivated person beyond a certain optimal level tends to be so preoccupied with a limited set of valued outcomes that he easily overlooks other information that may actually aid his performance (Vroom, 1964). Third, under the condition of high stress and anxiety, people tend to rely on such emotional defense mechanisms as rationalization and fixation rather than problem-solving behaviors (Kahn, 1960). They tend to be more preoccupied with anxiety-reducing defensive behaviors than effectively performing their tasks. All these psychological reactions to stress and anxiety lead to a decrement of performance. On the other extreme, low motivation lacks stimulation needed to get people to act. An optimum level of stimulation and performance thus occurs with a moderate level of motivation.

Several studies are germane to the performance model. For example, Vroom (1960) studied the relationship between ability and performance for supervisory personnel. He found a high positive correlation between ability and performance for supervisors who were high in motivation, a low but positive correlation for those supervisors who were moderate in motivation, and zero or slightly negative correlation for those who were low in motivation. Lawler

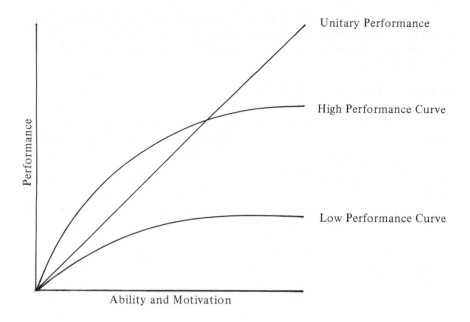

FIGURE 6-1. ABILITY, MOTIVATION, AND PERFORMANCE

(1966) also found that the relationship between job attitudes and performance became clearer when ability was introduced as an intervening variable. When the level of ability was low, an increase in motivation did not improve performance. But, when the level of ability was high, an increase in motivation was accompanied by an improved performance.

While the studies by Vroom and Lawler supported the interactive relationship between ability and motivation, a study by Anderson (1976) supported the inverted-U relationship between motivation and performance. Anderson's study reported that perceived stress displayed an inverted-U relationship with performance. Performance increased as the perceived stress increased up to a certain level. But, beyond that level performance decreased as the perceived stress intensified, and emotional coping behaviors such as rationalization, aggression, and withdrawal increased. This study implies that performance can be improved by creating an optimal level of motivational stress. This level of motivational stress can be created by increasing stimulation when the motivational level is low and by reducing perceived stress levels by helping individuals to effectively deal with problem-solving activities.

THEORIES OF JOB SATISFACTION

Job satisfaction means different things to different people. To some, it means the amount of needs actually satisfied (Maslow, 1954; McGregor, 1960), while to others it means the amount of anticipated need satisfaction or the valence of an outcome (Vroom, 1964). Lawler (1973) identifies four theoretical frameworks of job satisfaction: fulfillment theory, discrepancy theory, equity theory, and two-factor theory. In addition, Vroom (1964) proposed the valence theory of job satisfaction.

NEED FULFILLMENT THEORY

Fulfillment theory of job satisfaction has its root in Maslow's theory of needs (1954). Maslow indicated that satisfied needs no longer serve as determinants of behavior; unsatisfied needs dominate instrumental behavior leading to satisfaction. Unsatisfied higher-order needs are activated upon gratification of lower-order needs. This dynamic process of deprivation-domination-satisfaction-activation continues until physiological, safety, socialization, and self-esteem needs have been gratified, and the self-actualization need is activated. In essence, satisfaction of a need reduces its importance as a motivator, but it activates an unfulfilled need to motivate the person.

Cofer and Apply (1964), Lawler and Suttle (1974), and Wahba and Bridwell (1976) indicated that the deprivation-domination and satisfaction-activation propositions are only relevant in the case of the deprivation of existence needs. Agreeing with this observation, Maslow (1970) indicated that satisfaction of such higher-order needs as relation-oriented and growth-oriented needs strengthen their importance as motivators rather than reducing it. The implication of this revised need theory is that satisfaction of lower-order needs leads to lower motivation. But, satisfaction of higher-order needs leads to increased motivation. The types of need satisfaction moderate the satisfaction-motivation relationship.

According to fulfillment theory, the level of job satisfaction can be measured by the perceived amount of rewards a person has received from his work environment. People who are in need-fulfilling job situations will be more satisfied than those who are in less fulfilling job situations. The sum of gratification of various needs or satisfaction with various job facets constitutes the amount of total job satisfaction. While current satisfaction reduces motivational effort, anticipation of future satisfaction may increase it.

SATISFIERS AND DISSATISFIERS

Two-factor theory of job satisfaction proposed by Herzberg et al. (1957, 1959) seems to support the need fulfillment theory of job satisfaction. Two-factor theory divides job related incentive factors into two major categories: satisfiers and dissatisfiers. Satisfiers are those job factors that lead to job satisfaction and are largely associated with growth-oriented needs which stimulate personal growth and development. These satisfiers include such factors as challenging job, recognition, advancement, responsibility, and professional growth. Conversely, dissatisfiers are primarily associated with a person's existence and socialization needs and do not lead to job satisfaction beyond a level of satisfying these needs. They include such factors as pay, job security, working conditions, supervision, and company policy.

The major themes of two-factor theory are that 1) when workers are not satisfied with dissatisfiers, they become the major source of job dissatisfaction, but satisfaction with dissatisfiers neither leads to job satisfaction nor high performance, and 2) the presence of satisfiers tends to boost both job satisfaction and performance. However, a number of research findings do not support these themes. For example, Wernimont (1966) found that both intrinsic and extrinsic job factors could be the sources of both job satisfaction and dissatisfaction. Dunnette, Campbell, and Hakel (1967) reported that while some satisfiers were related to job satisfaction, dissatisfiers were not related to job dissatisfaction. Kosmo and Behling (1969) indicated that both satisfiers and dissatisfiers must be present in job situations to generate job satisfaction. Friedlander and Margulies (1969) indicated that such dissatisfiers as social climate and interpersonal relationships were important motivational factors for research and development personnel. Starcevich (1972) also reported that such satisfiers as achievement, ability utilization, challenging job, growth, recognition, and promotion· were ranked as important factors for both job satisfaction and dissatisfaction regardless of the occupational levels of respondents. Such dissatisfiers as fringe benefits, merit increases, working conditions, supervision, and job influence on home life were ranked among the least important for both job satisfaction and dissatisfaction. A job factor can be a source of both job satisfaction as well as job dissatisfaction, regardless of occupational levels.

These research findings generally agree that the same job factors can contribute to both job satisfaction and job dissatisfaction, and both satisfiers and dissatisfiers must be present in a work environment to enhance job satisfaction and performance. A dissatisfier such as pay can be a job satisfier and a determinant of performance when a person is motivated by existence needs. Also, the types of work groups moderate the positive and negative influence of satisfiers and dissatisfiers. For example, Friedlander (1966) reported that low performers were motivated primarily by socialization factors and to a lesser extent by recognition and advancement. Comparisons among the three potential motivators for high performers showed that intrinsic work was of greatest importance, recognition was second, and socialization was the least important. Hinrichs and Mischkind (1967) reported that when job satisfaction was compared for high and low satisfaction groups, satisfiers positively influenced the high satisfaction group, but had both positive and negative influences for the low satisfaction group. Dissatisfiers acted negatively for the high satisfaction group but positively for the low satisfaction group.

VALENCE-SATISFACTION THEORY

Herzberg's two-factor theory is primarily concerned with the determinants of job satisfaction and dissatisfaction and does not explain why certain job factors are preferred by a worker and how they influence his performance. In this sense, it is not a motivation theory but rather a theory of job satisfaction. Vroom (1964) perceived job satisfaction to be a future event rather than a past gratification, and he defines it as a valence of outcomes or an anticipation of need satisfaction. People are attracted to an object or incentive because it is perceived to be able to satisfy their needs. Job satisfaction is measured by the total amount of outcome valences available to an employee. The employee's motivation to produce then depends on the amount of anticipated outcome valences and the expectancy that his effort will result in task performance instrumental to receiving the valued outcomes.

March and Simon (1959) proposed a behavior search model similar to the valence-satisfaction model. According to this model, satisfaction reduces search behavior or motivation; however, the anticipated value of rewards increases the level of search behavior. The motivation to produce stems from 1) the present or anticipated state of dissatisfaction (needs), 2) the anticipated value of rewards (valence), and 3) the perceived relationship between performance and anticipated satisfaction (instrumentality of performance for the attainment of the rewards). A state of dissatisfaction is a necessary, but not a sufficient, condition for performance (Schwab and Cummings, 1970). It is necessary because some degree of dissatisfaction is needed to arouse search behavior. However, it is not sufficient because dissatisfied persons may not perceive the instrumental relationship between performance and satisfaction due to a lack of reinforcement experience.

Valence theory of job satisfaction can be compared with fulfillment theory and two-factor theories. The differences are: fulfillment theory defines job satisfaction as the amount of satisfied needs which reduces search behavior; two-factor theory defines it as a source of reinforcement which increases search behavior; and valence theory defines it as an anticipation of receiving valued outcomes. However, they all seem to agree that satisfied needs do not serve as determinants of behavior; unsatisfied needs stimulate behavior. The role of satisfied needs is to activate unsatisfied needs, strengthen stimulus-response association, and serve as the basis for estimating the level of anticipated need satisfaction.

DISCREPANCY THEORY

Discrepancy theory compares what a person actually receives with what he expects to receive from his job. Job satisfaction is determined by the difference between the actual reward level and the expected reward level. For example, Porter and Lawler (1968) defined job satisfaction as the extent to which rewards actually received meet or exceed the perceived equitable level of reward. As the difference between the two decreases, satisfaction increases. A failure to receive the perceived equitable level of rewards creates a feeling of job dissatisfaction. Locke (1969) adopted the concept of discrepancy for defining job satisfaction. He defined job satisfaction as the perceived difference between what a person actually receives and what he wants to receive. The difference between Porter et al. and Locke is that the former uses the equitable reward level as a basis for comparison, while the latter uses the aspiration level as a comparative basis.

This distinction is important for understanding their motivational consequences. When a person receives less than what he equitably expects to receive, he will be dissatisfied with his job and may reduce his performance level. On the contrary, people usually expect the level of aspiration to be higher than the actual achievement level. Thus, the difference between the actual achievement level and the aspiration level, if they are not far apart, tends to serve as a positive motivational force rather than a source of dissatisfaction. Thus, it seems more logical to see job satisfaction in terms of equitable rewards rather than aspiration levels.

An important feature of discrepancy theory is that job satisfaction involves more than knowing the actual reward level. In addition to knowing what a person has actually received, it is important to know what he expected to receive from his job to determine his level of job staisfaction. Two persons may have received the same amount of rewards, but their level of job satisfaction may differ depending on what they have expected to receive. One may be unhappy because what he has received was less than what he expected.

EQUITY-INEQUITY THEORY

Adams (1963a, 1965) extended the equity concept of discrepancy to accommodate social comparison in reward systems. As in the case of discrepancy theory, satisfaction is a function of a person's input-output balance. Satisfaction results from perceived equity, while dissatisfaction results from perceived inequity. However, Adams' theory of equity-inequity emphasizes the importance of other people's input-output ratios in determining a person's input-output ratio. The person determines his own input-output by comparing it with the perceived input-output ratios of his co-workers. If he perceives his input-output ratio is compatible with others' input-output ratios, he will be satisfied with the rewards he receives. If he perceives his ratio is larger than others,' he will perceive himself over-rewarded and may feel quilty. If he perceives himself under-rewarded in comparison with others, he will be dissatisfied.

The presence of perceived inequity (over or under-rewarded) creates tension which motivates people to reduce by changing their input-output balance. Though they may tolerate inequity for a period of time, they will eventually reestablish equity. Generally, people who feel over-rewarded may try to increase their productivity or improve the quality of their work if they are able to do so (Middlemist and Peterson, 1976). If they are not able to alter their input levels, they may select a new set of referent persons for comparison, or even attempt to lower their rewards by producing less under incentive systems. On the other hand, people who feel under-rewarded attempt to increase their rewards (outputs) by increasing the number of products under incentive systems or may attempt to reduce the quality as well as quantity of their work under non-incentive systems. The consequences of inequity under different pay conditions will be further discussed in Chapter 7.

When people are not able to alter the input-output balance by actually changing their productivity and/or the quality of their work, they may attempt to change the balance by cognitively distorting their perceived input-output ratios. For example, the feeling of being under-paid can be reduced by increasing intrinsic job satisfaction. An employee may insist that his pay is lower than others, but he does not mind because he likes his job. Another way of reducing perceived inequity is to use one's socioeconomic, educational, and racial backgrounds to modify his and/or others' input-output ratios. An Anglo-Saxon male with an Ivy League education may feel that his pay should be higher than a female worker with a college education even if she is a better performer than he is. Such a cognitive distortion has a limitation because it may create a feeling of self-deception and guilt.

SATISFACTION AND PERFORMANCE

The aforementioned theories identify four definitions of job satisfaction: need fulfillment or gratification, anticipated need satisfaction, perceived outcome valence, and perceived equity. Depending on how job satisfaction is defined, the theoretical position regarding satisfaction and performance differs. The relationship between satisfaction and performance has been the topic of study for several decades, and yet it continues to be a source of controversy among scholars and practitioners. There are basically three theoretical positions: 1) satisfaction causes performance (Argyris, 1957, 1973; Maslow, 1954, 1970; Herzberg et al., 1957, 1959; and Sutermeister, 1976); 2) performance causes satisfaction (Lawler and Porter, 1967; Porter and Lawler, 1968; and Greene, 1972); and 3) reward causes satisfaction and performance (Cherrington, Reitz, and Scott, 1971).

SATISFACTION-CAUSES-PERFORMANCE

Early human relationists have been interpreted as saying that employee morale determines the level of performance (see Mayo, 1933, 1945; Roethlisberger and Dickson, 1939; and Strauss, 1968). Their position seemed to be that organizational members have personal goals, attitudes, and values which they bring and hope to satisfy through their organizational participation. Organizations have to satisfy these personal expectations to induce employees to contribute their energies to the organization goal attainment. Thus, employee satisfaction was perceived to be an antecedent condition for productivity. This theoretical position reflects a popular belief that a happy worker is a productive worker, and it has been well accepted by practicing managers who want both employee morale and high productivity to prevail in their organizations.

Several theories imply that satisfaction is an important element for generating high performance. Need theory of job satisfaction implies that although current satisfaction reduces motivation or search behavior, satisfying experiences increase the anticipation of future need satisfaction. Thus, if job satisfaction is defined as an anticipated need satisfaction rather than current gratification, job satisfaction may increase the level of motivation and performance. In the same line of thinking, reinforcement theory implies that rewarded behavior is repeated, while nonrewarded behavior is discontinued. Satisfying experiences with a particular reinforcer strengthen the association between the reinforcer and its instrumental behavior. Finally, expectancy theory defines job satisfaction as the amount of oucome valences that one expects to receive. When one anticipates an increased outcome he values, the instrumental behavior that leads to such outcomes will increase.

Does job satisfaction automatically lead to increased performance? The answer is obviously no. The satisfaction-performance linkage is moderated by a number of factors. First, the types of needs moderate the linkage. As indicated earlier, lower-level needs can be easily satiated, and their satisfaction tends to reduce motivational importance. Unless their satisfaction activates higher-order needs, satisfaction only depresses motivational level. However, the satisfaction of higher-order needs increases their motivational importance stimulating instrumental behavior leading to further satisfaction.

Second, corollary to the types of needs are the types of organizational incentives. Substantive incentives can be given to workers regardless of their performance levels. Incentive rewards may satisfy workers, but may not motivate them to work harder unless their application is contingent upon the level of performance. Effectance incentive rewards, on the other hand, increase both job satisfaction and performance because they continuously provide the major source of satisfying higher-order needs, and their reinforcement is directly contingent upon task performance.

Finally, the perceived equity between a person's inputs and outputs in comparison with referent persons' input-output ratio moderates the satisfaction-performance linkage. A worker may be satisfied with existence needs and the intrinsically motivating nature of his job. However, if his input-output ratio is lower than referent persons' input-output ratios, his job satisfaction as well as performance will be reduced. When the worker perceives equity in the input-output balance or inequity in his favor, his level of performance will be either maintained or increased.

The conditions under which the satisfaction-causes-performance proposition prevails are: 1) satisfaction activates unfulfilled needs or an unfulfilled portion of the same needs; 2) the valence of incentive outcomes is attractive to the worker; 3) incentive application is contingent upon performance; and 4) the worker perceives equity in the input-output balance or inequity in his favor. When these conditions do not prevail in an organization, need satisfaction alone does not lead to improved performance. Although there may not be a direct satisfaction-causes-performance relationship visible in the short run, satisfaction is an important organizational goal because it helps to maintain healthy organizational members whose physical and psychic energies can be utilized for productive organizational endeavors. Argyris (1957, 1973) perceived the satisfaction of organizational members' needs as the key for developing a healthy organization in which people strive to achieve both individual and organizational goals. Job satisfaction may not have a direct influence on performance, but it influences performance in the long run by means of keeping healthy organizational members.

PERFORMANCE-CAUSES-SATISFACTION

Lawler and Porter (1967), Porter and Lawler (1968), and Lawler (1973) promoted the thesis that performance causes satisfaction. Rather than seeing satisfaction as a causal variable, they perceive it as a dependent variable which is a function of performance. Their argument is that differential performance levels lead to differences in reward levels which in turn produce variation in satisfaction. According to them, the types of rewards and the perceived equity of these rewards moderate the relationship between performance and satisfaction. Intrinsic rewards are more closely related to both job performance and job satisfaction than extrinsic rewards. Intrinsic rewards are the direct outcomes of task performance, and their effects on job satisfaction are direct and immediate. Extrinsic rewards on the other hand are independent of job performance, and their effects on the performers' satisfaction are contingent upon the performance-reward tie and the perceived equity. If the rewards are positively associated with performance levels and the perceived levels of rewards are equitable, the relationship between performance and satisfaction will be positive. If otherwise, the relationship will be either neutral or negative.

The performance-satisfaction linkage seems to be stronger and tighter than the satisfaction-performance linkage. The performance-causes-satisfaction proposition is supported when workers perform intrinsically motivating tasks, and extrinsic rewards are contingent upon performance. Organizations have some control over the distribution of intrinsic and extrinsic rewards. Work systems produce intrinsic rewards (see Chapter 9) and organizational reward systems control the application of extrinsic rewards (see Chapter 7). However, the satisfaction-causes-performance proposition is moderated by a number of individual factors such as ability, motivation, and role perception which are not under the direct control of an organization. Since the satisfaction-performance linkage is moderated by many factors not controlled by the organization, it can be expected that performance is more likely to result in satisfaction than satisfaction to result in high performance (Porter and Lawler, 1968).

REWARD-CAUSES-SATISFACTION

Cherrington, Reitz, and Scott (1971) are more specific in specifying the impact of reward on satisfaction. They argue that there is no inherent relationship between performance and satisfaction. Rather, both performance and satisfaction are caused by rewards. In their study, regardless of their performance levels, rewarded subjects expressed satisfaction, while poorly rewarded subjects expressed dissatisfaction. When lower performers were rewarded, they expressed satisfaction but they continuously performed at a low rate of productivity. When higher performers were poorly rewarded, they expressed dissatisfaction, and their performance declined substantially on their subsequent trails. When rewards were contingent upon performance, productivity was significantly higher than when rewards were not related to performance.

Both Porter et al. and Cherrington et al. agree that performance-based reward systems result in satisfaction. However, a difference between them seems to be that while performance is an essential part of Porter's model, reward is the key to satisfaction in Cherrington's model. Even nonperformance contingent reward systems can satisfy some workers—especially poor performers. Under the Cherrington's theoretical position, if both high performance and satisfaction are to be maintained, two conditions should prevail in the organization: 1) rewards are contingent upon performance and 2) perceived equity prevails in its reward system. When these two conditions do not exist in an organization, rewarded lower-performers may be satisfied, while poorly rewarded high-performers are dissatisfied. While satisfied lower-performers may or may not increase their performance, dissatisfied performers will either reduce their performance levels or leave the organization.

SATISFACTION AND PERFORMANCE CONTINGENCIES

The controversy over the relationship between satisfaction and performance can be resolved by specifying various contingency relationships among performance, reward, and satisfaction. Figure 6-2 elaborates performance-reward, reward-satisfaction, and satisfaction-performance contingencies. The performance-reward contingency implies that people are more likely to perceive their rewards to be equitable under performance-contingent reward systems than under nonperformance contingent systems. When rewards are not contingent upon performance, there is more room for people to feel that they are either under or over-paid in comparison with referent others.

However, performance-based reward systems do not automatically insure the perceived equity. The problem is that in many cases contingent rewards are

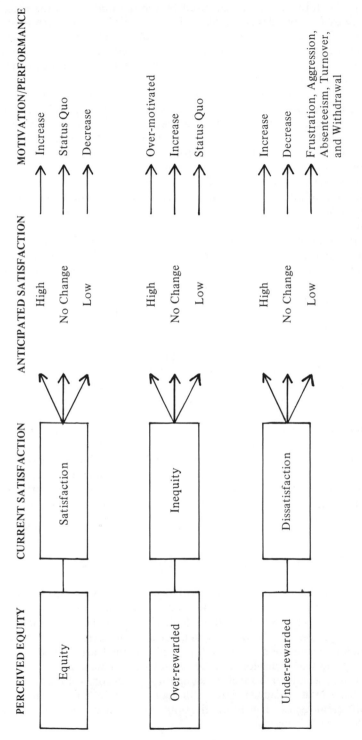

FIGURE 6-2.   REWARD-SATISFACTION-PERFORMANCE CONTINGENCIES

based on the performance levels perceived by the rewarder. When the perceived performance by the rewarder is at odds with that of the performer, the perceived equity that affects employee satisfaction may not prevail. Thus, it is necessary for the rewarder to communicate with his subordinates and have a better understanding on the perceived equity. The perceived equity is to a large extent affected by the rewarder's behavior.

Figure 6-2 also indicates that job performance is a function of current as well as anticipated satisfaction. The satisfied worker may raise his level of aspiration, anticipating satisfaction of unfulfilled needs or increased outcome valence. If his anticipated outcome valence is higher than what he perceives to be an equitable reward level, he will make an extra effort to achieve high performance. If the former is lower, so will be his motivation and performance.

When a worker feels over-rewarded, he may feel guilty and attempt to reduce the feeling of inequity by exerting high effort and being productive. However, if the gap between his anticipated outcome valence and equitable reward level is too wide, the increasing inequity may over-stimulate and cause him to be less effective. If the same level of inequity is expected to prevail, the worker may be motivated to reduce it by showing high productivity. If the anticipated outcome valence is expected to be lower than his perceived level of equitable rewards, he may either reduce or maintain his performance.

Job attitude largely depends on one's expectation that his effort will lead to valued incentives or outcomes. Thus, even if a person may not be satisfied with his current level of rewards, he may have a positive attitude toward his job if he anticipates his effort leading to increased rewards (Vroom, 1964; Schwab and Cummings, 1970; and Sheridan and Slocum, 1975). However, if the person perceives little or no chance for future job satisfaction, his performance will suffer and exhibit such dysfunctional behaviors as apathy, low morale, absenteeism, turnover, sabotage, strike, drug abuse, and other mind-altering behavior.

In summary, job satisfaction is influenced not only by the current level of rewards but also the antcipated level of rewards. If what he expects to receive from his job is higher than what he feels he should receive, he may be motivated to increase the instrumental behavior or performance leading to the anticipated rewards. If the former is lower than the latter, he will reduce his performance level. If the perceived equity prevails in the future, he will maintain his current rate of performance.

CONSEQUENCES OF JOB DISSATISFACTION

What happens when a person is not satisfied with his work environment for a prolonged period of time? If existence needs are not satisfied, the result is obvious; physical health will be deteriorated. If relation-oriented needs are not satisfied, the person will become psychologically alienated and depressed. If growth-oriented needs are not satisfied, he will become frustrated with his job. Though its effects on behavior may be less obvious, failure to satisfy higher-order needs may lead to emotional stress, apathy, aggression, sabotage, and other forms of behavioral maladjustment. Although behavioral manifestations may vary for different types of need deprivation, there is a general pattern of behavioral reactions to nonsatisfaction.

The first sign of job dissatisfaction is frustration. Frustration refers to a state of being disappointed. Frustration occurs when a person is prevented from obtaining a valued incentive or goal which has need-satisfying power. Internal and/ or external barriers interfere with a person's goal-directed behavior. Internal barriers include such personal factors as intelligence, skill, training, personality, money, and motivation. A person may want to have a professional job paying a high salary, but he cannot have it because he is lacking proper training in the field. External barriers include such organizational factors as structure, rules and regulations, reward systems, supervision and leadership, work group, and the job itself. The person may want to produce more to maximize his economic gains, but he cannot achieve this goal because pay is not contingent upon performance. Argyris (1957, 1973) pointed out that a number of organizational barriers prevent organizational members from satisfying their needs. Rigid organizational structure, specialization, rigid control, authoritarian leadership, and inflexible reward and punishment systems tend to restrict individual freedom and initiative, increase individual dependency on the organization, and depress personal growth. Under these circumstances, people experience frustration, psychological failure, and difficulty of resolving conflict.

When people are frustrated, their behaviors undergo distinct changes. Usually, healthy and unemotional persons may show signs of emotional stress and behavioral maladjustment. Often times, normal behavior is replaced by stereotyped and defensive behavior. In some extreme cases, the behavior becomes unpredictable and pointless. Reactions to frustration are numerous; they range from adaptive behavior to destructive aggression. Although the sequence of behavioral reactions to frustration is not clearly identified, Klinger (1975) speculates that frustrated behavior is usually followed by invigoration, aggression, depression, and recovery.

Invigoration

Invigoration refers to increased responses as a reaction to nonreinforcement. Invigoration occurs right after reinforcement is determinated or a goal-directed effort fails. During the period of extinction, people tend to behave with increased vigor, hoping this will lead to desired outcomes. They may repeat the same instrumental behavior or attempt new exploratory behavior. Frustration leads to behavioral invigoration because the blocked incentive is perceived to be more valuable. When people are frustrated, they tend to regard the incentive as more attractive than before (Brehm, 1972). When the blocked incentive becomes more attractive, other incentives tend to be less important (Adamson, 1971). Some people are over-involved in frustrated undertakings. Invigoration effect tends to disappear when the person perceives that the chance of goal-attainment becomes nil.

Aggression

When the person finds that his invigorated behavior does not achieve the desired outcomes, he becomes aggressive toward the reinforcing agent, other persons, or objects. Aggressive behavior means a hostile act associated with anger. When aggression against the frustration-causing agent is prevented, the energy may be directed to other subjects. For example, an employee may be frustrated by his supervisor, but he has learned not to express aggression toward his boss. So he waits until he can release his anger at his subordinates or family members. Aggression can be directed inward. When a person internalizes his frustration inwardly, he may appear calm and even tempered, but his emotion can be in turmoil. Unrelieved frustration can be manifested in forms of such psychosomatic reactions as asthma, hay fever, hypertension, migraine, and ulcer.

Depression And Withdrawal

When the state of frustration remains unrelieved over a period of time, the person reduces or stops his instrumental as well as aggressive behavior. Apathy or indifference toward what used to be valued incentives is a common form of depression and resignation. Depression is a dormant condition in which people have a state of mind described as "giving up." People in this state have low morale and withdraw themselves from all productive activities. People can be mentally or physically withdrawn. Mental withdrawal takes the form of apathy and indifference, while physical withdrawal takes the form of absenteeism and turnover. Mentally withdrawn people perform their jobs with a minimum level of interest or effort, while physically withdrawn people simply leave the field to avoid the frustration-causing agent.

Recovery

Individuals usually recover from frustration and depression. People modify their expectations and/or find substitute goals. They may adjust their expectations downward and respond positively to the attainment of these readjusted expectations. When one instrumental behavior for attaining a valued incentive is blocked, the person may try alternative behaviors during the invigoration and aggression phases. When one particular incentive is blocked, one may develop substitute incentives. One can subliminate his frustration through these alternative behaviors and substitute goals. An individual's commitment to several valued goals can also minimize the frustration effect of one valued goal. People who develop such coping strategies tend to be less susceptible to the frustration effect.

Intensity of frustration and recovery largely depend on the importance of the valued outcome and one's capacity to use an effective coping strategy. The more important the outcome is to the person, the stronger the frustration effect will be. For example, losing such valued outcomes as a satisfying job and a marriage partner may turn a fulfilling life situation into a barren one. Recovery depends on one's ability to adapt to new situations. This adaption process can be facilitated by learning various coping strategies. If the failure to attain valued outcomes is attributable to one's internal barriers such as ability, skill, and personality, it is important for him to overcome these limitations. Removing external barriers is also a means of facilitating the recovery process. An organization should remove any artificial barriers that unnecessarily frustrate its members' goal-attainment behavior and clarify path-goal relationships so that they effectively direct their energy toward their valued outcomes.

BEHAVIORAL PROBLEMS IN ORGANIZATIONS

Many behavioral problems in organizations are attributable to job dissatisfaction. Dissatisfaction with pay may cause people to leave or discourage them from showing up for work. Lack of socialization opportunity may cause people to minimize their psychological commitment to the organization. Job dissatisfaction may increase workers' apathy and indifference toward their work. Although a particular behavioral problem can be caused by a single need deprivation, most behavioral problems are caused by multiple factors. Employee turnover can be attributable to economic conditions, personal reasons, and/or job dissatisfaction. Economic and personal factors are beyond the control of management, and therefore they are beyond the scope of our discussion. However, many problems are attributable to job-related factors which the organization can influence. For example if job satisfaction is a function of a variety of job facets, job dissatisfaction results from the failure to satisfy a variety of employees' needs.

Figure 6-3 shows employees' relations to job dissatisfaction. Frustrated employees may react to their job dissatisfaction by forms of aggression and/or withdrawal. Aggression toward management takes the form of strike, sabotage, or theft. Psychological withdrawal is manifested in the form of apathy, alienation,

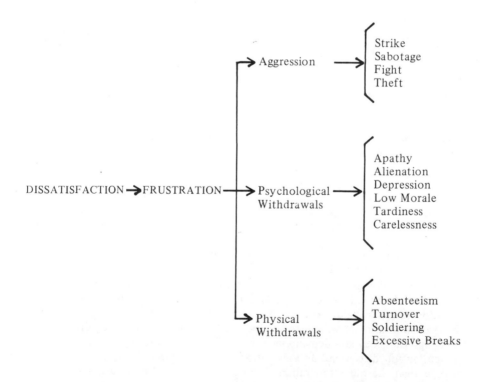

FIGURE 6-3. BEHAVIORAL PROBLEMS IN ORGANIZATIONS

low morale, and depression. Physical withdrawal takes the form of low productivity, absenteeism, and turnover. Since the general theme of the need deprivation cycle is discussed earlier, our attention will be focused on some specific behavioral problems which are common concerns of practicing managers.

STRIKE ACTIVITY

Strike activity is foremost among aggressive behavioral manifestations of job dissatisfaction. Unlike passive withdrawal such as apathy, absenteeism, work slowdown, and quitting, workers actively seek for improvement in economic and noneconomic pay-offs. What are the major causes of strike? It is hypothesized here that strikes are correlated with economic considerations, management-worker relations, and job alienation. The following observations tend to support this hypothesis.

The number of strikes increases during the period of low unemployment when work stoppages hurt the companies most and workers feel safer in finding employment opportunities. Flanagan, Strauss, and Ulman (1974) reported that during the period of 1960-1965, the number of strikes remained under 4,000 per year. Toward the end of the 1960s, there were at least 5,700 work stoppages each year. The rate has dropped to a level of 5,100 in the first part of the 1970s. The lowest unemployment rates in the latter part of the 1960s accounted for some of the increase in strikes. And when unemployment rose in the first part of the 1970s, the number of strikes fell. The rate of inflation and its effect on real income seem to contribute to the cause of strikes. The rapid inflation in the late 1960s and early 1970s may have been a factor for increased or at least sustained strike activities. The number of strikes was lower in the early seventies than the late sixties, but was still higher than that of the early sixties when the rate of inflation was relatively low.

Why then do these economic considerations lead to more strikes? From a psychological standpoint, in time of economic prosperity, workers' expectations regarding economic as well as noneconomic gains tend to be higher than what they actually receive. Workers' demands for better working conditions and higher-order need satisfaction tend to increase with the rising level of education and economic standard of living. Yet, an increasing rate of inflation tends to lower workers' perceived actual as well as future incomes. The gap between increased employee expectations and perceived lower actual incomes tends to augment pay dissatisfaction which in turn stimulates strike activity. The proportion of strikes attributable to such nonmonetary factors as plant administration, physical plant, safety, supervision, and work assignment has increased slightly in recent years (Flanagan et al., 1974).

Finally, although the evidence supporting job alienation as a major cause of strike activity is lacking, job alienation is nevertheless a contributing factor in addition to other major causes such as economic gains and working conditions. Workers will be more willing to support strike activities when they dislike their jobs, and they may also demand more economic rewards to compensate for their increasing job discontent. Job alienation seems to more adversely affect young people than the older generation. Young people reared in an affluent society, with an increasing level of education, tend to expect more from their jobs than their elders. Further, they seem to have less discipline for working under adverse working conditions. The well-publicized wildcat strike at the Vega plant, Lordstown, Ohio, attests to this observation. Also, job alienation is a concern of some union leaders such as Leonard Woodcock of Auto Workers and Charles Levinson of International Federation of Chemical and General Workers. Their concern is expected to be reflected in union contracts in forms of job enrichment, worker control, or codetermination of management.

ABSENTEEISM

Absenteeism refers to the worker's failure to report and remain at work as scheduled; holidays, day-offs, and vacation are not counted in estimating absenteeism. United States Bureau of Labor statistics indicated that the rate of part-week (less than a week) absenteeism has increased from 3.9 percent to 4.3 percent for the period of 1967-1972 (Hedges, 1973). During the same period, the rate of full-week (more than a week) absenteeism has increased from 2.1 percent to 2.3 percent. (The rate of absenteeism is derived from man-days lost divided by the sum of man-days lost and man-days worked.) Man-hours lost as a result of part-week absences averaged 43.8 million hours per week in 1972, and additional 59.4 million hours per week were lost from full-week absences. Absenteeism is costly to employers because they are often forced to pay fringe benefits for absent workers, produce products on overtime basis, use less skilled substitutes, and rely on less efficient production schedules.

Absenteeism is caused by a number of factors. Some are avoidable, while others are not. Illness and accidents frequently prevent workers from reporting for work. It is hypothesized here that avoidable absences are related to job satisfaction. Pay method seems to influence absenteeism. When pay is not contingent upon attendance and performance, absenteeism is expected to be high. It can be expected that absenteeism will be higher under salary paid than under piece-rate or hourly paid systems. Sick leave policy encourages absences because it pays for not reporting to work. The amount of pay is less closely related to absenteeism than paid method. In some instances, industries paying weekly wages tend to experience more employee absenteeism than low-paying industries (Flanagan et al., 1974). Workers who are satisfied with existence needs demand satisfaction of nonmonetary needs. When they are not able to satisfy these needs, they search for their satisfaction outside of the organization.

Socialization opportunity influences absenteeism and turnover. Vroom (1964) reported that jobs providing greater opportunities for social interaction tend to have lower absenteeism and turnover rates than jobs providing fewer socializing opportunities. Porter and Lawler (1965) reported that large-sized work groups reduce opportunities for social interaction and thus, exhibit high rates of absenteeism and turnover.

Leadership influences both absenteeism and turnover. Fleishman and Harris (1962) found that leadership style showing high employee consideration is associated with lower turnover and grievance rates. In general, considerate leaders tend to have more satisfied subordinates. However, the effect of considerate leadership on employee satisfaction depends on the kind of rewards that the leader controls and the degree to which the subordinates depend on the leader for their need satisfaction. A leader who has power to influence the rest of the organization is more effective in using a considerate leadership style than a low-influence leader (Wager, 1965).

Finally, job alienation causes high absenteeism. Absenteeism is highest among blue-collar workers, high among white-collar clerical workers, and lowest among managerial and professional groups (Hedges, 1973). The absenteeism rate reaches as high as 15 percent among assembly line workers (usually on Mondays and Fridays) whose wages are high but who find their jobs dull and repetitive. Absenteeism is also high among young workers, females, and nonwhites who are more likely to hold menial jobs providing no intrinsic job satisfaction. It is feasible that these workers are less disciplined in their work behavior and thus more prone to absenteeism. However, it is more likely that job alienation causes absenteeism than work behavior causes absenteeism. It can be possible that older, male, and/or white workers might show as high absenteeism as young, female, and/or nonwhite workers if the former group of workers were forced to take menial jobs.

TURNOVER

Although both absenteeism and turnover are related to job dissatisfaction, they have different effects on employee job satisfaction and performance. While absenteeism is a passive avoidance response to a problem, quitting a job implies an active solution to the problem. While the former solves little for the absentees or the organization, the latter can result in positive outcomes for both. A dissatisfied worker may find another job where he finds satisfaction. Also, an organization may attempt to design pay and promotion policy to discourage poor performing employees from staying.

Although turnover can have a positive impact on an organization, it is usually costly to the organization because it involves the expenditure of time and money for hiring and training new employees and may also mean a loss of valuable employees. Turnover can be higher among high-performers than lower-performers without mobility. While a dissatisfied high-performer may leave the organization, a dissatisfied low-performer may express their dissatisfaction by means of apathy, absenteeism, sabotage, and other nonproductive behaviors.

How serious is the problem of turnover? A survey conducted by the Administrative Management Society reported that the turnover rate was 21 percent among office workers in 1973; it was 19 percent in 1971 (Dailey, 1974). The turnover rate is expected to be higher among nonmanagerial employees reporting a 40 percent level and is still higher among assembly line workers, approaching as high as 275 percent a year (Lawler, 1973). (The turnover rate is obtained by dividing the total number of separations by average annual employment).

What causes turnover? The Bureau of National Affairs (1975) surveyed its policy forum members for the causes of turnover. The survey ranked the causes in the order of personal problems, pay dissatisfaction, job opportunity, supervision, working conditions, poor selection, and inadequate orientation for production and office workers. For managerial personnel, the rank was in the order of job opportunity, pay dissatisfaction, personal problems, poor selection, supervision, working conditions, and inadequate orientation.

Although some turnover is not under the control of the organization, most of it can be influenced by organizational factors. Some turnover can occur as a result of uncontrollable factors such as retirement, death, and health, but their share in total turnover is relatively small. According to the Administrative Management Society survey, only 10 percent of turnover can be considered unavoidable. This survey ranked the reasons for turnover in the order of another job (43%), dismissal (12%), leave city (11%), stay home (8%), return to school (7%), retirement (6%), pregnancy (5%), reduction in staff (3%), and others (5%). At least, about 58 percent of turnover (another job, dismissal, and staff reduction) in the survey can be influenced by the organization.

From these two surveys, one can speculate that turnover is to some extent attributable to job dissatisfaction; pay, job, supervision, and other managerial practices contribute to turnover. Pay is the single most important reason why people leave one organization for another one. If one can get more pay for performing the same type of task, holding other job factors constant, he will leave for another job. The studies reviewed by Lawler (1973, pp. 141-143) indicated that employees who said their pay was too low tended to leave, while those who said their pay was adequate tended to stay. Employees in high-paying industries appear to quit less frequently, but are as prone as, or even more prone than, workers in low-paying industries to be absent.

Finding a better job is a strong motive for a person to leave an organization. People search for other job opportunities when they feel their present jobs do not provide them with the incentive rewards they desire (I-N) and/or their contributions are not equitably rewarded (P-I). Equity theory indicates that when people feel they are under-rewarded in comparison with referent others, they search for ways of minimizing the feeling of inequity. Leaving the present job for another one is certainly an alternative. Finding a better job can mean a number of things. It can mean better pay, better social environment, and/or an intrinsically motivating job. Since turnover rates tend to be higher among workers in blue-collar jobs, it can be speculated that both pay and job discontent contribute to high turnover.

Finally, socialization and supervision affect turnover the same way they affect absenteeism. However, there is an indication that an employee's immediate work group environment, including co-workers and supervision, is a major cause of turnover; the causal relationship is relatively more clear in turnover than in absenteeism (Porter and Steers, 1973). In terms of motivational differences, Porter and Steers found pay and promotional considerations to be significant factors of turnover, whereas Brayfield and Crockett (1955) found job discontent tends to be more significantly related to absenteeism than to turnover. In general however, absenteeism and turnover are closely related to overall job dissatisfaction. In many cases, absenteeism progresses to turnover (Lyons, 1972). Overall job dissatisfaction is manifested in tardiness, absenteeism, and grievances, and gradually progresses toward termination. Dissatisfied workers may express intention to leave and then eventually leave the organization (see Atchison and Lefferts, 1972; Kraut, 1975; and Porter, Crampton, and Smith, 1976).

LOW PRODUCTIVITY

Does job dissatisfaction lead to poor performance? The relationship between job dissatisfaction and poor performance seems to be clearer than the relationship between job satisfaction and high performance. There are two ways job dissatisfaction can lead to poor performance. First, as we can see in Figure 6-3, it leads to a number of dysfunctional behaviors which all can contribute to low productivity. Lower productivity can result from such overt behavior as sabotage, strike, absenteeism, and turnover, and from covert behavior such as apathy, indifference, low morale, and resistance to change. Dissatisfied workers initially may try harder to increase productivity hoping their increased performance will lead to increased rewards. However, when their expectations are repeatedly not met, their disappointments lead to dysfunctional behavior.

Second, productive workers are more prone to job dissatisfaction. Job dissatisfaction results when what a person currently receives or expects to receive is less than what he feels he should receive. What he feels he should receive is determined by his perceived job qualifications, performance contributions, and job requirements. The better qualified and capable he is, the more rewards he feels he should receive from his job. The more he feels he should receive, the greater the chances for disappointment. Poor performers may expect less from their jobs and have less chances to be disappointed. In fact, when organizational rewards are not contingent upon performance, poor performers may be well satisfied, while high performers are dissatisfied. Under this circumstance, satisfied poor performers do not find any reason to increase their productivity. Thus, satisfaction will not lead to higher performance. If they feel over-rewarded, they can easily modify their perceived inputs to justify their perceived inequity without modifying their output levels. Dissatisfied high performers, on the other hand, may lower their output levels and cause lower performance for the organization. When the reward system creates a situation in which poor performers are satisfied while high performers are dissatisfied, it can be called *the double jeopardy principle* of reinforcement. Such a double jeopardy effect usually occurs under non-performance-contingent reward systems. It is hypothesized here that many poorly performing organizations are subject to this principle.

SUMMARY AND CONCLUSION

Job performance is affected by a number of factors. Motivation alone does not lead to increased performance. Ability and technology moderates the relationship between motivation and performance. The higher the levels of ability and motivation, the higher the level of performance will be. However, increasing motivation beyond an optimal level tends to produce a dysfunctional result because it is accompanied by an increasing level of anxiety. A high level of anxiety often disrupts performance.

The relationship between satisfaction and performance is not clear. Satisfaction may or may not lead to high performance depending on the perceived availability of valued outcomes and the perceived expectancy that a person's effort and performance will lead to receiving the valued rewards. If the person expects that his performance will lead to increased rewards which he values, the level of his motivational effort will increase; if he anticipates less, his motivational effort will be lower.

The relationship between job dissatisfaction and poor performance seems to be clearer than that between satisfaction and performance. Dissatisfaction leads to poor performance by means of apathy, absenteeism, turnover, sabotage, and strike. In addition, high performers are more vulnerable to job dissatisfaction because they tend to expect more from their jobs than low performers.

Job satisfaction is more closely related to the decision to join and remain in an organization than to the motivation to produce. The motivation to produce largely depends on the availability of valued outcomes (valence), the perceived instrumentality of performance for receiving incentive rewards, and the perceived expectancy that effort leads to performance. The task of satisfying employees is much easier than the task of motivating them because the former can be achieved by rewarding them while the latter requires such additional constraints as establishing performance-reward contingencies and designing motivating work systems. The remaining chapters deal with tasks of satisfying and motivating employees.

PART II

MOTIVATIONAL PROGRAMS

7

MOTIVATION BY FINANCIAL INCENTIVES

Labor costs usually comprise the largest expenditure in an organization. For many organizations, payrolls account for more than 50 percent of their total budgets. This percentage can be higher for service-oriented industries because their primary commodities are labor services. Pay systems present the greatest opportunity for management to increase productivity through their effective utilization. For an employee, pay is one of the most important rewards received from his employment. It can be an effective motivational tool if strategically applied as a means of arousing employee motivation. Yet, the role of pay in employee motivation and performance is one of the understudied subjects in the field of organizational psychology and behavior (Steers and Porter, 1975). Likewise, management frequently has done a poor job of utilizing pay systems as a means of arousing employee motivation (Lawler, 1971, pp. 11-12). Management usually considers pay as an economic outlay without assessing the returns it generates. Overall wage rates frequently are determined by such forces in the economic environment as competitors, unions, and governments. Within these overall wage level constraints, however, management should be able to influence individual pay rates reflecting performance differences if it wants to make the pay system effective.

This chapter examines ways of improving the effectiveness of pay systems. The reinforcement contingencies and schedules, discussed in Chapter 4, suggest that 1) the amount of pay should vary to reflect differences in performance; 2) an incentive reward should be paid regularly, 3) a ratio schedule is more effective in arousing motivation than an interval schedule; 4) incentives should be matched with needs; and 5) a partial reinforcement schedule can be a more effective motivational tool than a continuous schedule. Expectancy theory, presented in Chapter 5, also suggests that management can increase the effectiveness of pay systems by relating pay systems to employees' needs (I-N); tying performance to pay (P-I); and establishing a challenging but attainable reward system so that effort exertion leads to task performance and reward (E-P). These motivational theories will be reflected in designing effective pay systems.

MOTIVATIONAL VALUE OF PAY

Pay gains a motivational value when it is instrumental in satisfying an employee's needs. It can not only satisfy such basic needs as physiological and economic security, but also such higher-order needs as self-esteem and independence. However, the relative importance of pay as a motivational tool varies because pay can satisfy certain kinds of needs better than others. Pay has different meanings for people depending on their values, possessions, and economic needs. For example, pay seems to have a stronger motivational value to low-paid workers because it satisfies their physiological needs. Pay is still important to high-paid workers because it satisfies their need for self-esteem and independence. An understanding of the differences in motivational value of pay to different individuals can be useful for designing effective pay systems.

IMPORTANCE OF PAY INCENTIVE

How important is pay as a motivational incentive? Pay was considered the most important incentive during the period of scientific management (Taylor, 1911). Taylor perceived man as an "economic being" who wants to maximize economic gains. He proposed the use of piece-rate incentive systems to stimulate workers' productivity and to maximize their incomes. This view was challenged by the human relationists in the 1930s and 1940s who changed the concept of man from economic being to social being. The human relationists argued that worker behavior is influenced by such social factors as group norms, social pressures, and supervisory controls rather than economic factors (Roethlisberger and Dickson, 1939).

In the middle 1960s, increased attention was given to satisfying such higher-order needs as self-esteem and self-actualization. Maslow's need hierarchy concept (1954) and McGregor's theory of X and Y (1960) emphasized the concept of "self-actualizing man" in lieu of the "economic man" and "social man" concepts. Maslow's need hierarchy concept (1954) tended to underestimate the motivational value of pay beyond the level of satisfying economic and job security needs. For example, McGregor (1960, 1967) assumed that most people in this society were reasonably satisfied with lower-level needs, and these satisfied needs were no longer the motivators of behavior. Consequently, money primarily instrumental for satisfying physiological and security needs lost its motivational value.

Herzberg and his associates (1957, 1959) viewed money as a dissatisfier and underestimated the importance of pay as a motivator. To them, pay is important because it frequently becomes a major source of dissatisfaction, but it is not important as a motivator. Their literature survey (1957) found that the average worker ranked pay sixth in importance behind security, interest, opportunity for advancement, appreciation, company policy, and job content. Despite a general tendency of some behavioral scientists to undermine the importance of pay as a motivator, most workers and practicing managers take pay seriously, and it becomes a constant source of management-worker disputes. Also, several scholars recognize the importance of pay and devote their effort for studying the effect of pay on motivation and performance (Lawler, 1971; Porter and Lawler, 1968; and Nash and Carroll, 1975).

Why then do these workers, managers, and scholars take pay seriously? There are economic and psychological reasons for their concerns. Pay is an economic issue that concerns both employers and employees. For example, over the past decade, hourly compensation has almost doubled, while the productivity of the economy has shown a nominal increase. Labor bureau statistics indicates that while the hourly wage index in the private economy sector has increased to about 185 during the period of 1967-1975, the productivity index increased to around 115 during the same period (Norsworthy and Fulco, 1976). The increase in compensation has resulted in the increases of unit production cost and price. Are employees better off because of the wage increase? The answer is not necessarily yes. While their absolute wages increased, their real wages have remained almost unchanged. Since 1947, real wage has increased an average of 2.9 percent a year, while productivity has increased 2.8 percent a year. Maintaining a balance between wage, price, and productivity will remain as a common concern for everyone in the economy.

Pay is a powerful extrinsic incentive that can satisfy a number of needs. Pay is valued by employees because it not only provides the means of satisfying existence needs, but also symbolizes a number of things people value including material possession, status, power, and independency. Money is a versatile reinforcer which can be associated with a number of other reinforcers. It is essentially a neutral stimulus that takes value from its association with other valued incentives. Once it acquires a valence, it serves as an incentive as well as reinforcer. The instrumentality of pay will be further discussed later.

Pay can serve as a strong incentive for employees to increase productivity. Contrary to Herzberg's view that pay is a hygiene factor, there is some evidence that it serves as a motivator when contingent upon performance (Chung and Vickery, 1976; Lawler, 1971; and Pritchard and Curts, 1973). The incentive value of money largely depends on how it is acquired. Money acquired through pay has higher incentive value than money acquired through windfalls. A performance-contingent pay system is more powerful in arousing employee motivation than a nonperformance contingent pay system. Although people prefer hourly wage systems to piece-rate incentives (Schwab and Wallace, 1974), productivity is usually higher under incentive systems than under hourly wage systems.

Finally, dissatisfaction with pay leads to a number of dysfunctional behaviors. As indicated in Chapter 6, when organizational members are not satisfied with what they receive from the organization, they tend to reduce their commitments to the organizational endeavors. Pay dissatisfaction is measured by the difference between what they actually receive and what they feel they should receive. If the difference is against their favor, it leads to dissatisfaction. Pay dissatisfaction is manifested in forms of low motivation, sabotage, absenteeism, and quitting. These undesirable behaviors contribute to low productivity. Pay satisfaction is also considered a prerequisite for implementing a new managerial system. When people are not satisfied with pay, they will not respond positively to such motivational systems as job enlargement, job enrichment, and management by objectives.

RELATIVE IMPORTANCE OF PAY

Conceptually, pay can be important in satisfying employees' needs in the order of Maslow's need hierarchy: physiological, safety and security, socialization, self-esteem, and self-actualization. Although there is no direct evidence to test the relative importance of pay in satisfying these needs, a number of theories and empirical studies are germane to the study of relative importance and instrumentality of pay.

Pay has a motivational power because it buys the means of satisfying physiological needs. As man's survival depends on the satisfaction of physiological needs, these needs become the prime motivators of behavior if they are not satisfied. Maslow (1954) and McGregor (1960) postulated that these needs must be satisfied before other needs emerge as behavioral determinants. However, since most people in this society are reasonably satisfied with physiological survival needs, some researchers do not consider these survival needs important variables in motivational research (Hall and Nougain, 1968, Lawler and Porter, 1963).

Pay is instrumental for satisfying safety and security needs because it helps to insure against any possible financial disaster. Union demands for job security, buying life insurance, and saving money for rainy days are the prime examples of using money to satisfy safety and security needs. Higher-order needs emerge once these basic needs are satisfied. For example, Alderfer (1966) found that employees' satisfaction with fringe benefits is associated with increasing desire for peer group socialization. Hall and Nougaim (1968) found that as managers advance, their need for satisfying economic security decreases while their need for satisfying affiliation, esteem, and actualization increases.

Pay can facilitate satisfaction of socialization needs, but only indirectly. Money can buy the means for socialization such as memberships in clubs and food for parties, but it cannot buy friendship, love, and affection. Money, however, does free the individual from the fear of depriving physiological and security need satisfaction and allows him to search for satisfaction of other needs including socialization. Pay studies, reviewed by Lawler (1971), revealed that pay is not significantly correlated with socialization needs.

Pay can be directly instrumental for satisfying status, power, and self-esteem needs. How much money a person makes is frequently a measure of the person's worth to an organization and to society; thus pay becomes important to the satisfaction of status, power, and esteem needs. One's power motive is often expressed through the accumulation of economic means. When one's path to political power is blocked, he can sublimate his power motive through economic power.

Pay can be instrumental for satisfying achievement need but not self-actualization. When pay is tied to performance, it serves as a measure of achievement. When making money is endogenous to task performance, it can be a source of intrinsic motivation (Kruglanski, 1975). Activities directly related to monetary payoffs, such as gambling and entrepreneurial endeavors, are money-endogenous task performances.

Finally, pay is least likely to satisfy self-actualization. The role of money in satisfying self-actualization need is the same as that of satisfying socialization needs. It can buy the means of self-actualizing one's potentials, but it does not result in self-actualization. Alderfer (1969) found an insignificant relationship between the importance of pay and the strength of self-actualization need. In summary, pay is instrumental for satisfying physiological, security, status, power, esteem, and achievement needs, but is least likely to satisfy socialization and self-actualization needs.

VARIATIONS IN PAY IMPORTANCE

The importance of pay varies. First, it depends on the strength of a person's need structure. Pay can be important to a person who strives for the satisfaction of physiological and security needs. But as the person is reasonably satisfied with these needs, pay may lose its importance unless it can be instrumental in satisfying other needs. The motivational power of satisfying lower-level needs may be different from that of satisfying higher-order needs. Pay may have stronger impact on satisfying lower-level needs because they are more vital for survival.

Second, the importance of pay depends on how much a person receives. A prediction is that the more pay a person receives, the less important pay is to him (Lawler and Porter, 1963; Lawler, 1971, pp. 52-53). As the person becomes increasingly satisfied with high pay, he begins to attach less importance to pay. As the marginal utility of additional dollars decreases, it will take more dollars to make a raise meaningful to high-paid employees. Thus, it becomes necessary for management to develop motivational tools other than monetary incentives to continuously motivate high-paid employees.

Third, it also varies as a function of job levels. Managers tend to value pay as less important than workers (Centers and Bugental, 1966; Ronan, 1970). Lower-level managers tend to place a higher value on pay than do middle-managers (Porter, 1961). Top-level managers place less importance on pay than middle-managers (Lawler and Porter, 1963). The importance of pay also varies with different types of employment. For example, blue-collar workers seem to value pay more than white-collar workers. Likewise, unskilled workers seem to attack higher value on pay than skilled workers. The reason may be that higher-level and skilled jobs usually pay more than lower-level and unskilled jobs. In addition, higher-level and skilled jobs usually provide more and better opportunities to satisfy higher-order needs. Higher-level managers generally report high levels of need satisfaction, even when they are not highly paid (Porter and Lawler, 1965). Intrinsic motivation may compensate a lack of extrinsic motivation.

McClelland (1975) indicated that people with relatively low achievement motivation will work harder for increased financial rewards. It is not the task or the pay itself that interests them, but what it can buy. When the individual's possession increases, the importance of pay may be minimized and his efforts to produce may be reduced accordingly. People with high achievement motivation on the other hand, will be primarily motivated by their achievements. Offering additional financial incentives does not necessarily make them work harder, but they will expect their achievement to be recognized with rewards, including pay increase.

EMPLOYEES' PAY PREFERENCE

There are a variety of pay methods ranging from a simple piece-rate system to a more complex bonus plan. The value of a pay plan will increase if it is matched with the employees' pay preference. A number of studies report the results of employees' pay preferences. Mahoney (1964) reported that managers prefer straight salary payments over incentive payments such as stock option and profit-sharing plans. Managers also preferred individual pay plans to group plans. Industrial experiences with a salary-paid system for blue-collar workers seem to indicate that workers generally prefer the salary-paid system over the hourly-paid pay system (Hulme and Bevan, 1975). Also, there is some indication that workers prefer hourly wages to piece-rate incentives (Jaques, Rice, and Hill, 1951; Deci, 1972; and Schwab and Wallace, 1974).

In studying employees' pay preferences for seven compensation options early retirement, pay increase, shorter workweek, shorter workday, sabbatical leave, five Fridays off, and extra vacation), Nealey and Goodale (1967) found that blue-collar workers and foremen rated extra vacation, five Fridays, sabbatical leave, and shorter workweek ahead of pay increase. Some differences in pay preference were found among individuals with different personal backgrounds. Males rated the pay increase higher in preference than females; older workers rated their earlier retirement higher than did younger workers; shorter workday was ranked higher by females than males and higher by single than by married employees. In a similar study, Chapman and Ottemann (1975) found that extra vacation was most preferred while pay increase was the second in preference among public utility workers.

These studies imply that matching pay methods to workers' pay preferences will increase the incentive value of pay systems; the prefered pay methods can better satisfy employees' needs. Probably, cafeteria-style pay plans can be implemented to increase pay satisfaction. These plans allow employees to select the combination of cash payment and fringe benefits they want (Lawler, 1971, p. 198). Since the compensation package contains only preferred pay plans, the employees' perceptions of the valence of their pay packages will be increased. In addition to increasing the valence of the pay package, management should reinforce the instrumental relationship between pay amount and performance and insure the belief that motivational effort will be rewarded if it results in task performance.

PAY METHODS AND PERFORMANCE-INCENTIVE TIE

Expectancy theory indicates that the effectiveness of pay systems increases when task performance is instrumental for receiving valued incentives. When wages and salaries are not contingent upon performance, the pay system loses its motivational power and becomes a major source of employee dissatisfaction. The key to a successful utilization of a pay system is to reflect performance differences in individual pay. However, there are a number of questions to be asked in relating performance to pay. Should they be paid on an incentive or hourly basis? If an incentive plan is used, is there a reliable performance criterion? How often should workers be paid—daily, monthly, or annually? Finally, should workers' performance be measured on an individual or group basis? The effectiveness of various pay plans will be reveiwed in conjunction with these questions.

PIECE-RATE VERSUS HOURLY-RATE

Studies on compensation methods predict that a payment system based on a continuous ratio schedule, or piece-rate incentive, is more effective than a system based on a continuous interval schedule, or hourly-rate. Several early studies on pay systems reported that the use of incentive systems yielded higher productivity than that of hourly systems. Early studies by Taylor (1911) reported increased productivity due to an introduction of incentive systems. A government survey conducted by Ramond and his associates (1945) indicated that productivity under hourly-rate pay plans seldom exceeded 60 percent of that obtained under incentive plans. Further, considering all types of incentive plans, good, bad, and indifferent, average increase in productivity of 25 percent to 45 percent was obtained when the companies switched from hourly to incentive pay plans. Viteles (1953) also cited an increase in productivity of 16 percent when such a switch occurred. A similar study by Dale (1959) reported productivity increased by an average of 63 percent under incentive systems.

Bergum and Lehr (1964) reported that the subjects who received individual incentives performed better than those in the control group who were not rewarded. When the incentives were removed from the experimental group, the group's performance was poorer than that of the control group. Ayllon and Azrin (1965) reported that when the rewards were made contingent upon performance, patients in a mental hospital exhibited productive work behavior by spending more hours performing volunteer work. When the reward contingency was removed, the amount of hours decreased. Judging from these empirical studies, one may conclude that an incentive system which ties pay to performance can be expected to result in increased performance by 10 to 20 percent (Lawler, 1973, p. 119).

The use of incentive plans can be defended by expectancy or instrumentality theory of motivation (Galbraith and Cummings, 1967; Lawler and Porter, 1967; and Vroom, 1964). According to this theory, a person's motivation increases as he perceives the instrumentality of effective performance for obtaining the reward which he values. The instrumental relationship shows a direct support for an operant contingency. While the instrumentality theory concentrates on perception and value, the operant theory offers a way of empirically defining the valued reward (Schneider, 1974, p. 530). In other words, if a consequence of behavior is effective in controlling the rate of operant responses, rather than affecting perception and belief, it is considered a valued reward.

Most expectancy theorists and related empirical theorists (Arvey, 1972; Cherrington, Reitz and Scott, 1971; Galbraith and Cummings, 1967; Jorgenson, Dunnette, and Pritchard, 1973; Lawler, 1971; Lawler and Porter, 1967; and Schneider and Olson, 1970) generally confirmed the importance of the direct relationship between perceived or valued rewards and performance in affecting work behavior. In a comparative study on the impacts of different pay methods, Schwab (1973) reported that the attractiveness of pay and perceptions about the linkage between performance and pay were higher among incentive paid employees than among employees paid by hourly wages. Cammann and Lawler (1973) also reported that when workers perceived a close relationship between their pay and performance, they responded positively to the economic pay-off structure of the incentive plan.

In spite of the overwhelming evidence and theoretical support that incentive plans stand a better chance of success in motivating high productivity, the utilization of piece-rate incentive plans has declined over the years. A comparison of a 1968-1970 survey with similar surveys in earlier years suggests that there is a trend away from the use of incentive toward hourly methods in industries. United States Bureau of Labor statistics showed a decrease in the use of incentive plans for plantworkers from 20 percent in 1961-1963 to 14 percent in 1968-1970 (Cox, 1971) (Figure 7-1). A comparable labor survey indicated that 30 percent of plantworkers in all industries were paid on an IR basis in 1945 and 27 percent in 1958 (Stelluto, 1969).

A number of reasons are cited for the decrease of incentive pay systems.

Pay Methods	Manufacturing	Public Utilities	Wholesale Trade	Retail Trade	Services	All Industries	
						1968-70	1961-63
Time Payments	80%	99%	95%	90%	94%	86%	79%
Incentive Payments	20		5	10	6	14	20
Piece-rate	10				4	6	8
Individual	9				3	5	7
Group	1				1	1	1
Production Bonus	10			1	1	6	8
Individual	5			1	1	3	4
Group	5					3	4
Commission			5	8	1	2	3
Total	100	100	100	100	100	100	100

FIGURE 7-1. PAY METHODS FOR PLANT WORKERS IN URBAN AREAS

Source: Cox, J.H., "Time and Incentive Pay Practice in Urban Areas," *Monthly Labor Review*, 1971, 94, pp. 53-56. (Percentage figures less than 1 are not reported.)

First, there has been a change in the nature of industrial jobs which makes it difficult to measure individual outputs. Technological advancement in producing goods has reduced the portion of the work force engaged in blue-collar jobs where incentive pay mentods are commonly applicable. In addition, Belcher (1974, pp. 300-311), Roethlisberger and Dickson (1939), Viteles (1953), and Whyte (1955) pointed out that the installment of incentives, especially individual piece-rate, resulted in restriction of output. Workers feared that increased productivity might result in increased production standards, rate cuts, possible layoffs, impaired health, and loss of self-esteem. Lawler (1973, pp. 121-127) also listed several dysfunctional consequences of tying rewards to job performance. Individual incentive pay systems frequently led workers to compete among themselves for sharing limited resources and rewards and thus fail to develop cooperative behavior; to perform well in those aspects of jobs that were measured for determining the size of rewards while neglecting other aspects that were not measured but needed to be performed; and to feed invalid data to distort information flow and performance measuring mechanisms.

EQUITY THEORY AND P-I TIE

Not only do financial incentives often produce dysfunctional behavior of workers, but they operate with different effectiveness under different equity conditions, and some even suggest that they are detrimental to performance in intrinsic job situations. According to equity theory of pay, the way a person perceives the balance between his inputs and outputs, in comparison with relevant others' input-output balances, seems to be more important than the direct linkage between reward and performance in determining the effectiveness of a pay system. If the person's input-output ratio is perceived to be equitable to the relevant other's input-output ratio, a feeling of perceived pay equity exists. Conversely, if they are perceived to be inequitable, a state of inequity occurs—inequity being either overpaid or underpaid. The presence of inequity creates tension that motivates the person to reduce the feelings of inequity for modifying either his behavioral or cognitive modes (Adams, 1963a and 1965).

The behavioral mode of changing the input-output ratios (increasing or decreasing quantity and/or quality of a person's inputs and outputs), as a means of reducing inequity, presents an interesting observation to our discussion. According to equity theory, unlike an incentive pay system where workers will respond positively to maximize their economic gains, workers will respond to the same pay system according to the ways they perceive equity of their pay. Thus, some workers may reduce quantity output even if they are paid on a piece-rate basis.

Equity theory predicts that subjects who feel overpaid on an incentive plan will raise their inputs by producing a higher quality but lower quantity of products as a means of reducing inequity (Adams and Rosenbaum, 1962; Adams, 1963b; Adams and Jacobsen, 1964; Goodman and Friedman, 1969; and Wood and Edward, 1970). Subjects who feel underpaid on an incentive plan will raise their outputs by producing a higher quantity of low quality products (Andrews, 1967; and Lawler and O'Gara, 1967). Under an hourly plan, subjects who feel overpaid will raise their inputs by producing a higher quantity as a means of reducing inequity (Adams and Rosenbaum, 1962; Goodman and Friedman, 1969; and Pritchard, Dunnette, and Jorgenson, 1972). On the other hand, subjects who feel underpaid will reduce their inputs, quality and/or quantity, to achieve equity in their input-output ratios (Evan and Simmons, 1969; and Prithcard, et al., 1972). Figure 7-2 summarizes the likelihood responses of workers to inequity under overpaid and underpaid conditions.

A number of behavioral scientists (Opsahl and Dunnette, 1966; Wyatt, 1934) argued that individuals under performance-contingent pay systems do not necessarily exert higher motivational effort than individuals who are under nonperformance contingent pay systems if their tasks are repetitive, boring, destructive, or disliked. When the task is lacking opportunities for satisfying higher-order needs, a manipulation of monetary rewards does not produce long-term effects on performance. Even if an incentive system may temporarily re-lieve boredom, outputs under such a system may suffer if the task is disliked. Further, the utilization of contingent pay systems in an intrinsically satisfying task situation may be detrimental to employee motivation. Deci (1972) reported that when payments were made contingent upon performance in an intrinsically motivating task situation, the subjects' motivation to perform the task de-creased. When payments were not contingent, intrinsic motivation was not affected. Apparently workers do not like to feel they are performing their task for money.

The following observations can be made from these studies when they are viewed collectively. First, tying money to performance alone is not a sufficient condition for motivating workers to produce. The nature of tasks, perceived equity of pay, and perceived linkage between performance and pay are some additional factors that determine the effectiveness of a pay method. Intrinsic rewards are shown to be more powerful predictors of performance. Yet, mone-tary incentive, especially in the absence of intrinsic motivation, seems to be a viable predictor of performance. Perceived equity and job performance is higher under high incentive conditions as opposed to low incentive conditions. Per-ceived linkage between performance and pay is higher among incentive paid employees than among employees paid by hourly wage. In addition, the follow-ing conditions should prevail to make the incentive more effective (Nash and Carroll, 1975, pp. 209-210). The incentive plan should be simple enough to be understood by employees. Lack of understanding breeds suspicion and mis-trust. The plan should have carefully established standards and work methods. Poorly set standards and lack of standardized work methods can easily lead to

Condition \ Pay Method	Incentive-rate	Hourly-rate
Overpaid	Increase the quality of production at low volume	Increase the volume of production at low quality
Underpaid	Increase the volume of production at low quality	Reduce the volume and/or quality of production

FIGURE 7-2. INEQUITY ADJUSTMENTS UNDER OVERPAID AND UNDERPAID CONDITIONS

disputes questioning the fairness and equity of the standards and pay rates. There should be an acceptable procedure for changing standards when necessary. Changes in quality of raw materials, equipment, and work methods necessitate a change in output standards. Finally, the incentive plan must be accepted by the employees. It should have an appeal to workers in terms of its magnitude and fairness.

HOURLY WAGE VERSUS SALARY

Customarily, most blue-collar and lower-level rank-and-file workers are paid on an hourly basis, while managerial and professional personnel are paid on a salary basis. There are several explanations for these practices. First, the performance cycles of the jobs at lower-levels of an organization are relatively short and can be measured in hourly units. The hourly-rate pay system can closely relate individual performance to pay. Second, the low-level rank-and-file workers are assumed to be less committed to their organizations and thus less responsible for their time. If time clocks are removed, they will be less motivated to show up for work and thus encourage absenteeism. Finally, it is easier to compute the direct costs of products under an hourly system than under a salary system. The time clock provides information useful for accounting and managerial purposes.

Salaries are then generally paid to white-collar workers for the following reasons. The performance cycles of supervisory, managerial, and professional jobs in an organization are relatively long and cannot be measured in hourly units and the hourly system does not closely reflect one's contribution to his job. A salary method based on a weekly, biweekly, monthly, or yearly interval can be more relevant for paying these groups of workers. White-collar workers are assumed to be self-directed and more responsible for using their time, so it is not necessary to strictly control their attendance. Also, their services frequently require them to be outside of their offices; punching in and out of the offices may create unnecessary burdens on them. The organization may not be able to attract qualified personnel if it imposes the use of time clock and hourly-paid systems. Finally, there is no evidence that a salary-paid system encourages a high rate of absenteeism. Contrarily, there is evidence that eliminating time clocks and putting workers on salaries can sometimes lead to better attendance (Cannon Electric and Motorola, Lawler, 1971, pp. 193-195).

Undoubtedly, most workers will prefer to be paid on a salary basis rather than on a hourly basis because it will appeal to their needs for income stability and self-esteem. Whether it is advisable to switch an hourly-paid system to a salary-paid system for blue-collar workers is debatable. However, the answer seems to be somewhat positive. The reasons for this may be that 1) blue-collar workers are as responsible as white-collar workers for the use of their time; 2) they are interested in satisfying the needs for income stability and self-esteem as white-collar workers; 3) the switch usually improved the management-worker relationships; and 4) a well-designed salary-paid system does not encourage absenteeism. Yet, many firms still reason that the changeover from an hourly basis may increase absenteeism and tardiness and cause the loss of some valuable accounting and managerial information.

Despite some concerns, a number of companies have introduced the salary approach to paying blue-collar workers. Hulme and Bevan (1975) examined five companies' salary plans—Gillette, Polaroid, Kinetic Dispersion, Avon Products, and Black & Decker—for blue-collar workers. These plans are varying widely. Some deduct pay for absences under certain conditions, while others guarantee pay regardless of an absence or tardiness.

Although it is difficult to generalize the outcomes of the salary plans, the following observations can be made from their studies. The rate of absenteeism surged initially but subsided somewhat later. In some cases, the increase in absenteeism subsided without specific management actions, while in others extensive managerial controls were needed to curb the increase. Employee reactions to these plans were positive although they felt resistance initially. Finally, the underlying objective of these plans was to improve the management-employee relations by eliminating the differences between blue-collar and white-collar workers. The outcomes of these plans generally met this management expectation.

Hulme and Bevan (1975) concluded that paying salaries to all workers could be a worthwhile objective for many organizations as a way of improving management-employee relations. However, in view of some difficulties encountered in the implementation process, they offered the following major conditions necessary for probable success: Management-employee relations are open and operative, the labor force is reasonably stable, mature, and responsible; first level supervisors have the ability and personal confidence to use their judgment within the context of the plan; time-recording procedures generate adequate and accurate absence-control data and accounting information; prevailing absenteeism rates are not unusually high; advance communication of the purpose and operation of the plan are extended to all employees; management has good relations with a union, if there is one. Finally, the plan provides for unobstructed exercise of maximum management discretion.

INDIVIDUAL VERSUS GROUP INCENTIVES

Should incentive rewards be paid on an individual or group basis? The answer depends on the nature of the job, workers' pay preference, and managerial philosophy. Individualized incentive plans such as piece-rate, production bonus, commission, and merit-rate recognize individual contributions to the organization's goal attainment. These plans assume that job performance is a function of an individual effort, there is a set of discernable performance criteria which differentiate individual contributions, and workers enjoy some degree of competition among themselves. Group plans, on the other hand, assume that the job performance is a function of group effort and it is difficult to identify individual performance.

Piece-rate Plans

Individualized piece-rate plans, such as straight piece-rate and differential piece-rate, are the oldest and the most common form of wage payment (Taylor, 1911). Since payment is directly tied to the number of production units a worker produces, these plans are considered the most effective motivational means of paying employees. However, only about 5 percent of plantworkers were paid by individualized piece-rate plans in 1968-1970 (Figure 7-1) and the percentage is steadily declining. The primary reason for this decline is due to changes in the nature of industrial jobs which make it difficult to measure individual performance. Most jobs in an industrial world require a high degree of interdependency among workers, so one's performance is usually dependent upon other workers' performance. Further, since production standards frequently change whenever there are changes in raw materials, equipment, and work methods, the base piece-rates have to be changed accordingly, which frequently creates disagreement. However, individual piece-rates still prevail in such industries as apparel, textile, leather footwear, and cigar manufacturing where productivity primarily depends on individual effort.

Production Bonus Plans

Production bonus plans involve payments to workers for production above an established performance standard. The original production bonus plan was devised by Halsey in 1890. Fifty percent of labor cost savings were paid to individual workers who competed tasks in less than standard time. This plan is used where standard times are relatively loose. When tighter standards are used, full savings are paid to workers (Nash and Carroll, 1975, p. 196). About three percent of plantworkers received individualized production bonuses in 1968-1970 (see Figure 7-1).

Commission Plans

A commission plan is a form of incentives paid to salesmen and in a limited extent to maintenance and material-handling workers. Nash and Carroll (1975, pp. 197-198) reported that between 10 and 25 percent of companies pay salesmen on a straight commission basis. The rest use a combination of salary and commission. Although commission plans are considered effective in stimulating salesmen' activities, they also generate several negative consequences: 1) the hard-sell approach may alienate potential customers; 2) nonselling activities such as services often are ignored; and 3) salesmen do not have income stability. Similar incentive plans also are used to stimulate productivity for janitorial, truck driving, and material-handling personnel.

Merit-rate Plans

When compensation is paid on interval schedules such as hourly and salary plans, incentive reward takes the form of merit increase. Merit-rate plans are commonly applied to all types of employees in various industries with a possible exception of blue-collar workers. The Bureau of National Affairs' survey (1975) indicated that about 80 percent of small and 90 percent of large organizations applied merit-rate plans to all types of employees except a portion of blue-collar workers; about 40 percent of these organizations reported the application of merit-rate plans to blue-collar workers. Almost 99 percent of office workers were paid on interval pay schedules; about 58 percent of office workers received merit-rated increases in 1968-1970 (Cox, 1971); the rest received automatic pay rate increase or no increase at all.

The policy of relating individual performance to pay increment has a potential motivational value. However, in the absence of objective performance measurements, many organizations evaluate their employees' performance by rating employees on their job qualifications (knowledge, ability, education, training, and experience) and personality factors (attitude, cooperativeness, dependability, and adaptability). Although these performance criteria may be reliable indicators of a person's effectiveness on the job, they do not measure actual performance. Instead, these criteria measure the worker's potential for future performance. The measurement on such criteria may provide useful information for selecting, placing, and promoting employees rather than for rewarding their performance. Such an evaluation is a highly subjective process and is likely to distort the relationship between job performance and organizational rewards.

To minimize the effects of subjective elements in the evaluation process, many scholars and practitioners advocate result-oriented performance appraisal (Chung, 1973; Meyer, Kay, and French, 1965; and Thompson and Dalton, 1970). The result-oriented performance appraisal establishes performance goals in advance, and actual performance will be measured against these preset goals. However, it is doubtful that a human being is ever able to be totally objective in evaluating others' performance. Even if one wants to be objective, man's perceptual gestalt process introduces subjective elements. The result-oriented performance appraisal will be discussed further in Chapter 10.

Group Incentive Plans

Group incentives can range from a piece-rate plan to a bonus plan as is the case with individual incentives. Group incentive plans usually are applied to those job situations in which job performance demands a high degree of interdependency among workers and where individual performance is difficult to measure. The advantages of group incentive plans are: These plans encourage joint effort by group members to increase the group's outputs which increase the total size of incentive pay for the group. Group members exercise social control functions to either encourage good performance or discourage poor performance of coworkers. A close supervision may not be necessary to manage the work group. It is less expensive to manage a group incentive plan than an individualized incentive plan. From the clerical standpoint, the company does not need to measure and maintain individual performance records. Supervision costs will be less as the work group needs less close supervision. Finally, the group incentive plans coincide with the underlying philosophy of group-oriented management whereby group members participate in the managerial process. Also, it is more flexible to introduce job rotation under a group incentive plan than under an individualized plan. Job rotation adds some motivation value to the job by enlarging task and skill variety to an otherwise repetitive and boring job.

However, a major disadvantage of group incentive plans is that these plans may have a less motivational value because one's pay is not closely related to his individual performance. When a group incentive plan is applied to a large work group, the instrumental relationship between pay and performance will not be as clear as in small groups or individual plans (Marriot, 1949; Lawler, 1973, p. 119). However, it is hypothesized that productivity will be higher under a group incentive plan than under a nonincentive plan and that restrictive production norms are less likely to develop when a group incentive plan is used (Lawler, 1971, p. 129).

COMPANYWIDE INCENTIVE PLANS

Some companies have adopted companywide reward systems in lieu of or in addition to individual or group incentive plans. Under these plans, some key employees receive some form of extra payment as reward for their contributions to the company's profits. In a broad sense, most companywide incentive plans can be considered profit-sharing plans because employee benefits under these plans are related to the company's profits. Typically, the same incentive bonuses are paid to all qualified employees holding similar jobs regardless of their productivity. Such companywide incentive systems are used to eliminate the problem of measuring individual performance and to foster harmony among employees. Companywide incentive plans take various forms. Some plans allow employee participation in the management of the pay plans. Incentives are paid to employees either in cash or stock. The measurement of a company's productivity can be profit, sales, or labor cost savings. The more popular companywide incentive plans include the Scanlon plan, cash or deferred payment profit sharing plans, Employee Stock Ownership Plans (ESOP), executive bonus plans, and stock option plans.

The Scanlon Plan

The Scanlon Plan is a form of profit-sharing by which workers share the company profits contributed by labor-cost savings. The Scanlon plan allows workers to participate in the production committee which serves as a communication linkage between management and workers. The committee reviews company plans and workers' suggestions for improving productivity. If these plans and/or suggestions results in labor-cost savings and consequently increased profits, the amount of cost savings will be distributed to individual employees proportionately to their base pay. Sixty to a hundred firms use the Scanlon plan, and most of these firms are fairly small with about 1,000 employees (Nash and Carroll, 1975, p. 215). A study by Lesieur and Puckett (1969) indicated that the Scanlon plan resulted in high efficiency, reduction in resistance to change, improved management-labor relations, and better employee concerns for the organizational welfare. However, problems arise when the standards have to be modified due to changes in product mix (Jehring, 1967). These changes frequently lead to disagreement between management and workers concerning the new standards. Especially when there is a lack of trust between them, the problem of arriving at agreeable standards can be a difficult task. Managerial attitudes toward employees (Ruh, Wallacne, and Frost, 1973), a trusting relationship between management and workers, and group-oriented management (Geare, 1976) are important factors for determining the effectiveness of the Scanlon Plan.

Profit-Sharing Plan

The term *profit-sharing,* in a narrow sense, means any pay scheme by which employees share a portion of corporate profits, not just labor-cost savings, with management. There are a variety of profit-sharing plans, but basically they can be classified into three major types: cash plan, deferred payment, and combination. Under the cash plan, a portion of profits are distributed directly to the employees. A well-known cash plan is that of the Lincoln Electric Company. The company pays most of its profits to employees; an individual employee's bonus usually runs between 20 percent to more than 100 percent of his annual wage. The amount of bonus is not only determined by the company's profits, but also by the employee's performance rating (Nash and Carroll, 1975, p. 215).

The most popular profit-sharing plan is the deferred plan whereby the employee's share of profits is set aside for a future benefit such as retirement or disability. Deferred plans are considered an important motivational tool for management and an integral part of retirement plans for employees. By relating employees' bonuses to company profits, employees have an incentive to increase profits by being more productive on their jobs. And employees accumulate tax-deferrable incomes for their retirement. However, in recent years, both management and employees have begun to question the motivational value of the deferred plan. As inflation mounts and stock prices plunge, employees see the value of their profit-sharing holdings erode and thus prefer a cash plan over a deferred plan. To protect shareholders' interest, some companies such as Burlington Industries established a "guaranteed base" whereby, if the plan's portfolio falls below this base level, the company makes up the difference. Other companies such as Dart Industries and Rohr Industries discontinued their deferred plans and moved into more fixed-income oriented retirement plans (*Business Week,* December 7, 1974). The third type of profit-sharing plan combines the first two plans; a part of profit-sharing is deferred and the rest is distributed to employees in cash.

It was estimated that over 100,000 firms in the United States had profit-sharing plans and about 10 to 75 percent of corporate profits were paid to employees under these plans (Metzger, 1964). Metzger reported that approximately two-thirds to three-quarters of the firms surveyed claimed that their plans have improved operational efficiency, reduced costs, and lowered turnover. Another survey, reported in *Personnel Journal* (1972), found that the companies with profit-sharing plans performed better than those without the plans by 35 percent in sales, 47 percent in net worth, and 88 percent in profits per share for the period of 1952-1969.

Although there is little research on the relative effectiveness of various companywide plans, the following hypotheses can be drawn based on theoretical speculation. First, the Scanlon plan can have a stronger motivational value on employees' operational efficiency than other plans because it focuses on labor efficiency, which is under control of workers, and the workers participate in the management of the plan (Nash and Carroll, 1975, p. 217). Second, a cash plan can have a stronger motivational value than a deferred value. In addition, a reinforcement principle indicates that the incentive value of a reward decreases as its payment is delayed. Finally, a deferred plan can be more effective in reducing turnover and encouraging long-term commitments to the organization. Since deferred benefits will be realized in the long-run, the plan benefits employees with seniority.

Employee Stock Ownership Plans (ESOP)

An ESOP plan is similar to a profit-sharing plan. Both plans enjoy tax-deferred benefits for share-holdings and tax exemption on the earnings of the plans' trusts. Also, both plans encourage a high productivity and long-term commitment to their organizations. The difference is that fund contribution can be made to the ESOP trust even in years when the company has not made a profit, whereas contribution cannot be made if there is no profit under a profit-sharing plan. In addition, ESOP requires contribution be made in company stock, whereas benefits under a profit-sharing plan can be paid cash, stock, or other assets.

The principal purpose of ESOP is to give workers a piece of the action through ownership of the company and direct participation in sharing its profit. The ESOP trust can borrow money from banks to purchase a block of the company equity shares and distribute them to its employees on the basis of salary or other formula. The company then makes annual profit-sharing contributions to the trust which are tax deductable just as wages and salaries. But, they are treated as deferrable income for the employees. Profit-sharing contributions can be used to purchase more equity shares and/or to repay the bank loans and interests. By making a tax deductible contribution to the ESOP trust and having the ESOP repay the loan, the loan payment including principal and interest is tax deductible by the company (Tillman, 1975).

Ownership of a company will undoubtedly make a substantial difference in employee motivation as one's financial gains and ego are directly involved with the company's welfare. The idea of employee stock ownership was boosted by the recent action of Congress in passing the Employee Retirement Income Security Act of 1975. However, the acceptability and effectiveness of this plan remains to be seen because some union leaders are against any movement that leads workers to identify with management and stockholders. They fear that such a movement may undermine the union's bargaining position. Since its utilization is relatively new and is usually found in small companies, it is not yet certain how these plans will affect the relationships between management owner-employees, management and union, and employee-stockholders and non-employee-stockholders.

Executive Bonus Plans

Performance bonuses are paid to key employees of industrial organizations in relation to their profits. Generally, bonuses are paid to executives when the company's profits reach a minimum level of performance. The Conference Board (1972) reported that about two-thirds of manufacturers, 50 percent of retailers, and 40 percent of insurance firms in its survey had an executive bonus plan. Bourke (1975) defended the use of performance bonus plans by indicating that manufacturing firms with bonus plans generally have a greater return on sales and investment, and key managerial employees in bonus-paying companies enjoy a higher level of earning than do their counterparts in non-bonus-paying companies similar in size and activities. A comparative study of profit performance for 556 bonus-paying companies and 481 non-bonus-paying companies in durable goods manufacturing showed that the return on sales for the bonus group was 4.5 percent while that for the nonbonus group was 3 percent. The rates of return on net worth for both groups were 11.8 and 8.6 percents respectively.

Bourke (1975) indicated that there is a causal relationship between the performance bonus plan and profit performance. Companies in a breakeven or loss position have made drastic turnarounds when a managerial bonus plan was installed. Others have improved an already good performance level by relating bonuses not only to corporate profit but to individual performance under an MBO program. More than one-half of the nation's large corporations have bonus plans for their executives. However, performance bonus plans are more prevalent among durable goods manufacturing companies (over 52 percent) then in the nondurable goods manufacturing sector (about 42 percent).

Stock Option Plans

A stock option is a right to purchase a specific amount of stock at a specified price for a specified period. The option price frequently is lower than the market price at the time it is offered. Thus, the difference between the option price and the market price constitutes the value of the option. Stock options are usually offered to specific segments of managerial personnel as a compensation device and/or an ownership device. Either way, a stock option plan encourages executives' long-term commitment and job performance. The amount of stock that an individual executive can purchase usually is based on his salary. The Conference Board study (1972) reported that approximately 90 percent of the manufacturers and 85 percent of the retailers in its survey had a stock option plan limited to key employees, compared with 45 percent of the insurance firms, 36 percent of the banks, and 19 percent of the utility companies.

There are two types of stock option plans under the tax law—qualified and nonqualified—depending on whether the plan is qualified for capital gain tax benefits. A qualified option plan should meet the following requirements: 1) the option should be offered at the current market price; 2) the option can be exercised within a five-year period after the option date; 3) once the option is exercised, the purchaser should hold the stock for at least three years to qualify for tax benefits; and 4) the option cannot be exercised if there are other options outstanding. The option will be exercised if the stock price goes up or is expected to rise. Any income realized from exercising the option is taxed at the capital gains rate, up to but not exceeding 35 percent on all gains over $50,000. The Tax Reform Act of 1969, which raised the capital gains tax from the maximum rate of 25 percent to 35 percent and which reduced the maximum tax on current income to 50 percent, made the qualified option plans less attractive. In addition, the unfavorable stock market in the early 1970s made the qualified option plans further less popular among executives (Cook, 1976).

In reaction to the unfavorable development in exercising the qualified option plans, many companies and their executives have turned to other alternatives such as nonqualified option plans and performance share plans (Goddu, 1976). A nonqualified option plan gives up the capital gains tax benefits, but it is favored by many executives because of its flexibility. The stock option can be offered at below the market value, can have an unlimited exercise period, and can be exercised regardless of current stock holdings. Stock purchased under a nonqualified option plan needs to be held for six months to qualify for capital gains tax benefits. However, the amount of appreciation between the option price and the market value at the time of exercise is treated as ordinary income subject to the 50 percent maximum on earned income. The performance share plan is a cross between a performance bonus and a stock option. Contingent upon the organizational performance over a three to five year period, company executives receive the performance shares convertible to stock or cash. Thus, the plan encourages executives long-term commitments and operating results without tying it to stock price.

NONPERFORMANCE CONTINGENT PAYMENTS

There are a number of financial payments not tied to performance. Most fringe benefits such as pension premium, insurance premium, sick leave, health insurance premium, severance pay, unemployment benefit, paid vacation, paid rest period, Christmas bonus, and tuition refund are not directly contingent upon workers' performance. (Profit-sharing plans also are counted as fringe benefits, but these benefits are contingent upon the companywide performance.) According to a Chamber of Commerce report (1974), payments for fringe benefits averaged 32.7 percent of the surveyed companies' payroll. The average cost of these benefits was $3,230 a year per employee. The study also reported that larger firms tended to pay higher benefits than smaller firms. Fringe benefits for large companies have reached more than 35 percent of their payroll accounts. These benefits have expanded more than twice as fast as wages and salaries in U.S. industries. Fringes in real terms increased at the rate of 9.6 percent while salaries and wages increased at the rate of 3.9 percent per year between 1929 and 1967 (Oswald and Smyth, 1970). There are other types of nonperformance contingent payments such as across-the-board raises, cost-of-living adjustments, and seniority increases attached to direct compensation. All these nonperformance contingent payments will have no real effect on employees' work motivation and job performance because these payments are not related to their work motivation and actual job performance.

There are a number of reasons for the rapid growth of nonperformance contingent payments. Earlier in the century, some employers were motivated to provide their workers with various types of noncontingent payments for paternalistic reasons. As much as their employees were loyal to them, they may have felt obligated to take care of them. Such a benevolent approach became less popular and was replaced by external demands made by union, employees, and government. The growth of unions in the 1930s and 1940s pushed for increased benefits as a means of attracting new members. With increased opportunities for better education and employment, employees enjoy a higher standard of living and subsequently demand protection against any possible economic disasters. In addition, the Taft-Hartley Act of 1947 that required employers to bargain for pensions and group insurance programs encouraged unions to pursue fringe benefits. Governmental efforts to stabilize employee wages during World War II and the Korean War also exerted pressure for more fringe benefits in lieu of direct compensation increases.

The primary effects of noncontingent payments on employee motivation are to attract people to the organization, to free employees from the fear of economic deprivation, and to reduce turnover. But, such rewards do little to motivate a high level of performance beyond the line of duty. However, since such noncontingent payments help to increase employees' stakes in the organization as well as encourage cooperation among organizational members, its employees may feel responsible to better respond to such management efforts as job enrichment and MBO to increase organizational productivity. Also, management may negotiate with workers or unions to make some nonessential benefits such as paid vacations, shorter workdays, sabbatical leaves, and Christmas bonuses contingent upon workers' productivity. Since many employees prefer increases in such indirect payments to increases in direct payments (Chapman and Ottemann, 1975; Nealey and Goodale, 1967), some indirect payments can be used to yield a strong motivational value by relating them to performance.

EFFORT-REWARD EXPECTANCY AND PAY EFFECTIVENESS

An employee's belief that his effort will be followed by financial incentives (E-I) influences the effectiveness of a pay system. If the E-I expectancy is too low, people will be discouraged to exert motivational effort because they perceive that their effort will not be rewarded no matter how hard they try. On the other hand, if the E-I expectancy is too high, they may be satisfied with the pay system, but they will not exert a high level of motivational effort because they perceive that they will be rewarded regardless of their effort levels. Motivational effort will be high when the reward system is so designed that it requires a moderate level of effort from an employee before he is rewarded.

EFFECT OF E-I ON PAY EFFECTIVENESS

Well-intended incentive programs frequently fail to produce expected results, not because the value of the bonuses is small but because management has not counted the impact of the E-I expectancy on employee motivation in designing the incentive programs. For example, incentive bonuses are often given to only a small portion of employees, and thus the majority of employees do not expect that their efforts will lead to bonuses. Sales contests and productivity improvement bonuses are the prime examples of such bonuses, and most employees do not pay attention to these contests because they know in advance that their chances of receiving the rewards are almost zero. The opposite extreme also produces the same negative motivational result. For example, most nonperformance contingent rewards such as automatic across-the-board wage increases, Christmas bonuses, and various fringe benefits do not yield a motivational value because they fail to elicit the E-I expectancy.

Any incentive bonus system aimed at motivating a large number of employees should be designed so that most employees are able to receive the incentive bonuses if they work hard. However, the problem may be that since most incentive bonuses are supplementary payments added to a regular pay, it is often too expensive to reward a large number of employees with a meaningful dollar amount. If only a limited amount of money is available for incentive bonuses, a partial reinforcement schedule giving employees chances of winning bonuses will elicit the E-I expectancy if these chances are contingent upon job performance. When the sum of reward to be distributed is relatively small, partial reinforcement with a large variation in individual rewards is preferred to a continuous reinforcement with small sized rewards. When a given size of reward is divided into small pieces, the average size of reward will be too small to be meaningful. Partial reinforcement will make the average size of rewards attractive to recipients.

EFFECT OF E-P ON E-I

The E-I expectancy is determined by the belief that one's effort leads to task performance (E-P), and the extent to which the organization ties performance to pay (P-I). Since the performance-pay instrumentality was discussed previously, the present discussion will focus on the effect of the E-P expectancy on the E-I expectancy. The performance standard should be optimally designed to elicit a high level of motivational effort. The integrative expectancy theory, presented in Chapter 5, suggests that motivational effort will be higher when the E-P expectancy is moderate than when it is too high or too low. If it is too low, no matter how hard one tries, he cannot achieve the performance standard and will not be rewarded. If the E-P expectancy is too high, it will be easier to achieve the standard and be rewarded. However, it was pointed out in Chapter 5 that many simplified jobs do not motivate workers because their task performance is not perceived to be a function of their effort. There is some evidence that motivational effort does not increase with an increase of the E-P expectancy beyond a certain level (Atkinson, 1964; Atkinson and Feather, 1966; and Starke and Behling, 1975). In addition, we can hardly expect that economic payoff will be high for a task with a high E-P expectancy. The E-P expectancy is usually inversely related to economic payoff or valence.

Finding an optimum level of E-P expectancy is not a simple task because it varies for different individuals. For example, a person with a high achievement need will work harder under a reward situation where the odds are around 50 percent, while a person with a low achievement need prefers a situation where the odds are better than 50 percent (Atkinson, 1967). Also, the E-P expectancy changes with job experience. As an employee learns more job skills, the standard becomes looser and the old standard becomes less challenging. The performance standard should be adjusted periodically to keep the E-P expectancy at an optimal level in order to produce high motivational effort. However, if management frequently changes performance standards, it will be difficult to get acceptance for new standards and may even create feelings of distrust. The motivational implication of E-P expectancy for designing tasks will be further discussed in Chapter 9.

In summary, management can influence the E-I expectancy by changing either the E-P tie or the P-I tie. Management can influence the E-P expectancy by changing performance standards and the P-I instrumentality by manipulating pay rate and performance appraisal systems. Since management has an influence on the I-N tie and the E-I expectancy, managers' knowledge of pay methods and their integrity in administering pay plans are very important for determining their effectiveness. A well-designed pay system can easily lose its effectiveness if the employees suspect and distrust managerial integrity.

DIFFERENTIAL EFFECTS OF VARIOUS PAY METHODS

Pay methods discussed in the preceding section can be grouped into three major categories, depending on whether they are paid to employees on an individual, group, or companywide basis. Individual pay methods in each category can differ depending on the way they measure the performance of employees. Performance measurements range from relatively objective criteria such as production units, sales, and profits, to relatively subjective ones such as supervisory ratings. As pay methods differ in the way they are paid to employees and the way the pay bases are measured, they have different impacts on employee motivation and behavior. No one plan seems to satisfy all three motivational needs—individual motivation, group effort, and company loyalty of an organization.

Figure 7-3 presents a list of pay methods along with pay bases, motivational purposes, and their impacts on individual, group, and company-oriented behavior. Since the effectiveness of a pay plan not only depends on the way it is designed but also the way it is introduced and administered, the evaluative rating given to each plan should be considered general and tentative rather than specific and conclusive. Nevertheless, the following generalizations provide a guide for formulating a set of specific pay plans and a set of hypotheses for further studies on the relative effectiveness of various pay plans.

First, individual plans are generally rated high on individual motivation, but low on group motivation and organizational loyalty. While these plans encourage individual motivation by directly relating an employee's pay to his performance, they do not encourage, and sometimes even discourage, cooperative efforts because employees frequently compete for fixed rewards. The effects of individual plans on institutional loyalty can be rated as neutral or low because these plans neither encourage nor discourage institutional loyalty or any long-term commitment of employees to the organization. Since these plans are generally effective in arousing individual work motivation, they can be productively applied to task situations where job performance primarily depends on individual effort and can be individually measured in such objectively measurable performance units as production units, sales, costs, and profits. Merit-rating plans are rated medium on individual motivation because although the plans attempt to tie pay to performance, supervisory subjective judgments can easily distort the P-I tie.

Second, group plans are rated high on group effort, but medium on individual motivation and institutional loyalty. While an employee's pay is not directly related to his performance, the size of his pay depends on the degree to which the employee contributes to the joint effort of group members. When employees enjoy supportive relationships with co-workers, they may be able to develop institutional loyalty because the work group to some extent represents the institution to them. Group plans can be productively applied to task situations that require a high degree of interaction and cooperative effort among group members and where job performance cannot be measured on an individual basis.

Third, companywide plans are generally rated high on institutional loyalty, mostly medium on group effort, and medium to low on individual motivation. Since these plans place a major emphasis on organizational membership, benefits under these plans do not increase individual motivation. Rather, they tend to foster employees' institutional loyalty and long-term commitment. Although these plans do not affect group effort directly, they nevertheless emphasize a non-zero-sum game or at least do not encourage competition among members. The Scanlon plans and cash profit-sharing plans are rated medium on individual and group behavior. Although an employee's benefits are not directly related to his job performance, his overall benefits are indirectly related to his contribution to the company's profits. Also, his benefits are more current under these

Pay Plans		Performance Measurement	Individual Motivation	Group Effort	Institutional Loyalty
Individual	Piece-rate	Productivity	H	L	N
	Commission	Productivity	H	L	N
	Product Bonus	Productivity	H	L	N
	Merit-rate	Supervisor Rating	M	L	N
Group	Piece-rate	Productivity	M	H	M
	Commission	Productivity	M	H	M
	Production Bonus	Productivity	M	H	M
	Merit-rate	Supervisor Rating	M	H	M
Companywide	Scanlon Plan	Labor Cost Savings	M	M	H
	Profit-sharing	Profit	M	M	H
	Stock Option	Profit, Stock Price	L	M	H
	ESOP	Profit, Stock Price	L	M	H
	Fringe Benefits	Nonperformance Contingent	N	L	M

Rating scales: High (H); Medium (M); Low (L); and Neutral (N).

FIGURE 7-3. RELATIVE EFFECTIVENESS OF PAY SYSTEMS

plans than under deferred profit-sharing, ESOP, and stock option plans. Benefits under non-cash-paying plans are largely tied to the future performance of the company and its stock price. As nonperformance contingent payments, fringe benefits have little effects on individual work motivation and group effort, but will have some influence on institutional loyalty, as the institution provides the employee with some degree of economic security in times of personal difficulties.

Finally, Lawler (1973, p. 130) indicated that bonus plans would have stronger influence on individual motivation than merit-rate plans because bonus plans vary greatly from year to year in accordance with recent performance but merit-rated pay plans do not. One's overall pay under a merit-rate plan reflects both recent performance and performance over the years. But, his salary increment can be closely related to recent performance. Furthermore, since most bonuses usually are paid annually, employees find it difficult to relate their bonuses to specific performance or behavior. Consequently, both bonus and merit-rate plans will have about the same motivational effect.

In summary, no pay plan is effective in satisfying all three motivational needs of an organization—individual motivation, group effort, and institutional loyalty. A selection of a pay plan or a set of plans should reflect the nature of the tasks, the needs of organizational members, and the managerial philosophy of the employer to maximize the effectiveness of the reward systems. Since most organizations need all three types of employees' behavior with varying degrees of emphasis, they will probably need a set of diversified pay plans to encourage individual performance and still encourage group effort and institutional loyalty.

SUMMARY AND CONCLUSION

The effectiveness of pay systems as a motivational device increases when the type and amount of pay matches with employee needs (I-N), pay reflects the differences in performance (P-I), and the chance of receiving incentives is challenging but attainable (E-P-I). Depending on its design, a pay plan may or may not successfully elicit all these motivational elements of expectancy theory and thus exert a strong motivational value. For example, a well-designed individual incentive plan can increase the motivatonal value because it is designed to match with employee needs, the incentive magnitude is contingent upon job performance, and the employee earns the incentive reward as a result of effort and energy exertion. On the other hand, a fringe benefit cannot elicit work motivation because, while it may satisfy economic security needs, it fails to elicit the E-I expectancy.

A pay system based on a ratio schedule is more effective in arousing employee motivation than a pay system based on an interval schedule. The use of a ratio schedule is defended by expectancy theory of motivation, because a ratio schedule strengthens the perceived relationship between performance and reward (P-I). However, the utilization of pay systems based on a ratio schedule has been declining over the years due to the difficulty of measuring individual outputs in identifiable performance units. Jobs in a modern industrial world have become so highly interdependent and complex that individual contributions to an organization cannot be measured in production units.

Incentive rewards can be measured and paid to employees on an individual, group, or companywide basis. Individual pay plans are generally effective in arousing individual work motivation and thus can be productively applied to the task situations where job performance primarily depends on individual effort and can be measured individually in quantifiable output units. Group plans can be productively applied to task situations that require a high degree of interaction among group members and where job performance cannot be measured on an individual basis. Companywide plans are utilized to attract and maintain valuable employees, and benefits under these plans are usually related to the long-term performance of the organization. Fringe benefits have little effect on individual motivation and group effort, but are paid to employees to free them from the fear of economic disasters.

The effectiveness of a pay system not only depends on how it is designed but also how it is managed. A well-designed incentive system, from a mechanical standpoint, can easily fail to produce a positive motivation force, if a supervisor or management intentionally or unintentionally distorts the E-I expectancy and/or the P-I tie. For example, when employees increase productivity to maximize their financial gains under an incentive system, management may be tempted to adjust the pay rate or to raise the production standards. If this adjustment is made without the acceptance of employees, it often creates distrust between management and workers. Such distrust can easily be detected under a merit-rate pay plan because, in the absence of objective performance criteria, there is more room to disagree on one's performance between the superior and subordinates. When distrust and suspicion prevail in an organization, no pay plan can function as an incentive system that motivates people to positively respond to it. The importance and creation of a trusting and supportive organizational climate will be the major topics in the next chapter.

8

MOTIVATION THROUGH AFFECTIVE INTERACTION

People in organizations interact with each other to achieve personal as well as organizational goals. They perform organizational activities instrumental to achieving these goals. In the process of interacting within an organization, people develop either favorable or unfavorable sentiments toward one another, influencing the quality of their interactions. Interaction theorists argue that there is a positive relationship between interactions, sentiments, and activities (Homans, 1950; and Whyte, 1959). The more positive the sentiment among organizational members, the higher the rate of their interactions and the more activities they will carry out. The sentiments they hold will affect their reactions to their jobs, co-workers, and the organization. These affective reactions will be manifested in employees' work motivation and their commitment to the work group and organization.

For an individual, the effects of organizational interactions are directly and immediately felt at socialization level. Interactions with other members in an organization satisfy socialization needs for affiliation, belonging, and emotional support. Also, through interactions with others, other personal goals such as gaining recognition, power, and task accomplishment are achieved. An employee has a set of interaction patterns suitable to his own personality and life style. When his interaction patterns are not compatible to the existing organizational structure, work flow, and social climate, he will find it difficult to satisfy his socialization needs and impossible to draw support from others to achieve his goals. The compatibility between the individual and his work environment is important for predicting a person's affective reactions to his work environment, job satisfaction, and performance.

A number of organizational factors influence the quality and quantity of employee interactions, sentiments, and activities. This chapter discusses structural influence, the effect of leadership, and group dynamics on employee interactions and organizational compatibility. The chapter also investigates the behavioral process in which the structural design, leadership, and work group influence the affective reactions of employees which in turn affect employee job satisfaction and performance.

ORGANIZATIONAL DESIGN AND STRUCTURE

Organizational structure influences the frequency and intensity of inter-actions among organizational members. For example, the traditional organizational structure rigidly defines organizational relationships among work group members and between work groups. While such structured relationships increase role clarity for employees, they tend to restrict employee interactions. On the other hand, a flexible form of organization with loosely defined organizational relationships increases the natural flow of employee interactions. However, a flexible organizational structure may cause role ambiguity and conflict for employees creating job-related tension and dissatisfaction. No one design is right for all organizational situations. The selection of a particular design should reflect the requirements of the task, workers, and organizational environment.

DETERMINANTS OF ORGANIZATIONAL DESIGN

A number of organizational theorists suggest that various organizational factors should be taken into account in designing organizational structure (Lichtman and Hunt, 1971; Lorsch, 1970; Perrow, 1970; and Pugh, Hickson, Hinings, and Turner, 1969). Frequently mentioned factors include organization size, degree of task interdependency, degree of goal congruency between individual and organization, and technological environment.

The increase in organization size beyond a certain level seems to demand that the organization be highly structured and centralized (Pugh, et al., 1969). Structure and centralization are needed to manage the increased volume of interactions resulting from the increased number of employees. Porter and Lawler (1965), however, pointed out that although job satisfaction tends to be lower in large organizations, this finding is not conclusive. They argued that the subunit size is a more crucial determinant of employee satisfaction than total organization size. Small subunit size leads to cohesive work group and interpersonal satisfaction.

The degree of task interdependency is an important design factor. Katz and Kahn (1966) listed the organizational conditions under which an organization can be highly structured and centralized. These conditions occur when task interdependency between work groups is high, the tasks do not require creative skills, and identification with organizational goals is not required. When the opposite characteristics prevail, a flexible organizational design can be utilized for organizational effectiveness.

The degree of congruency between individual and organizational goals is another determinant of organizational design. When individual and organizational goals are congruent, a flatter organizational structure with more general supervision can be practiced. A number of human relationists (Argyris, 1964; Herzberg, 1968; Likert, 1961; McGregor, 1960; and Myers, 1970) suggest organizational restructuring away from the mechanical design to provide employees with more opportunities for participation in decisions, face-to-face interactions, and self-control.

Finally, technological environment also influences the type of organizational structure. Burns and Stalker (1961) indicated that a highly structured design can be suitable to an organization operating in a stable technological environment, while a flexible organizational structure may be suitable to an organization in a dynamic and uncertain technological environment. Woodward (1965) also found that flexible organizational structure, decentralized operation, and permissive leadership were successfully used in nonprogrammable batch production firms, while highly structured organizational design was successfully used in mass production firms.

Lawrence and Lorsch (1967) were concerned with the differentiation (division of labor) and integration (coordination) of organizational activities and indicated that the degree of environmental certainty would affect the modes of differentiation and integration. Greater environmental uncertainty and technological complexity would be reflected in greater differentiation of such organizational dimensions as subgroup goals, supervisory style, and structure. Highly differentiated industries then would use formal integrating agencies or integrators who could effectively interact with people in different functional groups. Organizations in a stable environment, on the other hand, would have a lesser degree of differentiation and rely on the bureaucratic mechanical process for integration.

Perrow (1970) was more specific in studying the contingency relationship between technology, task, and organizational structure. For example, when the task is highly programmable and has few exceptions, a formalized and mechanical organizational structure can be effectively applied. But, when the task is unprogrammable and has many exceptions, a more flexible organic organizational structure can be effectively used. Perrow stressed that management must adapt its organizational structure to fit the nature of the task and technological environment. The following discussion examines various organizational contingencies under which a particular form of organizational design can be productively utilized. Three major forms of organizational design—mechanical, linking-pin, and organic—will be considered.

MECHANICAL ORGANIZATIONAL DESIGN

The mechanical or traditional organizational structure consists of a hierarchical arrangement of work modules. Organizational activities are divided into various work modules composed of a limited number of related tasks, each requiring a set of similar skills and learning periods. Since workers are performing a limited number of tasks, they are expected to learn and follow the production methods quickly and to become experts in performing these tasks. These operation methods usually are prescribed by people other than the operators. Work relationships among peers and between hierarchical levels are formalized and controlled by rigid rules and regulations. The primary mode of interpersonal relationships is usually dyadic: management rarely uses the group approach to decision making, especially at lower organizational echelons.

Departmentalization by functional specialization is the most common mode of mechanical organizational design. Division of organizational activities by function and assignment of personnel with similar skills to appropriate functional departments enhances the opportunity for standardization and routinization of organizational activities, and increases the opportunity for managerial controls and accountability. Formal linkages between functional departments are through scalar chains, and departmental conflicts usually are brought to upper levels of management for resolution. While routinized activities are delegated downward, decision making is pushed upward.

Traditional organizational theorists assume that 1) labor is considered to be a production factor like capital, land, and other economic resources; 2) workers, through incompetence and apathy, cannot or do not wish to exercise self-control; 3) workers are too egocentric to care for the welfare of the organization; and 4) democracy is impossible due to the difficulty in accomodating opinions of the massive number of workers employed by large organizations. Under these assumptions, the primary concerns of traditional theorists are to maximize production efficiency through task specialization and specialized labor, and to increase managerial controls by hierarchical arrangements, impersonal rules and regulations, and accountability. Job holders are accountable for discharging duties according to prescribed rules and regulations. Because the manager is held responsible for the actions of his subordinates, the locus of decision making is pushed towards the top of the managerial hierarchy.

Mechanical organizational design seems to be suitable to an organization which essentially performs programmable tasks, has employees with lower-level maintenance needs, and operates in a stable and predictable market environment (Miles, 1975; Dalton and Lawrence, 1971; Van de Ven and Delbecq, 1974). When customer demands are accurately predicted, departmental activities can be easily planned and carried out with high-level coordination. Programmable tasks allow the production department to schedule and produce products to meet the market demand. Since overall organizational activities are predictable and programmable, most managerial decisions can be easily programmed and carried out by rank-and-file workers without going through the rigorous decision process. Only a few decisions may require top management's attention. Further, workers primarily motivated by hygiene factors cannot or may not wish to participate in making decisions.

Mechancial organizational design is widely used and is functional for maintaining stability in managing complex organizations. However, the mechanical approach to organizational design and managerial practice is likely to be less effective and efficient in performing nonprogrammable tasks that require a wide range of organizational resources, in dealing with employees with higher-order needs, and in responding to uncertain and dynamically changing environments.

Production methods that are not programmable and constantly present new problems can be neither precisely prescribed nor standardized, so employee training cannot be specific and simplified. Training needs to be general and should focus on the development of problem-solving capacities. Such tasks require participation of workers in the problem-solving process; all new problems cannot be pushed upward in the organizational echelons for solution. Employee participation is desirable for solving problems encountered in nonprogrammable task situations because workers are closer to and more familiar with the problems than is management. Furthermore, employee participation in the problem-solving process will help to satisfy workers' needs for interaction and control.

Many jobs in the changing world of technology require a high degree of interaction between functional groups and demand timely responses from these groups. For example, the marketing department conducts market feasibility studies, estimates sales volume, and coordinates with the research and development department for product development and with the production department for delivery schedules. Yet, the functional departmentalization tends to direct members' loyalty to their departmental subgoals which often creates interdepartmental conflicts. And conflict resolution between functional groups tends to be time-consuming and costly.

Although the mechanical organizational design is both widely used and effective in maintaining stability, it must be modified to accommodate the changing characteristics of the task, people, and technological environment. Two alternative organizational designs are: linking-pin organizational design to encourage employee participation in managerial process and organic organizational design to facilitate interactions between functional specialities.

LINKING-PIN ORGANIZATIONAL DESIGN

Likert (1967) pictured an effective organization as a set of interlocking groups, with each group linked to the rest of the organization through linking-pin persons who hold memberships in more than one group. Group activities are managed by group members, and their decisions rely heavily on group processes. The linking-pin structure provides the organization with an upward orientation in communication, decision making, and goal attainment.

Decisions made by groups at lower-levels are represented at higher levels of management by supervisors in linking-pin positions. By linking subgroup activities to managerial activities, the organization is able to integrate sub-units' activities into a concerted effort toward achieving organizational goals. The group process in decision making and the upward orientation in communication are unique features of the linking-pin organizational design. Figure 8-1 depicts the linking-pin process of overlapping groups.

The linking-pin organizational model assumes that organizational members have the desire and ability to exercise self-control, have the necessary information and skills to manage their own group activities, and are capable of responding to organizational demands in a responsible manner. It has been argued

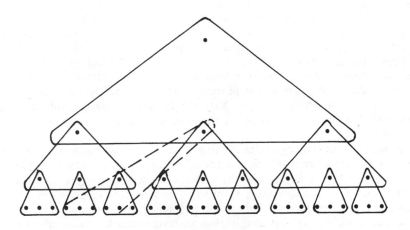

FIGURE 8-1. LINKING-PIN ORGANIZATION
(Adapted from Likert, R., *The Human
Organizations.* New York: McGraw-Hill,
1967, pp. 168-169.)

that a growing number of people in this society have reasonably satisfied their lower-level needs and are now able to strive toward satisfying higher-order needs. Today's workers generally are better trained than their elders. Due partly to the current surge in employee training programs, their abilities to perform demanding jobs and to function in groups have greatly increased. Furthermore, the manager, having participated in the decision-making process with his subordinates at one level and his supervisor and peers at another level, has gained the necessary information and understanding to coordinate and support the activities of his subordinates, superior, and peers and in the process has achieved personal as well as organizational goals.

The concept of linking-pin organization is often criticized for slowing the decision-making process. Although the group approach takes more time to arrive at decisions, employee participation generally results in high quality decisions, better subordinates' acceptance of these decisions, and facilitates the implementing process. Group approach management often improves employee morale and job performance. Thus, the advantages seem to outweigh this particular disadvantage.

Another concern with the linking-pin design centers on the problem of coordinating the functional groups. Although conflicts between lower-level subgroups can be resolved through the interactions of their supervisors, controversial issues tend to be passed upward rather than being resolved at the lower-level points of conflict. Functional subgroupings in a linking-pin organization may foster members' loyalty to their own subgroups, and this subgroup orientation may create the problems of intergroup conflict and lack of coordination. To deal with such problems, Likert (1967) suggested the concept of horizontal linkage to facilitate lateral interaction between functional groups for better communication and coordination. In this lateral arrangement, as shown in Figure 8-1, a manager in one subunit can serve as the leader of a group whose members are drawn from various functional groups to work on a given project. This cross-functional grouping is similar to the committee structure in a traditional organizational design. However, unlike the committee structure which usually is temporary in nature and is seldom vested with power other than advisory, a lateral linking-pin group is usually charged with the responsibility of solving specific problems. This lateral linking-pin process and the supervisory interactions in a high-level group can better facilitate coordination and conflict resolution processes between functional groups than the traditional organizational design. Yet, the linking-pin design still does not eliminate the problem of subgroup-orientation caused by functional departmentalization.

In sum, the linking-pin design is suitable to an organization which essentially performs nonprogrammable, unstructured, enriched jobs requiring joint efforts of group members, employs workers with the desire and ability to exercise self-control and the necessary skills to manage their own group activities, and operates in a complex but relatively stable technological and market environment. It will be less effective in dealing with organizational tasks that require a higher degree of interaction between functional specialities and demand timely responses from these groups to cope with drastic changes in the environment. A more flexible and dynamic organizational design is needed to cope with such an environmental demand.

ORGANIC ORGANIZATIONAL DESIGN

The need for adaptability to change calls for flexibility in organizational design. Organic organizational design introduces flexibility to make the organization adaptable to changes in internal as well as external environments. This form of organizational design is widely practiced in highly technological industires such as aerospace, computers, and electronics because they require a high degree of interaction as well as timely responses from various functional specialties. It is also becoming widely used in other business, military, and governmental organizations that want to meet the demand for flexibility and adaptability. The most salient characteristic of organic organizational design is the cross-functional grouping which exists on horizontal, vertical, and diagonal levels. In this arrangement, members of a number of functional specialities are pulled together to work on a specific project or problem for a finite time period.

There are several variations of organic organizational design. One is the project organization composed of members from several functional departments. This provides the project manager with line authority, and its members work for the project manager independent of their functional affiliations (Cleland and King, 1968; Galbraith, 1973). Since they are part of the project group rather than members of functional groups, they will be more loyal to the project and its manager than to the functional groups and their managers. Figure 8-2 presents a typical form of project organization which coexists with a traditional form of organization.

The major advantages of a project organization are that it 1) facilitates interactions between functional specialties usually on a face-to-face basis, 2) fosters a common goal of completing the project and at the same time minimizes functional group conflicts, 3) provides workers with enriching job ex-

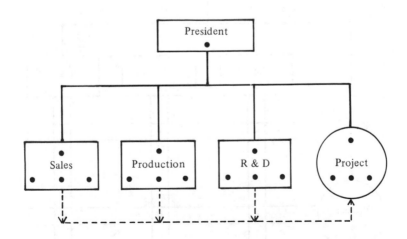

FIGURE 8-2. PROJECT ORGANIZATION

periences through participation in project management, and 4) is capable of responding to internal and external changes quicker than the traditional and linking-pin organizational designs. Some major disadvantages are that it duplicates efforts and facilities of functional specialties among the projects, creates complexity and instability in defining organizational relationships, and tends to create feelings of insecurity and instability among project members in their relationships with others due to the lack of permanency in project employment.

Matrix organizational structure is often suggested to overcome some of the disadvantages of project organization. Instead of separating project groups from the functional structure, a matrix organization superimposes a project structure on the functional structure (Cleland and King, 1968; Galbraith, 1973). Figure 8-3 presents a matrix organization in which persons often hold memberships in both functional and project groups. Authority and responsibility relationships in a matrix organization flow both vertically and horizontally throughout the organization. The functional managers have line authority over functional group members and perform personnel functions such as assignment, promotion, and salary adjustment, while the project managers have authority over their project members in carrying out their project activities. The functional managers are responsible for supporting the activities of both functional supervisors and project managers. The project managers have responsibility to secure necessary assistance from functional groups to carry out project activities.

The authority and responsibility relationships frequently violate traditional organizational relationships. For example, having dual membership violates the unity of command principle. The principle of unity of command indicates that

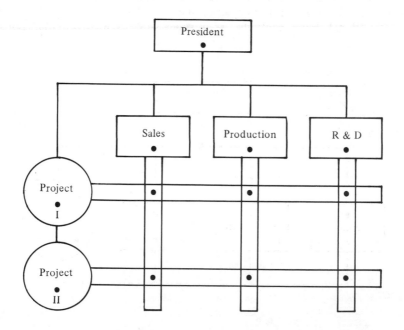

FIGURE 8-3. MATRIX ORGANIZATION

a subordinate should receive orders from one boss. Lateral interactions may violate the scalar principle. The scalar principle refers to following the line of authority for formal communication and coordination between individuals and groups and to allowing direct but informal interactions between them. The project or matrix organization allows direct, formal, and informal interactions between group members. Further, the traditional superior-subordinate relationship becomes more of peer-to-peer relationship in matrix organizations.

The complexity in organizational relationships often creates conflict and confusion between functional and project groups. However, this disadvantage can be outweighed by several advantages of a matrix structure. First, project members can have close ties with functional groups, so they can easily readjust to functional groups upon returning. Second, project group members can serve as coordinators between project and functional groups. Finally, the matrix organization is more flexible in utilizing manpower resources because both functional and project groups can share manpower. For example, an employee can spend a part of his time on a project and the remainder on functional group activities.

Another variation of the organic organizational design is the organization which loosely describes individual roles and their organizational relationships (Bennis, 1966, pp. 113-119; and Luthans, 1973, pp. 178-179). Basically, it has a pool of personnel that can be flexibly assigned to various tasks to meet particular demands of the organization at a particular time. The major characteristics of this free-form are that *(a)* its organizational units are highly result-oriented and are managed by group members; *(b)* organizational members maintain a high degree of interdependency, mutual trust and support; *(c)* its members often hold multigroup memberships and mutually share authority and responsibility; and *(d)* conflicts and problems are resolved through bargaining process and persuasive influence rather than supervisory arbitration. This form of organization can be found in professional groups such as university faculty, scientists in research departments, law firm partners, and engineers. They usually enjoy relatively equal status and have a loosely defined set of objectives.

Another free-form organization is the office landscaping approach to organizational design. Functional and project groups are organized on the basis of the need for interactions through functional or project ties. These groups are separated by an array of movable flower pots, planters, or other partitions in a huge office (Duffy, 1969). There are no permanent walls between groups; the office can be rearranged whenever changes are needed in interactional patterns within and among functional and/or project groups. The physical proximity is determined by the degree of interactions needed between groups. An example of office landscaping is shown in Figure 8-4. In this figure, project groups can move around the functional groups based on the need for interactions with them at different times.

Organic organizational designs are primarily suitable for organizations or organizational units that perform organizational tasks requiring a high degree of interaction between functional group members; deal with organizational members who have desire and capacity to exercise self-control; and operate in a dynamic, complex, and uncertain technological environment. In summary, organic organizational structures are utilized to meet the need for a high degree of interaction between functional groups and the need for adaptability to changes in a changing world of technology. Since these designs introduce

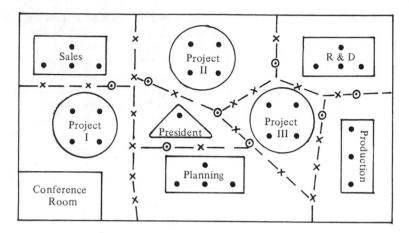

FIGURE 8-4. OFFICE LANDSCAPING ORGANIZATION

complexity and confusion in defining and structuring organizational relationships, they are not particularly suitable to an organization operating in a stable environment. The criteria for determining the merit and demerit of a particular organizational design are whether it facilitates interactions among organizational members and between functional group members whose activities are timely coordinated; instigates such organizational climate factors as autonomy, openness, supportiveness, and flexibility; and/or is compatible to the characteristics of the task, people, and other organizational realities.

LEADERSHIP PROCESS AND MOTIVATION

Leadership process has a significant influence on employee motivation because it controls not only the means of satisfying such maintenance needs as pay, job security, and socialization of employees but also the conditions for releasing such motivational needs as self-respect, achievement, and self-actualization. In addition to controlling the distribution of intrinsic as well as extrinsic rewards, the supervisory process influences employees' perceptions on the instrumental relationships between their effort and task performance (E-P) and between task performance and receiving incentive reward (P-I). A supportive and instrumental leader can enhance employees' perceptions on the E-P relationship by helping them to increase their capacity to deal with their organizational tasks. Also, the supervisor can enhance employees' P-I expectancy by tying incentive reward to performance. However, no particular leadership process is right for all employees and situations. The following reviews different leadership processes and attempts to specify organizational contingencies under which a particular leadership process can be effectively utilized.

TRAIT THEORY OF LEADERSHIP

For centuries writers have been interested in finding a set of predictable relationships between leaders' behavior and their subordinates' performance. An earlier attempt identified a finite number of personal traits of acknowledged leaders. An assumption underlying this approach was that acknowledged leaders tended to possess certain personality traits which could be used to identify and differentiate potentially successful and unsuccessful leaders. Trait researchers studied such personal characteristics as intelligence and emotional and physical makeups of leaders. For example, Stogdill (1948) reviewed twelve studies on personal traits and concluded that leadership ability was correlated with verbal facility, judgment, and intelligence, and that leaders tended to be taller than followers. Ghiselli (1963) found that managers with an intermediate level of intelligence tended to be more effective leaders than those with low or high levels of intelligence. Individuals with superior intelligence and conceptual ability might not find managerial jobs to be intellectually challenging. While there is agreement that personal traits are important factors for studying leadership behavior, there is little agreement among researchers regarding what constitutes effective leadership traits. The problem of the trait approach is that it ignores the differences in subordinates' traits and job-related situations. The trait approach overlooked the influence of followers and task situations in determining the effectiveness of leadership behavior.

BEHAVIORAL THEORY OF LEADERSHIP

A number of leadership researchers began to challenge the trait theory and turned their attention to behavioral theory of leadership. For example, Lewin, Lippitt, and White (1939) identified three types of leadership styles—authoritarian, democratic, and laissez-faire—and studied their influences on social climates in an organization. Early studies at the University of Michigan (Katz, Maccoby, and Morse, 1950; Katz, Maccoby, Gurin, and Floor, 1951) and at Ohio State University (Hemphill, 1949; Fleishman, Harris, and Burtt, 1955; and Stogdill and Coons, 1957) generally suggested that there are two types of leadership style—employee-oriented and production-oriented. Employee-oriented leadership is also called "employee-centered," "consideration," or "general supervision." Production-oriented leadership is also called "boss-centered," "initiating structure," or "close supervision."

Michigan studies generally indicated that supervisors with good production records appeared to rely on the employee-centered leadership style, while supervisors with low-producing records were more production-oriented. Employee-centered leadership was associated with higher job satisfaction and morale, whereas production-centered leadership was associated with low job satisfaction and poor morale. Similar studies conducted at Ohio State University found that increasing consideration was highly correlated with a lower grievance rate; a high degree of initiating structure was associated with a higher grievance rate. Later, Fleishman and Harris (1962) found that the grievance rate was lowest when both consideration and structure were high; when low consideration was coupled with low structure, the grievance rate was high. However, Ohio studies in general indicated that high structure and low consideration were closely related to high absenteeism, grievances, and turnover.

The relationship between production-orientation and people-orientation was initially considered to be a continuum existing on a unidimensional level. Some theorists felt that a leader should use one leadership style to be effective. For example, most traditional management theorists argued that an effective manager plans, organizes, directs, and controls his subordinates' activities toward the attainment of organizational goals (Fayol, 1916; Davis, 1951; Gulick, 1937; Urwick, 1943; and Koontz and O'Donnell, 1955). Human relationists, on the other hand, generally argued that a people-oriented leadership was more effective in arousing employee motivation and performance (Mayo, 1945; Roethlishberger and Dickson, 1939; Likert, 1961; and most early studies at the University of Michiagn). According to Likert, an employee-centered leader focuses his efforts on the human aspects of his subordinates' problems and on establishing a work group with high performance goals. Consequently, a supportive employee-centered leader develops a productive work group.

Contrary to this unidimensional view, most researchers view that the two leadership styles are relatively independent; a leader can be high or low on both production and people dimensions. Leadership researchers at Ohio State generally view leadership behavior in two-dimensional scales—structure and consideration. Their general positions seem to be that employee satisfaction and productivity increase when a supervisor uses a leadership style high on both consideration and structure, and that low consideration and high structure are associated with high absenteeism, grievances, turnover, and low productivity. Blake and Mouton (1964) also plotted leadership behavior on a two-dimensional graph. They argued that an effective leader employs a leadership style high on both production and people concerns.

Despite considerable efforts made by behavioral theorists to find a set of leadership principles, many studies have failed to find a consistent relationship between leadership style and performance (see Korman, 1966; and Fleishman, 1973). Fleishman, Harris, and Burtt (1955) found that in production departments there was a positive relationship between initiating structure (production-oriented leadership) and employee proficiency, but a negative relationship between employee proficiency and consideration. However, the relationships were reversed in staff departments. In their study, the differences in tasks moderated the relationship between a leadership style and its effectiveness. Graen, Dansereau, and Minami (1972) found that the leader's task-oriented behavior (initiating structure) greatly influenced the relationship between his employee-centered behavior (consideration) and the performance of his subordinates. The more consistent the leader was in performing his task-oriented role, the more accurately his subordinates could perceive the leader's behavior in performing his employee-centered role. The subordinates' perceptions of the leader's behavior then moderated the effectiveness of a leadership style.

The work of Woodward (1965) and Lawrence and Lorsch (1967), as reported earlier, indicated that the nature of technological environment not only influences the type of organizational design but also the type of leadership style. For example, Woodward found that closer supervision was exercised in continuous process production such as chemical and refinery processes than in mass production and unit production. Lawrence and Lorsch pointed out that supervisory style must vary with such situational factors as task, people, and technological environment to effectively manage the process of differentiation and integration of organizational activities.

CONTENGENCY THEORY OF LEADERSHIP

As it became evident that behavioral theories of leadership were not adequate to predict leadership effectiveness, situational or contingency theories of leadership have emerged to account for such situational variables as task, people, and organizational structure moderating the relationship between leadership style and its effectiveness. The major theme of situational theory of leadership is that no leadership style is absolutely right for all situations. The selection of a proper leadership style depends on the characteristics of the leader himself, the traits of his subordinates, and the specific requirements imposed by the task situation (Tannenbaum and Schmidt, 1958). An effective leader is capable of adapting his style to suit the task situation and the traits of his subordinates.

According to Fiedler (1967), the effectiveness of leadership depends on the favorableness of superior-subordinate relations, the position power of the supervisor, and the degree of task structure. He distinguishes between people-oriented and task-oriented leaders. According to this theory, task-oriented leadership is more effective when the superior-subordinate relations are favorable, the task is highly structured, and the supervisor has a relatively strong position power. It is also effective when the superior-subordinate relations are poor, the task is unstructured, and the position power is relatively weak. The people-oriented leadership is more effective when the superior-subordinate relations are neither favorable or unfavorable, the task is moderately structured, and the supervisor has a moderate position power.

The main thrust of the situational or contingency approach to leadership is that, instead of suggesting a particular leadership style for all situations, it forces the supervisor to search for a proper leadership style best suited to a given situation. To be effective, a leader should have an accurate perception of his own style and situational variables before he chooses a particular style or situation. The situational theory specifies contingencies under which a particular style can be most effective. It has practical implications for placing supervisors whose leadership styles are compatible to various situational variables or for changing one or two situational variables to be compatible with others. However, a major problem with the situational approach is that it does not clearly explain how and why one particular leadership style is more effective than the other. It fails to explain how a leadership style influences employee motivation and job performance.

PATH-GOAL THEORY OF LEADERSHIP

A newly emerging theory, referred to as path-goal theory of leadership, explains why and how leadership style influences employee motivation. According to this theory, a leader influences work motivation by affecting his subordinates' perceptions of their task goals, personal goals, and the paths to their goal attainment. Path-goal theory has its root in expectancy theory of motivation. For example, House (1971) and House and Mitchell (1974) postulate that a leader can influence employee motivation by making rewards available to satisfy employees' immediate or future needs (I-N), making these rewards contingent upon their task accomplishments (P-I), and helping employees to accomplish their assigned tasks (E-P). The acceptance of a leader by his subordinates increases to the extent that the subordinates see the leader as a source of their need satisfaction. Thus, the subordinate's motivation to work depends on the leader's ability to manipulate the valence of rewards, the instrumentality of receiving rewards, and the expectancy of getting the job done.

House and Mitchell (1974) integrated behavioral and situational theories within the framework of path-goal theory. They have attempted to study the effects of four leadership styles (directive, supportive, achievement-oriented, and participative) and two classes of situational variables (subordinate characteristics and work environmental factors) on employee perceptions regarding job satisfaction, acceptance of leader, and the E-P and P-I relationships. Subordinates' characteristics include authoritarian orientation, perceived ability, and locus of control. Locus of control refers to a belief that a person has control over the outcomes of his behavior. If one feels the outcomes to be under his control, the locus of control is said to be internal. If the outcomes are perceived to be controlled by other than himself, the locus of control is said to be external. Environmental factors include the task, work group, and managerial systems. The four major leadership styles will be reviewed in conjunction with these situational variables.

Directive Leadership

Directive leadership is similar to initiating structure that specifies employees' roles and path-goal relationships. This has a positive relationship with satisfaction and expectancies of subordinates who are engaged in ambiguous and non-programmable tasks, but it has a negative correlation with those who are engaged in well-defined tasks (House, 1971; House and Dessler, 1974). When the tasks, organizational procedures, and work methods are not clearly defined, a supervisor with a directive leadership style can clarify the path-goal relationships by providing his subordinates with the necessary information and guidance and by structuring their job-related factors. However, when the path-goal and work-related factors are clear to them, directive leadership is seen as a hinderance.

However, other studies do not support the above findings. For example, Stinson and Johnson (1975) reported that the relationship between initiating structure and satisfaction was more positive under conditions of high task structure than low task structure. Downey, Sheridan, and Slocum (1975) also reported that the supervisor's consideration was significantly related to the subordinates' work attitudes, job satisfaction, and affective motivational paths in both structured and unstructured task situations. These two studies do not support the path-goal prediction that the more unstructured the task, the more positive the relationship between initiating structure and job satisfaction.

Probably, the characteristics of subordinates moderate the relationship between initiating structure and job satisfaction. Subordinates who are high on authoritarianism may expect their supervisors to provide them with role and path-goal clarifications. Initiating structure by their supervisors may be considered as a source of help rather than a punitive element. Dessler (1973) pointed out that authoritarian workers performing routinized and repetitive tasks at the lower level of a manufacturing firm preferred a directive leadership, while non-authoritarian subordinates preferred a nondirective leadership. Sweney, Fiechtner, and Samoris (1975) also reported that a directive leadership (authoritarian) tended to meet the dependency needs of authoritarian subordinates (ingratiators). Ingratiators expect their supervisors to be directive.

It is also possible that both task ambiguity and subordinate authoritarianism simultaneously operate to reinforce the desirability of directive leadership. A literature review by House and Mitchell (1974) found that there is an interaction between subordinate authoritarianism and task ambiguity in manufacturing firms. Directive leadership not only meets the dependency needs of authoritarian subordinates but also is considered instrumental for clarifying role perceptions and path-goal relationships. Kerr, Schriesheim, Murphy, and Stogdill (1974) pointed out similar contingency factors. They reported that leader initiating structure has a positive influence on employee motivation when 1) the task is nonroutinized and satisfying, 2) performance pressure is created by sources other than the leader, 3) the subordinates are dependent on the leader for information and direction, 4) the subordinates are psychologically dispositioned toward the supervisory directiveness, and 5) they favorably perceive the demand for their services.

Unlike leader consideration or supportive leadership which tends to have a positive relationship with satisfaction and performance of subordinates, leader initiating structure or directive leadership has a confusing relationship, ranging from positive to negative, with employee job satisfaction and performance (see Schriesheim, House, and Kerr, 1976). It appears that the relationships between initiating structure and employee behavior are moderated by more contingency variables than are the relationships between leader consideration and behavior. However, in general, it can be said that directive leadership tends to be effective when the subordinates perceive supervisory directiveness to be instrumental for their task accomplishments.

Supportive Leadership

Supportive leadership is characterized by a considerate and friendly leader who shows concern for the well-being and needs of subordinates. Supportive leaders seek to gain acceptance from their subordinates by treating them with respect and dignity rather than through the use of formal authority. Supportive leadership is said to be effective in arousing employee motivation and job performance because it satisfies employees' needs for affiliation and belonging, and it leads to close cooperation between the supervisor and his subordinates for their productive activites. A number of studies reported that supportive leadership is highly correlated with positive attitudes, satisfaction, and in some cases job performance of subordinates (Katz, Maccoby, and Morse, 1950; Indik, Seashore, and Georgooulos, 1960; Korman, 1966; Likert, 1961; and Downey, Sheridan, and Slocum, 1975).

However, House and Dessler (1974) and House and Mitchell (1974) found no clear relationship between supportive-considerate leadership and employee attitudes and/or performance. Their reviews nevertheless indicate that supportive leadership is highly correlated with employee satisfaction under conditions of high task structure but not under low task structure. When tasks are highly structured, an effective leader provides his subordinates with consideration and support to reduce the frustration resulting from performing routinized tasks with little intrinsic motivation. When tasks are intrinsically motivating, employee job satisfaction is less likely related to supportive leadership. Results obtained by Dessler (1973), House and Dessler (1974), and Stinson and Johnson (1975) supported this view.

Path-goal theorists generally predict that supportive leadership will have its most positive effect on subordinate satisfaction with those who work on frustrating, stressful, or dissatisfying tasks. These workers will perceive supportive leaders as the major source of their need satisfaction. Although supportive leadership may not be as effective as under conditions of high task structure, it has a positive influence on subordinates' job attitudes and perceived motivation even under low task structure (Downey et al., 1975). This may be because leader consideration positively influences the subordinates' expectancy that they can better their performance under a supportive leader than under a directive leader.

Participative Leadership

Participative leaders share information and power with their subordinates in both decision-making and action processes. Mitchell (1973) identified at least four ways a participative leadership could have a positive impact on employee motivation as predicted by expectancy theory. First, it increases the clarity of path-goal relationships (E-P and P-I) Second, employees have a better chance of selecting organizational goals they highly value and thus tend to internalize these as their own goals. Third, the participative leader allows the work group to exercise social controls over its members. Finally, as employees internalize organizational goals, subordinates tend to exercise self-control for managing their own activities rather than relying on supervisory control. A number of studies supported the positive impact of participation on employee motivation (Coch and French, 1948; Likert, 1967; Maier, 1963; Myers, 1970; and Vroom, 1960).

However, the relationship between participative leadership and employee behavior is highly ambiguous and seems to be moderated by both the characterist of subordinates and the situational factors. For example, Vroom (1960) reported that workers with little need for independence and achievement generally did not positively respond to participative leadership. Runyon (1973) and House and Mitchell (1974) indicated that people who believe that what happens to them occurs because of luck or chance (external locus of control) do not positively respond to a participative leadership style. Those who believe that what happens to them occurs because of their effort (internal locus of control) tend to be more satisfied with participative leadership style. The amount of knowledge possessed by subordinates (Swinth, 1971) and the level of their intelligence (Calvin, Hoffman, and Hardin, 1957) seem to moderate the effectiveness of participative leadership. Subordinates with high intelligence and the necessary information relevant to the decision issues can contribute more to the participative decision processes than those without such qualities.

Regarding the moderating effects of task situation, House and Mitchell (1974) indicated that participative leadership is positively related to job satisfaction of employees performing ego-involving and nonprogrammable tasks. When employees are ego-involved in their jobs, they are more likely to have an influence in the decisions that affect them. When the tasks and organizational procedures are not well defined, participation by capable individuals serves as an effective means of clarifying path-goal relationships. The supervisor allows participants to define the path-goal relationships for themselves.

When tasks and subordinate characteristics are jointly considered, it can be generalized that workers with strong needs for independence and achievement will be satisfied with a participative leadership style especially when performing ego-involving and ambiguous tasks. However, when workers are performing repetitive tasks which are less ego-involving, the amount of subordinates' authoritarianism tends to moderate the relationship between leadership style and satisfaction. Subordinates with low authoritarianism tend to prefer a participative leadership style.

Achievement-oriented Leadership

An achievement-oriented leader sets challenging goals and expects his subordinates to achieve them. House and Mitchell (1974) hypothesized that achievement-oriented leadership would cause subordinates to strive for higher standards of performance and to have more confidence in the ability to meet challenging goals. Their study reported a positive relationship between the amount of achievement orientation of the leaders and the subordinates' expectancy that their effort would result in effective performance. More specifically, for subordinates performing ambiguous, nonrepetitive, and ego-involving tasks, the higher the achievement orientation of the leader, the more confidence subordinates exhibited that their efforts would pay off in effective performance. For subordinates performing well-defined and repetitive tasks, there was no significant correlation between achievement-oriented leadership and subordinate expectancies that their efforts would lead to effective performance. Litwin and Stringer (1968) reported that achievement-oriented leaders aroused an achievement-oriented climate in an organization.

Stringer (1966) advocated that managers can arouse achievement motivation of employees by using an achievement-oriented leadership style. Their job is to create an organizational climate in which achievement-oriented behavior is encouraged and rewarded. The strategy for arousing achievement motivation involves establishing the following managerial processes. First, task goals and performance standards have to be explicit so employees can compete against these goals and standards of excellence. Second, task goals and performance standards have to represent a moderate degree of risk or difficulty. Goals too difficult or too easy to achieve do not arouse achievement motivation. Third, when there is a change in the expectancy of goal-attainment, performance standards have to be changed to make them moderately difficult to achieve. Fourth, performance feedbacks have to be immediate and based on the progress that employees are making toward their goals. Fifth, organizational rewards should be related to performance. Sixth, the goal-oriented managerial system should be made, if possible, on an individual basis because the individual can better see the instrumental relationship between his effort and task accomplishment. Finally, supportive leadership enhances the chance for arousing achievement motivation because it reduces task-related anxiety and improves the expectancy that effort can result in effective performance. Once aroused, achievement-oriented behavior becomes self-motivating. Thus, the supervisor does not need to exercise close supervision on employees.

In summary, a supervisor has a significant influence on employee work motivation because he usually has some control over the distribution of incentive rewards. He controls such intrinsic job factors as participation, autonomy, and feedback, and has the power to give or withhold such extrinsic rewards as pay increase, promotion, and interpersonal reinforcement or punishment. Supervisory behavior is directly and indirectly related to both employee satisfaction and performance. The relationship between leadership style and satisfaction is generally positive when supportive leadership is utilized regardless of task and subordinate characteristics (Stogdill, 1974; Downey et al., 1975; and Weed et al., 1976). When several leadership styles are jointly used, a leader high in both initiating structure and consideration is liked best. The leader high in consideration but low in initiating structure is liked next best, and the leader high in initiating structure but low in consideration is liked least (Fleisheim and Hunt, 1973; and Weed et al., 1976).

The relationship between leadership style and job performance is not that clear. A leader who is considerate may be liked best but not necessarily be effective in stimulating employee performance unless his leadership style matches with subordinate personality and task type. Generally, a leader high in initiating structure gets better performance from authoritarian subordinates than from nonauthoritarian subordinates. But, when several contingency factors are interacted, leaders with high consideration and initiating structure get better performance results from nonauthoritarian subordinates performing ambiguous and difficult tasks than leaders with high initiating structure and low consideration from similar subordinates and task situations. Leaders with low structure and high consideration are least effective in dealing with authoritarian subordinates (Weed et al., 1976).

GROUP PROCESS AND MOTIVATION

The influence of a work group on employee behavior has been recognized by many behavioral scientists. The Hawthorne experiments conducted by Mayo and his associates in the late 1920s and early 1930s contributed to our awareness of group influence on employee motivation. Two major conclusions on the importance of the work group process can be drawn from the experiments. First, group productivity is more strongly affected by group norms than by financial incentives or physical working conditions. Second, supervisory behavior has an important impact on work group behavior (Mayo, 1945; Roethlisberger and Dickson, 1939). Barnard (1938) recognized the importance of informal groups in a formal organization. He emphasized that the informal group serves to aid communication, maintain group cohesiveness, and strengthen individual integrity, self-respect, and independence. Lewin's research in group dynamics (1947) continues to have an important impact on organizational behavior and management thought, group process is treated as a basic unit of organizational analysis. Sociometric techniques for studying interpersonal relations and group behavior facilitated the research of group influence on employee behavior. Work groups influence employee behavior—satisfaction and performance—because they not only satisfy employees' needs for affiliation and companionship but also control the means of achieving personal and organizational goals through social influences. Several group processes that influence group behavior will be discussed in the following sections.

GROUP NORMS AND COHESIVENESS

Group norms are behavioral guidelines existing in the group. By accepting these norms, members give the group power to regulate their behavior. The Hawthrone experiments (Roethlisberger and Dickson, 1939) provided some

insights into the impact that a group can have on employee motivation and productivity. In the relay-assembly test room, a work group developed a promanage-
ment norm that was supportive of high productivity. In this group, employee
motivation and productivity were high because productive behavior was rewarded by both the group and management. However, in the bank-wiring observation room, the work group developed an antimanagement norm that was
not supportive of high productivity. When an employee broke the group norms
and produced high performance, he was reprimanded by the group.

Asch (1952) demonstrated how simple it is for people to conform to group
norms. In his experiment, the subjects were to match a line in a card with one
of three lines shown in another card. The task was so simple and obvious that
most subjects in the control group matched the two lines without mistakes.
The subjects in the experimental group did not know that some group members
were instructed to give incorrect answers. The uninformed subjects, when faced
with unanimous choices by the other members, often gave the same incorrect
answers. Some of these subjects did not conform to the group norm; nevertheless, the degree of conformity was quite high. Milgram (1964) also found that
under social pressure, the uninformed subjects administered more physical pain
to other subjects than they would have on their own initiative.

Why then are people willing to conform to and comply with group norms?
First, people join groups because of their needs for affiliation, companionship, and emotional support. Furthermore, the group can assist an individual
in achieving his personal as well as group objectives. Like leadership, the work
group performs task-oriented functions and maintenance-oriented functions.
It not only facilitates interaction among members in carrying out group tasks,
but also undertakes activities that build group loyalty and at the same time
satisfies members' needs. Thus, the more the individual values the outcome of
group interaction, the more he is willing to conform to the group norms. Non-
conformity and noncompliance may cause withdrawal of these social outcomes.
On the other hand, people who do not value the outcome of group interaction
are less likely to conform to the group norms. For example, Whyte (1955)
found that employees who did not value the group outcomes, despite the group
pressure to restrict their productivity, produced a high quantity of products and
were rewarded by management. The differences in individual personality, sex,
and education also seem to moderate the group influence on employee behavior.
Steiner and Johnson (1963) reported that authoritarian employees are more
conforming than nonauthoritarians. When authoritarianism was combined with
need for social approval, the subjects were more likely to agree with expressed
opinions of their peers. Females and males with less intellectual ability showed
more conformity (DiVesta and Cox, 1960). College graduates conformed less
than those with less education (Milgram, 1964).

The group's power to influence its members' behavior increases as the internal
solidarity and psychological bond felt by its members increase. Group cohesiveness and conformity to norms are mutually reinforcing factors. The more cohesive the work group, the greater the likelihood that its members have similar
attitudes, values, and group norms. Also, the more cohesive the work group,
the greater the influence it can have on its members' behavior. Since group
norms in a cohesive work group are highly valued by its members, the acceptance or rejection by this group will be an important outcome for these members than noncohesive groups.

The degree of group cohesiveness affects the degree to which a work group can either help or harm the formal organization. When a cohesive work group develops group norms compatible to the organizational goals, the work group can be highly effective in achieving these goals. However, if the cohesive work group has a low work motivation, it can be associated with low productivity. Stogdill (1972) found that group cohesiveness is positively related to productivity under high work group motivation and negatively related to productivity under low group motivation routinized task situations. Likert (1967) indicated that through participative and supportive leadership, work groups can develop group norms compatible to organizational goals. Lawler and Cammann (1972) also favored democratic rather than autocratic leadership for developing cohesive work groups.

Cohesive work groups can be effectively utilized in organizations in several ways. First, when group norms are compatible to organizational goals, its members may internalize the organizational goals as their group goals. Internalized goals tend to intrinsically motivate people to achieve them. Second, when the task requires a high degree of interaction among group members, a cohesive work group can facilitate the needed interactions and thus carry out more group activities. Third, management can rely on the group for managing the group activities. Social controls of a cohesive work group are more powerful in influencing its members' behavior than management's formal controls, because the former have more direct and immediate impact on employee behavior. Finally, social controls minimize the need for close supervision. Supervisory personnel can utilize their time and energy for more valuable activities such as planning and problem-solving.

There are a number of factors that affect group cohesiveness. First, the more successful the group is in achieving its goals, the more likely it will become cohesive (Sherif and Sherif, 1953). Unsuccessful groups tend to be less cohesive, but not always. Second, the existence of superordinate goals such as a common enemy, external pressure, and common goals, tends to solidify group members. Thus, a losing athletic team can solidify its members by setting the winning of a game as a superordinate goal for the team. Third, the higher the status of a group, the more likely it will become cohesive. Higher-status groups tend to better satisfy the need for self-esteem. Fourth, people with similar attitudes, values, and behavioral patterns tend to stick together because they mutually reinforce each other's needs. In addition, the size of a group, its isolation from others, and its leadership have some influence on group cohesiveness. A supervisor can manipulate these factors to develop a cohesive work group.

GROUP SIZE AND EMPLOYEE BEHAVIOR

A review of literature reveals that group size has a significant effect on the interactions of group members, conformity and consensus, group participation, employee satisfaction, and job performance. Graicunas (1937) indicated that as the group size increases linearly, the number of possible interactions among group members increases geometrically. The increased number of possible interactions usually means fewer personal contacts with other members in the group. Hare (1952) explored the way in which groups of five and twelve affect the nature of interaction and consensus. He found that as the group size increased from five to twelve members, the amount of consensus decreased, and there was a tendency for subgrouping into two and three factions within the group of twelve members. Hare (1962) indicated that as group size increases, the quality and quantity of member participation in group discussions decrease. Increased group size tends to reduce employee participation and minimize the opportunity for sensitive exploration of other members' viewpoints (Hare, 1962; Delbecq, 1968).

However, there seems to be a lower limit of group size, below which opportunities for interaction and participation decline. Groups with two to three members tended to inhibit expression of disagreement and dissatisfaction, and the members of the small groups were more passive and restrained in their interactions. Bales and Borgatta (1952) in their comparisons of the interactions within groups ranging from two to six members found that six-member groups showed high solidarity and tension release. Slater (1958) reported that the optimum group size, in terms of member satisfaction, was five. Hackman and Vidmar (1970) reported a similar finding concerning the advantages of having a medium size group of four to five members for generating member satisfaction. Both smaller and larger groups were less effective in generating member satisfaction. These authors speculate that members in smaller groups feel uncomfortable because of their high personal visibility, and members in larger groups feel unhappy because of the problems of communication and coordination.

The relationship between group size and performance is not clear. While a few studies (Marriott, 1949; Hare, 1952) reported an inverse relationship between individual productivity and group size, other studies (Gibb, 1951; Watson, 1928) reported a positive relationship. Ziller (1957) and Cummings, Huber, and Arendt (1974) found the quality of group decisions improved with the increase of group size. A possible explanation may be that larger groups offer greater resources for problem solving and decisions, and may benefit from labor specialization. Also, performance advantages can be accrued with larger groups at the expense of decreased member satisfaction and increased time and difficulty in reaching a consensus among members.

A literature review by Thomas and Fink (1963) indicated that quality and quantity of performance were positively related to group size but only under specified conditions where mechanisms for communication and coordination were readily available or where such mechanisms could be developed. When the task involves less ambiguous problem-solving and participants are provided with clear decision-making procedures, a large group may contain individuals who can contribute to group problem-solving. However, when the task involves highly complex and ambiguous problem-solving, and decision processes are not clearly defined, a small group with professionally competent members may function more effectively. In addition, it is generally concluded that if the quality of the group decision is of considerable importance, a large group with seven to twelve is desirable because many inputs are available to group decision. If reaching a consensus is of primary importance, a small group with three to five will facilitate the decision process. The type of group decision process also affects the effectiveness of a group and will be discussed in the following section.

GROUP DECISION PROCESS

The effectiveness of a group problem-solving approach has been a major concern for many researchers for numerous years (Bunker and Dalton, 1976;

Barnlund, 1958; Levine, 1973; Lowin, 1968; Delbecq, Van de Ven, and Gustafson, 1975; Green, 1975; Schoner and Rose, 1974; Wood, 1972; and Wood,
1973). A review of their studies leads to a conclusion that the effectiveness of
a group decision process depends on the nature of the task, people, organizational level, and group process. In studying the comparative effectiveness of
group versus individual approach to problem-solving, several researchers indicate
that a group approach appears to be superior to an individual approach when the
tasks involve pooling additive bits of information, require a high degree of interaction among experts, and are interdependent for effective performance. The
individual approach seems to be superior to the group approach when the
tasks require a division of labor in which the performances of members are
linked in series, are performed individually, and involve individualistic thinking
processes.

The amount of participation by members in decision processes increases as
the decision-making level increases (Hellriegel and Slocum, 1976, pp. 181-182).
At the lower levels of an organization, supervisors make decisions or take upper-
level decisions and announce them. Group decision implies that the group members have some degree of autonomy and responsibility for their actions. Furthermore, the quality of inputs made by participants may increase as the decision
group involves higher-level personnel. This will be more so in an organization
where the information flow is centralized. A group approach will be less likely
utilized at the lower-levels of a hierarchically-oriented organization where decisions are rarely made at these levels.

Van de Ven (1974)and Delbecq, Van de Ven, and Gustafson (1975) indicated
that the proper use of interacting and nominal group techniques increases the
effectiveness of group decision processes. An interacting group technique refers
to an unstructured group discussion for obtaining and pooling ideas of interacting group members and the process of majority voting for decisions. An
interacting group process can be effectively used for synthesizing ideas, evaluating the generated ideas, and reaching group decisions. A nominal group technique refers to the process of soliciting ideas from noninteracting group members. An underlying assumption of this approach is that noninteracting group
members may have valuable ideas relevant to the problems but do not express
them. A round-robin approach is used to force these group members to express
their ideas, usually in writing. Then their ideas are evaluated through the interactive group process.

The nominal group process has some advantages over the interacting group
process because it utilizes the talents of noninteracting group members, generates a greater number of ideas, and increases the likelihood of balanced participation and representation of all members in the group. People often are inhi-
bited in group-settings because of their introverted characteristics or a few
dominant members. A nominal group process helps to release such barriers
(Chung and Ferris, 1971). However, when participants are both pervasively
aware of the existing problems and willing to communicate their ideas, a
nominal process is not superior to an interacting group process because all
members freely participate in the interactive process (Green, 1975).

GROUP COMMUNICATION PROCESS

A communication network refers to the system of behavioral exchanges
existing between organizational members. Communication networks in an or-

ganization show actual interaction patterns among members. Depending on how they are structured, communication networks can either facilitate or hamper these interactions. Employee performance and satisfaction can be seen as a function of the communication network. Performance and satisfaction can increase when the communication network in a group facilitates interactions among its members who are performing tasks requiring technical interdependency. On the other hand, both performance and satisfaction can decrease when the communication network is restrictive, thus hindering the desired interactions.

There are several communication networks that can be used in organizations. Figure 8-5 shows the five basic communication networks: wheel or star, Y, chain, circle, and all-channel. These networks are arranged in the order of communication controllability and restriction. The wheel network is the most restrictive and controllable, while the all-channel network is the least restrictive and open. Network research indicates that no one single network is suitable to all job situations and a number of organizational contingencies such as task, people, and structure must be considered in selecting an appropriate network.

Guetzkow and Simon (1955) studied the effects of communication networks on work group's ability to organize for task performance. They found that the more difficult it was to organize the group, the less efficiently the group performed. More specifically, the wheel groups organized earliest with the least difficult organizational problem; the all-channel groups organized slowly, but were eventually performing as well as the wheel groups; and the circle groups had difficulty in organizing and performed poorly. In all these groups, it was found that once an organizational structure was developed by the group, the task was quickly accomplished. This was true regardless of the type of communication network the group employed.

Burgess (1968) reviewed the results of eighteen network studies. He found that, at least for simple tasks, the wheel and all-channel networks tended to be more productive than the circle. On the other hand, the people in the circle were better satisfied with their interactions than those peripheral members of the wheel. Hellriegel and Slocum (1976) attempted to generalize the effects of communication networks on the following criteria: 1) degree of communication centralization, 2) number of possible communication channels, 3) leadership predictability, 4) overall group satisfaction, and 5) individual leader satisfaction. They reported that the wheel and Y networks provide the leader high degrees of information centralization and leadership predictability. The circle and all-channel networks provide him with low degrees of information control and pre-

| Wheel | "Y" | Chain | Circle | All-channel |

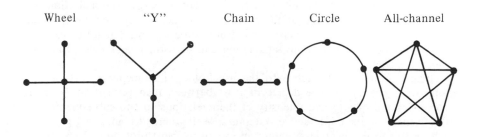

FIGURE 8-5. GROUP COMMUNICATION NETWORKS

dictability. However, subordinates' satisfaction tends to be higher with the all-channel and moderate with the circle and the chain networks. If the task requires a high degree of interaction among members, the all-channel network will be more effective than the wheel and Y networks.

Based on these researches, one can specify the following organizational contingencies under which a particular network can be effectively utilized. First, the wheel and downward networks are commonly utilized in a traditional organization where the supervisor controls the communication flow. Such networks can be effectively utilized for conveying organization messages such as instructions and procedures to employees performing relatively simple tasks. Passive and other-directed employees would respond to such networks more positively than self-directed employees. Power-oriented supervisors are more likely to use such networks because these networks allow them to preserve their power by controlling communication flows.

Second, the all-channel network is more appropriate for dealing with complex organizational problems requiring a high degree of interaction among experts. This network is representative of the communication flows in an organic organizational design where members freely interact within the work group. Also, such a network is suitable to a participative leader who encourages his subordinates to interact with other members for free information exchanges. Finally, the chain and circle networks can be used effectively for relaying messages in all types of organizations. Information is either informally channeled to other members without supervisory interference, or written reports are distributed. They may expedite information dissemination, but are not suitable for dealing with complex organizational problems requiring free information exchanges among experts.

ORGANIZATIONAL CLIMATE AND MOTIVATION

The preceding discussions focused on the relationship between organizational factors (structure, leadership, and group process) and organizational outcomes (satisfaction and productivity). The present discussion examines the process by which these organizational factors influence employee motivation and performance. Basically, organizational factors influence interactional patterns of employees, and members' sentiments or affective reactions toward one another develop as a result of their interactions. These sentiments or affective reactions constitute the climate in a group or organization, which in turn influences employee motivation and performance. In this context, organizational climate is seen as a set of intervening variables. They are influenced by such independent variables as structure, leadership, and group process, and can influence such organizational outcomes as job satisfaction and performance (Lawler, Hall, and Oldham, 1974).

Organizational climate refers to the psychological atmosphere existing in a group or organization. The degree of trust between management and workers determines the quality and intensity of their relationship and subsequently the effectiveness of their interactive outcomes. Well-intended managerial programs such as financial incentive systems and job enrichment programs often fail because of the failure to develop supportive and trusting relationships among organizational members, especially between management and workers. When workers distrust managerial integrity, they will be skeptical about the management effort to establish equitable pay systems. By the same token, when managers do not have confidence in their subordinates, they will hesitate to delegate managerial functions. Motivational programs such as incentive pay and management-by-objectives will never realize their potentials unless the emotion-ladden organizational climate is supportive and trusting enough to allow organizational members to search for rationality.

A number of studies reported that climate factors are positively related to employee satisfaction and performance (Ferris, 1969; Lawler, Hall, and Oldham, 1974; Likert, 1967; and Pritchard and Karasick, 1973). For example, Lawler et al. reported that climate factors are highly correlated with the satisfaction of higher-order needs and employee job performance. They also indicated that process factors (leadership and group) have a more direct and immediate influence and employee behavior than structural factors. Structural factors tend to have an indirect influence.

There are as many climate factors as there are climate researchers. The number of climate factors range from 8 (Halpin and Crofts, 1963) to 254 items (Payne and Pheysey, 1971). Why do we have so many climate factors and variations? Hellriegel and Slocum (1974) pointed out that, on a conceptual level, the organizational climate has well-defined boundaries between independent, intervening, and dependent variables. But, in moving from the conceptual to operational level, it is difficult to isolate climate factors from other organizational factors. Consequently, many researchers include a broad class of organizational factors in their climate studies (Likert, 1967; Litwin and Stringer, 1968; and Pritchard and Karasick, 1973).

Organizational climate is an important concept in studying organizational behavior because it dictates affective reactions of employees toward their jobs, co-workers, and organizational practices. However, much work has to be done to clearly define and measure the causal linkages between climate factors and independent variables (structure and process) or dependent variables (satisfaction and productivity). The trouble is that organizational climate is also influenced by job satisfaction and performance and can influence organizational structure, leadership, and group process. There is a question of redundancy between organizational climate and job satisfaction. While some scholars (Guion, 1973; Johannesson, 1973) argue that the two measures are redundant, other scholars (LaFollette and Sims, 1975; Payne, Fineman, and Wall, 1976; Schneider and Snyder, 1975) perceive a distinction between them. Further, performance and reward modify employees' affective reactions toward co-workers, their jobs, and management. Managerial styles can be modified as a result of organizational climate and employees' job performance. Until these causal relationships between climate factors and other organizational variables are more clearly defined and researched, the concept of organizational climate may be treated as a composite of various organizational variables including structural, process, and outcome factors.

WORKABLE FIT BETWEEN ORGANIZATIONAL COMPONENTS

Discussions on organizational structure, leadership process, and group process provide some clues as to how various organizational contingencies can be meshed together to arouse employee motivation and at the same time maximize organizational effectiveness. Although any attempt to find an organizational fit involving a large number of contingencies has a danger of over-simplifying complex organizational phenomena, such an attempt nevertheless will provide some insight into possible ways of harmonizing the demands of various organizational components. Figure 8-6 presents an overview of an organizational fit between organizational design, task, employees, leader, work group, and environmental demands. The horizontal dimension in the figure can be viewed as a continuum of the characteristics of these organizational components. For example, the continuum of organizational design ranges from a simplistic mechanical design to a complex organic design.

The following generalizations can be drawn for the contingency relationships shown in Figure 8-6. First, a mechanical organizational design may be suitable for managing low-skilled workers performing simplified programmable tasks existing in a stable environment. Directive and/or supportive leadership styles can be used depending an employee authoritarianism. Nonparticipative dyadic relationships between the supervisor and his subordinates can be maintained by the wheel and Y communication networks. Second, the linking-pin organization which relies on the group management process can be matched with nonprogrammable, intrinsically motivating jobs requiring joint efforts of qualified group members. Supportive and participative leadership styles generally are suggested for dealing with skilled workers with the ability and desire to manage or influence their work environment. The linking-pin organization is suggested for an organization operating in a complex but relatively stable technological environment. Finally, an organic organizational design can be matched with highly complex tasks existing in a highly dynamic industry. Such tasks often require a high degree of interaction between various functional experts. Timely responses from these functional specialties often are more important than maintaining an orderly organizational structure. Participative and goal-directed leadership styles are suggested for dealing with functional experts and professionals.

Figure 8-6 also implies that if these organizational components or contingencies are not compatible with each other, the mismatches will have negative impacts on organizational climate, employee satisfaction, and job performance. For example, if workers are either overqualified or underqualified for their jobs, they will be dissatisfied and frustrated. If a mechanical organizational structure is imposed on those employees performing nonprogrammable tasks in a dynamic industry, the organizational members cannot quickly respond to the changing task demands. There are a number of possibilities for mismatching the organizational contingencies, so managers should be alert to such possible mismatches. Furthermore, if there is any change or imbalance in the organizational fit, managers should take the necessary actions to establish a new workable balance.

SUMMARY AND CONCLUSION

A number of organizational contingencies are reviewed in this chapter because they influence employee interactions and sentiments which in turn affect job satisfaction and performance. Theoretically, environmental factors (sociocultural, econopolitical, and technomarket) influence the makeup of organizational design and behavioral process. Organizational structure, leader-

Organizational Design / Other Components	Mechanical Organization	Linking-pin Organization	Organic Organization (Project, Matrix, and Office Landscaping)
Task	Simplified, routinized, dull, and individualized tasks	Complex, enriched tasks requiring intraorganizational interactions	Complex, enriched tasks requiring intergroup interactions
Employee	Low-skilled workers with lower-order needs and high authoritarianism	Skilled workers with high-order needs and team work skills	Professionals with higher-order needs and self-control
Leadership	Directive or supportive depending on task and subordinate characteristics	Supportive and participative style	Participative, persuasive and achievement-oriented
Communication Network	Wheel or Y network	Circle or all-channel	All-channel
Environment	Stable, predictable market or technological Environment	Complex but relatively stable external environment	Complex and dynamic external environment

FIGURE 8-6. CONTINGENCY RELATIONSHIPS BETWEEN ORGANIZATIONAL COMPONENTS

ship, and group process then influence employees' affective reactions toward their work environment which in turn influence the organizational outcomes. When various organizational components are compatible to each other, their interactions will result in positive outcomes. The contingency relationships shown in Figure 8-6 suggest some ways of harmonizing the demands of various organizational components. As Kast and Rosenzweig (1970, p. 319) point out, the relationships between internal and external organizational components are too complex and dynamic to set forth any concrete statements about them. Nevertheless, the contingency relationships suggested in this chapter will provide managers with some insight into ways of creating an organizational environment in which employees can be motivated to achieve their individual as well as organizational goals.

The contingency concept implies that a number of factors can affect the organizational outcomes. It avoids the habit of searching for a single cause to solve organizational problems. A motivational problem can be created by one or more factors. Thus, it is necessary for the manager to investigate the characteristics of various organizational components and see if there are workable fits between them. Any lack of fit between these components usually signals the causes of the problems. When there is not, an attempt must be made to bring it about. A workable fit is not a static concept. Whenever there is a change in any one of the components, the organizational fit will be out of balance. The manager should be aware of changes in organizational components and be prepared to find new workable fits of different compositions of the components.

9

MOTIVATION THROUGH INNOVATIVE WORK SYSTEM

Work is more than an instrument for obtaining extrinsic rewards such as pay and promotion. It also can provide intrinsic motivation in the form of recognition, achievement, and growth. When work is not interesting and challenging, people will work only to the extent that it is necessary to satisfy biological and security needs. Once these low-order needs are reasonably satisfied, they will find their work drudgery and meaningless. Since today's workers are better educated and better off economically than their elders, they probably will find little value in holding jobs which they consider menial and lacking in challenge. They will expect their jobs to satisfy such high-order needs as self-respect and self-fulfillment, as well as lower-order needs.

When these high-order needs are not reasonably satisfied over a period of time, organizational members develop unhealthy attitudes and even pathological maladjustments to their work. They may actively rebel against work by restricting production, sabotaging the systems, and joining union activities, or they may passively withdraw from work through apathy, alienation, absenteeism, and low motivation. Such unhealthy attitudes and maladjustments prevent many organizations from best utilizing human resources. This neglect can cause higher costs, low productivity, poor product quality, and eventual business failure. Thus, making industrial jobs more interesting and challenging is not only crucial for satisfying workers' needs but also for maintaining productive organizations.

This chapter discusses several innovative work systems and their impacts on employee motivation and job performance. They will be discussed in the order of implemental expediency: 1) four-day work week, 2) flexitime, 3) job enlargement, 4) job enrichment, and 5) combined approach to job design. Although these programs can be implemented separately, they are expected to have a strong motivational potential when they are integrated into a motivational work system. This chapter also suggests several job design strategies based on expectancy theory. (A portion of this chapter is reported in Chung and Ross, 1977.)

INNOVATIVE WORK SCHEDULES

Innovative work schedule refers to any variation from the traditional five-day, fixed-time work week. There are several forms of innovative work schedules, but two types are predominant. The first is the four-day work week whereby employees work ten hours a day for four days a week. This program allows employees to fulfill their work commitment, and also leaves more free time for personal use. The second is a flexitime program. Workers organize their own work schedules to suit their personal needs and life styles without being forced to conform to rigid schedules.

FOUR-DAY WORK WEEK

The four-day work week has received more attention than the flexitime program in the United States. The American Management Association survey, conducted between August and September, 1971, indicated that 143 companies out of 1,056 companies studied (13 percent) reported the use of a four-day work week, and another 22 percent were studying the possibility of its implementation (Wheeler, Gurman, and Tarnowieski, 1972). The principal reasons for using such a program are based on traditional management concerns for increasing employee morale, productivity, and profit. This type of schedule helps management better utilize its resources by reducing absenteeism, turnover, and the number of production set-ups and shut-downs. Contrary to a criticism that the program allows employees to avoid working and glosses over real problems of job alienation (Herzberg, 1968), the shorter work week can serve as an incentive to employees. There are a number of reasons why. First, this program extends the weekend from two days to three. If the worker enjoys the extended weekends, he will be productive to reinforce the work system. If the worker does not maintain or exceed his previous level of productivity, management may return to the standard five-day work week. Second, this program helps reduce absenteeism because being absent a day means losing 25 percent out of a weekly pay check. Third, this program reduces the cost and time of travel to and from work by one round-trip a week which can mean quite a saving for those who commute a long distance. In addition, the commuter can avoid traffic congestion and the frustration and delay that accompany it. Finally, an employee on the four-day work week may be able to supplement his income with another job on a part-time basis.

However, Goodale and Aagaard (1975) reported that although nearly 70 percent of the employees in their survey were enthusiastic about the four-day work week, they showed fatigue and slowed down production. Nevertheless, this program was favorably accepted by its users. The American Management Association survey indicated that 66 percent of the 143 companies that have adopted the program reported increased productivity, 31 percent reported no change, and 3 percent experienced decreased productivity. No companies participating in the survey reported any deterioration in employee relations; 69 percent reported an improvement and 31 percent no change.

FLEXITIME

Flexitime was introduced in 1967 at the aerospace research and development plant of Messerschmitt-Bolkov-Blohm in Germany. This program was originally instituted to relieve traffic congestion during rush hours, but some employers as well as employees began to perceive it as an effective motivational device. It is estimated that in West Germany alone, some 3,500 companies have adopted the flexitime. This program has spread into other European countries, the United States, and Japan. However, rigid work rules and federal wage and hour regulations have restricted the use of this program in the United States.

The first major U.S. corporation to implement the flexible work schedule was John Hancock Mutual Life in Boston. John Hancock adopted the four-day work week plan for 2,000 office employees. However, for those employees whose schedules could not be adjusted to the shorter work week, the company adopted a flexitime plan whereby employees report to work between 7:30 and 9:00 a.m. and leave eight hours later, between 3:40 and 5:10 p.m. Department managers prepared work schedules with employees to determine their specific work schedules. All employees were required to work from 9:00 a.m. to 3:40 p.m., which was considered to be the core business hours. Because of the enlarged work day, the company could provide extended service to its customers.

Walker, Fletcher, and McLeod (1975) said that 78 percent of the employees in their survey reported improvement in the quality of office life because of flexitime schedules, and 94 percent did not wish to return to fixed working hours. In the same survey, 74 percent reported no changes in productivity, but 25 percent reported an increase because they were able to finish work they had started just before quitting. Previously, they would stop whatever they were doing at the regular quitting time.

Golembiewski (1974) also reported some positive results by using the flexitime in a company with employees ranging from laboratory helpers to scientists. After six months they responded favorably to 34 out of 36 questions related to the use of flexitime. A major attitudinal change occurred at supervisory levels; at the end of a year, responses to this program were more positive than at the end of six months.

Donahue (1975), after reviewing the use of flexitime in New York state's public agencies, outlined the following benefits and problems. Possible benefits are: it permits the agency to serve the public for extended hours; it reduces traffic congestion, it makes employees happier; it eliminates the use of tardiness penalty plans; and it helps to attract new employees. Potential problems are: it creates difficulties in scheduling meetings before and after core business hours; it imposes a need for accurate recording of employees' working hours; productivity may decline during early and late hours when supervisors may not be present; and it creates work scheduling problems.

RELATIVE EFFECTIVENESS

New work hours provide workers with incentives in the form of extended weekends or flexibility in scheduling their own work. The effectiveness of these programs, however, largely depends on the nature of the job and its work environment. Golembiewski, Yeager, and Hilles (1975) pointed out that the nature of the job must be carefully studied before a particular plan is adopted. For example, the flexitime program is not suitable to jobs with a high degree of interdependency due to the problem of scheduling. Also, it may not be suitable to a work situation which involves more than one shift. The four-day work week program seems to be more practical for manufacturing workers who operate on a continuous production line, while the flexitime schedule may appeal more to a clerical and service personnel. If employees value extended weekends more than flexible working hours, then the four-day work week will be a more effective motivational tool. However, the flexitime plan seems, on the whole, to be more psychologically meaningful because it offers workers a sense of control and freedom in determining their own work schedules. Furthermore, people have different psychological and physiological rhythms; some are more mentally alert and active early in the morning while others find peak functioning later in the day. The flexitime program allows them to adjust their work schedules to fit their psychological rhythms. Finally, setting one's own work schedule is generally regarded as a status symbol that only professional and managerial personnel enjoy. When this program is applied to rank-and-file employees, the element of prestige serves as an additional incentive.

JOB ENLARGEMENT

Job enlargement is often called *horizontal job loading* because it expands task elements horizontally. Instead of performing a fragmented job, the worker produces a whole unit or a major portion of a job. Though often viewed as interchangeable concepts, job enlargement and job enrichment can be separately implemented as distinct managerial strategies. The difference is that the former requires changes in the technical aspects of a job, while the latter involves changes in the behavioral aspects of an organization. Although enriching a job is said to have a stronger motivational impact on employees than enlarging a job technically, it is extremely complex and time-consuming to implement because it requires some changes in attitudes and values of organizational as well as societal members. Behavioral changes tend to arouse resistance from organizational members. Job enlargement, on the other hand, involves technical changes, which can be adopted more expediently than behavioral changes, and is therefore less likely to cause employee resistance. In addition, an optimally enlarged job possesses a number of motivational properties that can have a positive impact on some workers. Workers with low need for self-control and growth may be perfectly happy with enlarged jobs without job enrichment. Lastly, job enlargement should be considered as a prerequisite for introducing job enrichment programs. When the task is basically dull and meaningless, merely giving more authority and responsibility to the worker may not produce positive motivational results. The task should contain basic motivational characteristics (task variety, meaningful work module, performance feedback, ability utilization, and man-paced control) before workers are given managerial authority. If a task is properly enlarged, it will possess the following motivational characteristics.

TASK VARIETY

Under the influence of scientific management, many industrial jobs are so simplified that they can be easily standardized and mechanized. Advantages of simplification may be that jobs of this nature require little training and can be easily staffed by low-skilled workers. Management's dependency on skilled workers is minimized, and production workers are easily interchangeable. The reliance on low-skilled workers and low-cost training also helps to reduce personnel costs for management. The standardization and mechanization of production systems have made it possible to produce goods and services on a mass-production scale at low costs for massive consumption. Mechanization requires less mental and physical energy exertion; workers can produce more for less effort. Better pay and a high standard of living are realized as a result of the mechanization of production systems.

But, the problem with such mechanized jobs is that as workers become satisfied with lower-order needs, they demand satisfaction of higher-order needs. Industrial jobs designed according to the principles of scientific management are at odds with human needs for being creative and imaginative. Traditional production methods are not able to satisfy human needs beyond the level of biological survival and security. Thus the economic benefits expected from simplified jobs are easily offset by high costs of turnover, sabotage, and wage increase.

The dysfunctional aspect of repetitive jobs also can be explained by activation theory. According to this theory, the level of activation, which is defined as the extent of an organism's mental and physical energy release, is affected by stimulus intensity and variation (Duffy, 1962; Scott, 1966); the greater the intensity and variation of stimuli, the higher the level of activation. Repetitive tasks usually produce a limited number of unchanging stimuli, and subsequently lower the level of activation. This theory also indicates that there is an inverted-V relationship between activation level and performance. At low activation levels, performance is depressed due to the lack of alertness, the decrease in sensory sensitivity, and lack of muscular coordination. At intermediate levels, performance will be optimal; but at high levels, performance will be again depressed due to hypertension and loss of control.

Performance decrement is expected when performing repetitive tasks because such tasks will force repetition of a limited number of responses to a limited number of unchanging stimuli (Fiske and Maddi, 1961). Repetitive jobs increase boredom and daydreaming which, in turn, increase errors and accidents. Job enlargement is supported by the activation theory because the number of task variations is related to the level of activation; an intermediate number of task variations should be able to sustain an optimal level of activation as well as performance.

MEANINGFUL WORK MODULE

By combining related task components, the existing job becomes larger and closer to the whole work unit. As the worker performs the whole work unit or at least a major portion of a product or project, he can see his contribution to its completion. When the worker completes the given work module within a time unit which is psychologically meaningful and technically sound, he may find the job interesting and worthwhile. The time unit can range from one half hour to days, depending on the work cycle and attention level needed. Industrial experiences with job enlargement have shown that workers feel more responsible for the quality of their performance when they perform whole work units (Ford, 1973; and Walton, 1972).

Establishing work modules also makes it possible to introduce a job rotation program. An employee can perform several work modules, each having different sets of stimuli. Job rotation not only reduces boredom and monotony, but also may increase the level of mental and physical activities by introducing new sets of stimuli requiring different sets of responses. The enlarged job will have an especially high motivational value when the completion of these different work modules leads to the accomplishment of a final result, such as completing a major project. More specifically, Homans (1961) suggested that tasks be designed in such a manner that repeated activities lead to the accomplishment of some final result with reinforcements given at low frequencies until the final result is achieved.

However, a job should not be overly enlarged. As activation theory points out, overly enlarged jobs may be dysfunctional because they may generate hypertension and frustration on the part of workers. If the job is too complex to learn and perform, the worker may lose interest in doing the job, or he may lose control and be frustrated. Thus, if the job is too big to handle, it should be divided into several work modules so the worker can find it manageable. The key points for finding meaningful work modules are that when the worker completes a work module, he should be able to feel a sense of accomplishment, and each undertaking of a new work module should rejuvenate the level of activation.

PERFORMANCE FEEDBACK

When a worker performs a fractionated job with short performance cycles, he repeats the same set of motions endlessly without a meaningful finishing point. It is not only difficult to count the number of finished performance cycles, but even if counted, the information is meaningless. On the other hand, knowledge of results (KR) on enlarged jobs is psychologically meaningful because the worker's level of accomplishment can be measured and evaluated for organizational rewards.

Performance feedback, or KR, serves two motivational functions. First, KR serves as an external stimulus if added to a repetitive and dull task. According to Scott (1966), the activation level increases as KR is given; consequently the performance level can be sustained or improved at least temporarily. Second, KR can have a greater motivational value when it is internally mediated by the worker or the task than when it is externally introduced (Greller and Herold, 1975). Internally mediated KR is psychologically more relevant to the worker than externally introduced KR. Thus, the worker may be more willing to utilize the internal sources of KR for setting his performance goals or standards and evaluate his progress toward these goals (Chung and Vickery, 1976; Locke, 1968; Locke, Cartledge, and Koeppel, 1968; and Ronan and Latham, 1973).

There is some indication that the effect of KR on motivation in repetitive or monitoring tasks may be limited. Although high performance and least performance decrement were usually found in tasks where KR was given, several studies reported performance decrement in nonenlarged task situations. For example, Montague and Webber (1965) reported that although the manipulation of KR and monetary reward enhanced overall performance in a monitoring task, performance decrements in small magnitude occurred in all groups. Payne and Hauty (1955) also failed to deter performance decrement in their response time study. Freeman, Hafer, and Daniel (1966), in their study of the effect of extrinsic stimuli on brain functions, found that the electroencephalogram (EEG) pattern first showed signs of arousal when KR was given, but gradually declined over a period of time in a paired-associate learning situation.

The effect of KR on motivation, however, seems to have more sustaining power in enlarged or intrinsically motivating task situations. For example,

Gibbs and Brown (1955) reported sustaining higher performance from the subjects copying pages from books when KR was given than when it was with-
held. Although the task was repetitive in nature, the subjects might have perceived it as meaningful. Deci (1972) also reported the powerful effect of KR on
motivation in performing an intrinsically motivating puzzle-matching task.
Braunstein, Klein, and Pachla (1973) found the same result in student rating of
college faculty, thus substantiating the motivational effect of KR in specific
task situations.

ABILITY UTILIZATION

People derive satisfaction from jobs that permit the utilization of skills and
abilities. Enlarged jobs usually require more mental and physical abilities than
nonenlarged jobs. Several research findings confirmed the positive relationship
between ability utilization and job satisfaction. For example, Vroom (1962)
reported a positive correlation between opportunity for self-expression in the
job (the ability utilization) and job satisfaction for blue-collar workers. Kornhauser (1964) also reported a significant relationship between ability utilization
and mental health for both young and middle-aged workers across various occupational levels.

According to the expectancy theorists (Atkinson, 1964; Lawler, 1973;
Vroom, 1964), a task needs to be designed in such a manner that the worker's
exertion of effort and energy results in task accomplishment. Either too much
simplified or overly complex jobs are not motivational because their task
accomplishment is not closely related to effort exertion. Simplified jobs are less
motivating because they require low levels of ability and effort utilization. Since
the productivity of mechanized jobs depends primarily on machines, workers'
skills and abilities are not perceived to be principal determinants of task accomplishment. Also, overly enlarged jobs are not motivating because such jobs require
more skills and abilities than the workers possess, and thus create frustration and
prevent task accomplishment. However, enlarged jobs with optimum levels of
complexity allow effort to be closely related to task accomplishment, creating
a task situation which is challenging but attainable.

MAN-PACED CONTROL

Mechanization of production methods has reduced the amount of control
exercised by workers over their production speeds and work methods. The work
pace is controlled mechanically, and workers are expected to exert their
energies at regular and unchangeable rates of speed set by machines. Furthermore, work methods are standardized and uniformly applied to all workers
regardless of individual differences in skills, abilities, and work habits. As indicated elsewhere, machine-paced assembly operations make it possible to produce
goods and services for massive consumption, but are incongruent with one's
need to control his work environment. Under this circumstance, he may exert
control illegitimately by sabotaging the work system. The machine-paced production line is especially vulnerable to sabotage because the whole assembly
line depends on smooth operations of all workers and machines; one breakdown
by a single worker or machine can stop the whole production line.

Job enlargement makes it difficult to place workers on a machine-paced
production line. Since work modules are completed by workers with different

temperaments, work habits, and skill and ability levels, production speeds and work methods cannot be completely standardized. The man-paced production line has several advantages over the machine-paced one. First, it is motivational because it matches the worker's desire to control his work environment. Not only can the worker develop his own work methods and habits which are suitable to his personality, but he can also choose the work pace which best reflects his own work rhythm. Second, enlarged jobs organized around the man-paced production line may help to reduce employee turnover and absenteeism. If the worker achieves greater satisfaction when performing enlarged jobs, he will be willing to show up more consistently and will exert more effort when working.

Third, the man-paced system is less vulnerable to machine breakdown and sabotage. Since work modules are individualized, any individual man or machine breakdown will have little effort on the whole production line. Fourth, the man-paced production line is more flexible in terms of the number of products it can produce. This production system can easily be adjusted to reflect the changes in work methods and types of products to be produced. Fifth, the production system uses general-purpose equipment and machines which usually cost less than specialized machines used in the machine-paced production line. In addition, there is greater flexibility in assigning general-purpose machines than special-purpose machines to jobs. Finally, incentive pay systems can readily be adapted to the modular production system. Since the work is individualized and man-paced, it is easier to measure individual productivity.

The man-paced system, however, has several disadvantages. The rate of production can be lower than the rate which results from the machine-paced production line. Workers may have to exert more energy to produce about the same rate of production before the job enlargement. It may be difficult to produce large volumes of produce with the man-paced system. As the volume increases substantially, it often pays to shift the production system toward the machine-paced operation. Nevertheless, the advantages of using the man-paced production system offset its disadvantages. The crucial question to be asked is under what circumstances should management consider the use of man-controlled production systems. Managerial criterion for adopting this system can be whether it pays off in terms of high productivity and job satisfaction.

JOB ENLARGEMENT EFFECTS

A number of studies have attempted to measure the effects of new work systems on employee job satisfaction and performance. However, there are relatively few studies and industrial experiences that involve the use of only one type of work system based on either horizontal or vertical job loading. For this reason, it is difficult to test any performance prediction that a particular type of work system is superior to another in arousing employee motivation. Nevertheless, the following studies help in predicting motivational effects of job enlargement.

Conant and Kilbridge (1965), Guest (1957), Lawler (1969), Walker (1950), and Walker and Guest (1952) studied the effects of job enlargement (primarily horizontal loading) on employee motivation. Their studies concluded that job enlargement is more likely to improve employee satisfaction and product quality and, to a certain extent, reduce costs and increase productivity. However, job enlargement may create a situation in which workers have to exert more energy and effort to produce the same rate of production as before the jobs were enlarged. Enlarged jobs usually involve man-paced production methods that may sometimes reduce production speed and prevent optimal human movements. It is also possible that workers draw more job satisfaction from producing quality products than from producing a large quantity of low quality products. Thus, job enlargement is most likely to have a positive effect on employee satisfaction, have a positive influence on the quality of product, and have an affect on productivity.

Although job enlargement is much simpler to implement than job enrichment, potential users should be aware of its costs. In many instances, the existing assembly production lines need to be broken up and restructured into various work modules that can be considered natural work units and psychologically meaningful. Redesigning and balancing production lines are costly. Volvo estimated that a new work system would cost about 10 percent more than a comparable conventional auto plant. Further, workers as well as supervisors need to be retrained to adjust to new work systems. Outside consultants are usually invited to monitor the implementation process. Many companies experience drops in productivity during the initial stage of new work system implementation. Finally, under job enlargement workers perform more complicated jobs and may well demand higher wages.

In summary, a properly enlarged job possesses such motivational characteristics as task variety, meaningful work module, performance feedback, ability utilization, and man-paced control. These motivational properties can be functional for arousing job satisfaction of rank-and-file employees not particularly interested in performing overly demanding jobs. Furthermore, job enlargement is prerequisite for job enrichment. Unless the job is first enlarged to make it interesting, job enrichment which gives managerial authority to workers is meaningless. When the job is dull and repetitive, workers may want to work less rather than more. Although job enlargement incurs some costs, it can be recommended to employers on the basis of humanistic considerations and cost savings attributable to reduced absenteeism, lower turnover, and decreased product rejects.

JOB ENRICHMENT

Job enrichment is another form of motivational work system. It is often called *vertical job loading* and allows workers to participate in managerial processes previously restricted to managerial and supervisory personnel. It allows workers not only to perform more task components, but also to have more responsibility, autonomy, and control over the tasks they perform. Added to the motivational properties of enlarged jobs are such motivational characteristics of job enrichment as participation, goal-setting, group management, and autonomy and control. These motivational characteristics will have special appeals to those employees who strive for the satisfaction of such higher-order needs as self-actualization, competence, and growth. Experiences with job enrichment have shown that such a motivational program tends to be effective when workers are given enlarged jobs, participate in managerial decisions, and when work groups are responsible for managing their own group tasks. (AT&T, General Foods, Saab, and Volvo). Since the motivational characteristics of enlarged jobs were discussed earlier, the following sections present the motivational properties of job enrichment—employee participation, goal-setting autonomy, and group management.

EMPLOYEE PARTICIPATION

Both the traditional and job enrichment approaches to management involve essentially the same managerial functions—planning, organizing, performing, and controlling organizational activities. Planning includes setting goals and specifying action plans and programs. Organizing includes division of managerial activities and assignment of responsibilities to accomplish the tasks. The performing function is the actual phase of implementing plans and carrying out the tasks, utilizing workers' skills and abilities. Controlling is the feedback process for assessing actual performance against plans. The feedback information becomes the basis for recycling managerial functions for future activities. However, the difference between them is that, in the traditional approach, management alone plans, organizes, directs, and controls organizational activities, while leaving only the performance function to employees. Job enrichment, on the other hand, allows employees to perform all these managerial functions regarding their own jobs. Its goal is to make employees managers of their own jobs.

Participation of workers in managerial decisions influences not only employee job satisfaction but also job performance. Vroom (1964) pointed out that people become ego-involved in decisions which they have influenced. When they have participated in the decision-making process, they tend to internalize the organizational decision and feel personally responsible for carrying it out. Thus, the success or failure of a decision and subsequent action becomes their success or failure. Participation by employees tends to result in greater subordinate acceptance of decisions (Maier, 1963), and leaders trained in the group-decision method can elicit higher quality decisions (Maier and Hoffman, 1960). However, the quality of decision also depends on the quality and quantity of information that the participants have and the type of decision they are dealing with. For example, the quality is enhanced when the participants have the necessary information to make the decision (Swinth, 1971), and when the participants' goals are compatible to organizational goals.

When individual and organizational goals are in conflict or when the job lacks intrinsic motivation, the nonparticipative authoritarian approach may produce better results than the participative approach. Workers in any of these circumstances may not find any reason to set high standards and increase productivity; whereas authoritarian managers can influence workers' behavior by giving or withholding extrinsic rewards.

The participative approach generally produces favorable employee attitudes toward management, better relationships between supervisors and subordinates, greater upward communication, and greater subordinate acceptance of superiors as their representatives (Holder, 1972). All these factors contribute to greater employee satisfaction. However, the relationship between participation and productivity seems more ambiguous and complex than that between participation and employee satisfaction. Although several studies have shown a positive correlation with participation to job performance (Coch and French, 1948; Likert, 1971; and Whyte, 1955), the effectiveness of participation as a motivational tool depends on the establishment of goals by participants (goal-setting) and the degree of control that employees have over the means of carrying out the decisions (autonomy). The effects of participation are also tempered by individual differences in needs for independence and achievement. Vroom (1960) found that workers with little need for independence were not motivated to produce high performance. Steers (1975) also reported that goal specificity and performance feedback were significantly related to job performance for workers with high achievement need, while participation in goal setting was significantly related to the performance of low need achievers.

GOAL-SETTING RESPONSIBILITY

Motivation is goal-oriented behavior, and it does not exist without goals or objectives. If a job enrichment program is to be successful, workers should be involved in the goal-setting process for their work group. According to Likert (1967) and Odiorne (1970), participation itself does not guarantee high productivity unless workers' participation results in the establishment of high performance goals by the workers for themselves. High performance goals, as well as a supportive supervisory climate must be present if an organization is to achieve high productivity. According to Locke's report (1968), several studies showing a positive relationship between participation and high productivity have involved the actual establishment of high performance goals by the participants. This finding implied that goal-setting could be the key feature of employee participation.

Bryan and Locke (1967), Latham and Baldes (1975), Latham and Kinne (1974), Latham and Yukl (1975), and Ronan, Latham, and Kinne (1975) generally supported Locke's theory of goal-setting in producing high performance. For example, a study by Latham and Yukl (1975) compared the effects of assigned goal setting, participative goal setting, and "do your best" conditions on workers' productivity. This study reported that the participative goal-setting condition produced higher goals and productivity than did the assigned and "do your best" conditions.

Why is goal-setting behavior so effective in arousing high motivation and productivity? People have a tendency to set performance goals at higher levels than previous performance levels (Lewin, Dembo, Festinger, and Sears, 1944). The discrepancy between the goals and previous performance levels creates productive tension, which people are motivated to reduce. The attainment of these goals creates a feeling of success while any performance level lower than the goal levels or levels of aspiration is considered failure. Thus, people are motivated to achieve these goals not only to reduce the productive tension but also to experience the feeling of success. Past experiences of success or failure in task undertakings influence the new levels of performance goals. There is a general tendency for the levels to be raised following success, and lowered following failure (Atkinson, 1965; Moulton, 1965; and Feather, 1967). Therefore, setting consecutively higher but attainable goals is a key to successful task accomplishment.

Second, performance goals set by employees affect the level of motivation by influencing the expectancy, instrumentality, and valence of behavioral outcomes. Challenging but attainable performance goals will affect positively the expectancy that workers' efforts are needed and will result in task accomplishment (E-P). Task accomplishment produces such intrinsic incentive rewards as feeling of success, sense of achievement, and growth (P-I). These intrinsic rewards are highly instrumental in satisfying high-order needs such as self-respect and self-fulfillment (I-N). Especially employees with high achievement needs will be prone to become more ego-involved in achieving challenging goals because they may place higher value on such goal attainment (Atkinson and Feather, 1966; Mahone, 1960; Morris, 1967).

Finally, goal-setting provides employees with a sense of direction toward which their energies and efforts can be directed. Without such a direction, organizational members have to consume their energies in searching for alternative behavior patterns that can be accepted, or at least tolerated, by management and other members. By reducing unnecessary searching behavior, organizational members can concentrate their efforts on prescribed goal attainments. Goal-setting is a dynamic process by which individuals and organizations determine objectives and which becomes the basis for allocating resources to maximize the outcomes of their efforts.

Goal-setting systems have been used for managerial personel in the traditional management approach. Proponents of job enrichment have proposed that the goal-setting technique be applied to all levels of employees to achieve maximum effect on employee motivation (Herzberg, 1968; Myers, 1970; and Raia, 1974). However, the implementation of participatory goal-setting systems at lower levels of organizational hierarchy may not be practical because workers at these levels may not be technically and psychologically prepared to perform highly demanding jobs. Thus, it seems necessary to reexamine the simplistic notion of goal-setting systems applied to all levels of employees. Individual differences in technical and psychological readiness must be taken into account to increase the effectiveness of goal-setting systems in organizations. A diagnostic scheme to differentiate the individual difference factors will be presented in a later section.

AUTONOMY

To be most effective, job enrichment programs should go beyond the initial stage of allowing employees to participate in operational decisions. Employees should be given the authority to manage their own jobs. They should be allowed to have control over the means of achieving their task goals. They should be allowed to take risks, learn from their mistakes, review their progress, and assess their own accomplishments. When workers are given such a managerial authority, it should be unnecessary for managers to exercise close supervision, and they can then be available to employees for consultation, advice, guidance, and training. When autonomy is in fact working, managers can spend their time planning, trouble-shooting, and helping their supervisors. In some cases, the number of supervisory personnel can be reduced.

Autonomy is, however, frequently in conflict with the manager's desire to have control over, or to be informed of, subordinates' activities. The manager may delegate authority to workers, but he is still responsible for their actions. Consequently, even if he does not intend to interfere with workers' activities, his concern for productivity may lead him to review his subordinates' progress frequently. This behavior may make workers feel that they do not really have autonomy in managing their jobs.

The concept of autonomy, or self-management, seems contradictory to the managerial practice of a capitalistic economy which is primarily profit-oriented and has differentiated management and labor roles in the managing process. However, certain principles of self-management and representation are reflected in Likert's linking-pin organizational practice. The Likert thesis (1961, 1967) is that organizational members internalize organizational objectives when they are allowed to manage their own work group activities and participate in managerial decision-making through supervisory representation at the next high level of management. By linking subgroup activities to high level managerial groups, the organization should be able to integrate subunits' activities into a concerted effort toward obtaining organizational objectives. Furthermore, by having supervisors involved in group activities and, at the same time, linked to upper level managerial groups, both management and workers' desire to control and to be informed can be reasonably satisfied.

GROUP MANAGEMENT

Managerial autonomy can be granted to employees collectively or individually. But, most proponents and users of job enrichment programs prefer group action over the individualized approach (Ford, 1973; Howell, 1967; Likert, 1967; and Walton, 1972). The work group defines its task-goals, undertakes its tasks jointly, appraises its accomplishments and individual members' contributions to the group effort, and shares the outcomes of their accomplishments among its members. For example, self-managed work teams at General Foods, Topeka, Kansas, are given collective responsibility for managing day-to-day production problems. Assignments of individual tasks are subject to team consensus, and their tasks can be redefined by the team to accommodate individual differences in skills, capacities, and interests. In addition, the work group is responsible for 1) coping with manufacturing problems that occur within or between work groups, 2) temporarily redistributing tasks to cover absentees, 3) selecting members for plantwide task forces, 4) screening and selecting employees, and 5) counseling workers with performance problems.

There are several reasons for the group management approach. First, most jobs in industry are interdependent and require a high degree of interaction among work group members. Managers as well as workers have a responsibility for coordinating their efforts in achieving organizational or group goals. However, since these jobs are mutually interdependent, it is difficult to identify individualized goals, duties, and responsibilities. Second, a major strength of individualized management-by-objectives (MBO) programs is the strong personal responsibility an employee feels for his own goals. But, such an individualized program can lead an individual employee to pursue personal goals for which he alone is responsible to the point where organizational joint responsibilities are neglected. It can also create an unhealthy competition among workers when organizational rewards such as pay increase and promotion are based on an individualized MBO program.

Third, the group approach helps workers satisfy socialization needs on their jobs. As indicated in a previous chapter, work groups control the means of satisfying employees' needs for socialization and affiliation. Groups provide a sense of belonging and identification, reinforce feelings of self-worth and provide emotional support and comfort in times of emotional stress. Interaction by itself does not necessarily lead to satisfaction; interaction can yield either favorable or unfavorable sentiments among members. Since self-managing work group members are able to select their own peers as well as supervisors, their inter-actions will more likely be favorable. Also, the group framework allows members to accept and reinforce each other's feelings, thus ensuring positive relation-ships.

Finally, the group approach seems to have a strong influence on employee work motivation and performance. Since work groups control the means of satis-fying socialization needs, their members tend to comply with group norms and performance standards to maintain their membership. When someone continu-ously deviates from these norms and standards, initially he will be warned and eventually will face peer rejection in the form of kidding, ostracism, or hostility. Cohesive work groups have a stronger influence on employee motivation and performance than noncohesive groups because cohesive groups are more effec-tive in satisfying their members' needs. Since they are more willing to comply with group norms, the actions of the cohesive group members tend to be similar.

However, the application of self-management by workers seems to be limited in practice in organizations because it requires a set of organizational conditions that has to be met before workers are given managerial authority and responsi-bility. These conditions include satisfactory pay, trusting and supportive relation-ships among group members and between managers and workers, and harmoni-ous intergroup relations among many. Only when such a favorable climate prevails in the organization will its workers find the reasons and means for set-ting and maintaining high performance standards. Yet, not many organizations are free from the problem of meeting such organizational conditions.

JOB ENRICHMENT EFFECTS

The concept of job enrichment assumes that participation in decision making leads to greater acceptance of decisions by workers and thus increases employee motivation. However, there are a number of studies which indicate that partici-pation alone does not necessarily lead to high motivation and productivity un-less it results in high performance goals set by the participants for themselves (Bryan and Locke, 1967; Latham and Yukl, 1975; Likert, 1971; Locke, 1968; and Odiorne, 1970). There are a number of individual and organizational con-straints that may prevent the effective utilization of goal-setting systems. As indicated elsewhere, these constraints include workers' technical and psychologi-cal readiness to perform demanding jobs, pay, job security, and organizational climate. Further, it can be argued that workers will not set high performance goals unless their jobs have been horizontally enlarged to make them psychologi-cally meaningful. Thus, it is doubtful whether job enrichment alone can have a strong motivational impact on employee behavior. However, when these two types of work system are jointly applied under favorable circumstances, job enrichment can exert more influence on employee motivation than can job enlargement because the former provides workers with more opportunities for utilizing their abilities and for exerting control over their work environment.

In summary, job enrichment increases the motivational potential of a job through increased participation and self-management of workers in the managerial process. Yet, the implementation of this work system is difficult as it requires changes in behavioral systems which tend to be costly and time-consum-ing. First of all, workers need to be technically and psychologically prepared to perform demanding jobs so they may be able to gain satisfaction from performing them. In addition, the organization should be ready to create an organizational climate in which employees can pursue satisfaction of higher-order needs. When the employees are not reasonably satisfied with such hygiene factors as pay, job security, interpersonal relationships, and supervision, they will probably be preoccupied with need satisfaction of these hygiene factors. Such individual and organizational constraints in large part explain the reasons why new work systems are not widely used.

COMBINED APPROACH TO JOB DESIGN

Although there is a clear distinction between job enlargement and job enrichment, these two managerial strategies can be jointly applied to job design. It is predicted that job satisfaction and performance will be the highest when this combined approach is applied to designing jobs. The HEW report *Work in America* (1973) advocated that a work system should involve both enlargement and enrichment if it is to have a strong motivational influence on employee behavior. The report indicated that such a complete work system — not simply a job enlargement or job enrichment—resulted in an increase in productivity from 5 percent to 40 percent. A number of industrial experiences with the combined approach to job design tend to support such a prediction. Figure 9-1 shows the outcome of organizational experiences with this combined approach in nine companies in the United States and Europe. The outcomes are measured on three performance criteria: employee satisfaction, product quality, and quantity output. All nine companies reported improvement in employee satisfaction and product quality, while seven of them reported an increase in quantity output.

More specifically, AT&T reported that, after it had introduced the new work system into a service representatives' office at Southwestern Bell, the absenteeism rate in the experimental unit was 0.6 percent, compared with 2.5 percent in other groups; the errors per 100 orders were 2.9 as compared with 4.6 in the

Criteria Company	Improved Job Satisfaction	Improved Product Quality	Increased Quantity Output
AT & T (U.S.A.)	X	X	X
General Foods (U.S.A.)	X	X	X
Proctor & Gamble (U.S.A.)	X	X	X
Syntex (U.S.A.)	X	X	X
Texas Instruments (U.S.A.)	X	X	X
Imperial Chemical (British)	X	X	X
Philips (Netherlands)	X	X	X
Saab-Scania (Sweden)	X	X	—
Volvo (Sweden)	X	X	—

FIGURE 9-1. ORGANIZATIONAL EXPERIENCES WITH COMBINED JOB DESIGN

control group, and the 9 typists in the group were producing service order pages at a rate one-third higher than the 51 service order typists in the control group (Ford, 1973). At the General Foods' Topeka plant, the people involved in the new work system reported high job satisfaction, reductions in manufacturing costs through fewer quality rejects, a low absenteeism rate, and an increase in productivity. On the average, 77 people achieved the production level, which was estimated to require 110 employees if conventional engineering principles were adopted (Walton, 1972). Management of Syntex Corporation allowed two sales groups to set their own goals and work quality standards. As a result, sales increased 116 percent which was about 20 percent higher than that of control groups. Roche and MacKinnon (1970) and Paul, Robertson, and Herzberg (1969) also reported positive results in all three criteria at Texas Instruments and Imperial Chemical respectively.

The editor of *Organizational Dynamics* (1973) reported that the Philips' experience with job redesign improved employee morale, reduced production costs by 10 percent, and increased product quality. Saab-Scania reported improvements in employee attitudes, absenteeism, and product quality. However, there was no proof that productivity had increased as a result of job redesign at Saab-Scania. Volvo also reported drops in absenteeism and turnover and improvement in product quality, but there was no measurable improvement in production output. The general feeling among all these companies was that improved product quality and reduced labor problems such as absenteeism and turnover could cover the costs of redesigning the work systems.

The aforementioned industrial experiences with the new work systems seem to coincide with the research findings by Lawler (1969). According to Lawler, all ten studies reviewed reported that job redesign led to high product quality while six out of ten studies reported an increase in productivity as a result of job redesign. Based on these studies, he concluded that enlarged and/or enriched jobs produce greater employee motivation than do simplified jobs. The increased motivation means that employees will be more productive and quality conscious. However, the losses in machine assistance and optimal human movements means that employees have to exert more effort to maintain the pre-redesign production rate or may have to produce less to improve quality. Thus, it can be generally predicted that innovative work systems are more likely to lead to greater job satisfaction and higher work quality than to increased productivity.

JOB DESIGN STRATEGIES

Job design, especially the combined approach to job design, can have a significant influence on employee motivation because it contains the major motivational components as suggested in instrumental/expectancy theory of motivation. Job design affects the employee's expectancy that his effort leads to task performance (E-P), that task performance leads to intrinsic as well as extrinsic incentive rewards (P-I), and that these incentive rewards have the power of satisfying the person's needs (I-N). Workers respond to job design differently, reflecting individual differences in perceiving these motivational components. These differences often determine the effectiveness of new work systems. For example, not all workers are interested in performing demanding jobs, nor are they all motivated by higher-order need satisfaction. Also, not all organizations are able to supply adequate hygiene factors, such as pay and job security, and have a supportive climate for managerial innovation. Thus, these individual and organizational characteristics should be reflected in job design. Managerial strategies to job design involve matching task requirements with individual qualifications, tying performance to rewards, and differentiating tasks to satisfying different needs.

TASK DIFFICULTY AND INDIVIDUAL READINESS

Job design affects the expectancy that effort leads to task performance (E-P). It was indicated in a previous discussion that jobs either too simplified or too enlarged (or enriched) are motivationally dysfunctional because the performance of these jobs may not be a function of one's effort. When the job is too simplified or mechanized, it does not require any special effort or training on the worker's part and thus does not motivate him to exert mental as well as physical abilities. Performing an extremely enlarged or enriched job can by dysfunctional because the job is so complex that even a great deal of effort cannot lead to task accomplishment. The job may involve the utilization of high skills and abilities that the worker does not possess or is not willing to exert. The performance level is assumed to be highest at the point where the job is optimally designed so that one's effort results in high performance.

However, the optimal level of task design or difficulty varies for different individuals. Some can handle demanding jobs effectively and thus are reinforced by the successful accomplishment of their jobs, while others are not able to perform and are discouraged. Hulin (1975) indicated that there is an inverted-V relationship between task difficulty and job satisfaction and that the optimal level of job satisfaction varies for different workers. Contrary to the view that routinized and repetitive jobs lead to boredom and job dissatisfaction, some workers may find them suitable or even desirable (Reif and Luthans, 1972; Vroom, 1960). Hackman and Lawler (1971), Hackman and Oldham (1975), and Brief and Aldag (1975) also reported that individuals with higher-order needs generally display stronger relationships between core task attributes (task variety, task identity, autonomy, and feedback) and job satisfaction than do individuals lower in higher-order need strength.

The relationship between task attributes and individual differences is shown in Figure 9-2. This figure implies that employees with strong desire for and ability to perform demanding jobs (professional and managerial personnel) will find the highest level of job satisfaction and performance when their jobs are heavily enriched and complex, whereas workers with lower desire for and limited ability to perform demanding jobs (unskilled and semi-skilled) will find their optimal levels of job satisfaction and productivity when their jobs are relatively simple. Most skilled workers then will find their optimal levels of job satisfaction and productivity when their jobs are moderately enlarged and enriched.

The task difficulty index (TDI), shown in Figure 9-2, can be drawn from the task attributes (task variety, meaningful work module, performance feedback, ability utilization, man-paced control, group interaction, responsibility, and autonomy). The individual readiness index (IRI) is then derived from workers' skill levels and their psychological states. The skill levels measure workers' technical readiness for performing given tasks, while the psychological need levels measure their psychological readiness for undertaking the tasks. The inverted-V chart indicated that job satisfaction and performance increase when both TDI and IRI increase, but they decrease as the gap between TDI and IRI widens.

Figure 9-2 also implies that a worker's readiness (IRI) should be matched with the task difficulty (TDI) to maximize his job satisfaction and productivity. Motivational problems arise when the worker is either over-qualified or under-qualified for his job. If the TDI is substantially larger than the IRI, the gap probably can be minimized by 1) employee skill training, 2) developing need strength, 3) hiring skilled employees, 4) simplifying the jobs, and/or 5) de-enriching the jobs. On the other hand, if the IRI is substantially larger than the TDI, the gap probably suggests that the jobs must be enlarged and/or enriched, or people with less skill and ambition must be hired to staff the jobs.

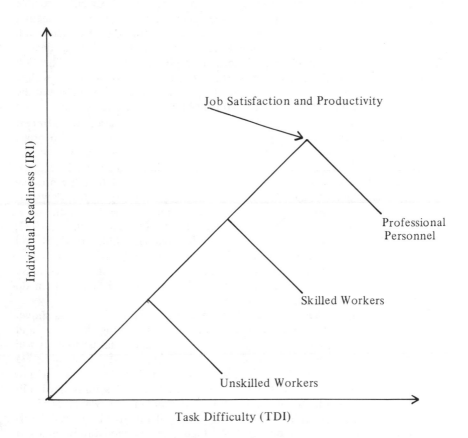

FIGURE 9-2. TASK DIFFICULTY AND INDIVIDUAL READINESS

(Adapted from Chung, K.H., and Ross, M.F., "Differences in Motivational Properties between Job Enlargement and Job Enrichment," *Academy of Management Review,* 1977 (forthcoming).

EFFECTS ON PERFORMANCE-REWARD TIE

Job design influences workers' perception of the performance-incentive reward tie (P-I) in two ways. First, workers performing enriched jobs can see a direct relationship between task accomplishment and feelings of achievement, recognition, and growth. If they perform successfully, they will be immediately reinforced by task accomplishment without going through supervisory evaluation. However, less productive workers will merely be frustrated when they can not accomplish their assigned demanding jobs. Thus, job enrichment is highly motivational for productive work groups but it can be a liability for unskilled workers.

Second, the E-P tie affects employees' perceptions of the P-I tie. When the task difficulty is low and every employee can perform the job, all will be rewarded for its completion regardless of effort level. On the other hand, if the task difficulty is too high, an average employee is not able to accomplish the task and will not be rewarded for his effort no matter how hard he may try. In either case, workers will perceive that their efforts are not related to performance (E-P) and that their reward or the outcome of their efforts is not related to task performance (P-I). Consequently, they will not be motivated to exert effort to accomplish their tasks. On the other hand, workers will be motivated to perform their tasks when these tasks possess an intermediate degree of performance difficulty because their perceptions of the E-P and P-I ties at this task difficulty level will be highly motivational.

MATCHING INCENTIVES WITH NEEDS

A critical task in developing an effective incentive-reward system is to match organizational incentives with individual needs (I-N). Figure 1-2 in Chapter 1 suggests a possible way of matching incentives with needs. This figure implies that workers who strive for the satisfaction of existence needs will be motivated by such extrinsic incentives as pay, job security, and working conditions (Myers, 1964). Such workers may easily tolerate or may even prefer simplified and routinized jobs (Vroom, 1960). Some workers are primarily motivated by socializing opportunities on their jobs. For example, Reif and Luthans (1972) found that unskilled workers prefer routinized tasks because these jobs provide them with opportunities to socialize or daydream without undue mental exhaustion and responsibility. Employees with higher-order needs or motivation seekers are then motivated by such intrinsic incentives as achievement, recognition, responsibility, and growth-opportunity.

Figure 1-2 also suggests various motivational programs which aim to produce appropriate incentives corresponding to employees with different sets of needs. Professional people are motivated by such incentives as achievement, recognition, responsibility, and growth opportunity. Thus, job enrichment is recommended to motivate employees with higher-order needs, while establishing an effective reward system and building a sociable organizational climate are suggested for workers with such maintenance needs as socialization and existence. However, it should be pointed out that a minimum-to-moderate level of job enlargement can be motivational even for maintenance seekers because such an enlarged job can be less boring and requires a minimum level of skill and responsibility.

JOB DIMENSIONS AND PSYCHOLOGICAL STATES

Hackman, Oldham, Janson, and Purdy (1975) explain how various job dimensions affect workers' psychological states, which influence their work outcomes. They indicated that positive personal and work outcomes (satisfaction, motivation, and performance) are derived from their job-related psychological states (meaningfulness of work, responsibility for outcomes, and knowledge of results). These psychological states are then created by the presence of five core job dimensions (skill variety, task identity, task significance, performance feedback, and autonomy). For example, a job becomes meaningful when it involves the use of different skills, the completion of a whole work unit, and a meaningful task. The motivational potential of a task increases as any one of these core job dimensions increases its motivational characteristics.

Hackman et al. proposed five implementing steps to generate the necessary motivational job dimensions: 1) formulating natural work units, 2) combining tasks, 3) establishing client relationships, 4) vertical job loading, and 5) establishing feedback channels. These implementing concepts are to increase the motivational potential of the job dimensions. The first action step is directly related to two of the core dimensions—task identity and task significance. Natural work units influence a sense of performing an identifiable work unit and a feeling of owning the job. The second action step, combining related tasks, affects task variety and task identity. As tasks are combined, the job becomes larger and requires a variety of skills. The establishment of direct contacts with clients influences skill variety, feedback, and autonomy. Workers have some degree of autonomy in dealing with clients and receive direct feedback from them. They also need interpersonal skills in interacting with clients. Vertical job loading increases the sense of responsibility of the workers for their performance outcomes.

Hackman and Oldham (1975) emphasized the importance of diagnosing the motivational potential of a job and studying the differences in individual need strength. Theoretically, the higher the motivational potential of a job, the higher the level of workers' affective reactions will be to the job. However, workers with strong growth need strength tend to respond more positively to enriched jobs than workers with lower growth need strength. Employee needs moderate the relationships between core job dimensions and affective reactions of the employees to their jobs.

The concepts of task difficulty index (TDI) and individual readiness index (IRI), presented in a previous section, are similar to Hackman's concepts of motivational potential score (MPS) and individual need strength. However, the differences between them are that while MPS involves five core job dimensions, TDI involves eight task attributes, and while Hackman's tool measures growth need strength, IRI concerns with both technical and psychological readiness to perform demanding jobs. The TDI also is divided into two major components—job enlargement and job enrichment. Further, the contingency relationships between TDI and IRI deal with the dysfunctional consequences of both over and under-enriched jobs.

Combining the Hackman et al. job dimension model with the motivational job characteristics presented in previous sections, a more comprehensive job dimension model is suggested in Figure 9-3. Figure 9-3 identifies nine core job dimensions (five job enlargement factors and four job enrichment factors), two

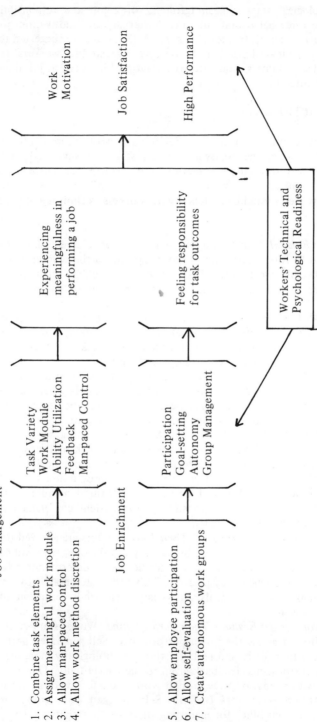

FIGURE 9-3. ACTION STRATEGY FOR JOB DESIGN
(Adapted from Hackman, J.R., Oldham, G., Janson, R., and Purdy, K., "A New Strategy of Job Enrichment," *California Management Review*, 1975, 17, p. 62).

critical psychological states (meaningfulness of a job and responsibility for outcomes), and three behavioral outcomes (internal work motivation, job satisfaction, and performance). In addition, seven action steps are suggested to create the nine core job dimensions. This figure also suggests that workers' technical and psychological readiness moderates the relationship between job dimensions and behavioral outcomes.

JOB DESIGN ACTION STEPS

If the job lacks motivational potential but the workers are ready to undertake demanding tasks, the following action steps are suggested to increase workers' work motivation, job satisfaction, and performance. These action steps are proposed to enhance the motivational potential of various job dimensions. Selection of any step should be matched with workers' technical and psychological readiness.

1. *Combine Related Task Elements.* A number of related task elements are combined to form a meaningful work module so the worker can perform an identifiable work unit. Task combination elicits such motivational properties as task variety, meaningful work module, and ability utilization.
2. *Assign Work Modules to Workers.* Workers are assigned the responsibility of performing identifiable units of work. The completion of these work units will provide them with performance feedback, sense of accomplishment, and sense of doing something worthwhile.
3. *Allow Self-control of Work Pace.* A man-paced production system allows the workers to speed up or slow down as long as they get the job done. This will provide them with a sense of control over the production system and satisfy their needs for independency and autonomy.
4. *Allow Discretion for Work Method.* After basic training, workers are given the opportunity to express their differences in work methods. Discretion is especially necessary for performing nonprogrammable jobs. This will provide them with a sense of control over the production system. If the workers have the ability and desire to perform demanding tasks with additional challenge and responsibility, job enrichment elements can be introduced into the work system.
5. *Allow Workers To Manage Their Own Jobs.* Workers are allowed to participate in the managerial process. Since they are the ones who will carry out the tasks, they should have some influence in determining what, how much, how, and when they perform. This action step may help employees to internalize their task goals and satisfy their needs for autonomy, control, and power.
6. *Allow Workers To Evaluate Their Performance.* Workers are given the responsibility to assess their own performance. Self-generated performance feedback is immediate and real and thus psychologically more meaningful than the performance feedback given to them externally. This will provide workers with a sense of pride in their work and a feeling of responsibility.
7. *Create Autonomous Work Groups.* Self-managed work groups are given collective responsibility for managing their group activities. They perform such managerial functions as planning, organizing, performing, and con-

trolling which are usually reserved for managerial personnel. This will increase the motivational potential of the job by giving them more autonomy and responsibility.

In addition to these job design factors, several peripheral factors can be implemented to enhance workers' affective reactions to their jobs. First, workers are provided with continuous education and training to increase their ability to deal with a variety of jobs. As performance is considered to be a joint function of ability and motivation, the education and training will positively influence the level of performance. Second, the pay level increases as the level of performance increases. When pay is not commensurate to the increased level of performance, motivation will be quickly subsided. Third, a facilitative leadership supportive to workers' goal-oriented behavior is encouraged. Leaders are often selected from the work groups and are responsible for team development and group decision making. Finally, status symbols differentiating managerial levels are minimized to give workers a sense of self-respect and self-worth. Status symbols usually downgrade lower-ranking personnel. The job enrichment program at General Foods (Topeka Plant) has many of the implementing concepts discussed above (Ford, 1972).

IMPLEMENTATION PROBLEMS

Despite considerable enthusiasm generated by job enlargement and enrichment concepts, many employers find it difficult to implement these programs in their organizations. A study conducted by Luthans and Reif (1974) indicated that out of 125 industrial firms surveyed, only five companies had made any formal efforts to enrich jobs. Even in these firms only a small portion of employees were affected by the job enrichment programs. For example, the job enrichment program at Texas Instruments, considered a pioneer in this field, has involved only about 10 percent of its total work force. Another 25 percent of the surveyed firms, however, have applied these programs to a small portion of their employees on an informal basis.

In addition to the tangible costs associated with job enlargement, there are several behavioral problems associated with an implementation of job enrichment. First, the practice of employee participation, especially management by consensus, is a time-consuming proposition. To be effective, the participatory management should be able to accommodate divergent viewpoints and cover a wide range of managerial decisions related to the work group. If it is used only for insignificant issues, employees may feel cheated and manipulated. Proponents of participatory management, however, indicate that this program can reduce time spent in implementing the new system because employees internalize the decisions, know what is expected of them, and are motivated to carry them out.

Second, employees will not positively respond to new work systems unless they are reasonably satisfied with lower-order needs such as economic and socialization. When these needs are not satisfied, employees become preoccupied with satisfaction of these needs; higher-order needs do not emerge as motivators of employee behavior. Although satisfying such lower-order needs as biological and security wants becomes less critical as the society becomes more affluent, people are never fully satisfied with these needs, and they, from time to time, become preoccupied with economic need satisfaction especially in times of economic recession. Furthermore, satisfying such relation-oriented needs as socialization, love, affection, trust, and openness is always a delicate task because people become more sensitive to socialization needs as a result of improved economic well-being, but they have less opportunity to satisfy them as the society becomes increasingly complex and mechanized.

Third, new work systems tend to sensitize workers to expect satisfaction of higher-order needs because they are usually told that the work systems are being redesigned to fulfill these needs. While raising the level of expectation is relatively a simple task, meeting the raised expectation is a complex one because the organization has to satisfy divergent needs of organizational members. Since the goals of organizational members as well as the organization and its subunits are to be synchronized into workable terms, it may be difficult for the organization to create a work environment in which individual members can fully and consistently satisfy their high expectations. Even if the organization is able to create an optimal climate, some individuals are not capable of deriving the benefits from it. When the raised expectation is not met, it then becomes a source of dissatisfaction which could have been avoided if the new work system had not been instituted.

Fourth, there are significant differences in individual responses to new work systems that have to be considered in task design. Blood and Hulin (1967), Hackman and Lawler (1971), and Turner and Lawrence (1965) found that people with rural backgrounds responded positively to job enrichment, but workers with urban backgrounds did not respond to the program in the same positive manner. Reif and Luthans (1972) also reported that unskilled workers prefer routinized tasks because these jobs require little thinking, training, and responsibility, and allow them to socialize or daydream on their jobs without impairing productivity.

Finally, job enrichment efforts can be impeded by labor unions. Unions may consider job enrichment to be an effort to exploit workers by giving them more responsibility for the same pay or an effort to alienate them from unions by reducing their dependency on union protection. Since most labor unions in their present form can survive only as protectors of exploited workers, successful job enrichment programs can be conceived as a threat to the existence of these unions. When such win-lose feelings prevail in the organization, any attempt to enrich jobs will be shattered by the uncooperative union by imposing restrictive work rules, adhering to legalistic procedures, or active sabotages. Management on the other hand may react to union attitudes by turning to paternalistic approaches such as higher wages and increased fringe benefits or by such scare tactics as threat of lay-offs and intimidation.

In essence, the combined approach to job design is a complex proposition because it has to deal with a variety of individual as well as organizational constraints and find a workable fit between individual and organizational motivational properties. As it is a complex phenomenon, job design planners often prescribe wrong programs for wrong problems. Sirota and Wolfson (1973) pointed out that many companies failed to implement productive work systems because they failed to diagnose real causes of employee problems and accordingly applied wrong remedies for them. Most motivational tools suggested by industrial psychologists are partial remedies to deal with a specific set of problems. Since they are not cure-all remedies, it is necessary for management to diagnose correctly the real causes of employee problems and prescribe a specific set of programs to deal with them.

SUMMARY AND CONCLUSION

Designing motivational work systems involves three major forms: flexible work schedules, job enlargement, and job enrichment. Flexible work schedules allow workers to fulfill their work commitment in a more flexible manner or in fewer days than the conventional five-day, fixed work schedules. There are two types of flexible work schedules—four-day work week and flexitime. Under the four-day work week program, the worker fulfills his work commitment in four-days and thus can enjoy three-day weekends. Flexitime allows employees to organize their own work schedules to suit their personal needs and life styles. Flexitime is psychologically more meaningful because it gives workers a sense of control and freedom in their work environment. When flexitime is added to enriched jobs, its characteristics will resemble those of professional and managerial jobs.

Job enlargement adds more task elements to an existing job. Unlike those who see it as a futile exercise of expanding the meaninglessness of a job, a properly designed job can have such motivational elements as task variety, meaningful work module, ability utilization, man-paced control, and feedback, and is considered to be a prerequisite to an implementation of job enrichment. Job enrichment gives workers the authority and responsibility to manage their own jobs. Employee participation in goal setting results in greater subordinates' acceptance of decisions and in high performance goals. Autonomy in managing their activities encourages workers to rely on their initiative and self control, and thus increases a sense of power as well as responsibility. But, the task of enriching jobs is more complex and requires high degrees of sophistication in dealing with people than does job enlargement because the former requires changes in behavioral systems in an organization while the latter primarily involves changes in technical aspects of a job.

It is predicted that job satisfaction and productivity will be higher when both job enlargement and enrichment are jointly applied to designing work systems than when they are applied individually. When they are utilized jointly, job enlargement makes the job more meaningful while job enrichment makes the worker feel more responsible on his job. Industrial experiences with this work system are generally favorable but with mixed results. Despite the considerable enthusiasm generated by the new trend in work systems, many jobs are not enriched, and only a small portion of the nation's work force is affected by this trend. Enriching a job is a difficult and expensive proposition because it has to satisfy a number of individual and organizational constraints before it elicits motivational forces. The following managerial strategies are suggested to deal with various individual and organizational constraints.

1. The task must be horizontally enlarged before it is vertically expanded. Giving workers who are performing simplified jobs more authority and responsibility may not produce any positive motivational result.

2. The workers should possess necessary skills or at least potential to perform their assigned tasks. When they are lacking necessary skills, increas-

ing responsibility and challenge may only create frustration for the workers. What they need may be job de-enrichment rather than enrichment.

3. The workers must be reasonably satisfied with lower-order needs such as monetary and socialization so that higher-order needs can emerge as motivators of behavior. When they are not reasonably satisfied with these needs, they will be preoccupied with low-level needs satisfaction.

4. The organization should promote a psychological climate in which its members, including workers, supervisors, and top management, are supportive of each other, trusty, and openly communicating with one another in dealing with day-to-day individual and organizational problems.

5. Job enlargement may be more suitable to workers at lower levels of organizational echelons because these workers may not be motivated by additional responsibility and challenge on their jobs. Further, enlarged jobs can be less boring and at the same time may not require a high degree of skill and responsibility.

6. Job enrichment can have strong motivational value to those employees who prefer challenge in performing demanding jobs, have abilities and skills to perform, and are motivated to satisfy higher-order needs.

7. It may be entirely possible that some workers may not be motivated by intrinsic motivation and thus do not respond to any new work systems. They may be happy with simplified jobs which give them opportunities to socialize.

10

MANAGEMENT BY OBJECTIVES AND PERFORMANCE APPRAISAL

Motivation is a goal-directed behavior. Goal-setting can serve as an impetus for releasing human motivation. Since such individual as well as organizational performance depends on employee motivation, management-by-objectives (MBO) can be an important tool. MBO is defined here as a managerial process by which the superior and his subordinates jointly assess their task goals, accomplishments. MBO can be seen as a special form of job enrichment which heavily emphasizes the goal setting process. MBO not only operationalizes the major concepts of job enrichment (participation, goal-setting, autonomy, and group management), but it also contains a result-oriented performance appraisal. Unlike the traditional management system which is directed by management's goals, MBO is managed by organizational goals jointly set by managers and workers. The theory is that employees tend to internalize task goals when they have influenced the goal-setting process. MBO as a concept is relatively simple. However, implementation of an MBO system is difficult because it involves the integration of various individual and group goals into a set of workable organizational goals. When an MBO system is mechanically introduced to an organization without taking into account the inner motivation of employees, it often fails to produce satisfactory results. This chapter will 1) discuss potential pay-offs of an MBO system, 2) present a set of specific action steps for implementing an MBO system, 3) discuss a result-oriented performance appraisal, 4) discuss potential problems associated with MBO, and 5) specify several organizational contingencies for effective utilization of MBO.

POTENTIAL PAYOFFS OF MBO

The concept of MBO involves several managerial functions such as planning, organizing, performing, and evaluating which are the core of the traditional management theories (Davis, 1951; Fayol, 1949; Gulick, 1937; and Urwick, 1964). Early management theories emphasize the importance of setting goals and distributing specific tasks to employees for their accountability. Organizational goals are primarily set by management and are imposed on employees for compliance in return rewards. This traditional management thinking is still widely practiced in industrial and government institutions and is even called

MBO. It may be called MBO because an organization is managed by goals under this system. However, such a system often fails to generate motivation because organizational goals usually represent those of management rather than those of employees.

The essence of MBO involves employee participation in goal-setting. The importance of employee participation was stressed by early behavioral scientists (Cock and French, 1948; Follett, 1942; and Mayo, 1945). These behavioral scientists emphasized employee participation in decision making as a means of gaining greater commitment to organizational goals and to enhance employees' intrinsic motivation. Drucker (1954) then synthesized the influences of the two schools of thought (traditional and behavioral) and further developed the concept of MBO that we are familiar with today. However, MBO as a managerial tool comes in a variety of forms and sizes. While some emphasize the planning and control functions of MBO, others use it as a method of developing objective performance criteria. While some use it as a motivational and communicational tool, some perceive it as a method of putting pressure on employees to increase productivity.

BRIEF HISTORY OF MBO APPLICATION

Drucker (1954) originally suggested MBO as an integrative managerial tool. He proposed the MBO philosophy and process as a method of integrating various goals of subunits of an organization to serve the corporate objectives. The original thinking of MBO seemed to be influenced by Alfred Sloan at General Motors in the 1920s. General Motors established decentralized operations with centralized control (Drucker, 1946). In Sloan's years at General Motors, divisional managers had to submit their estimates of operating results for which they were held accountable and were rewarded according to their accomplishments.

In the late 1950s MBO focused on the development of objective performance criteria for measuring the managers' contributions. For example, McGregor (1957) proposed a result-oriented performance appraisal as a reaction to managers' dissatisfaction with traditional trait-oriented performance appraisal. He suggested that each manager establish short-term performance goals for himself, and then be evaluated on the basis of his accomplishment. A number of companies such as a General Electric (Meyer, Kay, and French, 1965), Purex Corporation (Raia, 1965), and Texas Instruments (Hughes, 1966) have applied MBO-oriented performance appraisal systems and reported positive results in terms of improved communication and employee motivation.

In the 1960s and early 1970s, MBO was emphasized as a managerial tool for increasing employee motivation. As an integral part of job enrichment, MBO places an emphasis on employee participation in goal-setting, exercising autonomy in performing their jobs, and assessing their own performance (Herzberg, 1968; Likert, 1967; and Myers, 1970). The motivational approach to MBO stresses the development and integration of individual, as well as organizational, goals as a means of achieving mutual goals. Despite considerable enthusiasm generated by job enrichment concepts, as indicated in Chapter 9, MBO that relies heavily on employee participation and autonomy is not widely applied in organizations. Various individual and organizational factors such as job insecurity, lack of interpersonal competence, distrust among organizational members, and lack of support tend to prevent organizations from utilizing it effectively.

In recent years, MBO is reemerging as an integrative management system designed to orchestrate key managerial processes and activities into concerted efforts toward the attainment of organizational goals. The MBO process, as we shall see later, involves the establishment and execution of task goals, key performance responsibilities, action plans, and performance reviews. However, employee participation and autonomy in this process differ from one organization to another. Not all situations warrant an effective utilization of employee participation and automomy. The degree of participation and autonomy exercised by employees varies, reflecting the differences in task goals (specificity, difficulty, and relevancy), work environment or organizational climate (see Chapter 8), and individual technical and psychological readiness (see Chapter 9). Thus, the effectiveness of MBO depends on its user's ability to find a workable fit among these key organizational constraints. When all these contingencies are duly considered and matched in the process of implementing an MBO system, a full range of benefits can result from its utilization (see Luthans and Reif, 1974; Sirota and Wolfson, 1973; and Steers and Porter, 1964).

BETTER UTILIZATION OF RESOURCES

MBO signals organizational members the direction in which the organization is moving. Instead of reacting to the organizational environment passively and randomly, members actively search for the future state of their affairs and direct their energies and resources toward these future goals. Once these desired objectives are set, they tend to minimize the possibility of pursuing other potential goals due to the limited availability of resources. MBO leads to better utilization of organizational resources such as money, manpower, materials, and time. First, MBO forces managers to plan their activities to best achieve their organizational objectives. Planning reduces unnecessary search behavior and reduces the incidence of crash programs which tend to be more expensive than planned programs. Second, MBO forces managers to allocate limited organizational resources to achieve objectives most important to overall organizational missions. An order of priority is assigned to various objectives, and necessary resources are allocated on a priority basis. Third, MBO discourages individual and organizational activities which do not contribute to the attainment of organizational goals. Under MBO, both managers and employees frequently review the contributions they are making toward the goal attainment. Through this review process, they should be able to detect noncontributory activities and modify them. Finally, when members internalize organizational goals as their task goals, they will be motivated to direct and control their own activities to achieve these goals and will not need close supervision.

GOAL ATTRIBUTES AND MOTIVATION

A number of empirical studies cited in Chapter 9 indicate that goal-setting can result in higher performance of employees. In this chapter, discussion will be focused on the question of how MBO can be designed to increase employee motivation. This will be done within the theoretical framework of expectancy motivation. MBO can be effective in arousing employee work motivation if the task goals are set in such a manner that 1) goal-attainment is a function of effort exertion (E-P); 2) goal-attainment produces intrinsic as well as extrinsic incentives such as recognition, sense of achievement, promotion, and salary increase (P-I); and 3) these incentives have the power to satisfy employees' needs such as self-esteem and self-actualization (I-N). A number of research findings can be incorporated into this expectancy motivation framework to better explain why and how certain MBO attributes such as goal specificity, goal difficulty, and participation in goal-setting have impacts on employee satisfaction and job involvement by influencing motivational components of expectancy theory.

Goal Specificity and Clarity

The increase in goal specificity is positively related to job performance because it helps individuals see what is required from them to achieve specific goals (E-P). A goal-setting program (MBO) becomes motivationally effective because it specifies task-goals for work groups as well as individual employees (Latham and Yukl, 1975; Steers, 1975; and Steers and Porter, 1974). Goal clarity or specificity tends to be more closely related to job performance of employees with higher achievement needs than to those with lower achievement needs (Steers, 1975). Carroll and Tosi (1970) also reported that goal clarity seemed to be more important to managerial groups than to others. MBO also clarifies employees' role perceptions. Studies indicate that both role ambiguity and role conflict are directly related to poor performance outcomes (Hamner and Tosi, 1973; and House and Rizzo, 1972). But, role ambiguity is more pervasive in its adverse effects than role conflict (House and Rizzo, 1972; Johnson and Stinson, 1975; and Miles, 1976). These studies imply that when MBO clearly specifies task goals and workers' role perceptions, it can have a positive impact on employee job performance.

Goal Difficulty

Several laboratory studies indicate that goal difficulty is related to work motivation in an inverted-V relationship; work motivation increases as goal difficulty increases to a certain point (Atkinson, 1966; Hulin, 1975; and Steers and Porter, 1974). But when goals are believed to be too difficult, the MBO system may lose its credibility and create poor motivation. With moderately difficult task goals, the expectancy that effort leads to goal attainment tends to be the highest. However, differences in individual preference on goal difficulty should be taken into account when designing an MBO system. Studies indicate that individuals with high achievement needs tend to be more ego-involved in achieving challenging goals because they place a higher value on goal attainment (Atkinson and Feather, 1966; Heckhausen, 1967; Mahone, 1960; and Morris, 1967). Carroll and Tosi (1970) also reported that goal difficulty was associated with the increased effort among managers with high self-assurance, managers who perceived a close association between performance and reward, and experienced managers. But, it was associated with decreased effort among managers with low self-assurance and lack of experience.

Participative Goal-Setting

Goal-setting activity alone can positively affect the level of performance without a formal feedback program (Locke, 1968; and Locke, Cartledge, and Kneer,

1970). A number of studies, presented in Chapter 9, also indicate that the participative goal-setting program produces higher or harder goals and increased productivity than assigned and "do your best" goal-setting practices (Bryan and Locke, 1967; Locke, 1968; Latham and Baldes, 1975; Latham and Kinne, 1974; Latham and Yukl, 1975; Ronan, Latham, and Kinne, 1975). However, the relationship between participation and performance is highly ambiguous, and the effectiveness of a goal-setting system to a large extent depends on the differences in individual needs and the nature of the tasks. The effect of participation on performance tends to be positive for those employees with strong needs for independence and achievement (Vroom, 1960). Contrary to this finding, however, Steers (1975) reported that participation in goal-setting was more closely related to the performance of employees with low achievement needs. Carroll and Tosi (1970) also indicated that employee participation in goal-setting was not related to the perceived success of the MBO program nor in more favorable attitudes toward the program or the superior. However, participation in goal-setting tended to be positively correlated with increased effort for managers with high self-assurance but not for those with low self-assurance. Furthermore, the need for employee participation in goal-setting seems to be a function of the nature of the task being supervised. If the job is programmable and thus standardized, its performance standard is more or less predetermined and does not leave much room for employee participation. If the job is not programmable and its performance largely depends on employee motivation, as in research and development and marketing activities, employee participation in goal-setting may positively affect their motivation and job performance. In general, a participative MBO system can be effectively introduced to those employees with strong needs for independence and achievement in performing nonprogrammable jobs.

Performance Feedback

An MBO system has a built-in feedback mechanism. Knowledge of results (KR) is generated intrinsically from performing the job itself rather than supervisory evaluation. This internally generated feedback tends to be more authentic and motivational than that introduced externally (Cummings, Schwab, and Rosen, 1971; Greller and Herold, 1975). Employees can measure their actual performance against their goals, and the resulting information will provide them with either a feeling of success or failure. The feeling of success is associated with such intrinsic incentives as recognition, advancement, and growth. Such a feedback seems to be more important for individuals with high achievement needs (Steers, 1975; Heckhausen, 1967). These individuals tend to draw personal satisfaction from competing against some standard of excellence and from goal attainment for the sake of gaining a sense of accomplishment. Furthermore, an MBO system can generate meaningful performance feedback and thus increase the incentive value of a goal-setting system. In addition, extrinsic rewards such as performance bonus and promotion can be closely related to job performance under MBO. As an example, Feeney (1972) reported that performance feedback accompanied by positive reinforcement helped his company save an estimated $2 million in a three-year period.

OBJECTIVE PERFORMANCE CRITERIA

MBO provides a relatively objective performance criteria against which an employee's or a group's contributions to the attainment of organizational goals are measured and rewarded accordingly. As indicated earlier, the MBO performance system was developed as a reaction to managers' dissatisfaction with the traditional trait-oriented performance appraisal. The traditional method of performance appraisal evaluates contributions to an organization on the basis of such personal traits as initiative, intelligence, cooperation, and judgment, rather than achievement. For example, McGregor (1957) pointed out that both managers and employees resist the use of trait-oriented performance appraisal due to its unfairness. He then proposed the result-oriented performance appraisal (MBO) as a way of encouraging employees to use self-appraisal against short-term goals established for themselves.

McGregor's argument seemed to be well accepted and practiced by managers. For example, at General Electric, Meyer, Kay, and French (1965) compared managers using the work Planning and Review method (MBO-oriented performance appraisal) with the firm's traditional performance appraisal. They found that managers operating under the traditional method did not change their managerial behavior. Managers operating under MBO expressed favorable attitudes toward their superiors' effort to improve performance, willingness to try new ideas and suggestions, planning and utilizing their resources, and making use of performance appraisal. Thompson and Dalton (1970) criticized the traditional performance appraisal for not measuring the actual performance and for promoting a zero-sum game among employees. They indicated that an objective-focused approach (MBO) is productive in improving job performance, is future oriented rather than dewelling on past behavior, promotes an open and non-zero-sum game, and is flexible.

ORGANIZATIONAL EXPERIENCES WITH MBO

Although a number of companies practice MBO with seminars and meetings devoted to the subject, only a few companies seem to use it properly. Drucker, in his interview with the editor of *Organizational Dynamics,* indicated that many organizations are fascinated with the MBO procedures for the sake of following procedures without utilizing self-control (Dowling, 1974). About 83 percent of business firms claim to use MBO. However, the percentage of firms using it properly and getting positive results seems to be very low (Miglore, 1976). The poor utilization of MBO is comparable to that of job enrichment reported by Luthans and Reif (1974) in Chapter 9. Their study indicated that only a small portion of companies surveyed have applied job enrichment to a limited number of their employees. Several organizational experiences with MBO are reported in the following studies.

1. Meyer, Kay, and French (1965) reported a summary of their research findings at General Electric. Their study focused on the relative effectiveness of the traditional performance appraisal interview and the MBO oriented performance appraisal (Work Planning and Review). They found that the traditional appraisal interview had little influence on future job performance. Critical appraisal, however, led to defensive behavior on the part

of employees and had a negative effect on employee performance. Under the Work Planning and Review system (MBO), job performance was increased when task goals and deadlines are specifically established as a joint effort of the subordinate and his superior.

2. Raia (1965, 1966) investigated the impacts of MBO (Goals and Controls) on job performance at the Purex Corporation. His first study reported an increase in productivity and an increased awareness of the firm's goals due to the use of MBO. Prior to the MBO program, productivity was decreasing at the rate of .4 percent per month. After the program was instituted, it was increasing at the rate of .3 percent per month. However, the managers complained that participation was limited, and the program required a large amount of paper work. His second study reported a continuous increase in productivity in addition to improved managerial planning and control. However, many of the managers stated that the MBO program did not provide adequate incentives to improve performance, there was too much paper work, and it was not utilized at lower management levels. Also, an overemphasis on measurable goals was cited as a weakness.

3. Ivancevich, Donnelly, and Lyon (1970) studied the impacts of MBO on employee need satisfaction at two medium-sized companies. Their study reported that MBO was more effective in satisfying employees' needs when top-level executives were actively involved in the program implementation than when it was introduced by the personnel department. The top management's involvement in the program provided an impetus for a better understanding of its philosophy and mechanics throughout the entire organization. It was also found that the frequency of goal-setting and feedback sessions had some impacts on employee need satisfaction. Lower-level managers, however, complained about the amount of paper work required by the program and the difficulty of setting specific goals for their jobs.

4. Carroll and Tosi (1973) studied the managerial reactions to the MBO program at Black and Decker. Their interviews revealed that 35 percent of the managers perceived the MBO program as a performance appraisal tool, and 58 percent perceived it as a managerial tool for clarifying managers' roles and expectations. Forty-one percent felt that MBO led to the establishment of planning activities and target dates, and 31 percent felt that the MBO process forced supervisor-subordinate communication and feedback. However, some managers complained the excessive procedural requirements of the program and the inflexibility of modifying the goals once they had been established.

5. The editor of *Organizational Dynamics* (1974) reported the utilization of MBO at the Union Mutual Life Insurance. Union Mutual had combined MBO with Managerial Grid. Blake and Mouton's Managerial Grid (1964, 1969) was introduced to an existing MBO program to insure the process of achieving the corporate goals set by MBO. The Managerial Grid was used as a vehicle by which MBO could be carried out. The Grid training helped to develop the interpersonal competence of managers and their teamwork skills. The program, called "Grid-cum-MBO," helped the executives set high performance goals and function effectively as team members.

They previously were not concerned with return-on-investment goals and acted as autonomous professionals.

In summary, MBO can be defined as a process of defining and achieving organizational goals by joint effort of superior and subordinates. It can be seen as a management tool of assisting managers for execution of various managerial functions such as planning, organizing, directing and controlling. If MBO is properly designed, it can elicit the motivational characteristics (E-P, P-I, and I-N) of expectancy theory. It can be a motivational device for integrating individual and organizational goals into a mutually reinforcing system. Specific benefits are better utilization of resources, better planning and controlling, improved motivation and job performance, and increased superior-subordinate interaction. Some problems associated with MBO are excessive paper work and procedural requirements, difficulty of setting specific goals for some jobs, possible overemphasis on measurable goals, and demands for interpersonal competence and teamwork from employees.

MBO PROCESS AND ACTION STEPS

The actual process of implementing and managing an MBO system involves the several action elements. First, task goals should be established for individual work groups at various levels of the organization. Second, these goals need to be translated into action plans to guide their activities. Third, actions will be needed to carry out the activities. Fourth, performance reviews will be held periodically to assess progress toward the goals. Finally, annual performance appraisals will be held to relate performance to organizational rewards. These action elements are carried out through specific action steps. In outlining the MBO process, attention will be given to the motivational aspects of the program design. While it describes the mechanical aspects of implementing a MBO program, it will also discuss how and why each action can elicit the motivational attributes of task goals.

Step 1.   Arrange Organizational Goals in Means-Ends Chain

Organizational goals can be classified into three major categories: *(a)* overall organizational goals that need to be defined at the top management level, *(b)* task goals that need to be accomplished by various work groups, and *(c)* individual performance goals as derivatives of group task goals. In addition, there are individual personal goals that need to be accommodated in the process of achieving organizational goals. Organizational members contribute their efforts to the attainment of organizational goals as a means of achieving personal goals. MBO as a motivational tool will achieve the highest effectiveness when two sets of goals, individual and organizational, are meshed together for mutual reinforcement.

Organizational goals can be structured in a hierarchy of a means-ends chain in which the objectives (ends) of the subunits of an organization become the means of achieving the objectives of the next higher unit. The formulation of organizational goals can start with *(a)* the definition of long-range and short-term performance objectives at the top management level, *(b)* the derivation of task goals for each major department or division from the overall organizational objectives, *(c)* the derivation of task goals for each work group from the departmental goals, and *(d)* the establishment of individual task goals serving the task goal attainment of his work group. Figure 10-1 depicts the process of setting goals at various levels of an organization. Likert's linking-pin organizational structure is suggested as a vehicle by which task goals are formulated at various organizational levels and linked to overall objectives of the organization.

The linking-pin organizational process provides two-way communication channels through which organizational goals at higher levels are communicated downward to serve as a guide for formulating task goals at lower levels, and specific task goals at lower levels are communicated upward to serve the goals at higher levels. Any differences in goal-setting between organizational levels will be negotiated by supervisors in linking-pin positions. The linking-pin process should integrate individual as well as group activities at all levels toward obtaining overall organizational objectives. At the same time, organizational members at all levels exercise influence and reflect their interest in the process of formulating and achieving organizational objectives.

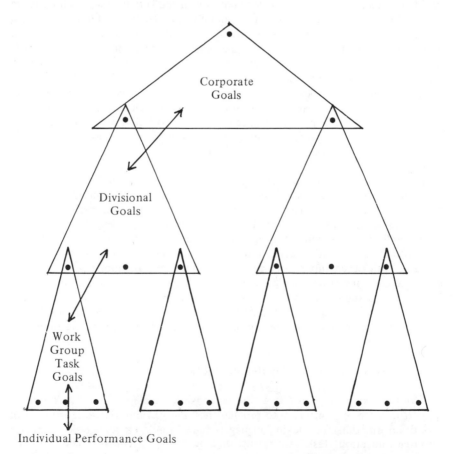

FIGURE 10-1. ORGANIZATIONAL GOALS IN MEANS-ENDS CHAIN

Step 2. Identify Key Performance Responsibilities

Organizational members of each work group participate in identifying the performance responsibilities for their work groups. Meeting these responsibilities will be contributory to the attainment of subgroup task goals and the overall goals of the organization. Unlike a general statement of organizational missions or long-range goals, task goals represent operational goals by which day-to-day organizational activities are planned, executed, and evaluated. Thus, goal-setting under MBO essentially involves the formulation of task goals in key areas of performance responsibility at all levels of the organization. The key areas of responsibility can then be classified into four major categories of activities: routinized, problem-solving, innovative, and individual development.

Routinized activities include a variety of ongoing and repetitive tasks that must be performed on a day-to-day basis. Most production, sales, and clerical functions are routinized activities. Problem-solving activities include a variety of nonscheduled or irregularly scheduled activities dealing with such problems as industrial accidents, absenteeism, machine breakdowns, and strikes. Such problems usually are related to day-to-day routinized activities, and solutions are essential for normal functioning of the day-to-day operations. Innovative activities involve a number of creative, developmental, and improvement-oriented activities that lead to the solution of persistent organizational problems or the introduction of new ideas, products, and behavioral patterns for better performance results. Individual activities involve a number of skill learning activities for improving current performance in technical and managerial activities, combating technical and managerial obsolescence, and preparing employees for additional responsibility and advancement. The formulation of individual development objectives provides a unique opportunity for management to integrate individual goals with organizational goals.

Every individual or work group performs all four categories of activities. However, the amount of time and energy one spends for each category will vary according to his position in the organizational hierarchy and functional specialization. For example, a production manager spends more time performing routinized and problem-solving activities than innovative activities, while personnel in research and development spend more time performing innovative activities than routinized activities. Rank-and-file workers tend to perform more routinized activities than supervisory personnel, and managerial jobs tend to be more complex and innovative than that of blue-collar workers, requiring nonroutinized activities such as problem-solving. However, as MBO increasingly demands employee participation in managerial processes, employees at all levels will have more opportunities for performing problem-solving, innovative, and personal development activities.

Step 3. Assign Priorities to Key Responsibilities

The third step of goal-setting is to establish a set of priorities for key areas of performance responsibility to provide the manager and his work group with useful information for making managerial decisions. These decisions involve resource allocation, task assignment, and performance control. The priorities can be ranked in the order of the activity's importance to the overall task goals, or a set of relative weights can be assigned to key performance responsibilities based on the amount of time or resources required to perform each of the key responsibilities. In some cases, both priority ranking and relative weights may be desirable for making appropriate managerial decisions. Thus, priority assignment requires two sets of judgments—qualitative and quantitative. The qualitative judgment deals with the importance of a task to the overall task goals; while the quantitative judgement involves a decision regarding the amount of resources needed to perform the assigned task or activity. A task may be highly important to the group, but its resource requirements may be too prohibitive to undertake. Thus, the selection of a certain task and its priority should be based on the trade-offs of these two sets of judgment.

Step 4. Define the Expected Outcomes of Key Responsibilities

The fourth step in the goal-setting process involves the development of expected outcomes for each of the key areas of performance responsibility. These statements of objectives become the targets for group as well as individual activities, and the criteria upon which performance progress review and appraisal will be carried out. If possible, the expected results should be expressed in tangible and measurable terms such as sales volume, costs, product units, profits, number of accounts, customer complaints, number of rejects, and target dates. This statement answers the questions of what, how much, at what costs, and by when. For example, a supervisory training group at XYZ corporation "undertakes a leadership training program for thirty supervisory personnel at the cost of $200 per person for five days beginning June 1." Note here that the purpose of this training program is to improve supervisory leadership skills. However, since it is difficult to quantify such a qualitative goal, the training activities or means leading to the qualitative goal are quantified and stated as expected outcomes. If one wants to measure the effectiveness of the training program, he can do so by measuring the changes in supervisory behavior by means of a survey or through observation. Figure 10-2 shows an example of setting specific goals.

A number of guidelines are developed to assist the work group in defining meaningful statements of expected results. A tentative statement of expected results for a major performance responsibility can be checked against the following criteria to increase its validity:

    a. The stated objective is challenging but attainable. Theory indicates that both motivation and performance increase when task goals can be achieved as a result of energy and effort exertion (E-P). Also, people want to utilize their ability for performing tasks.

    b. The stated objective should have a specific and identifiable target. If the statement does not have a specific target, no one will know how well the task performance is progressing. Specific goal statement not only assists the plan for specific actions but also provides tangible performance feedback (KR).

    c. The stated objective should have a specific time duration. A specific activity should be tied to a specified time-frame by indicating the duration and the completion date of the activity. This time-frame will serve as a milestone against which performance progress can be measured.

    d. The stated objective should specify costs. The cost factors give an indica-

226

PERSONNEL DEPARTMENT, XYZ CORPORATION				Progress Reviews:	
Prepared by:			Date:	Date:	
Reviewed by:			Date:	Date:	
Key Performance Responsibilities	Weight	Expected Results	Target Date	Actual Results	
1. Supervisory Training	30%	Complete leadership training for 50 supervisory personnel for 5 days starting June 1. Projected costs = $8,000	7/30		
2. Preparing skill Inventory	20%	Complete skill inventory for manufacturing personnel starting August 1. Projected costs = $6,000	9/30		
3. Campus Recruiting	10%	Visiting 10 university campuses to interview candidates starting October 10. Projected costs – $4,000	11/30		
4. - - - - - - -	- - -	- - - - - - - - - - - -	- - -		

FIGURE 10-2. SPECIFIC GOAL-SETTING FOR PERSONNEL DEPARTMENT

tion as to how many resources are needed to accomplish the task and help determine the benefits and priorities of various group activities.

e. The stated objective should be consistent with organizational goals. If it is not contributory to the higher-level goals, its undertaking means a waste of resources and will not be rewarded. The objective should be revised or abandoned completely.

f. The user should not be over-obsessed with measurable and tangible goal statements. There are some areas of organizational performance which cannot be quantified. Subjective judgment should be a part of overall performance appraisal.

Step 5.   Assigning Specific Tasks to Employees

Once task objectives are established, specific tasks should be distributed among work group members. The assignment of specific tasks is the first step toward formulating action plans because it specifies the question of "who" is doing "what." Task assignment provides a linkage between the work group and its members. The performance of these assigned tasks by individual members becomes the means of achieving both individual and group goals. Assigned tasks serve as the basis for formulating the individual performance goals and for developing personal development objectives. Individual performance goals are derived from the assigned tasks. Personal development objectives are established to prepare employees to undertake current as well as future performance goals.

The assignment of specific tasks serve several motivational functions. First, when tasks are assigned on the basis of individual interests and qualifications, employees can better align their personal goals with organizational objectives. Second, a specific task assignment increases goal clarity and specificity so that employees can better utilize their resources. Third, it provides employees with a sense of responsibility to accomplish their assigned tasks. Finally, it will give a sense of accomplishment when they achieve their performance goals.

The statement of individual performance goals or objectives may iterate the above goal-setting steps from one through three. But, the goal-setting process for individual members will be much easier since they have participated in the group goal-setting process. A group approach to goal-setting is more effective for integrating individual efforts and their performance goals into group efforts than an individualized approach because individual members know what other members contribute and how their individual efforts are related to each other. Individualized approaches to MBO can fail to produce positive results when they are not able to integrate and coordinate individual efforts toward the attainment of group or organizational goals.

Step 6.   Define Authority and Responsibility Relationships

The assignment of tasks will be meaningless unless it is accompanied with a clear understanding of "who" is responsible for "what" and "who" is authorized to do "what."   A failure to define and clarify organizational relationships in terms of work flow, authority, and responsibility often creates chaotic situations in an organization and leads to ineffective utilization of organizational resources. This is particularly true when a group approach to MBO is used and the job requires activities which cut across various functional lines. The sequencing of major activities with operationally responsible personnel attached to the major activities will not only help to avoid potential conflicts and confusions regarding the roles each employee and work group play but also provide them with the basis for formulating specific action plans. While the operating personnel are responsible for the execution of their assigned activities, the manager overseeing the overall activities such as department head or project manager is responsible for integrating and leading the activities of operating personnel toward the attainment of the task goals.

If the job involves a large number of activities and personnel, a responsibility charting technique such as the Managerial Responsibility Guide (Melcher, 1967) and the Responsibility and Authority Matrix Charts (Raia, 1974) can help managers describe the interfaces between operating personnel and work groups. Such a responsibility-charting technique provides a matrix of relationships between major tasks and responsibilities. However, such a responsibility chart is only a tool to assist the manager in clarifying organizational relationships. It should not be unnaturally imposed on employees to legislate their normal interactive patterns. A simplified responsibility chart is shown in Figure 10-3 as a part of an action planning device.

The distribution of authority tends to commensurate with that of responsibility. Since MBO, as a motivational device, relies more on self-control than on formal managerial control, the employee who has the operational responsibility should have the authority to make operational decisions related to his assigned tasks with the consultation or approval of his superior. These operational decisions may include utilization of necessary resources, selection of work methods, and coordination with other operational personnel. The parity between authority and responsibility is necessary if MBO is used as a motivational device. One cannot be held responsible for activities when he does not have control over the means for achieving them. The extra authority and power can be used arbitrarily and thus have negative impacts on others. When a group-oriented MBO program is used, the authority and responsibility should be shared by its members with the supervisor being the center of the authority and responsibility distribution.

Step 7. Develop Time Schedules for Performing Key Responsibilities

Activity scheduling involves determining the time requirements for completing key activities. A time schedule usually shows two types of time requirements: the target dates for completing each major activity and the amount of time required to complete each activity. The schedule can serve as a planning and control tool for managing key performance responsibilities. It is important for determining manpower and material requirements at each stage of performance and for reviewing the performance process when measured against the schedule. A careful assessment of resource availability is needed to see if the activities can be performed at the scheduled times. Activity scheduling, in essence, increases goal clarity or specificity by telling the employees what to do and when.

There are a number of techniques available to the work group or an employee for scheduling a series of activities. They range from a simple method of listing activities with dates to a complex PERT (Program Evaluation and Review

PERSONNEL DEPARTMENT, XYZ CORPORATION

Prepared by: _____   Date: _____

Reviewed by: _____   Date: _____

Key Performance Responsibilities	Task Assignments	Authority and Responsibility Relationships
1. Supervisory Training	Coordinator: Jack Jones Instructors: John Dow David Mind	1. General manager authorizes the training program. 2. Training director has the specific authority and responsibility for executing the program. 3. Coordinator consults with the affected departments.
2. Preparing Skill Inventory	Coordinator: Jane Miller Clerks: Jim Sheldon Henry Miller	1. General manager authorizes the program. 2. Coordinator consults with the manufacturing department. 3. Personal manager has the general responsibility for the task.
3. Campus Recruiting	Coordinator: Sam Antonio Interviewer: Mary Garner	1. General manager authorizes the campus visits. 2. Personel manager has the specific authority and responsibility for conducting the program. 3. Coordinator consults with the affected departments.

FIGURE 10-3. TASK ASSIGNMENT AND RESPONSIBILITY CHART

Technique). The simplest method lists major activities to be performed in a sequence along with starting and ending dates. If more than one individual is involved in performing these activities, it may be advisable to include the names of employees responsible for each major activity. The Gantt is another simple form of a scheduling technique. It shows the scheduled activities for each project in a sequence on horizontal lines, and actual progression of these projects are recorded parallel to the scheduled lines. PERT is a schematic presentation of the activities and events involved in a project. An activity is an operation whose performance is required, and an event is a point in time when an activity is completed and another is started. The strength of PERT is being able to incorporate uncertainties related to activities and events. Time estimates for completing these activities are based on probabilities. Since events are linked with activities, a PERT chart can serve as a milestone against which actual progress can be compared. Closely akin to PERT is a technique known as CPM (Critical Path Method) which is basically concerned with the tradeoff between costs and completion dates for complex projects. CPM is for scheduling projects with fewer uncertainties.

Step 8. Perform Assigned Tasks and Integrate Them Into Overall Goals

One aim of MBO is to increase employee participation in the managerial process at all levels of the organization so they may be able to internalize group and organizational objectives as theirs and thus exercise self-control in the process of achieving these goals. Since task goals for each work group are formulated through the process of "top-down" and "bottom-up" negotiations, they represent the aspiration of the work group members. When these members internalize the group and organizational goals and they are given autonomy to have control over the means of achieving these goals, it should be unnecessary for the supervisor to exercise close supervision over his subordinates. The supervisor's desire to be informed and have control over the subordinates' activities can be satisfied through periodic performance reviews. The supervisor and his subordinates are responsible for managing their group activities, and these activities are then integrated into overall organizational efforts to achieve their goals.

The linking-pin organizational concept, as discussed previously, can be applied to managing work group activities and integrating them into overall organizational efforts. Likert proposed the group approach to the goal-setting system (MBO) whereby the work group defines its task goals, accomplishes them, and appraises its accomplishments jointly. The supervisor then links his group's activities to high level work group activities. By this linking-pin process, the organization should be able to integrate activities at all levels into a concerted effort toward obtaining organizational objectives. A cohesive work group exercises social control functions by means of group norms, acceptance, and sanctions over the group members. The group's influence will be stronger when its members value their membership in the group. Likert (1967) reported that productive work groups tended to set higher goals than management's expectations and developed supportive relationships among employees and between the supervisor and his subordinates.

Step 9. Undertake Periodic Performance Process Reviews

Periodic progress review is an integral part of an MBO program as it provides employees with performance feedback telling how well they are progressing on their jobs. Performance feedback has a greater motivational value when it is internally generated by the employee or the job itself than when it is externally introduced (Greller and Herold, 1975). Performance review under MBO can be done by the employee by comparing his actual performance against the predetermined objectives and action plans. In addition, periodic progress review serves as a control function. It identifies any problem areas that need to be corrected and any performance goals that need to be modified. Unlike a traditional performance review which relies on the supervisor's subjective judgment, the performance progress review under MBO will be based on facts and figures. Thus, the supervisor and his subordinates' attention will be directed to how performance deviations should be dealt with rather than to deciding who should be blamed for the deviations. Further, since the performers are more familiar with their operations and have the knowledge of goals and action plans, the responsibility of progress review can be placed on them rather than on the supervisor. Such a progress review will facilitate the internalization of performance feedback. The role of supervisor then can be that of helping employees solve operational problems and to adjust any action plans or goals.

Another benefit of periodic performance review is that it adds flexibility to the MBO program and helps to clarify performance goals. By reviewing performance periodically, the supervisor and his subordinates have opportunities to review the validity of original goals, reassess the availability of resources, and study the possible impacts of environmental changes, which may necessitate the modification of original goals and action plans. In addition, periodic review sessions provide them with opportunities to clarify any misunderstanding among employees and between the supervisor and his subordinates regarding the assigned tasks or goals and the roles they have to play. Further, the increased opportunity for them to interact will help them to understand each other better on a personal level. Greater mutual esteem can be developed from these interactions when they are able to reinforce each other's needs.

Step 10. Conduct Annual Performance Review Session

The primary objective of an annual performance review is to provide a basis for rewarding employees for their contributions to the organizational goal attainment. While periodic performance reviews are designed to measure progress toward specific goals, to identify and solve operational problems, and to modify goals or action plans, annual performance review is designed to assess an employee's and the work group's contributions to the organization so that these contributions can be rewarded accordingly. Performance appraisal under MBO provides a solid foundation for evaluating an employee's or work group's contributions to the organization. Since performance appraisal presents an important and yet very difficult task for most managers, it deserves an elaborated discussion.

RESULT-ORIENTED PERFORMANCE APPRAISAL

It is performance appraisal time again. Am I getting a promotion this time? How much salary increment will I get? How well did I perform my job in the eyes of the supervisor? On what basis will I be evaluated? These are some of the questions that many employees are asking around appraisal time. In an effort to answer these questions, managers in organizations periodically evaluate the performance of their subordinates. The mode of performance appraisals takes a variety of forms. It may take a simple form of evaluative expression in terms of good or bad, or it may take a sophisticated form of evaluation criteria and procedures. The manager, while he is evaluating the performance of his subordinates, may or may not be aware of his subjective inclination in his evaluation. He may consciously or unconsciously like or dislike a certain person and tend to rate the person accordingly on some criteria. Or the manager may rely on quantitative criteria for he fears the use of inadequate subjective criteria. The manager makes a deliberate attempt to evaluate his employees on the basis of what they do rather than what they are, and yet finds that objectivity alone is not enough. In an attempt to understand the controversy on subjectivity and objectivity in performance appraisal, the present discussion will focus on the merits and demerits of the traditional or conventional method and the result-oriented method of performance appraisal.

TRADITIONAL PERFORMANCE APPRAISAL

A typical traditional method of performance appraisal includes three types of performance criteria: 1) demonstrated performance in terms of quantity and quality; 2) job qualifications such as education, experience, and training; and 3) personality factors such as attitude, creativity, initiative, and judgment. These criteria are measured according to the differences in excellence. The measurement scale usually ranges from the most desirable quality to the least desirable quality. Employees are rated on these criteria by their supervisors. The problem with these criteria is that they are rarely clear and are not objectively measured. Although the first criteria is aimed at measuring the demonstrated performance of employees, they often cannot be objectively measured because performance measurements are not clearly defined in advance. The lack of objective measurability then ushers in the subjective inclination of supervisors in rating the subordinates' performance. In the absence of objective performance criteria, there is a tendency for the supervisor to rate favorably those subordinates who reinforce his needs and/or have similar values while rating others poorly or rejecting them (Labovitz, 1969; Senger, 1971). Despite the apparent problem of the subjective process of performance appraisal, a large number of organizations are currently using this method. There are several reasons why such a subjective process with subjective criteria is practiced in performance appraisal.

First, it is difficult to quantify individual contributions to an organization. While it is feasible to define and measure organizational or group performance in quantifiable terms such as sales, costs, and profits, it is often difficult to define and measure individual performance in quantifiable terms. Especially when a person's performance depends on other persons' behavior and performance, it is extremely difficult to single out the employee's contribution in quantifiable measurement units. The lack of objective criteria, especially for positions other than those that are routine, necessitates the use of subjective criteria. Between the supervisor and subordinates, there are differences in perceiving what the person has to achieve in a certain position. The roles that a person must play and the objectives that he must achieve in the position are different for different individuals. In the absence of objective performance criteria, the manager hires individuals with proper job qualifications and desirable personalities and then evaluates their performance based on his views of their loyalty, attitude, and other personality factors.

Second, several researchers have indicated that some personality factors and qualifications such as leadership and supervisory styles, attitudes, role perception, ambition, education, and creativity are reliable indicators of a person's effectiveness on the job. For example, Likert (1967), Bennis (1966), Myers (1970), and others, prefer a supportive, democratic, and participative leadership style over authoritarian and laissez-faire leadership styles in an effort to improve supervisory effectiveness. Maslow (1968), McClelland (1961), and many others, have identified such high-order needs as achievement, growth, and self-actualization as genuine forces of human effectiveness and achievement. Porter and Lawler (1968) and others, agree that managers with inner-directed role perceptions, such as imaginative and independent qualities, are better job performers than those with other-directed role perceptions. Individuals with desirable personality characteristics tend to possess high potentials for effectiveness on the job and have better chances of succeeding in business.

The possession of desirable personality factors and job qualifications, however, does not automatically guarantee high performance. We often hear that a certain person is very intelligent and imaginative, but his job performance does not qualify him for further promotion. What good is it to have an individual with a high potential for success who doesn't demonstrate high performance in his job? Unless the possession of such desirable characteristics results in good performance on the job, the possession alone does not merit organizational reward and promotion.

Emphasis on personality factors as performance measures creates some undesirable consequences. The supervisor applies his subjective judgment in evaluating the subordinate's effectiveness on the job. What a man is worth is not measured by what he contributes to the success of the organization, but by what he does for his boss. Under these circumstances, the supervisor's view of the subordinate's loyalty, team play, attitude, and other personality factors is more crucial for the subordinate's success in the organization than his effectiveness on the job. Such an evaluation process is highly subjective, and the supervisor's judgment tends to be influenced by his personal biases, preferences, values, and idiosyncrasies.

Since the supervisor is the dispenser of organizational rewards and holds the key to success for his subordinates, he has power over his subordinates who are anxious to receive the rewards and to succeed. This is especially true in organizations where the subjective appraisal in the area of personality factors is practiced. The subordinates, in order to enhance their chances of success in the organization, must understand the subjective criteria and work hard to please the boss on these criteria. As they become sensitive to the supervisor's feelings, needs, and prejudices, and learn to conform to the supervisor's demands, their dependency on the supervisor tends to increase and their own sense of independence and self-esteem tends to decrease. Such an increased dependency and reduced independency tends to decrease a person's ability to try out his own ideas and to solve problems on his own strength.

Finally, the subjective process, although it may often generate biased responses, is a reality and is defended by interaction theorists. A human being has a natural tendency to perceive favorably, and react favorably to, the qualifications of other persons which satisfy his own needs. A subordinate who is constantly reinforcing the needs of his superior will be favorably perceived and rewarded. Social behavior is an exchange of material as well as nonmaterial goods. Persons who give much to others try to get as much from them, and persons who get much from others will give much to them. It is also natural for an individual, superior or subordinate, to dislike anyone who gets on his nerves consistently and disturbs harmonious interpersonal relationships in organizations.

Interaction theorists (Homans, 1950; Labovitz, 1969; Whyte, 1959) seem to support the subjective performance appraisal. For them, an organization is viewed as an interaction system. Organizational performance is then the outcome of the interactions among its members. Employees develop favorable or unfavorable sentiments toward the quality of interactions they are exchanging. The more positive the sentiment between organizational members, the higher the rate of interaction between them. Likewise, the higher the rate of interaction between the individuals in an organization, the more positive will be their sentiments toward each other. Thus, a high degree of favorable interaction creates an organizational climate in which a member is better able to align his goals with organizational goals, and such an alignment is the key to organizational effectiveness. In such a system, superiors and subordinates share an interdependent relationship in satisfying their respective needs. Since favorable interaction will lead to a high level of organizational performance, it is justifiable for an executive to reward and promote a subordinate who is loyal to him and has an interacting capacity with others (Labovitz, 1969).

RESULT-ORIENTED PERFORMANCE APPRAISAL

A result-oriented performance appraisal attempts to assess an employee's effectiveness on his job by measuring his accomplishments. Instead of evaluating a subordinate's contributions on the basis of his personality factors and job qualifications, the supervisor judges the subordinate for what he has accomplished on his job. Also, the result-oriented appraisal under MBO defines a set of predetermined goals against which actual performance will be measured. There are several advantages of using a result-oriented performance appraisal.

First, as indicated previously, the result-oriented performance appraisal directly measures actual performance results rather than performance predictors—personality factors and job qualifications. Its criteria are derived from job requirements instrumental to the attainment of organizational goals. Performance criteria include those criteria that can be quantitatively measured, and those that must be qualitatively judged. Quantitative criteria are relatively easier to define and measure because they are expressed in quantifiable business terms such as profit, cost, scrap rate, market share, absenteeism, and turnover. Qualitative criteria are difficult to define and measure because they are not readily expressed in quantifiable terms. However, through frequent interaction between the supervisor and his subordinates under MBO, they may come to better understand what is expected of them in performing nonquantifiable areas of their major performance responsibilities.

Second, unlike the traditional appraisal method which applies a same set of performance criteria for all levels of employees, the result-oriented performance appraisal under MBO differentiates performance goals for different levels and functions of an organization. As organizations require different talents for different jobs, they need to establish different performance criteria for varying jobs. Some jobs may require inner-directed and independent personality qualities, while other jobs require interaction-oriented characteristics for teamwork. The reliance on one kind of performance criteria for all jobs may lead to an unhealthy situation where the organization cannot cope with a variety of problems which require a variety of talents.

Finally, the result-oriented performance appraisal is an important aspect of MBO. It provides a basis for relating performance to organizational rewards. For example, performance data can be used to determine pay increase. A system of reward is one way to recognize excellent performance and serves as a stimulant to achieve higher performance. Failure to reward high performance may reduce the effectiveness of a goal-setting system. Furthermore, the maintenance of an equitable and fair reward system is necessary for maintaining a productive work group. The relationship between MBO and result-oriented appraisal is highly complementary; one without the other may cripple the motivational value of both systems. Goal setting can generate a motivational impact on employees by itself, but its motivation power will wear off if motivated behavior is not recognized and rewarded through a result-oriented performance appraisal. A result-oriented appraisal system recognizes good performance. But, without a clear understanding of performance goals, the evaluation of one's performance can be highly judgmental and arbitrary.

A number of researchers supported that the use of result-oriented performance appraisal combined with MBO produces better results than either MBO or result-oriented method alone. For example, Hughes (1966) reported that the combined approach used at Texas Instruments resulted in better employee acceptance and motivation than its previous system which stressed only historical performance. Ninety percent of salaried employees and 70 percent of managers felt the MBO performance appraisal was superior to the earlier system. Thompson and Dalton (1970) also indicated that although many managers claim the use of result-oriented performance appraisal, they tend to be arbitrary due to the lack of predetermined performance goals. To overcome this problem, they suggested the use of MBO approach to performance appraisal.

POTENTIAL PROBLEMS OF MBO

While MBO presents potential benefits, it also poses a number of potential problems. It is intuitively appealing to managers because of its potential benefits. But, many managers seem to find it difficult to implement MBO in their organizations. Kerr (1976) points out several problems and limitations associated with MBO. These problems often reduce the effective utilization of MBO in many organizations.

First, the premise that joint goal-setting among hierarchical unequals is possible is a tenuous assumption in most organizations. It may be possible in some organizations where mutually respecting and mature relationships prevail between superiors and subordinates. However, in most organizations, the hierarchical status differences prevent equal amount of influence among hierarchical unequals. When there is any conflict, the subordinates tend to subordinate themselves to the wishes of their superiors.

The idea that MBO must be implemented at all levels of an organization is questionable and misleading. Usually, managers at lower levels of organizational echelon do not have influence on goal-setting processes. The lower the hierarchical level, the less the manager can genuinely participate in MBO process. Once organizational goals are negotiated at high levels of the organization, lower level managers do not have an influential power to negotiate them. A bottom-up goal-setting process can be used to give them such a power, but it can be a costly process because it may have to rely on less well educated, trained, and informed personnel and because of the difficulty in coordinating divergent goals of subunits of an organization.

There are a number of problems of linking MBO to pay system. When MBO is linked to pay, employees may attempt to pad their performance goals, costs, and target dates in their favor. There is a problem of weighing the relative importance of various performance goals. It is necessary to adjust performance goals when there is a change in internal as well as external environment. Dynamic and unstable environment demands frequent changes in performance goals. Exceeding the predetermined performance goals does not necessarily mean good performance, but people may perceive it to be so. Performance goals could be achieved as a result of factors other than the performer's effort. There is no reliable formula for comparing actual results against predetermined goals.

MBO encourages goal-setting in quantifiable terms. But, it is seldom possible to write quantifiable objectives in the areas of innovation, creativity, leadership, and interpersonal relations. Attempts to measure employees' performance and reward them accordingly often lead them to be overly obsessed with quantifiable areas of performance while ignoring nonquantifiable areas. Also, it may lead them to compete against each other.

Finally, MBO is a static managerial tool which cannot be used in a dynamic and drastically changing organizational environment. A series of organizational, group, and individual goals have to be continuously renegotiated and readjusted. This readjustment process is time-consuming and costly; it is often impractical, if not impossible. The more complex and dynamic the task, the less any fixed goal statement is likely to be relevant.

Based on these observations, Kerr (1976) proposed a number of practical suggestions. He indicated that at least three features of MBO are worth keeping while other features are discarded: 1) the emphasis on goal-setting practice, 2) increased interactions between superiors and subordinates, and 3) providing opportunities for participation for those employees who desire it. Other MBO features to be discarded or at least to be carefully studied are 1) linking MBO to pay system, 2) considering MBO as an objective way of measuring performance, 3) focusing attention on only those quantifiable performance areas, 4) requiring paperwork for control and evaluation, 5) making the personnel department responsible for its maintenance, and 6) using prepackaged programs and costly consultants. Kerr argues that while the features worth keeping are related to positive performance results, the features to be discarded are closely related to dysfunctional behaviors.

CONTINGENCY APPROACH TO MBO

As Kerr indicated, MBO is not a care-free managerial tool. The potential user of MBO should be aware of various problems and limitations associated with its implementation and understand various organizational contingencies under which it can be effectively implemented. The following organizational contingencies are suggested as a guide for selecting a particular MBO system and for its effective utilization.

First, an MBO system requires a relatively stable internal and external organizational environment. Frequent changes in internal managerial structures, technological environment, and market situations necessitate accompanying changes in organizational goals, their priorities, and action plans to the point where these goals, priorities, and plans are no longer relevant and cannot serve as guidelines for planning organizational activities and for evaluating performance. Wickens (1968) indicated that organizational instability was a threat to the success of MBO because it demanded frequent changes in the priority of objectives and organizational problems. Furthermore, operational crises associated with such changes frequently divert the energies of employees from their goal-directed activities. Either traditional authoritarian management or a highly organic participative managerial system may be more suitable to deal with such unstable organizational conditions. The choice between these two systems then depends on the quality of employees in the organization and the technological complexity of their jobs. When the employees are capable of handling the technological complexity and of responding to turbulent environmental conditions, a participative management system can be effective for dealing with organizational uncertainties. However, when the employees are not capable of or not used to responding to such uncertainties, an authoritarian leadership may be effective at least in the short run.

Second, the performance dependency among work group members determines the type of goal-setting system. If job performance demands a high degree of dependency or interdependency among work group members, a group-oriented MBO system is preferred to an individualized MBO system. Many jobs in industry are highly interdependent and require a high degree of interaction among work group members and between functional groups. The group-oriented MBO system encourages joint efforts by group members at various levels of the organization. However, the group-oriented MBO is lacking individual motivation because it often fails to emphasize employees' personal performance responsibilities.

An individualized MBO program exerts a strong personal responsibility on an employee for his own performance goals. Thus, even if a group-oriented MBO is practiced, it is important to specify specific performance responsibility that each individual member feels personally responsible for. For example, winning a football game is a team effort. Yet, each individual member has a specific responsibility to perform in order to win. Individual performance is evaluated in the context of the player's contribution to the team effort. If individual performance alone is over-emphasized in work groups or athletic teams. an individual member will pursue his personal goals to the point where his responsibility to the team work is neglected.

Third, the differences in tasks determine the characteristics of performance objectives. Some performance objectives can be easily expressed in tangible and quantifiable terms such as sales volume, production units, costs, scrap rates, absenteeism, and turnover. These quantifiable objectives are usually applied to measure the performance of line managers. However, many performance objectives of staff managers in industrial organizations and public institutions do not easily lend themselves to such quantifiable measurements. For example, Kleber (1972) listed the six task areas where a result-oriented MBO is difficult to implement: 1) public relations, 2) engineering and research, 3) controller function, 4) educational institutions, 5) nonprofit organizations, and 6) governmental agencies. Managers in these task areas face a unique challenge of identifying and developing measurable objectives in addition to normal challenges that most line managers in industrial organizations encounter in defining and communicating their performance objectives.

The end results for carrying out the missions in these areas are often difficult to quantify and measure. However, it is possible to identify the activities that are the means of achieving their objectives. Once these activities are identified, they should be able to specify the expected outcomes of their activities in such measurable terms as the magnitude or number of services, target dates, and costs involved. For example, the U.S. Department of Health, Education, and Welfare (HEW) in its health service agency's MBO program utilizes performance milestone charts which lists activities to be achieved by specified dates within certain budget constraints (Brady, 1973). The performance of the agency is evaluated by comparing actual progress against the milestone charts. However, its quality has to be qualitatively judged.

Fourth, the purpose of performance appraisal differentiates the type of performance appraisal criteria. If the purpose is to reward current performance, management should focus on the performance criteria applied to the present task assignment. However, if the purpose is to identify one's performance potential at another job or managerial level, the performance criteria relevant to the new task assignment should be taken into account for replacement or promotion. Especially when one is considered for promotion to a managerial position, the traditional performance criteria involving personal qualifications and traits can be applied to judge his performance potential at the new job. When both MBO and traditional approaches are applied to performance appraisal, one's ability to function in different job situations can best be identified.

MBO is often accused of being short-term oriented by placing a heavy emphasis on current performance evaluated on short-term criteria. After all, short-term profits can be increased by reducing customer and maintenance services which may have adverse effects on long-term profits. Furthermore, a successful MBO program requires the development of employee skills which are not needed at the present moment but may be needed in the future. People move around to different jobs and are promoted to advanced positions which demand different job skills and interactional patterns. To prepare them to successfully encounter organizational mobilities and changes, personal developmental objectives should be incorporated as an integral part of an MBO program. Personal development is needed not only for better accomplishment of current task assignment but for increasing performance potential at different task assignments.

Fifth, since it is virtually impossible to define all aspects of managerial jobs, care must be given to those areas of managerial jobs not included in performance goals. It is rare to include such managerial functions as motivating employees and maintaining a trusting and supportive organizational climate as a part of a manager's performance objectives. Yet, such organizational variables can have a long-term impact on organizational as well as individual welfare. The MBO based performance appraisal system motivates people to focus their efforts on those objectives that can be easily quantifiable and measured, while ignoring some aspects of the job that are not quantifiable and yet important for smooth functioning of an organization. A manager may perform well on the quantifiable performance criteria, but may fail as a colleague, supervisor, and subordinate. Also, it may be possible that a manager can increase employee performance by being highly authoritarian or by using a zero-sum approach for a few years, while destroying morale and cooperative spirit among employees and sometimes causing them to leave. He may increase short-term profits at the expense of long-term benefits. The manager moves on to higher levels as a reward for his short-term performance showings on these hard performance criteria, while leaving permanent scars on his previous work groups. Thus, great care must be given to those qualitative aspects of the managerial job which may not be shown in the objective performance criteria.

Finally, an MBO system can be effectively applied to task situations where there are different means of achieving task goals, and the attainment of these goals greatly depends on employees' motivation and skill utilization. Through participation in goal-setting, employees internalize the organizational or group goals as theirs, and thus are motivated to achieve them. However, the implementation of such a job enrichment-oriented MBO system is highly complex because it has to integrate a variety of individual and group goals into a set of workable organizational goals.

Further, an effective utilization of MBO requires additional conditions to be met. The tasks that employees are performing have to be properly enlarged and relevant so the employees find them interesting and challenging. Employees should have the desire and ability to perform demanding jobs and to exercise self-control. A supportive and trusting climate has to prevail in the organization so that employees can exert their energies for task-oriented behavior rather than being preoccupied with such hygiene problems as fear of losing their jobs and interpersonal entanglement. Also, there should be a structural mechanism through which individual and group activities are integrated into concerted efforts toward the organizational goal attainment.

SUMMARY AND CONCLUSION

MBO is defined as a managerial process by which the superior and his subordinates jointly identify organizational task goals, achieve them, and assess their accomplishments. MBO as a management tool has emerged as a hybrid between traditional administrative theories and human relations movements. The administrative theories emphasized the importance of establishing and distributing organizational goals and tasks to those managers responsible for carrying them out, while the human relations theories emphasized the importance of participative management as a way of gaining employees' commitment to organizational goals. Drucker (1954) synthesized the influences of these two schools of thought and advanced the concept of MBO as a management tool.

MBO, however, means different things to different individuals. To some, it means communication of organizational goals set by upper level management downward so that lower level managers clearly understand what their performance responsibilities are. Goal clarity may help lower level managers and their subordinates better understand the direction in which the organization is moving and plan for their activities to accomplish their assigned tasks. When such a goal-oriented system is reinforced by a result-oriented performance appraisal system for dispensing organizational rewards, it can have a strong influence on employee motivation and performance. However, such a mechanical approach to MBO may not generate intrinsic motivation to those who do not internalize the organizational goals as theirs because these goals are imposed on them without their participation.

Participation in goal-setting helps the employees to internalize the organizational goals as theirs because they have influenced the formulation of these goals. Goal internalization is especially important to those employees who have the ability and desire to exercise self-control on their jobs. Such a participative MBO system fully realizes the motivational characteristics of job enrichment including goal-setting, participation, and autonomy. However, an actual implementation of such a participative MBO system is highly complex and difficult because it involves an organizational fit between enlarged tasks, employees with technical and teamwork skills, supportive organizational climate, and appropriate managerial control systems. When these peripheral organizational variables are not sufficiently developed, the participative system may not be able to yield a high motivational influence. Thus, the selection of a particular form of MBO should be based on a careful study of these organizational variables.

MBO is considered a powerful motivational tool. However, like all human systems, the effective utilization of MBO is at the mercy of its users. If the users carefully orchestrate the efforts of many individuals and groups toward their common goals and for mutual benefits, while various organizational contingencies are being duly considered, MBO will serve as a powerful managerial and motivational tool. However, if managerial judgment fails to account for various organizational contingencies, it will fail to produce positive results. Installing a MBO system does not turn poor managers into good managers. Instead, good managers use MBO as an effective management tool.

11

WORK MOTIVATION IN PERSPECTIVE

People join and work in organizations to satisfy their needs, while organizations need people to carry out their activities. People and their organizations are mutually interdependent for survival; any deficiency in satisfying these two sets of goals will lead to instability and failure of the cooperative systems. The attainment of these two sets of goals shares a common element—work motivation. Individuals as well as organizations attain the means of satisfying their goals through work motivation. Work motivation not only influences the level of organizational performance but also the level of outcomes that people value. Since the organization and its members depend on work motivation for their goal attainment, work motivation can be considered the key to their effectiveness and survival.

The study of work motivation has been the major concern for many scholars and practitioners in management and organizational behavior. As a result, the level of understanding of work motivation has increased considerably in recent decades. And yet, employee motivation still presents continuous problems that need to be solved. The solution requires an understanding of the changing nature of work and workers and a set of tools (theories and programs) to deal with them. This final chapter discusses the changing nature of work and workers, reviews major theories and programs of motivation, and draws some implications for managers in a nutshell form.

CHANGING NATURE OF WORK AND WORKERS

Work performs one of two roles. First, people may work because they enjoy it. They receive pleasure and a sense of self-fulfillment—intrinsic value. Second, work might be considered a necessary evil; people work because they have to. Work is not satisfaction-yielding in itself, but people work to earn money to buy the means of satisfying their needs—extrinsic value. In general, work is viewed as an institution through which people satisfy a variety of needs. Work can be intrinsically and extrinsically motivating because it not only provides the source of material existence, but also satisfies man's social and growth-oriented needs. Since it can satisfy a variety of human needs, it regulates the life of many individuals and binds them to reality—central life interest value.

Work satisfies a number of human needs. First of all, it satisfies financial needs. It is a means of survival for most workers. Financial rewards from work also represent economic security and measure one's value and contribution to society. Second, it satisfies social needs. The workplace provides opportunities for socializing and making friends. Also, those who do not work are often considered social dropouts. Third, it provides a source of self-esteem and self-respect. What one does at work usually demonstrates social status and the value that society puts on him. Fourth, it is a major institution through which an individual realizes his fullest potential. People toil to obtain what they want to accomplish. In essence, work satisfies many psychological needs. It helps an individual maintain a sense of balance and importance. This sense of psychological balance and importance counteracts with one's sense of impotence caused by the ever-increasing complexity and impersonality of the organizational world in which he spends the most of his working hours.

While most people consider work a means of satisfying a variety of needs, many blue-collar and even some white-collar workers seem to have difficulty perceiving work as a means of satisfying higher-order needs. The problem is that many jobs in our industrial world have lost the intrinsic value once found in the old economic system. Under the old system, workers usually performed the whole work unit, which gave them opportunities for expressing their individuality and creativeness. They utilized their skill and knowledge, controlled the production process and pace, and appreciated a sense of accomplishment when they finished the product.

Many jobs in today's industrial world have lost such a motivational value. Jobs are so big and complex that they have to be divided into small parts with each worker producing only a fragmented portion of a whole job. A fragmented job does not require learning and ability utilization. Even if the job requires skill utilization and learning, its fragmentedness fails to provide the worker with a sense of accomplishment. As technology progresses, even the simple fragmented jobs require education and skill training. When one acquires job skills and education, he may expect commensurating job satisfaction. Yet the repetitiveness and dullness of his job reduces the amount of job satisfaction.

Job satisfaction is closely related to the nature of job and job level. While high-level occupations possess psychologically meaningful job contents, low-level occupations are lacking in such motivational job contents. The HEW report *Work in America* (1973) indicated that more than 80 percent of the professionals (professors, mathematicians, lawyers, and journalists) would choose the same or similar work again, whereas 43 percent of white-collar workers, and only 24 percent of blue-collar workers would choose the same kind of work. A major reason cited for not choosing the same work was a lack of intrinsic job satisfaction. Coupled with job dissatisfaction is the growing sense of low social status and the inability to achieve prestige in their jobs. Blue-collar work is looked down on in our society (especially in urban areas.) Blue-collar workers are paid relatively less and have lower status in and out of their jobs. In a society where upward mobility is heavily emphasized, workers who remain in low-status jobs may suffer from impaired self-worth (Strauss, 1974).

Although blue-collar workers do not actively express job dissatisfaction, the fact that they will not choose the same type of work again seems to indicate that they are not fulfilling their needs in their jobs. Probably all they expect to gain from their jobs is the financial means to support themselves and their families and the opportunities to associate with co-workers. Thus, when they are asked whether they liked their work, their answers seem to be "yes, pay is good," "yes, I like the people I work with," or "it is not that bad," rather than answering "it is interesting or exciting." They seem to view their jobs as sources of extrinsic satisfaction rather than intrinsic satisfaction. When workers expect their jobs to be the means of satisfying economic and affiliation needs, less enlarged and enriched jobs will not create any serious problem of job satisfaction. However, when they expect their work to be the major source of intrinsic job satisfaction, unenlarged and unenriched jobs will create serious job dissatisfaction among workers.

The problem is that workers' expectations concerning their work seem to be changing. Young workers today seem to demand increased job satisfaction. They are better educated and better satisfied with lower-order needs than their elders. With increased social programs such as welfare and unemployment benefits, it is no longer necessary for anyone to work in order to survive. Relatively free from economic hardship, people are able to search for the satisfaction of aesthetic and psychological needs. A U.S. Department of Labor study (Quinn and Shephard, 1974) reported that about 36 percent of the labor force held a college degree in 1973, compared with less than 30 percent in 1969. More people are pursuing higher education than ever before, and this trend seems to be continuing. With the increased level of education, the level of aspiration seems to be rising. More people are searching for careers in technical, managerial, and professional fields.

Are the number of jobs in these technical, managerial, and professional fields increasing at the same rate of increased job seekers in the fields? The answer seems to be no. The Bureau of Labor Statistics (1975) estimated that there will be 140,000 surplus college graduates each year between 1980 and 1985. Technology will upgrade the jobs that some of these surplus graduates will get. However, others will be forced to take jobs that high school graduates would have taken in the 1960s. Some college graduates are taking white-collar, semiskilled, or even blue-collar jobs. Tight professional job markets may discourage some young people from going to colleges. However, the trend toward more education will not be subdued due to the lack of job opportunities. More parents are financially able to send their offsprings to colleges, and more people are motivated to self-actualization through education.

Another trend in the labor market is that there will be reduced supply of workers for many low-level occupations. Traditionally, low-status and low-wage jobs have been disproportionately filled by so-called disprivileged social groups, particularly blacks, immigrants, poor whites, and the least educated. However, more people in these social groups are improving their socioeconomic status and moving out of the low-level occupations. Wool (1976) projected that, while there will be increased supply of workers seeking high-status jobs between 1970 and 1985, the proportion of workers who will be available for low-level jobs is expected to be low. In 1970, 31.6 percent of the civilian labor force was engaged in the low-level occupations; it is expected to be 26.6 percent in 1985.

There are several implications of these labor market projections. First, there will be increased competition for entering preferred high-level jobs. More educated people will have to accept less preferred jobs and thus feel overqualified for these jobs. Second, although employers will have a greater choice of applicants with better education and training, they may be faced with motivational problems of these workers in low-level jobs. Finally, corollary to the first and second implications is that more jobs have to be enriched to accommodate the increasing number of workers searching for job satisfaction. If the society fails to provide them with intrinsically motivating jobs, many useful talents and educational investments will be wasted. Subsequently, job dissatisfaction will be widespread, and its accompanying behavioral problems will pluck the nation's productive capacity.

The challenge for the future is to increase the intrinsic value of work for all levels of jobs. Especially, attention should be given to such low-status occupational categories as blue-collar, white-collar, and skilled jobs in service industries. As the service-oriented economy expands, more people will be needed in service industries. Statistics complied by the Bureau of Labor Statistics (1970) indicated that by 1980, close to 70 percent of the work force—68 million workers—is projected to be in service industries. This trend indicates that we need to develop trained blue-collar, white-collar, and skilled workers to staff the service industries. Fortunately, many jobs in service industries are more enlarged and less boring than the fragmented jobs in manufacturing industries. However, many workers in service-oriented industries seem to suffer motivational problems because they do not enjoy their social status in and out of their jobs and are over-controlled by management.

Even those workers who do not aspire to pursue careers in technological and professional jobs will benefit from intrinsically motivating jobs. These workers may be originally motivated to satisfy lower-order needs. However, as they are better satisfied with economic needs, they may find performing nonenlarged, boring jobs unbearable. Many jobs designed to satisfy the materialistic needs of business owners, customers, managers, and employees have permitted workers to produce more production units in shorter periods of time. As a result, the standard of living has improved. However, workers cannot find intrinsic job satisfaction other than fulfilling economic needs. Therefore, they have ceased to get involved in their work beyond the necessary minimum to hold on to the jobs and turned their energies and interests toward their own little world of hobbies, families, and material possessions. The result is that their job performances tend to be mediocre.

Making the jobs more interesting and challenging at lower-level occupations will help to attract more young people to these job categories and also reduce the pressure for creating managerial and professional jobs to accommodate them. Along with the increased intrinsic job satisfaction will be the necessity for improving vocational education and job status of these workers. Removing pay and status differentiation between job categories seems to be a right direction for making low-status jobs more attractive. Job enlargement and enrichment can then be followed to provide intrinsic job satisfaction.

THEORETICAL OVERVIEW

Motivation theory views man as a rational being who takes actions leading toward goal attainment. The theory of motivation does not explain or predict all behavior. It distinguishes a motivated behavior from an existentialistic, frustrated, or physiological autoreflex behavior. Existentialistic behavior is not motivated behavior in the sense that people aimlessly act and react without knowing and thinking about the possible consequences of their behavior. Existentialism assumes that although people are free to act, they have only limited knowledge to act upon. Frustrated behavior lacks a goal-orientation and is not based on a rational choice. Frustration is an outcome of repeated failure to achieve goals. Frustrated people aimlessly or randomly react to their frustration. Physiological reflexes are automatic responses to external stimuli, without being subjected to the voluntary control of the respondent. This distinction is important, for it delineates the scope of motivational theory.

Traditionally, the primary concerns of motivation theories have centered around three major questions: 1) What are the forces that energize behavior? 2) What can influence human behavior toward a certain direction? 3) What moderates one's responses to internal as well as external stimuli? Although all theories of motivation have some relevances to all three questions, the first question is more closely related to the development of need theories; the second question is related to the development of incentive and reinforcement theories; and the third question is related to the development of cognitive and expectancy theories. The tendency to stress one particular question has led to the development of these partial theories involving a limited set of motivational determinants.

The development of partial theories of motivation has contributed to the intensive investigation of a particular set of motivational determinants. A partial theory can explain a motivational phenomenon occuring in a particular domain of motivation. However, the primary shortcoming of partial theories is that these theories tend to be so localized that they have no universal applicability in analyzing, understanding, and explaining a motivated behavior which involves a variety of motivational properties. The lack of a comprehensive model of motivation to deal with a variety of motivational components in organizations handicaps the managers, not only in understanding but also in finding a comprehensive and consistent approach to the problem of motivating employees. In the past, scholars in managerial motivation have recognized the significance of the major variables independently (needs, incentives, cognitive, and ability), but few researchers have attempted to deal with those major variables simultaneously. As a consequence, while much has been known about the separated areas of interest, little is known about the simultaneous interactions among these major variables.

A major theme of this book is that these partial theories are not necessarily exclusive but are complimentary to each other. The partial theories are integrated into a theoretical framework of expectancy motivation. The expectancy theory of motivation presented in this book indicates that motivated behavior is a function of 1) the expectancy that effort leads to task performance (E-P); 2) the instrumental relationships between task performance and incentive rewards (P-I); and 3) the valence (or the value of incentives) that the incentive rewards satisfy individual needs (I-N). This expectancy theory of motivation operationalizes the motivational concepts of expectancy theories advanced and subsequently modified by a number of expectancy theorists. By integrating the need and incentive theories of motivation into the theoretical framework of expectancy motivation, we can clearly define the expectancy concepts (valence, expectancy, and instrumentality) and operationalize these concepts in arousing employee motivation in organizations.

Several points illustrate the need for such an integration. First, most expectancy theorists define the concept of valence as an individual's desire for a particular outcome, but they do not specify what influences the strength of valence. It is contended in Chapter 4 that the valence of organizational incentives increases when the incentives are matched with employee needs. People are motivated by different needs and attach different values to incentives. Understanding the need structure of employees and the nature of organizational incentives will help management correctly match incentives with needs.

Second, there are several reinforcement principles that can be applied to strengthen the instrumental relationships between task performance and incentive rewards. The principle of timing indicates that the level of performance decreases as the reinforcement delays. The operant conditioning theory explains that the perceived instrumental relationship between performance and reward increases when reward is tied to performance. A partial reinforcement can be used to strengthen the perceived tie between reward and performance when the total size of reward is small (see Chapter 5 for expectancy theory and operant conditioning).

Finally, the expectancy that effort leads to task accomplishment can be influenced by one's past experience of task performance, level of ability and skill, and degree of skill requirement. The study of individual differences in technical and psychological readiness to perform the task and the nature of the task itself helps to explain and predict the way employees perceive the E-P expectancy. At the same time, an understanding of the characteristics of employees and their tasks can help management to train employees in job skills and/or redesign the tasks so that employees can develop a favorable perception of the E-P expectancy.

In summary, each of the partial theories has made important contributions to the study of work motivation. Need theories help us understand the role played by individual workers in the determination of employee work motivation. Incentive theories focus on the influences of organizational variables on work motivation (job content, power equalization, supervision, work group, and financial incentive). Cognitive theories study the perceptual responses of individuals and their influences on work motivation. When these partial theories are integrated into the theoretical framework of expectancy motivation, the integrated model of motivation is able to explain and predict the motivational process in organizations involving a number of individual and organizational variables. This integrative approach not only helps us understand the complexity of the motivational processes, but also helps us develop effective motivational programs to better achieve our individual as well as organizational goals.

MOTIVATIONAL PROGRAMS IN PERSPECTIVE

Managerial approaches to employee motivation have evolved through several historical stages: traditional approaches (scientific management and bureaucracy), the human relations movement, and contemporary approach. The traditional approaches to employee motivation appealed to the economic needs of employees as well as employers. These approaches assumed the worker was an "economic and rational being" who was motivated by the desire for economic betterment and who could maximize his economic gains by rationally evaluating and selecting the means of achieving economic ends. The nation's economy during the years between 1880 and 1930 could be characterized as a production-oriented economy which placed a primary emphasis on the efficiency of the productive systems. Employers were primarily interested in instituting elaborate production and managerial control systems that would enhance production efficiency. The motivational principles of the traditional approaches were to 1) design the most scientific and rational production methods and organizational processes, 2) define workers' performance standards, 3) train employees to perform their tasks in the prescribed manner, and 4) reward their performance by using incentive systems. The most effectively used motivation principle was to match pay to performance by using incentive systems. Mass production systems, better pay, and a higher standard of living were realized as a result of the traditional approaches. As they are better satisfied with lower-order economic needs, they begin to search for need satisfaction from social interactions on their jobs. The traditional models failed to consider the importance of psychological needs. The motivational value of task design was completely ignored in the scientific approach to management.

The human relations approach appealed to the socialization needs of employees. Employees are perceived to be more than economic beings; they are psychological beings affected by emotion and feeling. They are motivated not only by economic factors but by sociopsychological factors. An organization is considered to be a social system in which people interact and form social cliques and norms which guide the behavior of group members. Unlike the traditionalists who believed that productivity was a function of incentive pays, the human relationists argued that productivity is a function of group norms. The motivational strategies applied during this human relations movement were designed to satisfy employees' job security and socialization needs. A number of fringe benefits such as paid vacation, sick leave, unemployment benefit, severance pay, health insurance, and pension were introduced during this period. A number of social activities such as office parties, company picnics, Christmas party, and people-oriented supervision were advocated to increase the quantity and quality of social interactions in organizations. The human relationists assumed that employee morale leads to higher productivity and thus advocated that management is responsible for creating a happy workplace. The major contribution of the human relations movement was the realization of the importance of human elements in organizations. However, studies found that there is no significant relationship between employee satisfaction and productivity. Satisfaction can be increased by rewarding employees regardless of their performance; productivity is increased by tying reward to performance (P-I) and/or as a result of performing intrinsically motivating jobs (E-P). The human relationists ignored P-I and E-P motivational principles.

The contemporary approach emphasizes the satisfaction of such higher-order needs as self-esteem and self-actualization. Satisfaction of these needs seem to be derived from task performance rather than from rewards from extrinsic sources. It has been said that job performance is more likely to result in job satisfaction than satisfaction is to result in high performance. As a way of providing intrinsic job satisfaction, it has been suggested that job enlargement and job enrichment should be implemented. Through job enlargement and enrichment, workers perform interesting and challenging jobs and exercise managerial functions regarding their own jobs.

However, many managerial practitioners and scholars soon found that job enrichment is not suitable to all employees and organizations. Not all employees are motivated to satisfy higher-order needs. Not all organizations are ready to implement such a motivational program. Individuals differ in their technical and psychological makeups. Jobs require different levels of technical sophistication and different types of interpersonal and intergroup interactions. Organizations differ not only in their structural makeups but also in their psychological makeups. These differences in the tasks, people, organizational structural, and psychological makeups should be reflected in selecting a set of motivational programs. For those employees who have a low level of higher-order needs, job enlargement may be more suitable than job enrichment.

CONTINGENCY APPROACH TO WORK MOTIVATION

Traditional and human relations approaches to work motivation attempted to develop a set of universal principles that could be applied to all employees in all forms of organizations. For them, employees are motivated either by financial incentives or group norms. Unlike these traditional and human relations approaches, a contingency approach to work motivation argues that there is no one best way of motivating employees. People are motivated for a variety of reasons. Organizational incentives influence people in a variety of ways with varying degrees of efficacy. There are a number of motivational programs that are appropriate. But, the selection of a particular program depends on the particular circumstances in the specific situation.

SYSTEMS ANALYSIS AND ORGANIZATIONAL FIT

The contingency approach to motivation analyzes the characteristics of various organizational components (task, people, work groups, and managerial controls), studies the interrelationships between these components, and finds a workable fit between them so that their characteristics and demands are compatible to each other (Lawrence and Lorsch, 1967; and Dalton, 1971). Tasks differ in their programmability, skill requirement, performance interdependency, and motivational potential. Employees differ in their attitudes, motivation, job skills, interpersonal skills, and personal goals. Work groups differ in their norms, values, mutual commitments, cooperation and coordination, and institutional loyalty. Managerial controls involve the differences in organizational structure and design, reward systems, policies and procedures, leadership, and group processes. Figure 11-1 depicts the major organizational components and their characteristics.

Chapter 9 investigates the characteristics of tasks and employees, and attempts to specify the contingency relationships between them. Chapter 7 investigates the motivational value of various pay methods, and their contingency relationships with other components such as tasks and workers. Chapter 8 deals with the influences of organizational structure, leadership, and group process on work group behavior and affective motivation. An overview of overall contingency relationships between tasks, workers, work groups, and managerial controls are shown in Figure 8-6. These contingency relationships should not be viewed as conclusive statements that can be unequivocally applied to

solve motivational problems. Rather, they should be viewed as a way of understanding the complex interrelationships between various organizational components and as an aid to find a harmonious balance between them.

Correct diagnosis of the characteristics of organizational components and
their interrelationships is important for finding a workable fit between them
and for describing a motivational program. Failure to diagnose any one of these
components correctly will lead to a situation where a false fit exists, and any
motivational program based on this misfit will produce undesirable consequences.
Sirota and Wolfson (1973) and Hackman (1975) pointed out that many organizations fail to produce positive results from implementing job enrichment programs due to their failure to diagnose the real causes of employee problems.

BEYOND THE CONTINGENCY APPROACH

The contingency concept presents a useful guide to managerial actions. It
studies the characteristics (roles, functions, and demands) of various organiza-

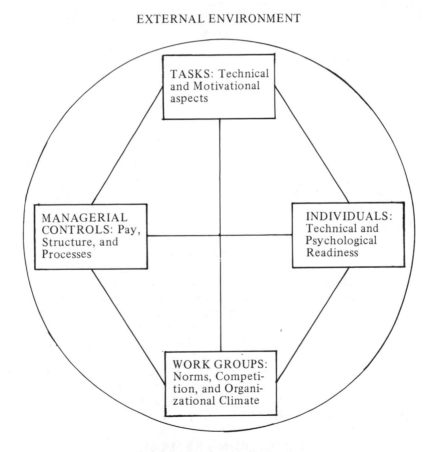

**FIGURE 11-1. WORKABLE FIT BETWEEN ORGANIZATIONAL
COMPONENTS**

tional components and finds a workable fit among them. An effective motivational system exists when the characteristics of the task, people, social climate, and managerial controls are compatible to each other. However, it does not provide the process skills with which the manager deals with changes in the organizational components which cause an imbalance in the organizational fit. Managers who apply the contingency concept should have the managerial skills needed to deal with the changes in organizations. Without the skills, the contingency concept may turn into a static managerial model which yields a set of universal principles of management (Moberg and Koch, 1975).

Organizational development (OD) presents the managerial skills necessary for dealing with organizational changes. OD refers to planned strategies for changes in the four major components (structure, people, social groups, and managerial controls) in an organization. The question of what to be changed and where to start the change will be revealed by a diagnostic analysis. Frequently, the needs for organizational changes are precipitated by the changes in tasks and people. For example, changes in technology lead to changes in the organizational tasks. Tasks become technologically more complex and demand higher degrees of job skills and interactions among functional specialists. Employee training in technological and interpersonal skills is needed to meet such demands. People in organizations, as they are better satisfied with lower-order needs, demand the satisfaction of higher-order needs from performing their jobs. These demands then necessitate changes in the jobs and organizational practices.

There are a number of planned strategies for changes ranging from sensitivity training to MBO. These strategies involve: 1) behavioral changes in workers, supervisors, work groups, and intergroup relations, 2) structural changes in organizational designs, policies, procedures, and programs, and 3) changes in technical aspects of the jobs. The techniques for dealing with behavioral changes include sensitivity training, T group, team building, inter-group team building, process consultation, confrontation, leadership training, managerial grid, and job enrichment. The techniques for dealing with structural changes include flexitimes, management-by-objectives, linking-pin process, project management, matrix organization, and changes in personnel policies, reward systems, and due processes. The techniques for dealing with technical changes involve job enlargement, work method modification, and mechanization.

OD places a heavy emphasis on the behavioral changes because the changes in attitudes, beliefs, perceptions, and sentiments (organizational climate) are the fundamentals of the changes in structural and technical aspects of an organization. Without the changes in organizational climate, structural and technical changes cannot alter interactional patterns of organizational members. However, the causal relationships between technostructural and climate factors are multidirectional. While climate factors influence the effectiveness of technostructural changes, they also are affected by the technostructural changes. Thus, if the organization wants to influence the behavioral patterns of its members, technical and structural changes should be accompanied by process skills to monitor the members' behavioral processes.

CONCLUDING REMARKS

Work motivation is important for workers, organizations, and society for maintaining their economic and psychological health. High productivity can be realized as a result of increased work motivation of the nation's work force. Productivity depends on employee motivation, ability, and technology. The level of employee ability and technological development increases as a function of motivation. Workers maintain psychological health when their needs are satisfied in their work place. Organizations can provide various means of satisfying the basic needs of their members. Maintenance needs can be met with pay and job security, affiliation needs are met with opportunities for socialization and participation, and growth-oriented needs can be satisfied with the opportunities for learning and utilizing their job skills. Increased productivity is the major source of these organizational incentives that can be applied to satisfy employees' needs. When an organization is economically healthy, it is able to experiment and expand motivational programs (pay increase, job security, socializing activities, job enlargement, and job enrichment) to satisfy employees' needs.

Some workers and union leaders seem to fear that increased productivity may lead to fewer jobs and will only benefit management. But, the truth is that decreased productivity reduces the competitive position of the company and the nation's economy in the domestic and international market, which necessitates a reduction of the employed labor force. When the organization is striken by low productivity, even the employed will suffer because the organization is not able to provide the means of satisfying employees' needs. When their needs are not reasonably satisfied over a prolonged period of time, employees will develop unhealthy or even pathological attitudes toward their work and organization. Behavioral maladjustments such as apathy, job alienation, absenteeism, turnover, sabotage, theft, and strike will prevent organizations from being productive in utilizing human resources. Such behavioral problems partially account for the high cost and poor quality of products and services and even lead to business failure.

Employee satisfaction does not necessarily lead to higher productivity. Satisfaction increases as a result of receiving rewards. When rewards are given to workers regardless of performance, satisfaction does not result in high performance. However, when high performance results in intrinsic and extrinsic rewards, both employee satisfaction and high productivity can result. Thus, the essential task of management is to create a work environment in which workers are motivated to contribute their efforts to achieve organizational goals as a means of achieving their personal goals. The following implications can be drawn from the theories and programs presented in this book to assist the managers who strive to create such a work environment in which both job satisfaction and productivity can be realized.

First, the manager should understand and manage the motivational process in organizations. The motivation process explains how individual and organizational variables affecting motivation are linked together and how their interactions result in employee satisfaction and performance. Individuals join and work in organizations to satisfy their needs (Chapter 3). Organizations have the means to satisfy these needs (Chapter 4). People differ in their responses to internal and external stimuli (needs and incentives), depending on how they perceive the outcomes of their behavior (Chapter 5). Work motivation increases when workers perceive that their effort leads to task accomplishment (E-P), task performance leads to receiving incentive rewards (P-I), and these rewards match with their needs (I-N).

Second, there are basically three types of motivation—extrinsic, affective, and intrinsic. They are primarily influenced by organizational reward systems, immediate work groups, and tasks respectively. Extrinsic motivation is aroused by administering such reward systems as financial incentives and promotion which are mediated externally (Chapter 7). The effectiveness of reward systems increases when the chance of obtaining the rewards is challenging but attainable, the amount of rewards reflects performance differences, and the rewards match with employee needs. Affective motivation dwells on man's desire to associate with others (Chapter 8). Affective motivation to comply with group norms and managerial practices increases when the workers are reinforced by the work group and their superior in their effort to satisfy their personal and task goals. Intrinsic motivation is derived from performing interesting and challenging tasks and appeals to the satisfaction of higher-order needs of employees (Chapter 9). It has a self-sustaining power; once installed, it provides the worker with a continued source of satisfaction. Intrinsic motivation increases when the task performance requires ability utilization and effort exertion, performance results in meaningful outcomes (task accomplishment, recognition, and advancement), and these outcomes satisfy the employee needs.

Third, job performance is influenced by many organizational components— tasks, work groups, managerial controls, and technological environment. Each component has a set of motivational properties that exert demands on other components. To function effectively, the organization should find a workable fit among them. For example, the task difficulty should be matched with individual readiness to perform it. A lack of fit between them leads to under or over-utilization of employee skills, which in turn leads to frustration. If the task demands timely responses from various functional specialties, an organic organizational design with behavioral training for the members is recommended. Management has no direct control over the behavior of workers, work groups, and technological environment. However, it can respond to their demands by modifying the characteristics of tasks and managerial controls.

Fourth, if employee satisfaction and performance levels are to be increased, management should be able to find a workable fit among the organizational components of a high order. The task must be intrinsically motivating. The employees are motivated to satisfy higher-order needs and have the necessary skills to perform the task. They possess interpersonal skills to interact with people with diverse professional backgrounds. Management allows them to participate in the decision-making process. When these conditions prevail in a work group or organization, the level of employee job satisfaction and performance will be the highest. However, such a workable fit of a higher order is not common in reality. Management should make a conscious and continuous effort to change the characteristics of various organizational components to arrive at the higher-order workable fit.

Finally, while management is striving to arrive at higher-order workable fits for its organizational tasks and employees, it should recognize the differences in tasks, people, work groups, and managerial controls in an organization. Thus, rather than trying to motivate the employees in an organization with the same approach, the organization differentiates its motivational programs to fit the characteristics of its employees. Operationally, some will be motivated by extrinsic incentives, while others will be motivated by enriched jobs. If more employees search for intrinsic motivation, more jobs need to be enriched. Or, more employees searching for extrinsic motivation or affective motivation need to be recruited for staffing less enriched jobs. The motivational strategy is to find workable fits for various work groups at different levels of the organization.

CASES
AND
DISCUSSION MATERIALS

MIDWEST ELECTRONICS

Midwest Electronics assembles and supplies printed circuit boards to major computer manufacturers and other electronics firms. It started as a small assembly operation in the early 1960s and has grown to the current size of eighty employees. Sam Harrison is the founder and president of Midwest Electronics. He received a master's degree in electrical engineering from a midwestern university in the late 1950s. Upon receiving a baccalaureate degree in the same field, he joined a major computer manufacturer and remained there until he left it to establish his own company.

Circuit board assembly contracts are received from computer and other electronic manufacturers. Detailed technical specifications are received, catalogued, and positioned. Assembly operations commence within a week of the receipt of orders, and finished circuit boards are shipped to the clients usually well within the specified dates. Quality and reliability are Sam's motto in dealing with clients. Since each activity has been precisely engineered to insure the optimum utilization of equipment and manpower, scrap losses are minimal. Midwest is well thought of by its clients for its products.

Midwest basically relies on manual labor to assemble the circuit boards. The circuit boards are laid on work benches, and the assemblers work along the bench to insert the electrical circuit components and other parts in each of the boards. The company hires practically anybody who has good health and good eyes. Good eyesight is very important to differentiate color-coded components and to read minute markings. Many of the employees are transient types including part-time students, housewives, and migrant farmers. They are hired and laid off to suit the volatile work load. The turnover rate runs more than 150 percent annually. Most employee turnovers are primarily attributable to employees' voluntary quittings and frequent layoffs.

Training of the new employee begins immediately, and becomes progressively more complex. The learner must learn to cut the lead within 1/8 inch length. Only when the cutting skill is developed, is the operator permitted to make the cuts at the required length. The operator is then allowed to learn such complex

This case was prepared by John Miller, an MBA candidate, Wichita State University, under the direction of Dr. Kae H. Chung.

tasks as lead forming and inserting the components into the printed circuit boards. This training process usually runs from four to six months depending on the dexterity and the attention level of the workers. Trainees are paid learners' wages which are lower than the regular wage rate. Trained workers are then paid regular wages which are about the same as the prevailing wage in similar industries in the region.

Time clocks are maintained to record the times of entry and departure of each employee. In addition, the time duration that each individual spends on a particular project is recorded to provide cost data for each project. Sam Harrison strolls around the plant to supervise and get involved with day-to-day activities of the workers. He knows most employees by their first names. There are four first line supervisors who closely consult with the president and supervise their subordinates. Sam is considered to be a warm person but strict in dealing with disciplinary problems. Absenteeism, tardiness, and horseplay frequently lead to dismissals.

Another influential managerial staff is Sam's brother John Harrison who is the vice president in charge of personnel and finance. He has an MBA degree from a midwestern university and has been with the company for the past three years. As a personnel manager, John is concerned with turnover problems. Those employees who quit Midwest Electronics join other electronic companies for better pay. Midwest has been a training ground for many productive employees of these firms. John is pondering on several motivational programs such as incentive pay, promotion, job enlargement, and job enrichment as managerial tools for dealing with the turnover problem.

DISCUSSION QUESTIONS

1. What is your analysis of the company's turnover problem?
2. How would you evaluate the company's employment and training policies?
3. Would an incentive pay system minimize the turnover problem?
4. Evaluate Sam Harrison's management or leadership style.
5. Would job enlargement and/or job enrichment help to alleviate the problem?
6. What are some other alternatives for the company if any of these programs are not implemented?

WHAT DO YOU DO WITH WILLIE JONES?

Willie Jones was late to work again. During the last twenty-six months his attendance has grown steadily worse. He no longer took any pride in the way he performed his job, and his association with fellow workers had practically ceased. Willie's problems all seemed to start about two years ago when Willie was moved from his production planning job to a circle saw operator's job. Because the company lost a large contract, Willie and several hundred other workers were bumped to lesser paying jobs.

At first, Willie seemed to adjust pretty well. He got along well with the foreman, and the fellow workers empathized with Willie. In December, four months after Willie got bumped, he began to complain of foot trouble. He claimed he couldn't stand on his feet for over half an hour before they would get numb. After three weeks of continuous complaining, Willie's foreman called Willie to the office to see what could be done to help.

Willie complained about his feet and commented that he sure would like to get his job back as a planner, because he could use that extra money. When Willie's foreman asked what Willie thought he's like to do if granted any job for which he was eligible, Willie asked about a trucker's job. The foreman said he thought it could be arranged and was quite happy to help get Willie a transfer; after all, it would help Willie get some of his money back due to a higher rate on the trucking job, but also Willie would be going to work for another foreman. In about two weeks, the transfer went through, and Willie became a fork-lift or goose driver.

Again things seemed to go well for Willie. The new foreman said Willie was slow, but new people were usually slow for the first couple of months. Willie seemed to like driving around the plant delivering parts orders. He seemed to be learning adequately but constantly mentioned how great it was to be a planner. Then, three months after Willie became a trucker, he missed his first day of work. When confronted by the foreman, Willie first told him he overslept and missed his ride. Later, he changed his story and said his feet and seat hurt from having to ride (drive) the bumpy goose around all day. In all the prior nine

This case was prepared by Larry McKean, a Master's degree candidate, Wichita State University, under the direction of Dr. Kae H. Chung.

years with the company Willie had maintained a good attendance record. Now things took a turn for the worse.

During the next three months Willie called in sick nine times and was tardy fifteen times. Furthermore, the work pace with which he did his job actually slowed down. There had been times when Willie delivered orders incorrectly, and one time he even backed into a post with a wagon and damaged an assembly. Routes which usually took ninety minutes to complete were now taking two and a half hours. Willie and his foreman had several short discussions. Willie would only say he would like to get his old planner's job back, because he sure could use the money. The foreman told Willie that if he did not improve his attendance and improve his production he would have to move him from the trucker job.

After two full weeks the foreman called Willie in and told him he would be transferred, beginning the next Monday, to be a scribe and trim worker. Willie did not say much, but the foreman could tell he was pretty low. After all he now had to take an even further drop in pay.

Willie worked as a scribe and trim man for two weeks. Most of the time he seemed to be daydreaming. When confronted with this situation Willie simply shrugged and said a dollar an hour was a lot to lose when it wasn't even his fault. The foreman watched Willie carefully. Since he was concerned about his safety, he decided to move him to another of his sections called smooth and burr. Maybe Willie would be more content here and for certain it would be safer.

Willie worked spasmodically in the smooth and burr section and kept his attendance record just clean enough to keep from getting fired. After all, by now everyone knew how much Willie wanted his planner's job back again.

Due to increases in the Company-Union agreement Willie was making six cents more per hour than his job as a planner some twenty-six months before. Willie always spoke well of the company and of the fair treatment he had received from the foremen. Willie knew that if the company could get a new contract, he and many of his friends could possibly get their old jobs back. How he longed for that. After all, if he was in his old job he would be drawing $1.39 per hour more than at present.

DISCUSSION QUESTIONS:

1. What are the factors that contribute Willie's problem?
2. Could this problem have been prevented? How?
3. What can be done to motivate Willie to do his present job better until when he returns to his old job?
4. Assuming that Willie has personal or family problems, what steps should be taken to improve his job attitude and performance?
5. How might this type of problem be prevented in the future?

NO NEWSPAPER STORY

Eastern Bupane Company retailed liquified petroleum gas (L.P.G.) to rural consumers in the Carolinas and West Virginia who lived beyond the limits of natural gas pipelines. L.P.G. is a member of the family of hydrocarbons similar to natural gas, but has the peculiar property of being transportable and storable as a liquid under pressure. However, it vaporizes quickly when the pressure is released.

Eastern Bupane Company delivered liquid L.P.G. to consumers who had bulk tanks either above or below ground. The firm also retailed heating equipment, water heaters, ranges, clothes dryers, and other gas burning appliances by preparing advertising copy and by staging sales campaigns at various retail outlets. He was given the title of director of advertising and sales promotion.

Harry did an outstanding job in advertising and sales and the store managers liked him and often requested his services. He enjoyed traveling around the states and did not complain about being away from home. Apparently he was quite happy with his job and his company. Some of the managers often remarked that "Harry is always in a good mood and lifts the spirits of employees by his beaming disposition."

After two and one half years of bubbling enthusiasm, Harry gradually seemed to lose interest in his work. The same managers began to remark that "Harry no longer has his old zip and enthusiasm, and he even fails to build enthusiasm for his promotional activities." Some managers complained that Harry had lost interest in his job and some even became reluctant to have him do any promotional work for them because he lacked spirit and failed to "pep up" the personnel.

After a series of complaints about Harry had reached the higher levels of management, he was called in by the vice-president in charge of merchandise sales, Mr. Osgood. After praising Harry for his splendid work in the past, and expressing his faith in his subordinate, he advised him of these recent complaints and asked Harry why he thought they were lodged against his work.

This case was prepared by Professor Leon C. Megginson of Louisiana State University as a basis for class discussion. From Leon C. Megginson, Human Resources: Cases and Concepts. © *1968 by Harcourt, Bruce Jovanovich, Inc. and reprinted with permission.*

Harry admitted that he no longer felt the same enthusiasm as he had originally possessed and promptly demanded a substantial raise in salary. Mr. Osgood expressed surprise that the employee would ask for a raise at a time when the effectiveness of his work was in question. Harry responded by saying that when he was hired by the sales manager, he was told that he would receive a raise in pay after working one year, if his work was satisfactory. He has been working as hard as possible, and yet, after two and one half years, no raise had come through.

The sales manager was on sick leave, but Mr. Osgood said that he would talk to him when he returned and see if such a promise had been made and if so, what could be done about it. In the meantime, he advised Harry to recapture his old enthusiasm and start doing a better job, or he might get fired instead of receiving a raise. The subordinate responded that he would not have to be fired, but that he would probably quit if the company failed to live up to its word.

The promotional work seemed to improve during the next months; at least the managers reported that Harry seemed more determined to do a good job, but that he still lacked his old sparkle.

When the sales manager returned from sick leave, he was questioned about the situation by Mr. Osgood. The manager said that he had told Harry that if merchandise sales increased 10 percent the first year, he would see that a raise would be given. However, in spite of the new employee's good work and fine promotional ideas, a mild economic recession in the area had prevented the sales from climbing as they should have done. He admitted, however, that without the promotional efforts, the merchandise volume would probably have been 10 percent lower.

The vice-president told the sales manager to talk with Harry and get the apparent misunderstanding cleared up.

The latter called the promotional man in, and after hearing Harry's complaint, the sales manager reminded him that the raise was contingent upon a 10 percent increase in merchandise. "Harry", said the manager, "if we have reaped a 10 percent increase in merchandise sales, I would have had sufficient ammunition to take to higher management to get you a raise. When the increase did not materialize, I thought you understood that I had no justifiable reason in requesting your raise. The fact that you said nothing for one and one half years indicated to me that you were fully aware of the situation. Now, like a bolt out of the blue, you suddenly start making demands. I think you are out of line, Harry. However, I will repeat my original proposal and if we have an increase of 10 percent this year, I will request your raise. However, the first thing you must do is change your attitude. In your present frame of mind, you cannot possibly accomplish very much."

Harry was not satisfied. He said that the increase failed to materialize because of a local depression and an ever increasing competitive situation. He asserted that if it had not been for his efforts, the appliance business would have decreased probably more than the state percentage.

Then, Harry aired another grievance. About two months previously, one of the branch managers was transferred from the field to the firm's headquarters to assist the sales manager with merchandise sales. This man had done an exceptional job in assisting managers to make personal contacts with customers. The resulting action had created spectacular results in a few places. These few outstanding results were featured in the company newspaper. Harry complained that he could do anything that the transferred manager could do, and many things that he could not do, such as making promotional signs, newspaper layouts, and designing direct mail circulars, as well as selling on the floor or in the field. Yet, in spite of all this, he had never received such a glowing write up in the paper. It seemed to him that the other man was being blown up whereas he was being belittled.

The sales manager explained that the manager had done an outstanding job in the past, but due to family trouble, he had slipped a great deal. Top management had decided that he should be tranferred to get him away from his family problems. The "build up" in the company paper was to give the concerned manager some praise for a job well done and also to give encouragement to an old employee who had done exceptional work in the past but had run into unavoidable private difficulties. "We are just trying to give some recognition to a fine old employee. We thought you would understand, Harry," said the sales manager.

Harry was promised that he would receive a write up in the paper in a later issue. This seemed to please him a great deal and he resumed his work with great vigor and the managers reported that he was doing a fine job.

After two future issues of the paper went to press with no mention of Harry Wegle, he wrote a letter of resignation. The vice president in charge of merchandise sales asked the disappointed man to come to his office for further discussion, but he refused and left the company's employment.

Further discussions with branch managers revealed that Harry had two distinquishing characteristics; first, he cheerfully expended his abundant energy in the performance of his duties; and second, he had a deep seated craving for praise and recognition from his superiors.

DISCUSSION QUESTIONS

1. Analyze and discuss Harry's problem from (a) Harry's and (b) his supervisors' viewpoints.
2. Could Harry's problem have been prevented? How?
3. Is the basis for determining Harry's pay increase justified? Would you raise his pay? Explain your decision.
4. How would you evaluate the newspaper story?
5. What would you do to motivate Harry if you were his supervisor?

RECOGNITION WON'T BUY BREAD

Steve Marks does not particularly like the performance appraisal and merit increase system his company uses but he has to live with it. Not much better nor worse than most others, it works on the pool of money available concept. For example:

> If the total payroll for his fiscal year is one million dollars (and if business is stable and cash available) a fixed percentage is established for promotions and merit increases for the coming period. If this fixed percentage is 5 percent, a pool of money is set aside for salary increases amounting to $50,000.
>
> Although usually not official policy, the effect of this pool of money concept is to force each supervisor to increase wages (give raises) in his work area to the point which on the average will not exceed 5 percent of his current direct payroll.
>
> In theory the supervisor is to reward the better producer with a large increase and give the average worker only a nominal increase. The marginal employee should receive no merit increase whatsoever.
>
> However, in practice, the situation is often quite different. Faced with the 5 percent rule, a supervisor such as Steve Marks finds that he cannot use his merit pool in a way which will fully reward the most competent performers. In practice, *almost everyone* gets some merit increase to keep the complaints to a minimum.

Steve Marks describes the inequities of the merit review system as it operates in his organization and tells of other recent experiences:

"Most everyone has to get some kind of increase or you have a near rebellion on your hands. I hate to admit it, but the average performer ends up getting the average (5 percent) merit increase. If the guy is a cut below average he gets 2-3 percent. Anything less than that and the man is insulted. So . . . that leaves 7-8 percent for the top contributors. As a raise it's not bad, but it's only 2-3 percent more than Mr. Average, hardly an incentive for extra output!

This case is from Robert D. Joyce, Encounters in Organizational Behavior. *New York: Pergamon Press, 1972, pp. 128-130. Reprinted with Permission.*

"The system really bothered me until I attended a short management seminar which our company sponsored. Seventeen supervisors attended the program which was conducted by some big name management consultant from New York.

"This consultant made a big issues out of the fact that we place far too much emphasis on money and raises. *He said that money doesn't motivate people! Then he went on to list his* findings on what *did* motivate people. I don't remember the order exactly, but it was something like this:

> Challenging Work
> Interesting Work
> Variety of Work
> Freedom of Action
> Responsibility
> Sense of Accomplishment
> Personal Growth and Development
> Recognition
> Friendly co-workers
> Good Working Conditions
> Salary

"Imagine! *Salary was at the bottom of the list!* At first it was hard to believe, but when I thought about it I could see that all of those other things were pretty important too. Somehow I felt a little less concerned about merit review limitations for better employees at the conclusion of the seminar.

"The week after the seminar I reviewed the performance of one of my top people. We use an anniversary date (from date of employment) to stagger reviews, and this man had completed his first full year with the company.

"Remembering what I had learned at the management seminar, I stressed the man's contributions and made a special point of recognizing his individual achievements since he had been hired. Then we spoke of ways to enrich his job, to make it more interesting and challenging. We even set objectives for the coming months and yardsticks for measuring goal achievement. I was pretty proud of myself until we got around to the specific amount of his merit increase.

"He was really upset. 'Five percent?' he said. 'Is that all I'm worth after all those words about what a great job I've done? Save those fancy words for some other guy . . . recognition won't buy bread at my store?

DISCUSSION QUESTIONS

1. Analyze and discuss Steve Marks' dilemma.
2. Analyze this case from the viewpoint of:
   (a) Job dissatisfaction (hygiene factors).
   (b) Job satisfaction (motivators).
3. Does *company policy and procedure* most affect employee job satisfaction or dissatisfaction? Explain.
4. Does the *supervisor or manager* most affect employee job satisfaction or dissatisfaction? Explain.
5. One prominent industrial psychologist has said that money (in the form of

wages and wage increases) must be considered in *two* distinct ways:
(a) Money for membership.
(b) Money for motivation.
Can you explain the difference between the two?
6. Discuss this case in terms of Maslow's *Hierarchy of Human Needs.*

CONTINENTAL PIPES

Continental Pipes produces a wide range of pipe valves for plumbing and building industries. Faced with sluggish earning performance in recent years, the company has decided to introduce a motivational program. The program is called the management-by-results (MBR). Unlike the management-by-objectives whereby employees participate in goal-setting process, employees' task goals are assigned by management. Don Webster, Personnel Director, explains the rationale behind the program as follows:

> Management-by-results is a way of communicating and distributing organizational objectives to employees. It is nothing more than deciding where we are going and how we get there. It cuts away extraneous foilages to keep the goals in sight and get the employees to adopt and focus on the goals. As the work becomes too big to be handled by one person, he needs to delegate a part of his job to others. The best way to delegate one's work to others is not only to assign the job but also define what its expected results should be. When one knows what is expected of him, he can do a better job because he can concentrate his effect on the assigned task. The results expected by anyone should be a part of the results expected of the man above and finally that of the enterprise. The accuracy by which the organizational objectives can be planned for each employee and for the interlocking with the overall organization is one of the major strengths of the management-by-result.

The performance of employees is evaluated against the predetermined goals at the end of the year. Performance points are assigned to each employee based on the percentage of task goal attainment. These points are assigned to employees collectively or individually according to the dependency of task performance. If the performance of an employee is an outcome of his independent effort, the employee will receive performance points calculated on an individual basis. If the performance is an outcome of a joint effort, performance points will be calculated on a group basis.

This case was originally prepared by Ron Westburg and Leslie Fiechtner. Wichita State University.

Most sales personnel receive independently calculated performance points, while production personnel receive group-oriented performance points. The total sales and production goals are jointly set by the sales manager, the production manager, the controller, the president, and the executive vice president. Historical performance records, general economic trend, and various internal managerial conditions are the main bases for determining performance goals for the company. The sales manager then assigns sales goals for individual sales personnel based on their past performance, territory, and sales experiences. The production manager assigns production goals for each work group.

The company pays annual performance bonuses to its employees. The annual incentive fund is determined at the end of the fiscal year, and this fund is paid out to individual employees within 60 days of the closing of the fiscal year. Ten percent of the company's earnings before taxes is set aside to pay for tax obligations and as a part of retained earnings. Fifty percent of the remainder is applied to the incentive fund. The total incentive fund is divided by the total performance points assigned to all employees to determine the value of each performance point. For example, if the incentive fund amounts to $70,000 and the total performance points are 3,500, each performance point will be worth $20. If an employee receives 80 performance points, his performance bonus will be $1,600.

The incentive program was instituted in 1974 so that employees could receive incentive bonuses. However, due to the the sluggish performance of building and plumbing industries in general, the company was not able to create the incentive fund. Inventories were increased, but the sales were down. A production supervisor commented, "My people worked hard to increase production. But, I don't see any production bonus coming to them. Yes, we all are very disappointed." A salesman also complained that he tried harder than previous years but with no increased sales volumes. Projecting the earning performance for 1975 and 1976, Mr. Webster commented, "The picture is brighter for the future than in 1974. They will have some incentive bonuses, but not very much."

DISCUSSION QUESTIONS

1. Is the management-by-results different from the management-by-objectives? Discuss major similarities and differences between them.
2. What would be possible reasons for using the management-by-results rather than the management-by-objectives? Would the company be better off if it had used the management-by-objectives?
3. What are the potential benefits and limitations of the management-by-results program?
4. Evaluate the incentive bonus plan. Use the concepts of valence, instrumentality, and expectancy of the cognitive theory presented in the textbook.
5. What are some benefits and limitations of the incentive plan? Discuss potential problems associated with such a performance appraisal.
6. Propose your own performance bonus plan and explain the rationale for suggesting such a plan.

THE GREAT PIZZA FIASCO

Old West Food Corporation is a closely held family corporation which specializes in the processing of delicatessen type food items. These foods include pre-made sandwiches, potato salad, macaroni salad, cole slaw, and a small line of bachelor dinners. The bachelor dinners typically consist of assorted cold cuts, cheese, a tomato wedge, pickle, and noodle or potato salad.

These items are sold through several smaller chain stores and assorted small markets where customers make a selection from a refrigerated case.

For the most part, Old West was never known for innovation in product development. Product ideas came from two major sources:

1. Company officers would discuss (at regular meetings) the new delicatessen products being introduced at supermarkets by the big name brand food processors. Ideas which looked good were copied and introduced in Old West packaging. This was not considered unethical because only minor product differences were required to invalidate a product infringement claim by competition. Old West still had to make its product attractive, tasty, and fresh. Often Old West felt its copies were much better than the original versions.
2. Old West salesmen would often come up with ideas after visiting these retail outlets and talking to merchants. The merchants would discuss customer comments and preferences and make useful suggestions.

For ten years since it was founded, Old West had been run by Gerald Meyerson and his brother Roger. Gerald is President and handles Purchasing and Processing Operations. Roger is Vice-President and is in charge of Sales and Finance. The organization then had the structure shown in Figure C-1.

About two years ago, Phillip Miles was hired as an executive assistant to Gerald. Miles was a production expeditor with five years of experience at a large aerospace organization. Miles was also Gerald Meyerson's son-in-law. Gerald had

---

This case is from Robert D. Joyce, Encounters in Organizational Behavior. *New York: Pergamon Press, 1972, pp. 77-80. Reprinted with Permission.*

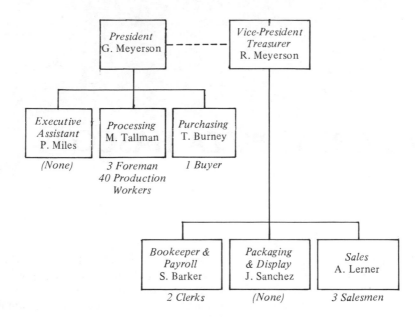

FIGURE C-1

always liked Miles and did not object too vigorously when his only child persuaded him to hire her husband. Phillip was just the man to add new blood to a tired, unimaginative organization.

In January of last year, Old West introduced an individual sized pre-baked frozen pizza. The idea again was not new, but it was a radical step for Old West in two ways:

1. Processing operations had to be expanded to include flash ovens and fast freeze cabinets.
2. Old West products were now in retail freezer cases as well as the cool delicatessen cases. New market potential existed.

The frozen pizza caught on quickly and production was brisk and profitable. Gerald Meyerson was elated. The pizza was Phillip Miles' idea. Phillip set up the operation and gave it the energy and drive it needed.

Gerald confided to Phillip that the organization needed more of the aggressiveness which Phillip demonstrated. It needed new ideas, incentives, and systems from modern industry. Gerald asked if Phillip could think of something else which would inspire the organization.

Miles reflected on the backgrounds of key people:

Marty Talman Age 43. 2 years of college, 15 years experience in food production, with Old West 7 years as Processing Manager. Talman hired his three foremen personally. They are very loyal. Production has, surprisingly, few major problems.

Tom Burney Age 37. Former assistant Bookkeeper at Old West. He became Purchasing Agent when that position was created 3 years ago. He is assisted by one buyer.

Sylvia Barker Age 32 and divorced. Five years experience in bookkeeping prior to Old West. Six years with Old West. Moved up to her present spot in 1963. No formal education beyond high school, but a very hard worker. She arrives early and leaves late — a regular career girl.

Joe Sanchez Age 39. Art major in college, but did not finish. Great eye for design of boxes, trays, and plastic display packages. Works by himself and with vendors. A lot of sales success must be attributed to his package designs. Three years at Old West.

Al Lerner Age 51. Al has been selling food all his life. He looks like he enjoys his product, too. Not too hot at administration though. The salesmen seem to come and go. No incentives.

Incentives, thought Miles, were the key!

The following month Phillip Miles outlined his incentive plan to Gerald and Roger Meyerson. All people involved with new products were to be included in the *New Product Bonus Pool*. This would include Talman, his three foremen; Burney (but not the girl buyer), Sanchez, Lerner, his three salesmen; and, of course, Miles. Sylvia Barker was not involved in the development-production-sales cycle and was not to be included.

The plan would work like this:

New Products were to be emphasized. A product was considered new until its sales exceeded $100,000. One percent of the wholesale sales price of each of these new products (up to $100,000 in sales) would be set aside in a pool. This would be divided at the end of the year. The amount each person got would depend upon:

1. The amount of money in the pool
2. The number of pool members involved
3. Salary level of each. Pool shares would be weighted slightly based upon salary.

Gerald Meyerson bought the idea over the objections of his brother, Roger, who saw it as unwarranted salary increases in disguise. Gerald, however, felt that it would provide incentives for new ideas, better methods, greater sales, and increased profits. Above all, it would increase individual motivation through sharing in company success.

The formal announcement was made in March at a meeting with the key people. Gerald Meyerson gave the following illustration of possible bonus amounts:

Assume ten new products this year with average sales of $75,000 each. At 1 percent of sales, this creates a new product pool of $7,500 $75,000 x 10 x 1 percent). With 11 people in the pool the bonus would average almost $700 each.

Response to the plan was enthusiastic and a new spirit of togetherness seemed to prevail. Five new products were successfully introduced by August. Two others had been initiated, but taste and appearance problems sharply curtailed sales.

In October, several problems began to develop. Talman and Burney checked with Sylvia Barker to see how the pool size was growing. Syliva snapped that she had no idea. She claimed she had only gross sales figures and suggested they see Roger Meyerson for the detailed new products sales information. When Talman asked Roger Meyerson, he was told the pool was coming along fine, but that he (Roger) was busy at the moment and could not provide the exact number.

By November, it appeared that seven new products would be involved, and that average sales would be nearer $50,000 than $75,000.

At the end of the year each person received his bonus with his regular paycheck. No announcement was made as to the amount each received, but when individuals started discussing the matter, it appeared that the bonuses varied from $150 to $300. The totals were much smaller than expected and the range was surprisingly large.

Tammy Brown, a payroll clerk, told her boyfriend in Processing that Phil Miles got a check for almost $500. The word spread rapidly. Lerner asked Gerald Meyerson about it directly. Meyerson replied that Miles' check included some travel expense he had incurred. Lerner was hardly satisfied.

Everyone felt that they had been misled as to bonus amounts. The salary differential made it very vague. On top of that, there are too many people in the pool. Miles had hired a technician to assist him during the year. Had he been included? Miles had no comment.

Gerald Meyerson was disgusted. "Try to do something for your people and they get greedy," he complained to Miles. Early in January, he issued a curt memo which ended the new product bonus. In its place he substituted a one-time only flat salary increase of 5 percent for all persons who had been on the new products bonus.

"That should end that," he announced. It did not. Sylvia Barker and one of Al Lerner's salesmen quit the next week.

DISCUSSION QUESTIONS

1. In what ways did the incentive plan produce *positive* or contributive employee behavior?
2. In what ways did the incentive plan produce *negative* employee behavior?
3. Was proper implementation and follow-up conducted? Explain.
4. How did Gerald Meyerson compound the problem?
5. Discuss this case in terms of:
   (a) Leadership style.
   (b) Effective communication.
6. How can sound behavioral elements be built into any incentive plan?

ARE YOU SATISFIED WITH YOUR JOB?

Job satisfaction means different things to different people. It can mean monetary rewards that the person receives, social interaction enjoyed on the job, or the job that one enjoys performing. Although the satisfactions with monetary rewards and social interactions do not necessarily lead to high performance, they are nevertheless important for workers to release their energies for productive endeavors. Satisfaction with the job itself is the key to job satisfaction and high performance. One way to measure overall job satisfaction is to investigate the extent to which the worker is satisfied with various facets of his or her work environment. However, if one wants to measure the extent to which an employee is satisfied with his or her job itself, it can be done by assessing the motivational potential of the job and by comparing the job's motivational potential with the worker readiness to the job. Exhibit A measures the motivational characteristics of a job. Exhibit B measures the individual readiness to a job.

The motivational potential or task difficulty index is derived from various task attributes. Each task attribute is measured on a nine-point scale, ranging from one, meaning its insignificance, to nine, meaning its significance. The sum of these attribute scores is divided by the number of task attribute items to arrive at an index. The individual readiness index is derived from an individual's skill level and psychological readiness. The skill level shows the person's technical readiness while the need state shows the worker's psychological readiness for dealing with the job. These individual characteristics are measured on a nine-point scale, and then the sum of these scores will be divided by the number of readiness items to arrive at an individual readiness index.

If the motivational potential (task difficulty index) is either substantially higher or lower than the worker's readiness (individual readiness index), the difference usually signals job dissatisfaction. The worker is either over-qualified or under-qualified for the job. Work motivation will be higher when they are closer to each other. The difference between the two indices suggests that either the jobs or people have to be changed. An analysis of responses to each item will provide the necessary information regarding the specific aspects of the task or employee training that have to be changed. For example, if the job is lacking a challenge to the worker, an additional task element or responsibility can be introduced to the job.

EXHIBIT A. TASK ATTRIBUTE SURVEY

Items	1 Very Little	2	3	4	5 Somewhat	6	7	8 Very Much	9
1. Does employee motivation make a major difference in job performance?									
2. To what extent does the employee perform different activities requiring a variety of job skills?									
3. To what extent does the worker perform the whole unit or a major portion of a product?									
4. Does the job provide a meaningful performance feedback?									
5. Does the job require a high degree of technical knowledge or skills?									
6. To what extent does the worker have control over his or her work method and pace?									
7. To what extent does the job provide the worker with opportunities to interact with co-workers or clients?									
8. To what extent does the worker feel responsible for the task accomplishment?									
9. To what extent does the worker have autonomy in utilizing his or her own time and other resources?									

EXHIBIT B. INDIVIDUAL READINESS SURVEY

Items	1	2	3	4	5	6	7	8	9
	Very Little				Somewhat			Very Much	
1. To what extent is the worker satisfied with his or her pay?									
2. To what extent does the worker have job security in the organization?									
3. How well is the worker technically prepared to perform the job?									
4. How well can the worker interact with his or her co-workers or clients?									
5. How well can the worker perform his or her job with a minimum level of supervision?									
6. Does the worker have the desire to hold the responsibility for the task accomplishment?									
7. To what extent is he committed to the organization?									

EVERY EMPLOYEE IS AN ASSOCIATE

Delta Corporation is an electronic company located in a medium-sized city in the Midwest. It manufactures calculators and cash registers and distributes them throughout the country and aboard. As most manufacturers in electronic products, Delta Corporation experiences the cyclincal ups and downs in business volumes and faces keen competition from other producers in the same field in and out of the country. Although it is not a leading producer, the company has been a viable competitor in the field and has been enjoying a fair share of the market. One of the contributing factors to its vitality is known as the quality of labor. Although it is a unionized company, the company has had less problems with the labor than other competitors. While other companies have experienced frequent labor problems such as lay-offs, work stoppages, high turnover, and high absenteeism, the company has not experienced any serious labor problems in recent years.

Sam Bolenz is the director of personnel at Delta Corporation. Describing the quality of his people, he said "they are hard working people. Most of them have rural upbringings and maintain Puritan work ethics." As a major employer in this area, the company is known as a "people-oriented" company. Its pay scales and fringe benefits are not the best but competitive. However, the company is known as a leader in employee training and development. As a response to recent development in employment enrichment, the company undertook an experimental program which focused on the improvement of quality of organizational life for its employees. Mr. Bolenz described the theme of the program, "We try to make every employee an associate rather than a helping hand." Everyone is called an associate and becomes the boss in managing his or her own job. The initial step was to do away with time clocks. Associates record their own working hours at a designated area. They report to work between 6:30 a.m. and 9:30 a.m. and leave between 3:30 p.m. and 6:30 p.m. in the afternoon. People work to meet their own share of work without unnecessary constraints imposed by the clock. There is not an abrupt rush to leave the building when the eight hours are up. They usually complete the work they have started or at least don't drop the things they are working on when the bell rings.

This case was prepared by John Miller, an MBA candidate, Wichita State University, under the direction of Dr. Kae H. Chung.

Every associate is on a salary basis. Any overtime compensation has to be prearranged between the supervisor and his subordinates. In addition, many of the status symbols are removed. There are no privileges for managers. There are no special parking lots for managers and no executive dining room. All associates are covered by the same type of fringe benefits. There is no status differential between office and plant associates. Plant associates receive the performance reports regarding their products—who bought them and how much, and how they like the products. Plant associates are trained to test their own equipment and inspect the quality of their products. Qualtiy assurance personnel work with the plant associates.

There are no time dependent sequential assembly operations. Plant associates are organized into teams. Each team is responsible for specific assembly operations or work modules. Team leaders distribute work assignments for their associates. Work assignments are frequently rotated among team members. The teams work like families. Job applicants are reviewed by the appropriate work team before they are hired; the team's rejects usually are not hired. Team leaders are also selected or approved by the team members.

Mr. Bolenz considers the program not a major success but satisfactory. Voluntary absenteeism rates have leveled off at about 1.2 percent after an initial rate of 2.1 percent at the beginning of the program. Asked about the change in productivity, Mr. Bolenz said, "Well, it is hard to measure the change in productivity attributable to the program. This thing (productivity) is affected by so many factors that one can hardly single out the effect of the program on productivity." But, talking to other managers, the case writer figured that there wasn't much change in productivity. In some cases, it was suspected that productivity might have been dropped somewhat due to the abolishment of scientifically engineered sequential assembly operations.

Intrigued by these lukewarm responses from managers, the case writer further pursued his inquiries into their responses to the program and its future. The following responses are the comments made by a team leader, a union steward, and the general manager.

Team Leader: "I don't mind calling them associates. But, it (the flexitime) creates some headaches for me. Some days, I need people early in the morning to meet the rush order. But, everybody shows up late. Another thing, it sometimes takes too much time to figure out who is doing what. It looks like everyone likes a certain job better than others."

Union Steward: "Every now and then, the company lays off workers. They now call us their associates. I got to see whom they are gonna lay off and how they are gonna lay off."

General Manager: "I heard a rumor that the union is zeroing in on us as its target. I guess they (national union officials) consider us soft-headed and think we may easily give in to their demands. I hope it is just a rumor. If it is true, I wonder what Sam wants to do about it."

DISCUSSION QUESTIONS:

1. Do you consider the company's employment enrichment program a success or a failure? Explain why.
2. What contributes the drop in absenteeism? Would the employees positively respond to the experimental program? Explain why or why not.

3. How would you explain the lack of improvement in productivity?
4. If you are the chief executive of the company, would you continue the program or dismiss it? What are some of the things to be considered if you decide to continue it? What would the possible consequences be if you decide to drop it now?
5. How do you interpret the comments made by the team leader, the union steward, and the general manager?
6. What are some generalizations you can make regarding some basic ingredients that have to prevail in implementing such a program?

JOB ENRICHMENT AT AT&T

ANATOMY OF ENRICHMENT

In talking about job enrichment, it is necessary to go beyond such high-level concepts as "self-actualization," "need for achievement," and "psychological growth." It is necessary to specify the steps to be taken. The strategy can be broken down into these aspects—improving work through systematic changes in (a) the module of work, (b) control of the module, and (c) the feedback signaling whether something has been accomplished. I shall discuss each of these aspects in turn.

WORK MODULE

Through changing the work modules, Indiana Bell Telephone Company scored a striking success in job enrichment within the space of two years. In Indianpolis, 33 employees, most of them at the lowest clerical wage level, compiled all telephone directories for the state. The processing from clerk to clerk was laid out in 21 steps, many of which were merely for verification. The steps included manuscript reception, manuscript verification, keypunch, keypunch verification, ad copy reception, ad copy verification, and so on—a production line as real as any in Detroit. Each book is issued yearly to the customers named in it, and the printing schedule calls for the appearance of about one different directory per week.

In 1968, the year previous to the start of our study, 28 new hires were required to keep the clerical force at the 33-employee level. Obviously, such turnover had bad consequences. From every operating angle, management was dissatisfied.

In a workshop, the supervisors concluded that the lengthy verification routine calling lot confirmation of one's work by other clerks, was not solving the basic problem, which was employee indifference toward the tasks. Traditional "solutions" were ineffective. They included retraining, supervisor complaints

This material is an excerpt from Robert N. Ford, "Job Enrichment Lessons from AT&T," Harvard Business Review, *Jan-Feb., 1973, pp. 96-106. Copyright © 1972 by the President and Fellows of Harvard College; all rights reserved. Reprinted with permission.*

to the employees, and "communicating" with them on the importance to customers of error-free listing of their names and places of business in the directories. As any employee smart enough to be hired knows, an incorrect listing will remain monumentally wrong for a whole year.

The supervisors came up with many ideas for enriching the job. The first step was to identify the most competent employees, and then ask them, one by one, if they felt they could do error-free work, so that having others check the work would be pointless. Would they check their own work if no one else did it?

Yes, they said they could do error-free work. With this simple step the module dropped from 21 slices of clerical work to 14.

Next the supervisory family decided to take a really big step. In the case of the thinner books, they asked certain employees whether they would like to "own" their own books and perform all 14 remaining steps with no verification unless they themselves arranged it with other clerks—as good stenographers do when in doubt about a difficult peice of paperwork. Now the module included every step (except keytape, a minor one).

Then the supervisors turned their attention to a thick book, the Indianapolis directory, which requires many hands and heads. They simply assigned letters of the alphabet to individuals and let them complete all 14 steps for each block of letters.

In the past, new entries to all directories had moved from clerk to clerk; now all paperwork connected with an entry belonging to a clerk stayed with that clerk. For example, the clerk prepared the daily addenda and issued them to the information or directory assitance operators. The system became so efficient that most of the clerks who handled the smaller directories had charge of more than one.

In defining modules that give each employee a natural area of responsibility, we try to accumulate horizontal slices of work until we have created (or recreated) one of these three entities for him or her:

1. A customer (usually someone outside the business).
2. A client (usually someone inside the business, helping the employee serve the customer).
3. A task (in the manufacturing end of the business, for example, where, ideally, individual employees produce complete items).

CONTROL OF THE MODULE

As an employee gains experience, the supervisor should continue to turn over responsibility until the employee is handling the work completely. The reader may infer that supervisors are treating employees unequally. But it is not so; ultimately, they may all have the complete job if they can handle it. In the directory-compilation case cited—which was a typical assembly-line procedure, although the capital investment was low—the supervisors found that they could safely permit the employee to say when sales of advertisements in the yellow pages must stop if the ads were to reach the printer on time.

But that was only one element in the total module and its control. The directory clerks talked *directly* to salesmen, to the printer, to supervisors in other departments about production problems, to service representatives, and to each other as the books moved through the production stages.

There are obvious risks on the supervisors' side as they give their jobs away, piece by piece, to selected employees. We have been through it enough to advise, "Don't worry." Be assured that supervisors who try it will say, as many in the Bell System have said, "Now, at last, I feel like a manager. Before I was merely chief clerk around here."

In other studies we have made, control has been handed by the supervisor to a person when the employee is given the authority to perform such tasks as these:

- Credit ratings for customers.
- Ask for, and determine the size of, a deposit.
- Cut off service for nonpayment.
- Make his or her own budget, subject to negotiation.
- Reject a run or supply of material because of poor quality.
- Talk to anyone at any organizational level when the employee's work is concerned.
- Call directly and negotiate for outside repairmen or suppliers (within the budget) to remedy a condition handicapping the employee's performance.

FEEDBACK

Definition of the module and control of it are futile unless the results of the employee's effort are discernible. Moreover, knowledge of the results should go directly to where it will nurture motivation—that is, to the employee, People have a great capacity for mid-flight correction when they know where they stand.

One control responsibility given to excellent employees in AT&T studies is self-monitoring; it lets them record their own "qualities and quantities." For example, one employee who had only a grade-school education was taught to keep a quality control chart in which the two identical parts of a dry-reed switch were not to vary more than .005 from an ideal dimension. She found that for some reason too many switches were failing.

She proved that the trouble occurred when one reed that was off by .005 met another reed that was off by .005. The sum, .010, was too much in the combined component and it failed. On her own initiative, she recommended and saw to it that the machine dies were changed when the reeds being stamped out started to vary by .003 from the ideal. A total variance of .006 would not be too much, she reasoned. Thus the feedback she got showed her she was doing well at her job.

This example shows all three factors at work—the module, its control, and feedback. She and two men, a die maker and a machine operator, had the complete responsibility for producing each day more than 100,000 of these tiny parts, which are not unlike two paper matches, but much smaller.

Compared with workers at a plant organized along traditional lines, with batches of the reeds moving from shop to shop, these three employees were producing at a fourtold rate. Such a minigroup, where each person palys a complementary part, is radically different psychologically from the traditional group of workers, where each is doing what the others do.

REFERENCES

Adams, J.S., "Inequity in Social Exchange," in L. Berkowitz (ed.), *Advances in Experimental Social Psychology*, Vol. 2. New York: Academic Press, 1965, 267-300.

Adams, J.S., "Toward an Understanding of Inequity," *Journal of Abnormal and Social Psychology*, 1963, 67, 422-436 (a).

Adams, J.S., "Wage Inequities, Productivity, and Work Quality," *Industrial Relations.* 1963, 3, 1-16 (b).

Adams, J.S. and Jacobsen, P.R., "Effects of Wage Inequities on Work Quality," *Journal of Abnormal and Social Psychology*, 1964, 69, 19-25.

Adams, J.S., "Inequity in Social Exchange," in Berkowitz, L. (ed.), *Advances in Experimental Social Psychology*. New York: Academic Press, 1965, 2, 267-300.

Adams, J.S. and Rosenbaum, W.B., "The Relationship of Worker Productivity to Cognitive Dissonance About Wage Inequities," *Journal of Applied Psychology*, 1962, 46, 161-164.

Adamson, R. "Contrast Effects and Reinforcement," in M.H. Appley (ed.), *Adaptation Level.* New York: Academic, 1971.

Alderfer, C.P., "An Organizational Syndrome," *Administrative Science Quarterly*, 1967, 12, 440-460.

Alderfer, C.P., "An Empirical Test of a New Theory of Human Needs," *Organizational Behavior and Human Performance*, 1969, 4, 142-175.

Alderfer, C.P., *Human Needs in Organizational Settings.* New York: Free Press, 1972.

Alderfer, C.P., Kaplan, R.E., and Smith, K.K., "The Effect of Variations in Relatedness Need Satisfaction on Relatedness Desires," *Administrative Science Quarterly*, 1974, 19, 507-532.

Allport, F.H., *Social Psychology.* New York: Houghton Mifflin, 1924.

284

AMACOM's Editor, "Job Redesign on the Assembly Line: Farewell to Blue-Collar Blues?" *Organizational Dynamics,* 1973, 2, 51-67.

Anderson, C.R., "Coping Behaviors as Intervening Mechanisms in the Inverted-U Stress-Performance Relationship," *Journal of Applied Psychology,* 1976, 61, 30-34.

Andrews, I.R., "Wage Inequity and Job Performance: An Experimental Study," *Journal of Applied Psychology,* 1967, 51, 39-45.

Appley, M.H. (ed.), *Adaptation Level Theory.* New York: Academic, 1971.

Argyris, C., *Integrating the Individual and the Organization.* New York: Wiley, 1964.

Argyris, C., *Personality and Organization.* New York: Harper and Row, 1957.

Argyris, C., "Personality and Organization Theory Revisited," *Administrative Science Quarterly,* 1973, 18, 141-167.

Arvey, R.D., "Task Performance as a Function of Perceived Effort-Performance and Performance-Reward Contingencies." *Organizational Behavior and Human Performance,* 1972, 8, 423-433.

Aronoff, J. and Litwin, G.H., "Achievement Motivation Training and Executive Advancement," *Journal of Applied Behavioral Science,* 1971, 7, 215-229.

Asch, S.E., *Social Psychology.* Englewood Cliffs, N.J.: Prentice-Hall, 1952.

Asch, S.E., "The Effects of Group Pressure Upon the Modification and Distortion of Judgments," in E.E. Maccoby, T.E. Newcomb, and E.L. Hartley (eds.), *Readings in Social Psychology.* New York: Holt, 1958.

Atchison, T.J. and Leffert, E.A., "The Prediction of Turnover Using Herzberg's Job Satisfaction Technique," *Personnel Psychology,* 1972, 25, 53-64.

Atkinson, J.W., *An Introduction to Motivation.* Princeton: D. Van Nostrand, 1964.

Atkinson, J.W., "Motivational Determinants of Risk-Taking Behavior," *Psychological Review,* 1957, 64, 359-372.

Atkinson, J.W., "Some General Implications of Conceptual Development in the Study of Achievement Oriented Behavior," in M.R. Jones (ed.), *Human Motivation: A Symposium.* Lincoln, Neb.: University of Nebraska Press, 1965.

Atkinson, J.W., Bastian, J.R., Earl, R.W., and Litwin, G.H., "The Achievement Motive, Goal Setting, and Probability Preferences," *Journal of Abnormal and Social Psychology,* 1960, 1, 27-36.

Atkinson, J.W. and Feather, N.T., (eds.), *A Theory of Achievement Motivation.* New York: John Wiley, 1966.

Atkinson, J.W. and Raynor, J.D., *Motivation and Achievement,* New York: Winston and Sons, 1947.

Ayllon, T. and Azrin, N.H., "The Measurement and Reinforcement of Behavior of Psychotics," *Journal of Experimental Analysis of Behavior,* 1965, 8, 357-383.

Bales, R.F., *Interaction Process Analysis:* A Method for the Study of Small Groups. Reading, Mass.: Addison-Wesley, 1950.

Bales, R.F. and Borgatta, E.F., "Size of Group as a Factor in the Interaction Profile," in A.P. Hare, E.F. Borgatta, and R.F. Bales (eds.), *Small Groups.* New York: Knopf, 1955, 396-413.

Bandura, A., *Principles of Behavior Modification.* New York: Holt, Rinehart, and Winston, 1969.

Barnard, C.I., *The Function of the Executive.* Cambridge: Harvard University Press, 1938.

Barnlund, D.C., "A Comparative Study of Individual, Majority, and Group Judgment," *Journal of Abnormal and Social Psychology,* 1959, 58, 55-60.

Beach, F.A. and Jordan, L., "Sexual Exhaustion and Recovery in the Male Rat," *Quarterly Journal of Experimental Psychology,* 1956, 8, 121-133.

Belcher, D.W., "Toward a Behavioral Science 'Theory of Wages," *Journal of Academy of Management,* 1962, 5, 102-115.

Belcher, D.W., *Wage and Salary Administration.* Englewood Cliffs, N.J.: Prentice-Hall, 1974.

Bennis, W.G., *Changing Organizations.* New York: McGraw-Hill, 1966.

Bennis, W.G., Berkowitz, N., Affinito, M., and Malone, M., "Authority, Power and the Ability to Influence," *Human Relations,* 1958, 11, 143-155.

Bentham, J., *An Introduction to the Principles of Morals and Legislation.* Oxford: Clarendon, 1875.

Berger, C.J., Cummings, L.L., and Heneman, H.G., "Expectancy Theory and Operant Conditioning Predictions of Performance under Variable Ratio and Continuous Schedules of Reinforcement," *Organizational Behavior and Human Performance,* 1975, 14, 227-243.

Bergum, B.D. and Lehr, D.J., "Monetary Incentives and Vigilance," *Journal of Experimental Psychology,* 1964, 67, 197-198.

Berlyne, D.E., "The Reward Value of Indifferent Stimulation," in D.J. Tapp (ed.), *Reinforcement and Behavior.* New York: Academic Press, 1969, 205-211.

Black, R.W., "On the Combination of Drive and Incentive Motivation," *Psychological Review,* 1965, 72, 310-317.

Blackwood, R.D., *Operant Control of Behavior.* Akron, Ohio: Exorium Press, 1971.

Blake, R.R. and Mouton, J.S., *Building a Dynamic Corporation Through Grid Organization Development.* Reading, Mass.: Addison-Wesley, 1969.

Blake, R.R. and Mouton, J.S., *Group Dynamics: Key to Decision Making.* Houston: Gulf Publishing Company, 1961.

Blake, R.R. and Mouton, J.S., *The Managerial Grid.* Houston: Gulf Publishing Company, 1964.

Blauner, R., "Extent of Satisfaction: A Review of General Research," in T.W. Costello and S.S. Zalkind (eds.), *Psychology in Administration.* Englewood Cliffs, N.J.: Prentice-Hall, 1963, 80-95.

Blood, M.R. and Hulin, C.L., "Alienation, Environmental Characteristics, and Worker Responses," *Journal of Applied Psychology,* 1967, 51, 284-290.

Blumberg, P., *Industrial Democracy.* New York: Schocken Books, 1968.

Bolles, R.C., "Reinforcement, Expectancy, and Learning," *Psychological Review,* 1972. 79. 394-409.

Bolles, R.C., *Theory of Motivation.* New York: Harper and Row, 1967.

Bourke, J.T., "Performance Bonus Plans: Boon for Managers and Stockholders," *Management Review,* 1975, 64, 13-18.

Brady, R.H., "MBO Goes to Work in the Public Sector," *Harvard Business Review,* 1973, 51, 65-74.

Braunstein, D.N., Klein, G.A., and Pachia, M., "Feedback Expectancy and Shifts in Student Ratings of College Faculty," *Journal of Applied Psychology,* 1973, 58, 254-258.

Brayfield, A.H., and Crockett W.H., "Employee Attitudes and Employee Performance," *Psychological Bulletin,* 1955, 52, 396-424.

Brehm, J.W., *Responses to Loss of Freedom.* Morristown, N.J.: General Learning Press, 1972.

Brief, A.P. and Albag, R.J., "Employee Reactions to Job Characteristics: A Constructive Replication," *Journal of Applied Psychology,* 1975, 60, 182-186.

Broodling, L.A., "Relationship of Internal-External Control to Work Motivation and Performance in an Expectancy Model," *Journal of Applied Psychology,* 1975, 60, 65-70.

Brown, J.S., "Gradients of Approach and Avoidance Responses and Their Relation to Level of Motivation," *Journal of Comparative and Physiological Psychology,* 1948, 41, 450-465.

Brown, J.S., *The Motivation of Behavior.* New York: McGraw-Hill, 1961.

Bruner, J.S. and Goodman, C., "Value and Need as Organizing Factors in Perception," *Journal of Abnormal and Social Psychology,* 1947, 42, 33-44.

Bruning, J.L., "Direct and Various Effects of a Shift in Magnitude of Reward on Performance," *Journal of Personality and Social Psychology,* 1965, 2, 278-281.

Bryan, J.F. and Locke, E.A., "Goal Setting as a Means of Increasing Motivation," *Journal of Applied Psychology,* 1967, 51, 274-277.

Buchanan, B., "Building Organizational Commitment: The Socialization of Managers in Work Organizations," *Administrative Science Quarterly,* 1974, 19, 533-546.

Bunker, D.R., and Dalton, G.W., "The Comparative Effectiveness of Groups and Individuals in Solving Problems," in P.R. Lawrence, L.B. Barnes, and J. W. Lorsch (eds.), *Organizational Behavior and Administration.* Homewood, Ill.: Richard D. Irwin, 1976, 199-203.

Bureau of National Affairs, *Labor Policy and Practice—Personnel Management.* Washington, D.C.: Bureau of National Affairs, 1975.

Bureau of National Affairs, *Wage and Salary Administration: Personnel Policies Forum.* Washington, D.C., 1972.

Burgess, R.L., "Communication Networks: An Experimental Reevaluation," *Journal of Experimental Social Psychology,* 1968, 4, 324-337.

Burke, R.J., "Are Herzberg's Motivators and Hygienes Unidimensional?" *Journal of Applied Psychology,* 1966, 50, 317-321.

Burns, T. and Stalker, G.M., *The Management of Innovation.* London: Tavistock Publications, 1961.

Cammann, C. and Lawler, E.E., "Employee Reactions to a Pay Incentive Plan," *Journal of Applied Psychology,* 1973, 58, 163-172.

Campbell, A. and Converse, P.E. (ed.), *The Human Meaning of Social Change.* New York: Russell Sage Foundation, 1972.

Campbell, J.P., Dunnette, M., Lawler, E.E., and Weick, K.E., *Managerial Behavior, Performance, and Effectiveness.* New York: McGraw-Hill, 1970.

Capdevielle, P. and Neef, A., "Productivity and Unit Labor Costs in the United States and Abroad," *Monthly Labor Review,* 1975, 98, 28-32.

Carroll, S.J. and Tosi, H.L., "Goal Characteristics and Personality Factors in an MBO Program," *Administrative Science Quarterly,* 1970, 15, 295-305.

Carroll, S.J. and Tosi, H.L., *Management by Objectives.* New York: Macmillan, 1973.

Cartwright, D. and Zander, A., *Group Dynamics: Research and Theory.* Evanston, Ill.: Row, Peterson & Co., 1960.

288

Centers, R. and Bugental, D.E., "Intrinsic and Extrinsic Job Motivation among Different Segments of the Working Population," *Journal of Applied Psychology,* 1966, 50, 193-197.

Chalupsky, A.B., "Incentive Practices as Viewed by Scientists and Managers of Pharmaceutical Laboratories," *Personnel Psychology,* 1964, 17, 395-401.

Chamber of Commerce, *Employee Benefits, 1973.* Washington, D.C.: U.S. Chamber of Commerce, 1974.

Chapanis, A., "Knowledge of Performance as an Incentive in Repetitive, Monotonous Tasks," *Journal of Applied Psychology,* 1964, 48, 263-267.

Chapman, J.B. and Ottemann, R., "Employee Preference for Various Compensation and Fringe Benefit Options," *Personnel Administrator,* 1975, 20, 31-36.

Cherrington, D.J., Reitz, H.J., and Scott, W.E., "Effects of Reward and Contingent Reinforcement on Satisfaction and Task Performance," *Journal of Applied Psychology,* 1971, 55, 531-536.

Chung, K.H., "A Markov Chain Model of Human Needs: An Extension of Maslow's Need Theory," *Academy of Management Journal,* 1969, 12, 223-234.

Chung, K.H., "Developing a Comprehensive Model of Motivation and Performance," *Academy of Management Journal,* 1968, 11, 63-74.

Chung, K.H. and Ferris, M.J., "An Inquiry of the Nominal Group Process," *Academy of Management Journal,* 1971, 14, 520-524.

Chung, K.H. and Ross, M.F., "Differences in Motivational Properties between Job Enlargement and Job Enrichment," *Academy of Management Review,* 1977 (forthcoming).

Chung, K.H. and Vickery, W.D., "Relative Effectiveness and Joint Effects of Three Selected Reinforcements in a Repetitive Task Situation," *Organizational Behavior and Human Performance,* 1976, 16, 114-142.

Church, R.M., "The Varied Effects of Punishment on Behavior," *Psychological Review,* 1964, 70, 360-402.

Cleland, D.I. and King, W.R., *Systems Analysis and Project Management.* New York: McGraw-Hill, 1968.

Coch, L. and French, J.R.P., "Overcoming Resistance to Change," *Human Relations,* 1948, 1, 512-532.

Cofer, C.N. and Appley, M.H., *Motivation: Theory and Research.* New York: Wiley, 1964.

Collier, G. and Bolles, R., "Some Determinants of Intake of Sucrose Solutions," *Journal of Comparative and Physiological Psychology,* 1968, 65, 379-383.

Conant, E.H. and Kilbridge, M.D., "An Interdisciplinary Analysis of Job Enlargement: Technology, Costs, and Behavioral Implications," *Industrial and
Labor Relations Review,* 1965, 18, 377-395.

Conference Board, Inc., *Top Executive Compensation.* New York: The Conference Board, Inc., 1972.

Cook, F.W., "Stock Options at the Crossroads," *Personnel,* 1976, 53, 18-26.

Costello, T.W. and Zalkind, S.S., *Psychology in Administration.* Englewood
Cliffs, N.J.: Prentice-Hall, 1963.

Cox, J.H., "Time and Incentive Pay Practices in Urban Areas," *Monthly Labor
Review,* 1971, 94, 53-56.

Crandall, V.J., Solomon, D., and Kellaway, R., "Expectancy Statements and
Decision Time as Functions of Objective Probabilities and Reinforcement
Values," *Journal of Personality,* 1955, 24, 192-203.

Crespi, L.P., "Amount of Reinforcement and Level of Performance," *Psychological Review,* 1944, 51, 431-457.

Crespi, L.P., "Quantitative Variation of Incentive and Performance in the White
Rat," *American Journal of Psychology,* 1942, 55, 467-517.

Cummings, L.L., Huber, G.P., and Arendt, E., "Effects of Size and Spatial
Arrangements on Group Decision Making," *Academy of Management
Journal,* 1974, 7, 460-475.

Cummings, L.L. and Schwab, D.P., *Performance in Organizations.* Glenview,
Ill.: Scott, Foresman and Company, 1973.

Cummings, L.L., Schwab, D.P., and Rosen, M., "Performance and Knowledge
of Results as Predeterminants of Work Motivation," *Journal of Applied
Psychology,* 1973, 58, 397-418.

Cummins, R.C., "Leader-Member Relations as a Moderator of the Effects of
Leader Behavior and Attitude," *Personnel Psychology,* 1972, 25, 655-660.

Dachler, H.P. and Mobley, W.H., "Construct Validation of Work Motivation:
Some Theoretical Boundary Conditions," *Journal of Applied Psychology
Monograph,* 1973, 58, 397-418.

Dailey, D.C., "1973 AMS Office Turnover Survey," *Management World,* 1974,
3, 3-6.

Dale, J.D., "Increase Productivity 50% in One Year with Sound Wage Incentives," *Management Methods,* 1959, 15, 38-42.

Dalton, G.W., "Motivation and Control in Organizations," in G.W. Dalton and
P.R. Lawrence (eds.), *Motivation and Control in Organizations.* Homewood, Ill.: Irwin and Dorsey, 1971, 1-35.

Dalton, G.W., and Lawrence, P.R., *Motivation and Control in Organizations.*
Homewood, Ill: Irwin and Dorsey, 1971.

Dalton, G.W., Lawrence, P.R., and Greiner, L.E., *Organizational Change and Development*. Homewood, Ill.: Irwin and Dorsey, 1970.

Darwin, C.R., *The Origin of Species*. London: J. Murray, 1906.

Dashiell, J.F., "A Quantitative Demonstration of Animal Drive," *Journal of Comparative Psychology*, 1925, 5, 205-208.

Davis, R.C., *The Fundamentals of Top Management*. New York: Harper & Row, 1951.

DeCharms, R., *Personal Causation: The Internal Affective Determinants of Behavior*. New York: Academic Press, 1968.

Deci, E.L., "The Effects of Contingent and Noncontingent Rewards and Controls on Intrinsic Motivation," *Organizational Behavior and Human Performance*, 1972, 8, 217-229.

Deci, E.L., "Effects of Externally Mediated Rewards on Intrinsic Motivation," *Journal of Personality and Social Psychology*, 1971, 18, 105-115.

Deci, E.L., *Intrinsic Motivation*. New York: Plenum Publishing, 1975.

Deci, E.L., "Intrinsic Motivation, Extrinsic Reinforcement, and Inequality," *Journal of Personality and Social Psychology*, 1977, 22, 113-120 (B).

Deci, E.L., "Notes on the Theory and Metatheory of Intrinsic Motivation," *Organizational Behavior and Human Performance*, 1975, 15, 130-145.

Delbecq, A.L., "The World Within the Span of Control," *Business Horizons*, 1968, 11, 45-56.

Delbecq, A.L., Van de Ven, A.H., and Gustafson, D.H., *Group Techniques for Program Planning*. Glenview, Ill.: Scott, Foresman, 1975.

Dermer, J., "The Interrelationship of Intrinsic and Extrinsic Motivation," *Academy of Management Journal*, 1975, 18, 125-129.

Dessler, G., *An Investigation of the Path Goal Theory of Leadership*. Unpublished Doctoral Dissertation, Bernard M. Baruch College, City University of New York, 1973.

Dinsmoor, J.A., "Punishment: I. The Avoidance Hypothesis," *Psychological Review*, 1954, 61, 34-46.

DiVesta, F. and Cox, L., "Some Dispositional Correlates of Conformity Behavior," *Journal of Social Psychology*, 1960, 52, 259-268.

Dollard, J. and Miller, N.E. *Personality and Psychotherapy*. New York: Mcgraw-Hill, 1950.

Donahoe, J.W., Schulte, V.G., Moulton, A.E., "Stimulus Control of Approach Behavior," *Journal of Experimental Psychology*, 1968, 78, 21-30.

Donahue, R.J., "Flexible Time Systems: Flex Time Systems in New York," *Public Personnel Management*, 1975, 4, 212-215.

Dowling, W.F., "Conversation with Peter F. Drucker," *Organizational Dynamics,* 1974, 2, 34-53.

Downey, H.K., Sheridan, J.E., and Slocum, J.W., "Analysis of Relationships Among Leader Behavior and Satisfaction: A Path-Goal Approach," *Academy of Management Journal,* 1975, 18, 253-262.

Downey, H.K., Sheridan, J.E., and Slocum, J.W., "The Path-Goal Theory of Leadership: A Longitudinal Analysis," *Organizational Behavior and Human Performance,* 1976, 16, 156-176.

Drucker, P.F., *Concept of the Corporation.* New York: Day, 1946.

Duffy, E., *Activation and Behavior.* New York: Wiley, 1962.

Duffy, F., *Office Landscaping: A New Approach to Office Planning.* Geneva, Switzerland: Anbar Publications, 1969.

Dufort, R.H. and Kimble, G.A., "Changes in Response Strength with Changes in the Amount of Reinforcement," *Journal of Experimental Psychology,* 1956, 51, 185-191.

Dufort, R.H. and Wright, J.H., "Food Intake as a Function of Duration of Food Deprivation," Journal of Psychology, 1962, 53, 465-468.

Dunnette, M.D., "Factor Structure of Unusually Satisfying and Unusually Dissatisfying Job Situations for Six Occupational Groups." Paper presented at Midwest Psychological Association, Chicago, April, 1965.

Dunnette, M.D., Campbell, J.P., and Hakel, M.D., "Factors Contributing to Job Satisfaction and Job Dissatisfaction in Six Occupational Groups," *Organizational Behavior and Human Performance,* 1967, 2, 143-174.

Dunstan, J.L., *Protestantism.* New York: Washington Square Press, 1961.

Durand, D.E., "Effects of Achievement Motivation and Skill Training on the Entrepreneurial Behavior of Black Businessmen," *Organizational Behavior and Human Performance,* 1975, 14, 76-90.

Dyer, L. and Parker, D.F., "Classifying Outcomes in Work Motivation Research: An Examinstion of Intrinsic-Extrinsic Dichotomy," *Journal of Applied Psychology,* 1975, 60, 455-458.

Edwards, W., "Behavioral Decision Theory," *Annual Review of Psychology,* 1961, 12, 473-498.

Edwards, W., "Probability-Preferences in Gambling," *American Journal of Psychology,* 1953, 66, 349-364.

Edwards, W., "The Theory of Decision Making," *Psychological Bulletin,* 1954, 51, 380-417.

Edwards, W., "Utility, Subjective Probability, Their Interaction, and Variance Preferences," *Journal of Conflict Resolution,* 1962, 6, 42-51.

Egan, D.M., "Executive Performance Appraisal," *Academy of Management Proceedings,* Atlanta, Georgia, 1971, 75-80.

Epley, S.W., "Prediction of the Behavioral Effects of Aversive Stimulation by the Presence of Companions," *Psychological Bulletin,* 1974, 81, 271-283.

Evan, W.M. and Simmons, R.G., "Organizational Effects of Inequitable Rewards: Two Experiments in Status Inconsistency," *Administrative Science Quarterly,* 1969, 14, 224-237.

Evans, M.G., "The Effects of Supervisory Behavior on the Path Goal Relationship," *Organizational Behavior and Human Performance,* 1970, 5, 277-298.

Fayol, H., *General and Industrial Administration.* London: Pitman, 1949. (Translated by C. Storrs from the original work published in French, 1916.)

Feather, N.T., "Level of Aspiration and Performance Variability," *Journal of Personality and Social Psychology,* 1967, 6, 37-46.

Feather, N.T., "Mower's Revised Two Factor Theory and the Motive-Expectancy-Value Model," *Psychological Review,* 1963, 7, 500-515.

Feeney, E.J., "At Emery Air Freight: Positive Reinforcement Boosts Performance," *Organizational Dynamics,* 1973, 1, 41-50.

Feeney, E.J., "Performance Audit, Feedback and Positive Reinforcement," *Training and Development Journal,* 1972, 26, 8-13.

Feldstein, M., "Unemployment Compensation: Its Effect on Unemployment," *Monthly Labor Review,* 1976, 39-41.

Ferguson, G., "Motivation and the Motivator," *Best's Insurance News, Life Edition,* 1965, 66, 24-27.

Ferster, C.B. and Skinner, B.F., *Schedules of Reinforcement.* New York: Appleton-Century-Crofts, 1968.

Fiedler, F.E., "Predicting the Effects of Leadership Training and Experience from the Contingency Model," *Journal of Applied Psychology,* 1972, 56, 114-119.

Fiske, D.W. and Maddi, S.R. (eds.), *Functions of Varied Experience.* Homewood, Ill.: Dorsey Press, 1961.

Flanagan, R.J., Strauss, G., Ulman, L., "Worker Discontent and Work Place Behavior," *Industrial Relations,* 1974, 13, 101-123.

Fleishman, E.A., "A Relationship Between Incentive Motivation and Ability in Psychomotor Performance," *Journal of Experimental Psychology,* 1958, 56, 78-81.

Fleishman, E.A. and Harris, E.F., "Patterns of Leadership Behavior Related to Employee Grievances and Turnover," *Personnel Psychology,* 1962, 15, 43-56.

Fleishman, E.A., Harris, E.F., and Burtt, H.E., *Leadership and Supervision in Industry*. Columbus, Ohio; Ohio State University, Bureau of Education Research 1955.

Fleishman, E.A. and Hunt, J.G., "Twenty Years of Consideration and Structure," in E.A. Fleishman and J.G. Hunt (eds.), *Current Developments in the Study of Leadership*. Carbondale, Ill.: Southern Illinois University Press, 1973.

Fleishman, E.A. and Peters, D.R., "Interpersonal Values, Leadership Attitudes, and Managerial Success," *Personnel Psychology*, 1962, 15, 127-143.

Fodor, E.M., "Group Stress, Authoritarian Style of Control, and Use of Power," *Journal of Applied Psychology*, 1976, 61, 313-318.

Follett, M.P., *Freedom and Coordination*. London: Management Publications Trust, 1949.

Follett, M.P., "The Psychology of Consent and Participation," in H.C. Metcalf and L. Urwick, *Dynamic Administration: The Collected Papers of Mary Parker Follett*. New York: Harper & Brothers, 1942, 210-229.

Ford, R.N., "Job Enrichment Lessons from AT&T," *Harvard Business Review*, 1973, 51, 96-106.

Fowler, H. and Troplod, M.A., "Escape Performance as a Function of Delay of Reinforcement," *Journal of Experimental Psychology*, 1962, 63, 464-467.

Freedman, N.L., Hafer, B.M., and Daniel, R.S., "EEG Arousal Decrement During Paired-Associate Learning," *Journal of Comparative Physiological Psychology*, 1966, 61, 15-19.

French, E.G., "Effects of Interaction of Achievement Motivation and Intelligence on Problem Solving Success," *American Psychology*, 1957, 12, 399-400 (abstract).

Freud, S., *Instincts and Their Vicissitudes*. (Translated by A.A. Brill.) New York: Basic Books, 1959. (Original publication in 1915.)

Freud, S., *Beyond the Pleasure Principle*. London: Hogarth, 1948.

Freidlander, F., "Motivations to Work and Organizational Performance," *Journal of Applied Psychology*, 1966, 5, 143-152.

Friedlander, F. and Margulies, N., "Multiple Impacts of Organizational Climate and Individual Value Systems Upon Job Satisfaction," *Personnel Psychology*, 1969, 22, 171-183.

Galbraith, J., *Designing Complex Organizations*. Reading, Mass.: Addison-Wesley, 1973.

Galbraith, J. and Cummings, L.L., "An Empirical Investigation of the Motivational Determinants of Past Performance: Interactive Effects Between Instrumentality, Valence, Motivation, and Ability," *Organizational Behavior and Human Performance*, 1967, 2, 237-257.

Gallerman, S.W., *Motivation and Productivity.* New York: American Management Association, 1963.

Geare, A.J., "Productivity from Scalon-type Plans," *Academy of Management Review,* 1976, 1(3), 99-108.

Georgopoulos, B.S., Mahoney, G.M., Jones, N.W., "A Path-Goal Approach to Productivity," *Journal of Applied Psychology,* 1957, 41, 345-353.

Ghiselli, E.E., "Managerial Talent," *American Psychologist,* 1963, 18, 631-641.

Gibb, J.R., "Effects of Group Size and Threat Reduction on Creativity in a Problem-Solving Situation," *American Psychologist,* 1951, 6, 324.

Gibbs, C.B. and Brown, I.D., "Increased Production from the Information Incentive in a Repetitive Task," Medical Research Council, Applied Psychological Research, Great Britain, 1955, No. 230.

Goddu, G.A., "Trends in Executive Compensation Plans," *Management Review,* 1976, 65, 49-53.

Golembiewski, R., "Flexi-time and Some of Its Consequences: Some Modest 'Structural' Intervention," *The New Technology in Organizational Development Conference.* New Orleans: NIL Institute, February 18-19, 1974.

Golembiewski, R., Yeager, S., and Hilles, R., "Factor Analysis of Some Flexitime Effects: Attitudinal and Behavioral Consequences of A Structural Intervention," *Academy of Management Journal,* 1975, 18, 500-509.

Gomperz, T., *Greek Thinkers.* (Translated by G.G. Berry.) London: John Murray, 1904.

Goodale, J.G. and Aagaad, A.K., "Factors Relating to Varying Reactions to the 4-day Workweek," *Journal of Applied Psychology,* 1975, 60, 33-38.

Goodman, P.S. and Friendman, A., "An Examination of Adams' Theory of Inequity," *Administrative Science Quarterly,* 1971, 16, 271-288.

Goodman, P.S. and Friedman, A., "An Examination of Quantity and Quality of Performance Under Conditions of Overpayment in Piece Rate," *Organizational Behavior and Human Performance,* 1969, 4, 265-374.

Goodman, R.A., "On the Operationality of the Maslow Need Hierarchy," *British Journal of Industrial Relations,* 1968, 6, 51-57.

Gordon, T.J. and Leblew, R.E., "Employee Benefits, 1970-1985," *Harvard Business Review,* 1970, 48, 93-107.

Graen, G.B., "Instrumentality Theory of Work Motivation: Some Experimental Results and Suggested Modifications," *Journal of Applied Psychology,* 1969, Monograph 53, 1-25.

Graen, G., Dansereau, F., and Minami, T., "Dysfunctional Leadership Styles," *Organizational Behavior and Human Performance,* 1972, 7, 216-236.

Graicunas, V.A., "Relationship in Organization," in L. Gulick and L. Urwick (eds.), *Papers on the Science of Administration*. New York: Institute of Public Administration, 1937, 181-187.

Green, T.B., "An Empirical Analysis of Nominal and Interacting Groups," *Academy of Management Journal*, 1975, 18, 63-73.

Greene, C.N.,"Causal Connection Among Managers' Merit Pay, Satisfaction, and Performance," *Journal of Applied Psychology*, 1973, 58, 95-100.

Greene, C.N., "The Satisfaction-Performance Controversy," *Business Horizons*, 1972, 15, 31-41.

Greiner, L.E., "Red Flags in Organization Development," *Business Horizons*, 1972, 15, 18-23.

Greller, M.M. and Herold, D.M., "Sources of Feedback: A Preliminary Investigation," *Organizational Behavior and Human Performance*, 1975, 13, 244-256.

Guest, R.H., "Job Enlargement: A Revolution in Job Design," *Personnel Administration*, 1957, 20, 9-16.

Guetzkow, H. and Simon, H.A., "The Impact of Certain Communication Nets Upon Organization and Performance in Task-Oriented Groups," *Management Science*, 1955, 1, 233-250.

Gulick, L., "Notes on the Theory of Organization," in L. Gulick and L. Urwick *Papers on the Science of Administration*. New York: Institute of Public Administration, 1937.

Gurin, G., Veroff, J., and Feld, S., *Americans View Their Mental Health*. New York: Basic Books, 1960.

Guttman, N., "Equal-Reinforcement Valves for Sucrose and Glucose Solutions with Equal-Sweetness Valves," *Journal of Comparative and Physiological Psychology*, 1954, 47, 358-361.

Guttman, N., "Operant Conditioning, Extinction, and Periodic Reinforcement in Relation to Concentration of Sucrose Used as Reinforcing Agent," *Journal of Experimental Psychology*, 1953, 46, 213-224.

Hackman, J.R., "Is Job Enrichment Just a Fad?" *Harvard Business Review*, 1975, 53, 129-138.

Hackman, J.R. and Lawler, E.E., "Employee Reactions to Job Characteristics," *Journal of Applied Psychology*, 1971, 55, 259-286.

Hackman, J.R. and Oldham, G.R., "Development of the Job Diagnostic Survey," *Journal of Applied Psychology*, 1975, 60, 159-170.

Hackman, J.R., Oldham, G.R., Janson, R., and Purdy, K., "A New Strategy for Job Enrichment," *California Management Review*, 1975, 17, 57-71.

Hackman, J.R. and Porter, L.W., "Expectancy Theory Predictions of Work Effectiveness," *Organizational Behavior and Human Performance,* 1968, 3, 417-426.

Hackman, R. and Vidmar, N., "Effects of Size and Task Type on Group Performance and Member Reactions," *Sociometry,* 1970, 33, 37-54.

Haire, M., "The Incentive Characteristic of Pay," in I.R. Andrews (ed.), *Managerial Compensation.* Ann Arbor, Mich.: Foundation for Research on Human Behavior, 1965, 13-17.

Hall, D.T. and Nougaim, K.E., "An Examination of Maslow's Need Hierarchy in an Organizational Setting," *Organizational Behavior and Human Performance.* 1968, 3, 12-35.

Halpern, G., "Relative Contributions of Motivator and Hygiene Factors to Overall Job Satisfaction," *Journal of Applied Psychology,* 1966, 50, 143-152.

Halpin, A.W. and Crofts, D.B., *The Organizational Climate of Schools.* Chicago: University of Chicago, Midwest Administration Center, 1963.

Halpin, A.W. and Winer, B.J., "A Factorial Study of the Leader Behavior Descriptions," in R.M. Stogdill and A.E. Coons (eds.), *Leader Behavior: Its Description and Measurement.* Columbus, Ohio: Ohio State University, Bureau of Business Research, 1957, 39-51.

Hamner, T.H., and Dachler, H.P., "A Test of Some Assumptions Underlying the Path Goal Model of Supervision: Some Suggested Conceptual Modifications," *Organizational Behavior and Human Performance,* 1975, 14, 60-75.

Hamner, W.C. and Foster, L.W., "Are Intrinsic and Extrinsic Rewards Additive: A Test of Deci's Cognitive Evaluation Theory of Task Motivation," *Organizational Behavior and Human Performance,* 1975, 14, 398-415.

Hampton, D.R., Summer, C.E., and Webber, R.A., *Organizational Behavior and the Practice of Management.* Glenview, Ill.: Scott, Foresman, 1973, 1-24.

Hardesty, D., Trumbo, D., and Bevan, W., "The Influence of Knowledge of Results on Performance in a Monitoring Task," *Perceptual and Motor Skills,* 1963, 16, 629-634.

Hare, A.P., *Handbook of Small Group Research.* Glencoe, Ill.: Free Press, 1962.

Hare, A.P., "A Study of Interaction and Consensus in Different Sized Groups," *American Sociological Review,* 1952, 17, 261-267.

Harlow, H.F., "The Nature of Love," *American Psychologist,* 1958, 13, 673-685.

Harlow, H.F. and Suomi, S.J., "Nature of Love—Simplified," *American Psychologist,* 1970, 25, 161-168.

Harrison, Roger, "Sources of Variation in Manager's Job Attitudes," *Personnel Psychology*, 1960, 13, 425-434.

Hartley, J., "Experience with Flexible Hours of Work," *Monthly Labor Review*, 1976, 99(5), 41-42.

Heckhausen, H., *The Anatomy of Achievement Motivation.* New York: Academic, 1967.

Hedges, J.N., "Absence from Work—a Look at Some National Data," *Monthly Labor Review*, 1973, 96, 24-30.

Hellriegel, D., and Slocum, J.W., "Organizational Climate: Research and Contingencies," *Academy of Management Journal*, 1974, 17, 255-280.

Hellriegel, D., and Slocum, J.W., *Organizational Behavior Contingency Views.* St. Paul, Minn.: West Publishing, 1976.

Hemphill, J.K., *Situational Factors in Leadership.* Columbus, Ohio: Ohio State University, Bureau of Educational Research, 1949.

Heneman, H.G., "An Empirical Investigation of Expectancy Theory Predictions of Employee Performance," *Psychological Bulletin*, 1972, 78, 1-9.

Herzberg, F., "The Motivation-Hygiene Concept and Problems of Manpower," *Personnel Administration*, 1964, 27, 3-7.

Herzberg, F., "One More Time: How Do You Motivate Employees?" *Harvard Business Review*, 1968, 46, 53-62.

Herzberg, F., *Work and the Nature of Man.* New York: The Mentor Executive Library, 1966.

Herzberg, F., Mausner, B., Peterson, R., and Capwell, D., *Job Attitudes: Review of Research and Opinion.* Pittsburgh: Psychological Service, 1957.

Herzberg, F., Mausner, B., and Snyderman, B., *The Motivation to Work.* New York: John Wiley, 1959.

Hicks, H. G., *The Management of Organization.* New York: McGraw-Hill, 1967.

Hinrichs, J.R. and Mischkind, L.A., "Empirical and Theoretical Limitations of Two-Factor Hypothesis of Job Satisfaction," *Journal of Applied Psychology*, 1967, 51, 191-200.

Hofstede, G.H., *The Game of Budget Control.* London: Tavistock, 1968.

Holder, J.J., "Decision Making by Consensus," *Business Horizons*, 1972, 15, 47-54.

Homans, G.C., *Social Behavior: Its Elementary Forms.* New York: Harcourt, Brace, and World, 1961.

Homzie, M.J. and Ross, L.E., "Runway Performance Following a Reduction in the Concentration of a Liquid Reward," *Journal of Comparative and Physiological Psychology*, 1962, 55, 1029-1033.

House, R.J., "A Path Goal Theory of Leader Effectiveness," *Administrative Science Quarterly,* 1971, 6, 3, 321-338.

House, R.J. and Dessler, G., "The Path Goal Theory of Leadership: Some Post Hoc and a Priori Tests," in J.G. Hunt and L.L. Larson (eds.), *Contingency Approaches to Leadership.* Carbondale, Ill.: Southern Illinois University Press, 1974.

House, R.J. and Mitchell, T.R., "Path-Goal Theory of Leadership," *Journal of Contemporary Business,* 1974, 3, 81-97.

House, R.J. and Rizzo, J.R., "Role Conflict and Ambiguity as Critical Variables in a Model of Organizational Behavior," *Organizational Behavior and Human Performance,* 1972, 7, 467-505.

House, R.J., Shapiro, H.J., and Wahba, M.A., "Expectancy Theory as a Predictor of Work Behavior and Attitude: A Re-evaluation of Empirical Evidence," *Decision Sciences,* 1974, 5, 481-506.

House, R.J. and Wahba, M.A., "Expectancy Theory in Managerial Motivation: Review of Relevant Research," in H.L. Tosi, R.L. House, and M.D. Dunnette (eds.), *Managerial Motivation and Compensation.* East Lansing, Mich.: Graduate School of Business Administration, Michigan State University, 1972.

Howell, R.A., "A Fresh Look at Management by Objectives," *Business Horizons,* 1967, 10, 51-58.

Huberman, J., "Discipline Without Punishment," *Harvard Business Review,* 1964, 42, 62-68.

Hughes, C.L., "Why Goal Oriented Performance Reviews Succeed and Fail," *Personnel Journal,* 1966, 45, 335-341.

Hules, S.H. and Firestone, R.J., "Mean Amount of Reinforcement and Instrumental Response Strength," *Journal of Experimental Psychology,* 1964, 67, 417-422.

Hulin, C.L., "Effects of Changes in Job Satisfaction Levels on Employee Turnover," *Journal of Applied Psychology,* 1968, 52, 122-126.

Hulin, C.L., "Individual Differences and Job Enrichment—The Case Against General Treatments," in R.M. Steers and L.W. Porter (eds.), *Motivation and Work Behavior.* New York: McGraw-Hill, 1975, 425-436.

Hulin, C.L. and Blood, M.R., "Job Enlargement, Individual Differences, and Worker Responses," *Psychological Bulletin,* 1968, 69, 41-55.

Hull, C.L., *A Behavior System.* New Haven: Yale University Press, 1952.

Hull, C.L., *Principles of Behavior.* New York: Appleton Century, 1943.

Hulme, R.D. and Bevan, R.V., "The Blue-collar Worker Goes on Salary," *Harvard Business Review,* 1975, 53, 104-112.

Hunt, J.G. and Hill, J.W., "The New Look in Motivational Theory for Organizational Research," *Human Organization,* 1969, 28, 100-109.

Hunt, J.M., "Intrinsic Motivation and Its Role in Psychological Development," in D. Levine (ed.), *Nebraska Symposium on Motivation.* Lincoln, Neb.: University of Nebraska Press, 1965, 189-282.

Indik, B.P., Seashore, S.E., and Georgopoulos, B.S., "Relations Among Criteria of Job Performance," *Journal of Applied Psychology,* 1960, 44, 195-202.

Irwin, F.W., "Stated Expectations as Functions of Probability and Desirability of Outcomes," *Journal of Personality,* 1953, 21, 329-335.

Ivancevich, J.M., "Changes in Performance in a Management by Objectives Program," *Administrative Science Quarterly,* 1974, 19, 563-574.

Ivancevich, J.M., Donnelly, J.H., Lyon, H.L., "A Study of the Impact of Management by Objectives on Perceived Need Satisfaction," *Personnel Psychology,* 1970, 23, 139-151.

Jablonsky, S.F. and DeVries, D.L., "Operant Conditioning Principles Extrapolated to the Theory of Management," *Organizational Behavior and Human Performance,* 1972, 7, 340-358.

Jacques, E., *Equitable Payment,* New York: John Wiley, 1961.

Jacques, E., Rice, A.K., and Hill, J.M., "The Social and Psychological Impact of a Change in Method of Wage Payment," *Human Relations,* 1951, 4, 315-340.

James, L.R. and Jones, A.P., "Organizational Climate: A Review of Theory and Research," *Psychological Bulletin,* 1974, 81, 1046-1112.

James, L.R. and Jones, A.P., "Organizational Structure: A Review of Structural Dimensions and Their Conceptual Relationships with Individual Attitudes and Behavior," *Organizational Behavior and Human Performance,* 1976, 16, 74-113.

Jehring, J.J., "A Contrast Between Two Approaches to Total Systems Incentives," *California Management Review,* 1967, 10, 7-14.

Jenkins, M., "The Effect of Segregation and the Sex Behavior of the White Rat as Measured by the Obstruction Method," *Genetic Psychology Monograph,* 1928, 3, 455-571.

Johnson, E.M. and Payne, M.C., "Vigilance; Effects of Frequency of Knowledge of Results," *Journal of Applied Psychology,* 1966, 50, 33-34.

Johnson, T.W. and Stinson, J.E., "Role Ambiguity, Role Conflict, and Satisfaction," *Journal of Applied Psychology,* 1975, 60, 329-333.

Jorgenson, D.D., Dunnette, Marvin, and Pritchard, R.D., "Effects of the Manipulation of a Performance-Reward Contingency on Behavior in a Simulated Work Setting," *Journal of Applied Psychology,* 1973, 57, 271-280.

Kahn, R. L., "The Prediction of Productivity," *Journal of Social Issues*, 1956, 12, 41-49.

Kahn, R. L., "Productivity and Satisfaction," *Personnel Psychology*, 1960, 13, 275-286.

Kahn, R. L., "The Work Module—A Tonic for Lunchpail Lassitude," *Psychology Today*, 1973, 6, 35-39 and 94-95.

Karczower, M., Freygold, K., and Blum, N., "Effect of Amount, Percentage of Reinforcement and Deprivation Condition on Runway Time," *Psychological Reports*, 1962, 11, 406.

Kast, F.E. and Rosenzweig, J.E., *Organization and Management: A Systems Approach*. New York: McGraw-Hill, 1970.

Katz, D., "The Motivational Basis of Organizational Behavior," *Behavioral Science*, 1964, 9, 131-146.

Katz, D. and Kahn, R. L., "Leadership Practices in Relation to Productivity," in D. Cartwright and A. Zander (eds.), *Group Dynamics*. Evanston, Ill.: Row Peterson, 1960, 554-570.

Katz, D and Kahn, R. L., *The Social Psychology of Organizations*. New York: Wiley, 1966.

Katz, D., Maccoby, N., Gurin, G., and Floor, L., *Productivity, Supervision, and Morale Among Railroad Workers*. Ann Arbor, Mich.: University of Michigan, Institute for Social Research, 1951.

Katz, D., Maccoby, N. M., and Morse, N., *Productivity, Supervision, and Morale in an Office Situation*. Ann Arbor, Mich.: University of Michigan, Institute for Social Research, 1950.

Katzell, R. A., "Contrasting Systems of Work Organization," *American Psychologist*, 1962, 17, 102-108.

Kazdin, A. E., *Behavior Modification in Applied Settings*. Homewood, Ill.: The Dorsey Press, 1975.

Kazdin, A. E. and Klock, J., "The Effect of Nonverbal Teacher Approval on Student Attentive Behavior," *Journal of Applied Behavior Analysis*, 1973, 6, 643-654.

Kerr, S., "On the Folly of Rewarding A, While Hoping for B," *Academy of Management Journal*, 1975, 18, 769-783.

Kerr, S., "Overcoming the Dysfunctions of MBO," *Management by Objectives*, 1976, 5, 13-19.

Kerr, S., Schriesheim, C., Murphy, C. J., and Stogdill, R. M., "Toward a Contingency Theory of Leadership Based upon the Consideration and Initiating Structure Literature," *Organizational Behavior and Human Performance*, 1974, 12, 62-82.

Keys, A., Brozek, J., Henschel, A., Mickelsen, O., and Taylor, H., *The Biology of Human Starvation.* Minneapolis: University of Minnesota Press, 1950.

Kim, J. S. and Hamner, W. C., "Effect of Performance Feedback and Goal Setting on Productivity and Satisfaction in an Organizational Setting," *Journal of Applied Psychology,* 1976, 61, 48-57.

King, J.W., "Speed of Running as a Function of Goal-box Behavior," *Journal of Comparative and Physiological Psychology,* 1956, 49, 474-476.

Kleber, T.P., "The Six Hardest Areas to Management by Objectives," *Personnel Journal,* 1972, 51, 571-575.

Klein, S.M., "Pay Factors as Predictors to Satisfaction: A Comparison of Reinforcement, Equity, and Expectancy," *Academy of Management Journal,* 1973, 16, 598-610.

Klinger, E., "Consequences of Commitment to and Disengagement from Incentives," *Psychological Review, 1975, 82, 1-21.*

Knott, P. D., "Effects of Frustration and Magnitude of Reward in Selective Attention, Size Estimation, and Verbal Evaluation," *Journal of Personality,* 1971, 39, 378-390.

Knowles, M. S., "The Manager as Educator," *Journal of Continuing Education and Training,* 1972, 2, 97-105.

Kolasa, B. J., *Introduction to Behavioral Science for Business.* New York: Wiley, 1969.

Kolb, D. A., Rubin, I. M., and McIntrye, J. M., *Organizational Psychology.* Englewood Cliffs, N. J.: Prentice-Hall, 1971.

Kopelman, R. E. and Thompson, P. H., "Boundary Conditions for Expectancy Theory Predictions of Work Motivation and Job Performance," *Academy of Management Journal,* 1976, 19, 237-258.

Korman, A. K., "Consideration, Initiating Structure and Organizational Criteria: A Review," *Personnel Psychology,* 1966, 19, 349-362.

Kornhauser, A. W., *Mental Health of the Industrial Worker: A Detroit Study.* New York: Wiley, 1962.

Kosmo, R. and Behling, O., "Single Continuum Job Satisfaction Vs. Duality: An Empirical Test," *Personnel Psychology,* 1969, 22, 327-334.

Koteskey, R. L., "A Stimulus-Sampling Model of Partial Reinforcement Effect," *Psychological Review,* 1972, 79, 161-171.

Kraut, A. I., "Predicting Turnover of Employees from Measured Job Attitudes," Organizational Behavior and Human Performance, 1975, 13, 233-243.

302

Kruglanski, A. W., "The Endogenous-Exogenous Partition in Attribution in Theory," *Psychological Review,* 1975, 82, 387-406.

Labovitz, G. H., "In Defense of Subjective Executive Appraisal," *Academy of Management Journal,* 1969, 12, 293-307.

LaFollette, W. R. and Sims, H. P., "Is Satisfaction Redundant with Organizational Climate?" *Organizational Behavior and Human Performance,* 1975, 13, 257-278.

Lahiri, D. K. and Srivastva, S., "Determinants of Satisfaction in Middle-Management Personnel," *Journal of Applied Psychology,* 1967, 51, 254-265.

Lamberth, J., Goueux, C., and Davis, J., "Agreeing Attitudinal Statements as Positive Reinforcers in Instrumental Conditioning," *Psychonomic Science,* 1972, 29, 247-249.

Langdale, J. A., "Toward a Contingency Theory for Designing Work Organizations," *Journal of Applied Behavioral Science,* 1976, 12, 199-214.

Latham, G. P. and Baldes, J. J., "The 'Practical Significance' of Locke's Theory of Goal Setting," *Journal of Applied Psychology,* 1975, 60, 122-124.

Latham, G. P. and Kinne, S. B., "Improving Job Performance Through Training in Goal Setting," *Journal of Applied Psychology,* 1974, 59, 187-191.

Latham, G. P. and Yukl, G. A., "Assigned Versus Participative Goal Setting with Educated and Uneducated Wood Workers," *Journal of Applied Psychology,* 1975, 60, 299-302.

Latham, G. P. and Yukl, G. A., "Effects of Assigned and Participative Goal Setting on Performance and Job Satisfaction," *Journal of Applied Psychology,* 1976, 61, 166-171.

Lawler, E. E., "Ability as a Moderator of the Relationship Between Job Attitudes and Job Performance," *Personnel Psychology,* 1966, 19, 153-164.

Lawler, E. E., "A Correlational-casual Analysis of the Relationship Between Expectancy Attitudes and Job Performance," *Journal of Applied Psychology,* 1968, 52, 462-468 (a).

Lawler, E. E., "Equity Theory as a Predictor of Productivity and Work Quality," *Psychological Bulletin,* 1968, 70, 596-610 (b).

Lawler, E. E., "Job Design and Employee Motivation," *Personnel Psychology,* 1969, 22, 426-435.

Lawler, E. E., *Motivation in Work Organizations.* Monterey, Calif.: Brooks/Cole, 1973.

Lawler, E. E., *Pay and Organizational Effectiveness: A Psychological View.* New York: McGraw-Hill, 1971.

Lawler, E.E. and Cammann, C., "What Makes a Work Group Successful?" in A. Morrow (ed.), *The Failure of Success.* New York: Amacom, 1972.

Lawler, E. E., Hall, D. T., and Oldham, G. R., "Organizational Climate: Relationships to Structure, Process, and Performance," *Organizational Behavior and Human Performance*, 1974, 11, 132-155.

Lawler, E. E., and O'Gara, P. W., "Effects of Inequity Produced by Underpayment on Work Output, Work Quality, and Attitudes Toward Work," *Journal of Applied Psychology*, 1967, 51, 403-410.

Lawler, E. E. and Porter, L. W., "Antecedent Attitudes of Effective Managerial Performance," *Organizational Behavior and Human Performance*, 1967, 2, 122-142.

Lawler, E. E. and Porter, L. W., "The Effect of Performance on Job Satisfaction," *Industrial Relations*, 1967, 7, 20-28.

Lawler, E.E. and Suttle, J.L., "A Causal Correlational Test of the Need Hierarchy Concept," *Organizational Behavior and Human Performance*, 1972, 7, 265-287.

Lawrence, P.R. and Lorsch, J., *Organization and Environment: Managing Differentiation and Integration*. Boston: Graduate School of Business Administration, 1967.

Leavitt, H.J., *Managerial Psychology* (2nd ed.). Chicago: The University of Chicago Press, 1964.

Lerner, M.J., "Evaluation of Performance as a Function of Performer's Reward and Attractiveness," *Journal of Personality and Social Psychology*, 1965, 1, 355-360.

Lesieur, F.G. and Puckett, E.S., "The Scanlon Plan Has Proven Itself," *Harvard Business Review*, 1969, 47, 109-118.

Levine, E., "Problems of Organizational Control in Microcosm: Group Performance and Group Member Satisfaction as a Function of Differences in Control Structure," *Journal of Applied Psychology*, 1973, 53, 186-196.

Levinson, H., "Management by Whose Objectives," *Harvard Business Review*, 1970, 48, 125-134.

Levitan, S.A. and Johnston, W.B., "Job Redesign, Reform, Enrichment—Exploring the Limitations, *Monthly Labor Review*, 1973, July, 35-42.

Lewin, K., *The Conceptual Representation and the Measurement of Psychological Forces*. Durham, N.C.: Duke University Press, 1938.

Lewin, K., *A Dynamic Theory of Personality*. New York: McGraw-Hill, 1935.

Lewin, K., *Field Theory and Social Science*. New York: Harper, 1951.

Lewin, K., "Frontiers in Group Dynamics," *Human Relations*, 1947, 1, 5-41.

Lewin, K., *Principles of Topological Psychology*. New York: McGraw-Hill, 1936.

Lewin, K., Dembo, T., Festinger, L., and Sears, P.S., "Levels of Aspiration," in J.M. Hunt (ed.), *Personality and the Behavior Disorders.* New York: Ronald, 1944, 333-378.

Lewin, K., Lipitt, R., and White, R.K., "Patterns of Aggressive Behavior in Experimentally Created 'Social Climate,' " *Journal of Social Psychology,* 1939, 10, 271-299.

Lewis, D.J., "Partial Reinforcement: A Selective Review of the Literature Since 1950," *Psychological Bulletin,* 1960, 57, 1-28.

Lichtman, C.M. and Hunt, R.G., "Personality and Organization Theory: A Review of Some Conceptual Literature," *Psychological Bulletin,* 1971, 76, 271-294.

Likert, R., "Motivation: The Case of Management," in H. Koontz and C. O'Donnel, (eds.), *Management: A Book of Readings.* New York: McGraw-Hill, 1964, 335-365.

Likert, R., *New Patterns of Management.* New York: McGraw-Hill, 1961 and 1967.

Litwin, G.H. and Stringer, R.A., *Motivation and Organizational Climate.* Boston: Division of Research, Graduate School of Business Administration, Harvard University, 1968.

Locke, E.A., "Job Satisfaction and Job Performance: A Theoretical Analysis," *Organizational Behavior and Human Performance,* 1970, 5, 484-500.

Locke, E.A., "The Motivational Effects of Knowledge of Results: Knowledge of Goal Setting," *Journal of Applied Psychology,* 1967, 51, 324-329.

Locke, E.A., "Toward a Theory of Task Motivation and Incentives," *Organizational Behavior and Human Performance,* 1968, 3, 157-189.

Locke, E.A. and Bryan, J.F., "The Effects of Goal Setting, Rule-learning and Knowledge of Score on Performance," *American Journal of Psychology,* 1966, 79, 451-457.

Locke, E.A. and Bryan, J.F., "Knowledge of Score and Goal Level as Determinants of Work Rate," *Journal of Applied Psychology,* 1969, 53, 59-65.

Locke, E.A., Cartledge, N., and Kneer, C., "Studies of the Relationship Between Satisfaction, Goal-Setting, and Performance," *Organizational Behavior and Human Performance,* 1970, 5, 135-158.

Locke, E.A. Cartledge, N., and Koeppel, J., "Motivational Effects of Knowledge of Results: A Goal-Setting Phenomenon?" *Psychological Bulletin,* 1968, 70, 474-485.

Logan, F.A., *Incentive.* New Haven: Yale University Press, 1960.

Logan, F.A., "The Role of Reinforcement in Determining Reaction Potential," *Journal of Experimental Psychology,* 1952, 43, 393-399.

Logan, F.A. and Wagner, A.R., *Reward and Punishment*. Boston: Allyn and Bacon, 1966.

Lorsch, J.W., "Introduction to Structural Design of Organizations," in G.W. Dalton, P.R. Lawrence, J.W. Lorsch (eds.), *Organizational Structure and Design*. Homewood, Illinois: Irwin, 1970, 1-16.

Lowin, A., "Participative Decision Making: A Model, Literature Critique, and Prescriptions for Research," *Organizational Behavior and Human Performance*, 1968, 3, 68-106.

Luthans, F., *Organizational Behavior*. New York: McGraw-Hill, 1973.

Luthans, F. and Kreitner, R., *Organizational Behavior Modification*. Glenview, Illinois: Scott, Foresman, 1975.

Luthans, F. and Reif, W.E., "Job Enrichment: Long on Theory, Short on Practice," *Organizational Dynamics*, 1974, 2, 30-43.

Lyons, T.F., "Turnover and Absenteeism: A Review of Relationships and Shared Correlations," *Personnel Psychology*, 1972, 25, 271-281.

McClelland, D.C., *The Achieving Society*. Princeton, N.J.: Von Nostrand Reinhold, 1961.

McClelland, D.C., "Business Drive and National Achievement," *Harvard Business Review*, 1962, 40, 99-112.

McClelland, D.C., "Comments on Professor Maslow's Paper," in M.R. Jones (ed.), *Nebraska Symposium on Motivation*. Lincoln, Nebraska: University of Nebraska Press, 1955.

McClelland, D.C., "Money as a Motivator: Some Research Insights," in Steers, R.M., and Porter, L.W. (eds.), *Motivation and Work Behavior*. New York: McGraw-Hill, 1975, 523-534.

McClelland, D.C., "Risk-taking in Children with High and Low Need for Achievement," in J.W. Atkinson, (ed.), *Motives in Fantasy, Action, and Society*. Princeton, N.J.: Van Nostrand, 1958, 288-305.

McClelland, D.C., "That Urge to Achieve," *Think Magazine*, 1966, 32, 19-23.

McClelland, D.C., "Toward a Theory of Motive Acquisition," *American Psychologist*, 1965, 20, 321-333.

McClelland, D.C., "The Two Faces of Power," *Journal of International Affairs*, 1970, 24, 29-47.

McClelland, D.C. and Atkinson, J.W., "The Projective Expression of Needs: I. The Effect of Different Intensitites of the Hunger Drive on Perception," *Journal of Psychology*, 1948, 25, 205-222.

McConkey, D.D., "Writing Measurable Objectives for Staff Manager," *Advanced Management Journal*, 1972, 37, 10-16.

McDougall, W., *An Introduction to Social Psychology.* London: Methuen and Company, 1908.

McGregor, D., *The Human Side of Enterprise.* New York: McGraw-Hill, 1960.

McGregor, D., *The Professional Manager.* New York: McGraw-Hill, 1967.

McGregor, D., "An Uneasy Look at Performance Appraisal," *Harvard Business Review,* 1957, 35, 89-94.

Mackworth, J.F., "The Effect of True and False Knowledge of Results on the Detectability of Signals in a Vigilance Task," *Canadian Journal of Psychology,* 1964, 18, 106-117,(a).

Mackworth, J.F., "Performance Decrement in Vigilance, Threshold, and High-speed Perceptual Motor Tasks," *Canadian Journal of Psychology,* 1964, 18, 209-223 (b).

Madsen, C.H., Becker, W.C., and Thomas, D.R., "Rules, Praise and Ignoring: Elements of Elementary Classroom Control," *Journal of Applied Behavior Analysis,* 1968, 1, 139-150.

Mahone, C.H., "Fear of Failure and Unrealistic Vocational Aspiration," *Journal of Abnormal Social Psychology,* 1960, 60, 253-261.

Mahoney, T., "Compensation References of Managers," *Industrial Relations,* 1964, 3, 135-144.

Maier, N.R.F., *Problem-solving Discussions and Conferences: Leadership Methods and Skills.* New York: McGraw-Hill, 1963.

Maier, N.R.F., *Psychology in Industry.* Boston: Houghton-Mifflin, 1955.

Maier, N.R.F. and Hoffman, L.R., "Financial Incentives and Group Decision in Motivating Change," *Journal of Social Psychology,* 1964, 64, 396-378.

Maier, N.R.F. and Hoffman, L.R., "Using Trained 'Developmental' Discussion Leaders to Improve Further the Quality of Group Decisions," *Journal of Applied Psychology,* 1960, 44, 247-251.

Mann, R.D., "A Review of the Relationship Between Personality and Performance in Small Groups," *Psychological Bulletin,* 1959, 56, 241-270.

Manners, G.E., "Another Look at Group Size, Group Problem Solving, and Member Consensus," *Academy of Management Journal,* 1975, 18, 715-724.

March, J.G. and Simon, H.A., *Organizations.* New York: Wiley, 1958.

Marriott, R., *Incentive Wage Systems.* London: Staple Press, 1968.

Marriott, R., "Size of Working Group and Output," *Occupational Psychology,* 1949, 23, 47-57.

Marx, M.H., "Interaction of Drive and Reward as a Determiner of Resistance to Extinction," *Journal of Comparative and Physiological Psychology,* 1967, 64, 488-489.

Maslow, A.H., *Motivational and Personality.* New York: Harper, 1954, 1970.

Masters, J.L., "Effects of Social Comparison Upon Subsequent Self-Reinforcement Behavior in Children," *Journal of Personality and Social Psychology,* 1968, 10, 391-401.

Mawhinney, T.C. and Behling, O., "Differences in Predictions of Work Behavior from Expectancy and Operant Models of Individual Motivation," in T.B. Green and D.F. Ray (eds.), *Academy of Management Proceedings,* 1973, 29, 383-389.

Mayo, E., *The Human Problems of an Industrial Civilization.* New York: Macmillan, 1933.

Mayo, E., *The Social Problems of an Industrial Civilization.* Boston: Division of Research, Harvard Business School, 1945.

Megginson, L.C., *Personnel: A Behavioral Approach to Administration.* Homewood, Ill.: Richard D. Irwin, 1967.

Megginson, L.C. and Chung, K.H., "Human Ecology in the Twenty-first Century," *Personnel Administration,* 1970, 33, 46-56.

Melcher, R.D., "Roles and Relationships: Clarifying the Manager's Job," *Personnel,* 1967, 44, 33-41.

Merton, R.H., "Bureaucratic Structure and Personality," in A. Etzioni (ed.), *Complex Organizations.* New York: Holt, Rinehart and Winston, 1961.

Metzer, R., Cotton, J.W., and Lewis, D.J., "Effects of Reinforcement Magnitude and of Order of Presentation of Different Magnitudes of Runway Behavior," *Journal of Comparative and Physiological Psychology,* 1957, 50, 184-188.

Metzger, B.L., *Profit Sharing in Perspective.* Evanston, Ill.: Profit Sharing Research Foundation, 1964.

Meyer, H.H., Kay, E., and French, J.R.P., "Split Roles in Performance Appraisal," *Harvard Business Review,* 1965, 43, 123-129.

Middlemist, R.D. and Peterson, R.B., "Test of Equity Theory by Controlling for Comparison Co-workers' Effort," *Organizational Behavior and Human Performance,* 1976, 15, 335-354.

Migliore, R.H. "A History of Management by Objectives," in R. Albanese (ed.), *Southwest Division Academy of Management 1976 Proceedings,* Eighth Annual Meeting, San Antonio, Texas, March, 1976, 131-135.

Miles, R.E., "Human Relations or Human Resources?" *Harvard Business Review,* 1965, 43, 148-163.

308

Miles, R.E., *Theories of Management*. New York: McGraw-Hill, 1975.

Miles, R.H., "A Comparison of the Relative Impacts of Role Perceptions of Ambiquity and Conflict by Role," *Academy of Management Journal,* 1976, 19, 25-35.

Milgrams, S., "Group Pressure and Action Against a Person," *Journal of Abnormal and Social Psychology,* 1964, 69, 137-143.

Mill, J.S., *Principles of Political Economy*. New York: Appleton, 1965.

Miller, D.W. and Starr, M.K., *The Structure of Human Decisions*. Englewood Cliffs, N.J.: Prentice-Hall, 1967.

Miller, L., *The Use of Knowledge of Results in Improving the Performance of Hourly Operators*, General Electric Company, Behavioral Research Service, 1965.

Misumi, J. and Shirakash, S., "An Experimental Study of the Effects of Supervisory Behavior on Productivity and Morale in a Hierarchical Organization," *Human Relations,* 1966, 19, 297-307.

Mitchell, T.R., "Expectancy Models of Job Satisfaction, Occupational Preference and Effort: A Theoretical, Methodological and Empirical Appraisal," *Psychological Bulletin,* 1974, 81, 1053-1077.

Mitchell, T.R., "Motivation and Participation: An Integration," *Academy of Management Journal,* 1973, 16, 670-679.

Mitchell, T.R. and Albright, D.W., "Expectancy Theory Predictions of the Satisfaction, Effort, Performance and Retention of Naval Aviation Officers," *Organizational Behavior and Human Performance,* 1972, 8, 1-20.

Mitchell, T.R. and Biglan, A., "Instrumentality Theories: Current Uses in Psychology," *Psychological Bulletin,* 1971, 76, 432-454.

Moberg, D.J. and Koch, J.L., "A Critical Appraisal of Integrated Treatments of Contingency Findings," *Academy of Management Journal,* 1975, 18, 109-124.

Montague, W.E. and Webber, C.E., "Effects of Knowledge of Results and Differential Monetary Reward on Six Uninterrupted Hours of Monitoring." *Human Factors,* 1965, 7, 173-180.

Moreno, J.L., "Contributions of Sociometry to Research Methodology in Sociology," *American Sociological Review,* 1947, 12, 287-292.

Morris, J.L., "Propensity for Risk Taking as Determinant of Vocational Choice: An Extension of the Theory of Achievement Motivation," *Journal of Personality and Social Psychology,* 1967, 3, 328-335.

Morrisey, G.L., *Management by Objectives and Results*. Reading, Mass.: Addison-Wesley, 1970.

Morse, J.J. and Lorsch, J.W., "Beyond Theory Y," *Harvard Business Review,* 1970, 48, 61-68.

Moulton, R.W., "Effects of Success and Failure of Level of Aspiration as Related to Achievement Motives," *Journal of Personality and Social Psychology,* 1965, 1, 399-406.

Murray, H.A., *Explorations in Personality.* New York: Oxford University Press, 1938.

Myers, M.S., *Every Employee a Manager.* New York: McGraw-Hill, 1970.

Myers, M.S., "Who Are Your Motivated Workers?" *Harvard Business Review,* 1964, 42, 73-88.

Nash, A.N. and Carroll, S.J., *The Management of Compensation.* Monterey, Calif.: Brooks/Cole, 1975.

Nealey, S.M., "Pay and Benefit Preference," *Industrial Relations,* 1964, 3, 17-28.

Nealey, S.M. and Goodale, J.G., "Worker Preferences Among Time-off Benefits and Pay," *Journal of Applied Psychology,* 1967, 51, 357-361.

Nord, W.R., "Beyond the Teaching Machine: The Neglected Area of Operant Conditioning in the Theory and Practice of Management," *Organizational Behavior and Human Performance,* 1969, 4, 375-401.

Nord, W.R., "Improving Attendance Through Rewards," *Personnel Administration,* 1970, 33, 37-41.

Norsworthy, J.R. and Fulco, L.J., "Productivity and Costs in the Private Economy, 1975," *Monthly Labor Review,* 1976, 99(5), 3-11.

Odiorne, G.S., *Management-by-Objectives.* New York: Pitman, 1970.

Oldham, G.R., "The Motivational Strategies Used by Supervisors: Relationships to Effectiveness Indicators," *Organizational Behavior and Human Performance,* 1976, 15, 66-86.

Opsahl, R.L. and Dunnette, M.D., "The Role of Financial Compensation in Industrial Motivation," *Psychological Bulletin,* 1966, 66, 94-118.

Oswald, R. and Smyth, J.D., "Fringe Benefits on the Move," *American Federationist,* 1970, 77, 18-24.

Oxley, G.M. and Oxley, G.B., "Expectations of Excellence," *California Management Review,* 1963, 6, 13-22.

Patten, T.H., "OD, MBO, The R/P System: A New Dimension in Personnel Administration," *Personnel Administration,* 1972, 35, 14-26.

Patterson, C.H., "A Unitary Theory of Motivation and Its Counseling Implications," *Individual Motivation,* 1964, 20, 17-31.

Paul, W.J., Robertson, K.B., and Herzberg, F., "Job Enrichment Pays Off," *Harvard Business Review*, 1969, 47, 16-78.

Pavlov, I.P., *Conditioned Reflexes*. Oxford: Clarendon Press, 1927.

Payne, R.B. and Hauty, G.T., "Effect of Psychological Feedback Upon Work Decrement," *Journal of Experimental Psychology*, 1955, 50, 343-351.

Payne, R. and Pheysey, D., "G.G. Stern's Organizational Climate Index: A Reconceptualization and Application to Business Organizations," *Organizational Behavior and Human Performance*, 1971, 6, 77-98.

Peak, H., "Attitude and Motivation," in M.R. Jones (ed.), *Nebraska Symposium on Motivation*. Lincoln: University of Nebraska Press, 1955, 149-188.

Perin, C.T., "A Quantitative Investigation of the Delay of Reinforcement Gradient," *Journal of Experimental Psychology*, 1943, 32, 38-51.

Perrow, C., *Complex Organizations: A Critical Essay*. Glenview, Ill.: Scott, Foresman, 1972.

Perrow, C., *Organizational Analysis: A Sociological View*. Belmont, Calif.: Wadsworth, 1970.

Personnel Journal Editor, "As You Were Saying—Share Profits Don't Freeze Them," *Personnel Journal*, 1972, 54, 51.

Peters, R.S., *The Concept of Motivation*. New York: Humanities Press, 1958.

Pfaffmann, C., "The Pleasures of Sensation," *Psychological Review*, 1960, 67, 253-268.

Platt, J.R. and Gay, R.A., "Differential Magnitude of Reward Conditioning as a Function of Predifferential Reward Magnitude," *Journal of Experimental Psychology*, 1968, 77, 393-396.

Porter, L.W., "A Study of Perceived Need Satisfactions in Bottom and Middle Management Jobs," *Journal of Applied Psychology*, 1961, 45, 1-10.

Porter, L.W., "Job Attitudes in Management: I. Perceived Deficiencies in Need Fulfillment as a Function of Job Level," *Journal of Applied Psychology*, 1962, 46, 375-384.

Porter, L.W., *Organizational Patterns of Managerial Job Attitudes*. New York: American Foundation for Management Research, 1964.

Porter, L.W., Crampton, W.J., and Smith, F.J., "Organizational Commitment and Managerial Turnover: A Longitudinal Study," *Organizational Behavior and Human Performance*, 1976, 15, 87-98.

Porter, L.W. and Lawler, E.E., *Managerial Attitudes and Performance*. New York: Irwin-Dorsey, 1968.

Porter, L.W. and Lawler, E.E., "Properties of Organization Structure in Relation to Job Attitudes and Job Behavior," *Psychological Bulletin*, 1965, 64, 23-51.

Porter, L.W. and Steers, R.M., "Organizational, Work, and Personal Factors in Employee Turnover and Absenteeism," *Psychological Bulletin,* 1973, 80, 151-176.

Premack, D., "Reinforcement Theory," in D. Levine (ed.), *Nebraska Symposium on Motivation.* Lincoln: University of Nebraska Press, 1965, 123-180.

Pritchard, R.D., "Effects of Varying Performance-Pay Instrumentalities on the Relationship Between Performance and Satisfaction: A Test of Lawler and Porter Model," *Journal of Applied Psychology,* 1973, 58, 122-125.

Pritchard, R.D., "Equity Theory: A Review and Critque," *Organizational Behavior and Human Performances,* 1969, 4, 176-211.

Pritchard, R.D. and Curts, M.I., "The Influence of Goal Setting and Financial Incentives on Task Performance," *Organizational Behavior and Human Performance,* 1973, 10, 175-183.

Pritchard, R.D. and DeLeo, P.J., "Experimental Test of the Valence-Instrumentality Relationship in Job Performance," *Journal of Applied Psychology,* 1973, 57, 264-270.

Pritchard, R.D., DeLeo, P.J., and Von Bergen, C.W., "A Field Experimental Test of Expectancy-Valence Incentive Motivation Techniques," *Organizational Behavior and Human Performance,* 1976, 15, 355-406.

Pritchard, R.D., Jorgenson, D.D., Dunnette, M.D., "The Effects of Perceptions of Equity and Inequity on Worker Performance and Satisfaction," *Journal of Applied Psychology,* 1972, 56, 75-94.

Pritchard, R.D. and Karasick, B.W., "The Effects of Organizational Climate on Managerial Job Performance and Job Satisfaction," *Organizational Behavior and Human Performance,* 1973, 9, 126-146.

Pritchard, R.D. and Sanders, M.S., "The Influence of Valence, Instrumentality, and Expectancy on Effort and Performance," *Journal of Applied Psychology,* 1973, 57, 55-60.

Pugh, D.S., Hickson, D.J., Hinings, C.R., and Turner, C., "The Context of Organizational Structures," *Administrative Science Quarterly,* 1969, 14, 91-114.

Quinn, R. and Shephard, L., *The 1972-1973 Quality of Employment Survey.* Ann Arbor, Mich.: Survey Research Center, Institute for Social Research, The University of Michigan, 1974.

Raia, A.P., "Goal Setting and Self Control," *Journal of Management Studies,* 1965, 2, 34-53.

Raia, A.P., *Management by Objectives.* Glenview, Ill.: Scott, Foresman, 1974.

Raia, A.P., "A Second Look at Management Goals and Controls," *California Management Review,* 1966, 9, 57-58.

Ramond, Albert and Associates, *Bulletin,* 1945. War Production Board.

Rand, B., *The Classical Psychologists* Boston: Houghton Mifflin, 1912.

Reif, W.E. and Luthans, F., "Does Job Enrichment Really Pay Off?" *California Management Review*, 1972, 14, 30-37.

Reimann, B.C., "Dimensions of Structure in Effective Organizations: Some Empirical Evidence," *Academy of Management Journal*, 1974, 17, 693-708.

Reinharth, L. and Wahba, M.A., "Expectancy Theory as a Predictor of Work Motivation, Effort Expenditure, and Job Performance," *Academy of Management Journal*, 1975, 18, 520-537.

Reynold, W.F. and Pavlik, W.B., "Running Speed as a Function of Deprivation Period and Reward Magnitude," *Journal of Comparative and Physiological Psychology*, 1960, 53, 615-618.

Reynolds, G.S., *A Primer of Operant Conditioning.* Glenview, Ill: Scott, Foresman, 1968.

Richter, C.P., "Animal Behavior and Internal Drives," *Quarterly Review of Biology*, 1927, 2, 307-343.

Roberts, K.H., Walter, G.H., and Miles, R.E., "A Factor Analytic Study of Job Satisfaction Items Designed to Measure Maslow Need Categories," *Personnel Psychology*, 1971, 24, 205-220.

Roche, W.J. and MacKinnen, N.L., "Motivating People with Meaningful Work," *Harvard Business Review*, 1970, 48, 97-110.

Roethlisberger, F.J. and Dickson, W.J., *Management and the Worker.* Cambridge: Harvard University Press, 1939.

Ronan, W.W., Latham, G.P., and Kinne, S.B., "The Effects of Goal Setting and Supervision on Worker Behavior in an Industrial Situation," *Journal of Applied Psychology*, 1973, 57, 302-307.

Rosen, A.J. and Ison, J.R., "Runway Performance Following Changes in Sucrose Rewards," *Psychoneurosis Science*, 1965, 2, 335-336.

Ruh, R.A., Wallace, R.L., and Frost, C.F., "Management Attitudes and the Scanlon Plan," *Industrial Relations*, 1973, 12, 282-288.

Runyon, K.E., "Some Interactions Between Personality Variables and Management Styles," *Journal of Applied Psychology*, 1973, 57, 288-294.

Salancik, G.R., "Interaction Effects of Performance and Money on Self-Perception of Intrinsic Motivation," *Organizational Behavior and Human Performance*, 1975, 13, 339-351.

Saleh, S.D. and Grygier, T.G., "Psychodynamics of Intrinsic and Extrinsic Job Orientation," *Journal of Applied Psychology*, 1969, 53, 446-450.

Schachter, S., *The Psychology of Affiliation.* Stanford, Calif.: Stanford University Press, 1959.

Schneider, B., "Organizational Climate: Individual Preferences and Organizational Realities Revisited," *Journal of Applied Psychology*, 1975, 60, 459-465.

Schneider, B. and Olson, L.K., "Effort as a Correlate of Organizational Reward System and Individual Values," *Personnel Psychology*, 1970, 23, 313-326.

Schneider, B. and Snyder, R.A., "Some Relationships Between Job Satisfaction and Organizational Climate," *Journal of Applied Psychology*, 1975, 60, 318-328.

Schneider, C.E., "Behavior Modification in Management: A Review and Critique," *Academy of Management Journal*, 1974, 17, 528-548.

Schoner, B. and Rose, G., "Quality of Decisions: Individual Versus Real and Synthetic Groups," *Journal of Applied Psychology*, 1974, 59, 424-432.

Schrank, R., "Work in America: What Do Workers Really Want?" *Industrial Relations*, 1974, 13, 124-129.

Schriesheim, C.A., House, R.J., and Kerr, S., " *Organizational Behavior and Human Performance,"* 1976, 15, 297-321.

Schwab, D.P., "Impact of Alternative Compensation Systems on Pay Valence and Instrumentality Perceptions," *Journal of Applied Psychology*, 1973, 58, 308-312.

Schwab, D.P. and Cummings, L.L., "Theories of Performance and Satisfaction: A Review," *Industrial Relations*, 1970, 9, 408-430.

Scott, W.E., "Activation Theory and Task Design," *Organizational Behavior and Human Performance*, 1966, 1, 3-30.

Scott, W.E., "The Effects of Extrinsic Rewards on Intrinsic Motivation," *Organizational Behavior and Human Performance*, 1975, 15, 117-129.

Scott, W.G., and Mitchell, T.R., *Organization Theory*. Homewood, Ill.: Irwin and Dorsey, 1972.

Seashore, S.F., *Group Cohesiveness in the Industrial Work Group*. Ann Arbor: Institute for Social Research, University of Michigan, 1954.

Senger, J., "Managers' Perceptions of Subordinates' Competence as a Function of Personal Value Orientation," *Academy of Management Journal*, 1971, 14, 415-423.

Seward, J.P. and Proctor, D.M., "Performance as a Function of Drive, Reward, and Habit Strength," *American Journal of Psychology*, 1960, 73, 448-453.

Seward, J.P., Shea, R.A., and Davenport, R.H., "Further Evidence for the Interaction of Drive and Reward," *American Journal of Psychology*, 1960, 73, 370-379.

Sheppard, H.L. and Herrick, N.Q., *Where Have All the Robots Gone*. New York: The Free Press, 1974.

Sheridan, J.E. and Slocum, J.W., "The Direction of the Causal Relationship Between Job Satisfaction and Work Performance," *Organizational Behavior and Human Performance,* 1975, 14, 159-172.

Sherif, M. and Sherif, C., *Groups in Harmony and Tension.* New York: Harper and Row, 1953.

Sherman, A.R., *Behavior Modification: Theory and Practice.* Monterey, Calif.: Brooks/Cole Publishing, 1973.

Sipowicz, R.R., Ware, J.R., and Baker, R.A., "The Effects of Reward and Knowlecge of Results on the Performance of a Simple Vigilance Task," *Journal of Experimental Psychology,* 1962, 64, 58-61.

Sirota, D. and Wolfson, A.D., "Pragmatic Approach to People Problems," *Harvard Business Review,* 1973, 51, 120-128.

Skinner, B.F., *Science and Human Behavior.* New York: Macmillan, 1953.

Skinner, B.F. and Ferster, C.G., *Schedules of Reinforcement.* New York: Appleton-Century-Crofts, 1957.

Slater, P.E., "Contrasting Correlates of Group Size," *Sociometry,* 1958, 21, 129-139.

Slocum, J.W., "Motivation in Managerial Levels: Relationship of Need Satisfaction to Job Performance," *Journal of Applied Psychology,* 1971, 55, 312-316.

Smith, A., *The Wealth of Nations.* London: Old Authors Farm, 1776.

Smith, R.L., Lucaccini, L.F., and Epstein, M.H., "Effects of Monetary Rewards and Punishments on Vigilance Performance," *Journal of Applied Psychology,* 1967, 51, 411-416.

Spence, K.W., *Behavior Theory and Conditioning.* New Haven: Yale University Press, 1956.

Spence, K.W., *Behavior Theory and Learning.* Englewood Cliffs, N.J.: Prentice-Hall, 1960.

Spence, K.W., "The Role of Secondary Reinforcement in Delayed Reward Learning," *Psychological Review,* 1947, 54, 1-8.

Spencer, H., *Principles of Psychology.* New York: Appleton, 1899.

Starcevich, M.M., "Job Factor Importance for Job Satisfaction and Dissatisfaction Across Different Occupational Levels," *Journal of Applied Psychology,* 1972, 56, 467-471.

Starke, F.A. and Behling, O., "A Test of Two Postulates Underlying Expectancy Theory," *Academy of Management Journal,* 1975, 18, 703-714.

Steers, R.M., "Effects of Need for Achievement on the Job Performance-Job Attitude Relationship," *Journal of Applied Psychology,* 1975, 60, 678-682.

Steers, R.M., "Factors Affecting Job Attitudes in a Goal-Setting Environment," *Academy of Management Journal,* 1976, 19, 6-16.

Steers, R.M., "Task-Goal Attitudes-Achievement, and Supervisory Performance," *Organizational Behavior and Human Performance,* 1975, 13, 392-403.

Steers, R.M. and Porter, L.W., "The Role of Task-Goal Attributes in Employee Performance," *Psychological Bulletin,* 1974, 81, 434-452.

Steiner, I. and Johnson, H., "Authoritian and Conformity," *Sociometry,* 1963, 26, 21-34.

Stelluto, G.L., "Report on Incentive Pay in Manufacturing Industries, *Monthly Labor Review,* 1969, 92, 49-53.

Stinson, J.E. and Johnson, T.W., "The Goal-Path Theory of Leadership: A Partial Test and Suggested Refinement," *Academy of Management Journal,* 1975, 18, 242-252.

Stogdill, R.M., "Group Productivity, Drive, and Cohesiveness," *Organizational Behavior and Human Performance,* 1972, 8, 26-43.

Stogdill, R.M., *The Handbook of Leadership: A Survey of Theory and Research.* New York: Free Press, 1974.

Stogdill, R.M., "Personal Factors Associated with Leadership," *Journal of Applied Psychology,* 1948, 25, 35-71.

Stogdill, R.M. and Coons, A.E., *Leader Behavior: Its Description and Measurement.* Columbus, Ohio: Ohio State University, Bureau of Business Research, 1957.

Stone, E.F., "The Moderating Effect of Work-Related Values on the Job Scope-Job Satisfaction Relationship," *Organizational Behavior and Human Performance,* 1976, 15, 147-167.

Stone, E.F. and Porter, L.W., Job Characteristics and Job Attitudes: A Multivariate Study," *Journal of Applied Psychology,* 1975, 60, 57-64.

Strauss, G., "Workers: Attitudes and Adjustments," in J.W. Rosow (ed.), *The Worker and the Job.* New York: The American Assembly, 1974, 73-98.

Stringer, R.A., "Achievement Motivation and Management Control," *Personnel Administration,* 1966, 29, 3-5, 14-16.

Susman, G.I., "Automation, Alienation and Work Group Autonomy," *Human Relations,* 1972, 25, 171-180.

Sutermeister, R.A., "Employee Performance and Employee Need Satisfaction: Which Comes First?" *California Management Review,* 1971, 13, 43-47

Sutermeister, R.A., *People and Productivity.* New York: McGraw-Hill, 1976.

Sweney, A.B., "Developing Principles for Motivational Management," Air Force Office of Scientific Research, Project No. 2001, 1975.

Sweney, A.B., Fiechtner, L.A., and Samores, R.J., "An Intergrative Factor Analysis of Leadership Measures and Theories," *Journal of Psychology,* 1975, 90, 75-85.

Swinth, R.L., "Organizational Joint Problem-Solving," *Management Science,* 1971, 18, B69-B79.

Tannenbaum, A.S., *Controls in Organizations.* New York: McGraw-Hill, 1968.

Tannenbaum, R. and Schmidt, W.H., "How to Choose a Leadership Pattern," *Harvard Business Review,* 1958, 36, 95-101, and 1973, 51, 162-180.

Taylor, F.W., *The Principles of Scientific Management.* New York. Harper and Row, 1911.

Taylor, F.W., "Time Study, Piece Work, and the First Class Man," in H. F. Murrill, *Classics of Management.* New York: American Management Association, 1960, 67-76.

Thomas, E.J. and Fink, C.F., "Effect of Group Size," *Psychological Bulletin,* 1963, 60, 371-384.

Thompson, P.H. and Dalton, G.W., "Performance Apprisal: Managers Beware," *Harvard Business Review,* 1970, 48, 149-157.

Thompson, R.F. and Spencer, W.A., "Habituation: A Model Phenomenon for the Study of Neuronal Substrates of Behavior," *Psychological Review,* 1966, 73, 16-43.

Thorndike, E.L., *Animal Intelligence.* New York: Macmillan, 1911.

Tillman, F.A., "Employee Stock Ownership Plans," *Today's Manager,* 1975, 5, 26-29.

Tolman, E.C., "Operational Behaviorism and Current Trends in Psychology," Proceedings, 25th Anniversary Inauguration Graduate Studies. Los Angeles: University of Southern California, 1936, 89-103.

Tolman, E.C., "The Determiners of Behavior at a Choice Point," *Psychological Review,* 1938, 45, 1-41.

Turner, A.N. and Lawrence, P.R., *Industrial Jobs and the Worker.* Boston: Harvard University Graduate School of Business Administration, 1965.

Uhrbrock, R. S., "Music on the Job: Its Influence on Worker Morale and Production," *Personnel Psychology*, 1961, 14, 9-38.

Underwood, B. J., *Experimental Psychology.* New York: W. W. Norton, 1953.

U. S. Bureau of Labor Statistics, "The U. S. Economy in 1980," *Monthly Labor Review,* 1970, 93, 3-34.

U. S. Bureau of Labor Statistics, *Handbook of Labor Statistics.* Washington, D. C.: Department of Labor, 1974.

U. S. Department of Health, Education, and Welfare, *Work in America.* Cambridge, Mass.: MIT Press, 1973.

U. S. Department of Labor, *Job Satisfaction: Is There a Trend?* Washington, D. C.: U. S. Department of Labor, Manpower Administration, Manpower Research Monograph No. 30, 1974.

Urwick, L., *The Elements of Administration.* New York: Harper & Brothers, 1943.

Van de Ven, A. H., "Group Decision-Making and Effectiveness: An Experimental Study," *Organization and Administrative Sciences,* 1974, 5, 1-110.

Van de Ven, A. H., "Nominal Versus Interacting Group Processes for Committee Decision-Making Effectiveness," *Academy of Management Journal,* 1971, 14, 203-212.

Van de Ven, A. H. and Delbecq, A. L., "A Task Contingent Model of Work-Unit Structure," *Administrative Science Quarterly,* 1974, 19, 183-197.

Van de Ven, A. H. and Delbecq, A. L., "The Effectiveness of Nominal, Delphi, and Interacting Group Decision Making Process," *Academy of Management Journal,* 1974, 17, 605-621.

Veblin, T., *The Instinct of Workmanship in the State of the Industrial Arts.* New York: Macmillian, 1914.

Viteles, M. S., *Motivation and Morale in Industry.* New York: W. W. Norton, 1953.

Von Neumann, J. and Morgenstern, O., *Theory of Games and Economic Behavior.* Princeton, N. J.: Princeton University Press, 1957.

Vroom, V.H., *Some Personality Deterimants of the Effects of Participation.* Englewood Cliffs, N. J.: Prentice-Hall, 1960.

Vroom, V. H., "Ego-involvement, Job Satisfaction and Job Performance," *Personnel Psychology,* 1962, 15, 159-177.

Vroom, V. H., *Work and Motivation.* New York: Wiley, 1964.

Vroom, V. H. and Deci, E. L. (eds.) *Management and Motivation.* Baltimore: Penguin, 1970.

Wager, L. W., "Leadership Style, Influence, and Supervisory Role Obligations," *Administrative Science Quarterly,* 1965, 9, 391-420.

Wahba, M. A. and Bridwell, L. G., "Maslow Reconsidered: A Review of Research on the Need Hierarchy Theory," *Organizational Behavior and Human Performance,* 1976, 15, 212-240.

Walker, C. R., "The Problem of the Repetitive Job," *Harvard Business Review,* 1950, 28, 54-59.

Walker, C. R. and Guest, R. H., *The Man on the Assembly Line.* Cambridge, Mass.: Harvard University Press, 1952.

Walker, J., Fletcher, C., and McLeod, D., "Flexible Working Hours in Two British Government Offices," *Public Personnel Management,* 1975, 4, 216-222.

Walters, R. W. and Associates, *Job Enrichment for Results: Strategies for Successful Implementation.* Reading, Mass., Addison-Wesley, 1975.

Walton, R. E., "How to Counter Alienation in the Plant," *Harvard Business Review,* 1972, 50, 70-81.

Walton, R. E., "Innovative Restructuring of Work," in J. M. Rosow (ed.), *The Worker and the Job.* Englewood Cliffs, N.J.: Prentice-Hall, 1974.

Wanous, J. P. and Lawler, E. E., "Measurement and Meaning of Job Satisfaction," *Journal of Applied Psychology,* 1972, 56, 95-105.

Ware, J. R., Baker, R. A., and Sheldon, R. W., "Effect of Increasing Signal Load on Detection Performance in a Vigilance Task," *Perceptual and Motor Skills,* 1964, 18, 105-106.

Warm, J. S., Hagner, G. L., Meyer, D., "The Partial Reinforcement Effect in a Vigilance Task," *Perceptual and Motor Skills,* 1971, 23, 987-993.

Warner, L. H., "A Study of Sex Drive in the White Rat by Means of the Obstruction Method." *Comparative Psychology Monograph,* 1927, 4, Serial No. 22.

Waters, L. K. and Roach, D., "A Factor Analysis of Need-Fulfillment Items Designed to Measure Maslow Need Categories," *Personnel Psychology,* 1973, 26, 185-190.

Watson, G. B., "Do Groups Think More Efficiently than Individuals?" *Journal of Abnormal and Social Psychology,* 1928, 23, 328-336.

Weber, M., *The Protestant Ethic and the Spirit of Capitalism.* (Translated by T. Parsons," London: Allen and Unwin, 1930 (originally published in 1921).

Weber, M., *The Theory of Social and Economic Organization.* (Translated by A. M. Henderson, and T. Parsons.) New York: Oxford University Press, 1947.

Weed, S. E., Mitchell, T. R., and Moffitt, W., "Leadership Style, Subordinate Personality, and Task Type as Predictors of Performance and Satisfaction with Supervision," *Journal of Applied Psychology,* 1976, 61, 58-66.

Weidenfeller, E. W., Baker, R. A., and Ware, J. R., "Effects of Knowledge of Results (True and False) on Vigilance Performance," *Perceptual and Motor Skills,* 1962, 14, 211-215.

Weiss, R. F., "Deprivation and Reward Magnitude Effects on Speed Throughout the Goal Gradient," *Journal of Experimental Psychology,* 1960, 60, 384-390.

Wernimont, P. F., "Intrinsic and Extrinsic Factors in Job Satisfaction," *Journal of Applied Psychology*, 1966, 50, 41-50.

Wernimont, P. F., Toren, P., and Kappel, H., "Comparison of Sources of Personal Satisfaction and of Work Motivation," *Journal of Applied Psychology*, 1970, 54, 95-102.

Wexley, K.N. and Nemeroff, "Effectiveness of Positive Reinforcement and Goal Setting as Methods of Management Development," *Journal of Applied Psychology*, 1975, 60, 446-450.

Wheeler, K., Gurman, R., and Tarnowieski, D., *The Four Day Week: An AMA Research Report*. New York: American Management Association, 1972.

White, B. L., "Study of Employee Attitudes Toward a Wage Incentive Plan," *Personnel Practice Bulletin*, 1959, 15, 30-38.

White, R. W., "Motivation Reconsidered: The Concept of Competence," *Psychological Review*, 1959, 66, 297-334.

Whyte, W. F., "An Interaction Approach to the Theory of Organization," in M. Haire (ed.), *Modern Organization Theory*. New York: Wiley, 1959, 155-183.

Whyte, W. F., *Money and Motivation*. New York: Harper, 1955.

Wickens, J. D., "Management by Objectives: An Appraisal," *Journal of Management Studies*, 1968, 5, 365-379.

Wiener, E. L., "Knowledge of Results and Signal Rate in Monitoring: A Transfer of Training Approach," *Journal of Applied Psychology*, 1963, 47, 214-222.

Wiener, E. L. and Attwood, E. A., "Training for Vigilance: Combined Cueing and Knowledge of Results," *Journal of Applied Psychology*, 1968, 52, 474-479.

Wiener, M., "Word Frequency or Motivation in Perceptual Defense," *Journal of Abnormal and Social Psychology*, 1955, 31, 214-218.

Wikstorm, W. S., *Management by and with Objectives*. New York: National Industrial Conference Board, 1968.

Williams, J. L., *Operant Learning: Procedures for Changing Behavior*, Monterey, Calif.: Brooks/Cole, 1973.

Wist, E. R., "Amount, Delay, and Position of Delay of Reinforcement as Parameters of Runway Performance," *Journal of Experimental Psychology*, 1962, 63, 160-166.

Wolf, A. V., *Thirst: Psychology of the Urge to Drink and Problems of Lack of Water*. Springfield, Ill.: Charles C. Thomas, 1958.

Wolf, M. M., Giles, D. K., and Hall, R. V., "Experiments with Token Reinforcement in a Remedial Classroom," *Behavior Research and Therapy*, 1968, 6, 51-64.

320

Wood, I. and Edward, E., "Effects of Piece-rate Overpayment on Productivity," *Journal of Applied Psychology*, 1970, 54, 234-38.

Wood, M. T., "Effects of Decision Processes and Task Situations on Influence Perception," *Organizational Behavior and Human Performance*, 1972, 8, 417-427.

Wood, M. T., "Power Relationships and Group Decision-Making in Organizations," *Psychological Bulletin*, 1973, 74, 280-293.

Woodward, J., *Industrial Organization: Theory and Practice*. London: Oxford University Press, 1965.

Woodworth, R. S., *Dynamic Psychology*. New York: Columbia University Press, 1918.

Woodworth, R. S., *Psychology*. New York: Holt, Rinehart and Winston, 1921.

Wool, H., "Future Labor Supply for Lower Level Occupations," *Monthly Labor Review*, 1976, 99(3), 22-31.

Wyatt, S., *Incentives in Repetitive Work: A Practical Experiment in a Factory*. Industrial Health Research Board Report No. 69. London: H.M. Stationery Office, 1934.

Yankelovich, D., *The New Morality*. New York: McGraw-Hill, 1974.

Yinon, Y., Bizman, A., and Goldberg, M., "Effect of Relative Magnitude of Reward and Type of Need on Satisfaction," *Journal of Applied Psychology*, 1976, 61, 325-328.

Young, P. T. and Shuford, E. H., "Quantitative Control of Motivation Through Sucrose Solutions of Different Concentrations," *Journal of Comparative and Physiological Psychology*, 1965, 48, 114-118.

Young, P. T., *Motivation and Emotion*. New York: Wiley, 1961.

Yukl, G. A. and Latham, G. P., "Consequences of Reinforcement Schedules and Incentive Magnitudes for Employee Performance: Problems Encountered in an Industrial Setting," *Journal of Applied Psychology*, 1975, 60, 294-298.

Yukl, G. A., Wexley, K. N. and Seymore, J. D., "Effectiveness of Pay Incentives Under Variable/Ratio and Continuous Reinforcement Schedules," *Journal of Applied Psychology*, 1972, 56, 19-23.

Zaleznick, A., Christensen, C.R., and Roethlisberger, F.J., *The Motivation Productivity, and Satisfaction of Workers*. Boston: Harvard University, Graduate School of Business Administration, Division of Research, 1958.

Zeaman, D., "Response Latency as a Function of the Amount of Reinforcement," *Journal of Experimental Psychology*, 1949, 39, 466-483.

Ziller, R. C., "Group Size: A Determinant of the Quality and Stability of Group Decisions," *Sociometry*, 1957, 20, 165-173.

INDEX

324